D0203123

A TO Z OF
AMERICAN WOMEN
IN THE
VISUAL ARTS

CAROL KORT AND
LIZ SONNEBORN

Facts On File, Inc.

Facts On File, Inc.
132 West 31st Street
New York, NY 10001

Library of Congress Cataloging-in-Publication Data

Kort, Carol.
    A to Z of American women in the visual arts/Carol Kort and Liz Sonneborn.
        p. cm.
    Includes bibliographical references and index.
    ISBN 0-8160-4397-3
    1. Art, American—Dictionaries. 2. Women artists—United States—Dictionaries.
    I. Sonneborn, Liz. II. Title.

    N6505 .K59 2002
    704'.042'097303—dc21   2001040231

Facts On File books are available at special discounts when purchased in bulk quantities for businesses, associations, institutions or sales promotions. Please call our Special Sales Department in New York at (212) 967-8800 or (800) 322-8755.

You can find Facts On File on the World Wide Web at http://www.factsonfile.com

Cover design by Cathy Rincon

Printed in the United States of America

VB Hermitage 10 9 8 7 6 5 4 3 2 1

This book is printed on acid-free paper.

To my brother Roy, a true artist
— C. K.

To my mother
— L. S.

CONTENTS

ACKNOWLEDGMENTS

Georgia O'Keeffe, one of America's greatest modern painters and one of the more than 130 premier women artists profiled in this book, once observed: "Nobody sees a flower—really—it is so small—we haven't time—and to see it takes time, like to have a friend takes time."

I am deeply indebted to my friends for taking the time to support and encourage me during this project. For their invaluable suggestions, I would especially like to thank longtime friends Sloat Shaw and Lois Schklar, who are themselves talented professional artists. Naomi Lomba-Gomes, of Boston University's College of General Studies, and Sharon Valient, a specialist in early American naturalist painters, were also helpful.

For inspiration, I was fortunate to have had as my neighbor Berta Margoulies, a sculptor featured in this book. For years I could look into her yard, a veritable sculpture garden, and delight in her beautifully evocative bronze statues. In addition, *A to Z of American Women in the Visual Arts* would not have been possible without the able assistance of my editor, Nicole Bowen, and her assistant Gene Springs.

In the twilight of her years, Anna Mary Robertson Moses, better known as the popular folk artist Grandma Moses, asserted that "life is what we make it, always has been, always will be." If I have made anything of my life, it is largely because of my loving, caring, and creative family—Michael, Eleza, and Tamara.

— C. K.

AUTHORS' NOTE

Several criteria were used to determine which artists to include in *A to Z of American Women in the Visual Arts*. Apart from space limitations, we wanted to represent artists from a variety of mediums, such as painting, sculpture, printmaking, graphic arts, photography, architecture, and crafts. We also tried to focus on artists who spanned America's rich and varied history, from colonial times to the present, and who represented a panoply of geographic, cultural, and socioeconomic backgrounds. Our final consideration was women in the visual arts about whom we could supply easily accessed and substantial bibliographical material for further reading. Regrettably, we could not include many distinguished and noteworthy American women artists who belong in this book.

INTRODUCTION

Whether 17th-century portraiture or 21st-century computer-generated art, women in America have created an impressive body of artwork. Furthermore, long before the first European settlers arrived in the colonies, Native American women artists had been making exquisitely rendered crafts, such as richly decorated clothing, ceramics, and baskets.

In spite of myriad obstacles, including family responsibilities and limited access to art education and training, faced by female artists throughout America's history, these determined and talented women evolved from amateur to professional, first-rate artists. Although the achievements of American women in the visual arts have often been overlooked by the male-dominated art world, with the advent of the women's movement that took hold in the United States in the early 1970s, there has been considerable progress. As art writer Nancy G. Heller points out, women artists have finally become "more active, successful, and visible." Still, for women who have chosen to become artists in spite of the impediments, it has not been easy.

When asked to name the best-known American female artist, the most likely response is impressionist painter and printmaker Mary Cassatt (1844–1926), whose father reportedly said he would almost rather see his daughter dead than have her study art. However, Cassatt's mother conceded that "a woman who is not married is lucky if she has a decided love for work of any kind, and the more absorbing it is the better."

What of the roster of estimable American women artists who preceded Cassatt, but who never achieved her level of fame? For the most part, their names and the works they produced are unfamiliar because art history textbooks and survey courses often ignored them. For example, Henrietta Deering Johnston (1670–1728), probably the first professional American female artist and the first American artist of either gender to work in pastels, was a successful entrepreneur who took up portraiture when her ailing husband could no longer work. He remarked that without his wife's income, their family could not have survived. Johnston managed to produce more than 40 drawings and sell them to the wealthy citizens of Charleston, South Carolina. She worked when she was not fighting off Indian attacks, nursing her husband, tending to household chores, or raising several stepchildren. A critic called Johnston's pastels "direct and uncompromising," an apt description of the frontier artist herself. Surely Johnston and her pastel portraits deserve to be mentioned in the development of beaux arts in the United States.

America's first professional sculptor, Patience Lovell Wright (1725–86), used wax as her medium. An uneducated, spirited widow who supported her children by selling her delicate work, Wright also supported the American Revolution and, having declared that women are "always useful in grand events," daringly spied on the British. Meanwhile, prolific Frances (Fanny) Flora Bond Palmer (1812–76) produced more lithographs for Currier and Ives than any other artist who worked for the illustrious firm. Another example of a female artist whose name should be recognized is the 19th-century sculptor Emma Stebbins (1815–82), creator of a magnificent bronze fountain in New York City's Central Park. Every day thousands of people pass by *The Angel of the Waters,* but how many of them know who made it?

Edmonia Lewis, the first important African-American sculptor, was born around 1843. The daughter of an Indian mother and a black father, she overcame prejudice, and even a brutal beating by a vigilante mob, and went on to carve exquisite neoclassical figures, especially of women, from marble. "I have a strong sympathy for all women who have struggled and suffered," she wrote. Cecilia Beaux, a little-known painter from Philadelphia, has been compared in stature with John Singer Sargent. The prizewinning Beaux wondered why critics described her as a woman portraitist, instead of focusing on her paintings. "They don't write about *men* painters," she wryly observed. Finally, how many people realize that the image of President Franklin D. Roosevelt that appears on the United States dime is an example of the work of the accomplished figurative African-American sculptor and art educator Selma Hortense Burke?

It is impossible to know the names of many early American female folk artists, who were self-taught and produced, anonymously, superb traditional crafts as quiltmakers and needleworkers. Their work is described in *Artists in Aprons: Folk Art by American Women* as "extraordinary art by ordinary women." In later years, American women artists were better trained and educated, but they often continued to be ignored critically and commercially. During the 1985–86 season, only one of the solo exhibitions at the Museum of Modern Art, and none at the Guggenheim, Whitney, or the Metropolitan Museums (all in New York City), was by a woman.

Susan Macdowell Eakins, a prominent painter and lithographer, was not given a solo exhibition until 35 years after her death. Her acclaimed husband, Thomas Eakins, regarded his wife as the best female painter of her time, but that did not stop her from subordinating her career to his. The accomplishments of Anni Albers, perhaps the most influential abstract textile artist of the 20th century, are lost in the shadow of those of her husband, fellow Bauhaus theorist Josef Albers. Although both Max Ernst and his wife, Dorothea Tanning, were prominent surrealist painters, it is Ernst's reputation that endures. Tanning admitted that while her marriage was satisfying, it definitely hampered her career. The talented abstract expressionist Lee Krasner was primarily known as Jackson Pollock's wife, and then as his widow, until she was rediscovered in the 1970s. "She never got a fair shake as a painter or as a human being," commented one art critic, but Krasner chose to promote and publicize Pollock's work over her own. In art writer Lucy Lippard's landmark study *From the Center: Feminist Essays on Women's Art,* she noted that "the woman artist has tended to be seen either as another artist's wife, or mistress, or as a dilettante. Probably more than most artists, women make art to escape, overwhelm, or transform daily realities."

The reasons why American women have chosen to become professional artists are as diverse as the women themselves. Esteemed photographer Margaret Bourke-White was given her first camera by her mother, whom she considered her role model. For sculptor Berta Margoulies, childhood memories of war and insecurity shaped the expressionist humanity of her art. Painter, printmaker, and sculptor Louise Bourgeois says that everything she creates comes from something personal, some memory or emotional experience, and that she became an artist "to find a mode of survival." On the other hand, Jane Freilicher paints because she has to have something to refer to *beside* herself: "Otherwise my painting would be thin." Contemporary architect Maya Lin is less sure about the source of her creativity. "I do not see the [artistic] process as being under my control," she wrote. "It is a process of percolation, with the form eventually finding its way to the surface." For mixed-media digital artist Michi Itami, it was crucial that she aesthetically capture her Japanese-American family's horrific experiences of internment during World War II. "All of us have a story to tell, and understanding and empathy are increased when we share our stories," Itami said. As for the folk artist Ann Mary Robertson Moses (Grandma Moses), she once observed that if she had not started painting, she would have raised chickens.

Throughout the centuries, American women artists have displayed perseverance. Landscape painter Charlotte Buell Coman, for example, began painting when she was 40 and did her best work after she turned 80. The self-taught African-American folk artist Clementine Hunter labored in southern plantations picking cotton or as a kitchen maid. In her putative spare time, she painted stylized genre scenes of life among rural black people and sold her pictures for a quarter, or gave them away. (After her death in 1998, her primitive paintings sold for as much as $3,000 in fashionable art galleries.) Painter Alice Neel produced an unflinchingly realistic self-portrait of herself, nude, at 80; she became prominent only very late in her career.

There are also many profiles in courage. Post-modernist artist Eva Hesse attended a 1969 solo show of her work at New York's Whitney Museum of American Art in a wheelchair because that same year she had been diagnosed with brain cancer. From her hospital bed, Hesse directed the construction of a compelling latex, wire, and fiberglass structure that appeared in the show. Nell Blaine, known for her beautiful brushwork and lush interiors, painted from a wheelchair after contracting polio. She retrained herself to paint with her left hand. "Don't make a big deal of it," she told an art writer. "I don't." And the influential sculptor Louise Nevelson said, with gusto, late in her life, "I still want to do my work, I still want to do my livingness. . . . I recognized what I had, and I never sold it short. And I ain't through yet!" She died at age 86. However, even self-assured Nevelson had experienced a sense of isolation in the male-dominated art world, and she reportedly appreciated the support she received from younger emerging female artists.

A major breakthrough for American women artists came in 1987 when the National Museum of Women in the Arts opened its doors in Washington, D. C. For the first time, a museum focused attention exclusively on art made by women and celebrated women's diverse achievements over the centuries. "Old Masters are one thing; old mistresses are quite another," wrote art history professor Alexandra Comini, commenting on the need for the museum.

Although few women artists are as well known as their male counterparts, American women artists are finally coming into their own. They are getting more critical and commercial acclaim from gallery directors and museum curators, and they are being taken more seriously by art critics and the public. But the professional women artists of today should not forget those who paved the way—many of whom are still unknown and waiting to be rediscovered. As photorealist painter and sculptor Audrey Flack said in 1970 in *Art Talk:* "Art is continuous discovery into reality, an exploration of visual data which has been going on for centuries, each artist contributing to the next generation's advancement."

Art never stands still, and neither do artists. Some of today's female artists are experimenting with technology through computer and digital art, while others erect massive site-specific installations or probe the nature of spiritual and mystical forces, combining, as Alice Aycock put it, "science and magic." Abstract art is still popular, as is highly politicized statement art. But painting beautifully, or with unabashed emotion, is no longer considered reactionary, even though modernism once deemed it so. No matter what their style, medium, or background, the professional female artists profiled in this book have one thing in common: Each has made an important, lasting contribution to the art world. Surely it is time to learn more about them and their remarkable works of art.

— C. K.

ABBOTT, BERENICE
(1898–1991) *Photographer*

Berenice Abbott was one of the most accomplished American photographers of the 20th century. Her compelling body of work, which spanned six decades and two continents, is characterized by its pioneering documentary approach and its exacting artistry. "The photographer's act," she wrote in 1964, "is to see the outside world precisely, with intelligence as well as sensuous insight."

Shortly after Berenice was born in Springfield, Ohio, on July 17, 1898, her parents were divorced. She was raised by her mother, was separated from her siblings during her early years, and had little contact with her father. Without question, Abbott wanted to escape the Midwest and her unhappy childhood as soon as she could. After attending Ohio State University in Columbus for one semester, she dropped out and headed for New York City.

Abbott arrived in New York in 1918 in the middle of a snowstorm and a flu epidemic. Nonetheless, she loved the city and quickly befriended artists and writers who lived in her neighborhood, bohemian Greenwich Village. She signed up for journalism courses at Columbia University but after a few weeks opted to try her hand at sculpture.

Then she decided she could be poor "just as easily in Europe as in America." So on March 21, 1921—with only a few dollars and a one-way ticket in her pocket—Abbott sailed for France.

In Paris she looked up one of her New York friends, the surrealist painter Man Ray, who had become a financially successful portrait photographer. For a time Abbott studied sculpture and drawing at the Kunstschule in Berlin, but she recognized that she could not support herself as an artist and returned to Paris in search of a job. In 1923 Man Ray hired her as his darkroom assistant, claiming he wanted someone who had no knowledge of photography, whom he could train and mold. Within two years Abbott had mastered the technical side of photography; she seemed to have an almost uncanny sense of lighting, clarity, and precision. During her lunch break, she asked friends to stop by Man Ray's studio and pose for her. They praised her straightforward but illuminating portraits, and Abbott began charging her sitters modest fees. "I took them different from his [Man Ray], particularly the women," she noted.

In 1926 Abbott set up her own studio and spent three years taking penetrating photographs of French and expatriate luminaries such as Jean Cocteau, Marcel Duchamp, André Gide, James

Joyce, Djuna Barnes, and Edna St. Vincent Millay. Abbott described the way she worked: "I treated every session as though I had never taken a photograph before in my life, relying on the moment, on my reaction to the sitters. . . . It all came spontaneously with each person." On June 8, 1926, she held her first one-person show, *Portraits Photographiques.* Many more one-person exhibitions at major museums in Europe and America would follow. She also participated in notable group shows, beginning in 1928 at the *Salon des Independants,* which was considered the first avant-garde group exhibition in Paris.

One day, while visiting Man Ray's studio, Abbott noticed pictures of Paris taken by Eugene Atget, a 70-year-old, relatively unknown French photographer who had completed a documentary study of the city that covered a 30-year period. The impact of Atget's prints, she recalled, was "immediate and tremendous . . . a sudden flash of recognition—the shock of realism unadorned." Two years later she met Atget; wearing an enormous new overcoat, he had come to her studio to be photographed. However, when she went to his apartment to show him the finished portrait, she was told that he had died. From that moment, Abbott steadfastly promoted Atget as one of the world's great photographers. After purchasing 1,500 glass-plate negatives and 8,000 prints from his estate, Abbott went on to publish a book of his photographs, *The World of Atget* (1964), in which she extolled his attributes as a master photographer: "A relentless fidelity to fact, a deep love of the subject for its own sake, a profound feeling for materials and surfaces and textures, a conscious intent in permitting the subject photographed to live by virtue of its own form and life." In fact, Abbott could have been describing her own oeuvre.

In 1929 Abbott returned to the United States. Influenced by Atget's "realism unadorned," she embarked on a monumental project: to systematically record the vibrant, changing face of New York City. Initially she used a small handheld camera. But by 1932 she had switched to a large-format camera that enabled her to capture more details in

her dramatic black-and-white prints. She also employed modernist photographic techniques such as dynamically framed or asymmetrical compositions and flattened pictorial space. Abbott took pictures of ordinary people and places as well as New York's historic landmarks and architectural wonders, including one of her most celebrated photographs: a glittering view of New York at night taken from the top of the Empire State Building. But she also focused on newsstands, subway stations, and the bustling streets of the Lower East Side.

Obsessed by the idea of chronicling on film *all* of New York, as it changed from day to day, she plodded on, without financial assistance, for six years. She supported herself by taking freelance assignments at *Life* and *Fortune* magazines and helped create a photography program at the New School for Social Research, where she taught classes for 25 years. In 1934 the Museum of the City of New York exhibited 41 of Abbott's New York City photographs. The show was critically acclaimed, and a year later she was paid by the Works Project Administration of the Federal Art Project to continue her documentation of the city. The culmination of her mammoth project was the publication of *Changing New York* (1939), a book with photographs by Abbott and text by Elizabeth McCausland. Abbott's decade-long urban study has been called the finest record ever made of an American city. "The city was full of change, of contrasts, of contradictions, and Abbott attempted to render them all together in one critical moment in each of her photographs," explained Hank O'Neal, her principal biographer.

A few years later Abbott wrote an influential and popular bestseller entitled *A Guide to Better Photography* (1941; reissued in 1953). She also marketed her own inventions of photographic equipment, having received four U.S. patents for photographic devices. Looking for another new challenge, Abbott turned to the largely unexplored field of scientific photography, even though she had no background in physics. "Surely scientific truth and natural phenomena are as good subjects for art as are man and his emotions, in their infi-

A self-portrait of photographer Berenice Abbott
taken with a device she invented—
the Abbott Distorter
(AP/Wide World Photos)

nite variety," she asserted. In 1958 she joined the physical science committee of Education Services, Inc., in Cambridge, Massachusetts, which resulted in an exhibition at the Massachusetts Institute of Technology and three secondary school textbooks illustrated with her imaginative scientific photographs. O'Neal, author of *Berenice Abbott: American Photographer* (1982), speculated that her scientific pictures may well be viewed in future years as her outstanding contribution to photography. And *New York Times* art critic Hilton Kramer wrote that Abbott was a pioneer in the photographic elucidation of scientific discourse.

Abbott's last major project, which she began in 1954, was to follow U.S. Route 1 from the coast of Maine down to Florida, recording, as she explained it, the familial as well as "the fantastic and unex-

pected, the ever-changing and renewing . . . reality containing unparalleled beauties." Abbott fell in love with Maine and its hardworking, unpretentious residents. In 1956 she impulsively purchased a rundown stagecoach inn built in 1810, in a small town in Maine whose population numbered 52. After spending 10 years renovating the house, she moved to Maine permanently. Although she gave up her studio in New York, she never severed her ties with the city she had memorialized.

Abbott received numerous honorary doctorates and awards, including the First International Erice Prize for Photography in 1987 and the International Center of Photography's Infinity Award for Master of Photography in 1989. That same year the New York Public Library sponsored a major retrospective exhibition of her work; it traveled throughout America and to Tokyo. In December 1999, the New York Public Library held another show, this time of her science "illustrations." Abbott once defined photography as a "friendly interpreter between science and the layman." It should not, she said in a 1951 speech, attempt to imitate other mediums. "It has to walk alone; it has to be itself."

Berenice Abbott died at her home in Maine on December 9, 1991, at the age of 93. Although her early work had at times been overlooked by museums and galleries, in part because she was a female photographer, she enjoyed great critical success during her long, distinguished career. When asked what she considered her best photograph, Abbott replied, "The one I will take tomorrow."

Further Reading

Abbott, Berenice. *Changing New York,* with text by Elizabeth McCausland. New York: E. P. Dutton, 1939. (Reprinted as *New York: in the Thirties.* New York: Dover Publications, 1973.)

———. *A New Guide to Better Photography.* New York: Crown Publishers, 1953.

———. *The World of Atget.* New York: Horizon Press, 1964.

O'Neal, Hank. *Berenice Abbott: American Photographer,* with an introduction by John Canaday. New York: McGraw-Hill, 1982.

Vestal, David. *Berenice Abbott/Photographs,* with a foreword by Muriel Rukeyser. Washington, D.C.: Smithsonian Institution Press, 1990.

Yokelson, Bonnie. *Berenice Abbott: Changing New York.* New York: New Press, 1997.

— C. K.

ALBERS, ANNI (Annelise Fleishmann)
(1899–1994)   *Textile Designer, Graphic Artist, Printmaker*

During her long and illustrious career, Anni Albers was one of America's foremost and most influential contemporary weavers and textile designers, as well as a notable printmaker. As a devout modernist, she valued both aesthetics and technology, and she adhered to her own tenet: "We [artists] learn courage from our art work. . . . We learn to dare to make a choice to be independent."

Born Annelise Fleishmann on June 12, 1899, in Berlin, Germany, Anni studied art at home while she was a teenager. In 1922 she enrolled in the weaving workshop at the Bauhaus, an innovative school of design in Weimar that integrated art, architecture, and crafts. She would have preferred to study painting or glass, but weaving was one of the few workshops open to women.

Initially Fleishmann considered weaving "as sissy as working with threads." However, she soon changed her mind. For one thing, she was encouraged by her instructors to "take chances, even if that meant groping and fumbling." She also adopted the Bauhaus philosophy that the nature of the materials determined the direction of the work. That helps explain why she opted for spare symmetrical abstract designs, often in muted colors, instead of the busy floral patterns or narratives that were popular at that time.

In 1925 she married fellow Bauhaus student Josef Albers, who would become an acclaimed painter and color theorist. Five years later, Albers was awarded a diploma from the Bauhaus, having designed a sound-absorbing drapery material of cellophane, chenille, and cotton that was both functional and aesthetically appealing. When

Adolf Hitler closed the design school in 1933, the Alberses—who were both respected teachers there—emigrated to the United States, in part because Anni Albers was Jewish. The Jewish Museum in New York paid for their passage.

The next year the couple joined the faculty at North Carolina's newly established, progressive Black Mountain College. For 15 years, Albers, who by then had become an American citizen, was an assistant professor of art in charge of the college's weaving workshop. The Alberses decided to leave North Carolina in 1949 and settled in New York City. That same year Albers became the first weaver to have a solo show at the Museum of Modern Art. Her unique fabrics were well received both by critics and the public. In 1950 Josef Albers was named chair of the department of design at Yale University, so he and his wife moved to New Haven, Connecticut. No longer teaching, Anni

Influential textile artist Anni Albers and her husband, Josef Albers, arriving in America in 1933
(AP/Wide World Photos)

Albers concentrated on textiles that used nontraditional materials. She also wrote two seminal books, *Anni Albers: On Designing* (1959) and *Anni Albers: On Weaving* (1965), and designed Jewish ritual objects such as ark curtains.

It was during this productive period that Albers, influenced by her research into ancient Peruvian and Mexican textiles, created "pictorial weavings"—a term she used to designate small works of art composed of geometric studies. Although she advocated using a hand loom, Albers also recognized the value of sewing machines and industrial fibers. "Not only the materials themselves," she asserted in *On Designing,* "which we come to know in a craft, are teachers. The . . . more mechanized tools, our machines, are our guides too." She was equally comfortable making functional industrial draperies and bedspreads for textile manufacturers as she was creating small wall hangings that she had framed, placed behind glass, and put on display as fine art.

In 1961 Albers was the recipient of a medal for craftsmanship from the American Institute of Architects, but by that time she had turned to graphics as her preferred medium. "In the many years that I was a weaver I learned to respect their [textiles] suggestive power," she explained in an exhibition catalog. "Now that graphics is my medium, I again acknowledge their [textiles'] formative influence. Thus, signing my name to a work, I do it realizing the debt I owe them."

Albers moved to California in 1963, where her husband had been invited to participate in the Tamarind Lithography Workshop. Feeling like a "useless wife . . . just hanging around," Albers tried her hand at printmaking. As with her weavings, she let line determine the form. Her work was so successful that she was invited to return to Tamarind as a fellow. She went on to experiment with numerous printing processes such as embossing, photo-offset, and silk screen. In 1967 she produced her last pictorial weaving, and when the Alberses moved to Orange, Connecticut, in 1970, she left her looms behind. However, her prints, like her textiles, were based on small geometric forms that were repeated. They exuded a mysterious, cerebral quality, just as her weavings had.

Paula Wisotzki, in *North American Women Artists,* points out that, ironically, "despite Albers's success in destroying the boundaries between art and craft with her weavings, her prints, beyond reproach as part of the 'high art' tradition, seem to have secured her reputation."

In 1980 Albers received the rarely awarded gold medal for "uncompromising excellence" from the American Crafts Council. She taught at several art institutes and universities and was awarded five honorary doctorates. Albers's textiles and prints have been shown worldwide, including a retrospective exhibition that originated at the Guggenheim Collection in Venice in 1999, traveled to Germany and France, and in June 2000 closed at the Jewish Museum in New York City, the same museum that in 1966 had commissioned her to create a textile memorial to victims of the Holocaust. In his essay in the exhibition's accompanying catalog, Nicholas Fox Weber, executive director of the Josef and Anni Albers Foundation, noted that Albers was very much a modernist, valuing everything from water-repellent fibers to plastic. She would complain about "craft people," saying that they should "simply look at what they were wearing to understand the value of mechanization." Yet while Albers may have created pop jewelry made from sink strainers, bath chains, and paper clips, she also disliked industry's reliance on designers who worked on paper and never on the loom.

Anni Albers, through her life and work, inspired other women in her field, such as RUTH ASAWA and SUE FULLER, to experiment with fiber and design. She died at age 94, on May 9, 1994, one of the last survivors of the celebrated Bauhaus group.

Further Reading

Albers, Anni. *Anni Albers: On Designing*. Revised Edition. Middletown, Conn.: Wesleyan University Press, 1965.
———. *Anni Albers: On Weaving*. Middletown, Conn.: Wesleyan University Press, 1965.

Barbo, Gene, and Nicholas Fox Weber. *Anni Albers: Drawings and Prints.* New York: Brooklyn Museum, 1977.

Weber, Nicholas Fox, and Pandora Tabatabai Asbaghi. *Anni Albers.* New York: Guggenheim Museum/Abrams, 2000.

— C. K.

ALVAREZ, MABEL
(1891–1985)   *Painter, Printmaker*

Southern California artist Mabel Alvarez was one of the first female modernists to explore alternative religions and philosophies in her work. She began as a regional impressionist but was better known for her "dreamscapes"—evocative paintings and prints imbued with symbolic meaning.

Born on November 28, 1891, on the island of Oahu, Hawaii, Mabel Alvarez was encouraged at an early age to develop her interest in art. Her father, a prominent and affluent Spanish-born physician, instilled a strong sense of accomplishment in his children. In fact, Mabel's brother Walter was nominated in 1968 for a Nobel Prize for his contributions to physics.

In 1906 the Alvarez family moved to Los Angeles, California, where Mabel studied art with several instructors, including William Cahill, a prominent impressionist. He taught his young student to appreciate vivid, natural outdoor colors and instructed her in the use of fluid, abbreviated brush strokes. Alvarez's first impressionist painting was displayed at the Los Angeles Museum (now the Los Angeles County Museum of Art) in 1917. Around that time, she also worked on a large mural in San Diego, California, and on several notable academic drawings and richly hued oil portraits. One of them, *Self-Portrait* (1923), shows the artist wearing a gaily decorated large-brimmed chapeau. According to her diary, when she was not mastering color, line, and form, Alvarez enjoyed shopping for flamboyant hats.

Alvarez was very much part of the freethinking modernist movement in Southern California that flourished from about 1910 until World War II

and featured previously unknown but talented women painters. According to Ilene Susan Fort, in *Independent Spirits: Women Painters of the American West, 1890–1945,* "artistic investigations of a more introspective character engaged Southern California modernists, and these [female] painters responded with imaginative figurative, symbolic, and abstract paintings."

Increasingly interested in experimental art forms of a more introspective nature, Alvarez found herself influenced by the then-popular philosophical writings of Will Levington Comfort, an avid proponent of Theosophy, an eclectic system of religious belief and practice based on Eastern mystical insight. Alvarez was also influenced by the work of artists who were willing to delve into their own mysterious private worlds. In a diary entry in 1919, she wrote about a painter whose works she had recently seen: "A dream world of the spirit—nothing of the material physical world—strange and lovely color and compositions and subjects. He worked entirely from within." She also noted that for her there was no point to painting unless the inspiration came "straight from the center."

That same year, in 1919, Alvarez had a meeting with Stanton Macdonald-Wright, a progressive artist who cofounded synchromism, a modernist movement that focused on the purely abstract use of color. He introduced her to the European avant-garde, and Alvarez soon moved beyond regional impressionism, although she continued to emphasize the importance of color.

Beginning in 1925 Alvarez created what she called "dreamscapes"—symbolic works that explored the psyche and spiritual themes. Her goal was to express on canvas or paper her private dream world. One of her best-known dreamscapes, *Dream of Youth* (1925), comprised of ethereal maidens floating eerily in a kind of allegorical, heavenly green garden, exemplifies the artist's decision to stress symbolism over form. Alvarez often used various hues of green to create, as Ilene Susan Fort explains it, a "calm, gentle mood, suggestive of the spiritual harmony

"Dreamscape" painter and printmaker
Mabel Alvarez, circa 1915
(Courtesy Archive of American Art, Smithsonian Institution,
Washington, D.C., and Laband Art Gallery,
Loyola Marymount University)

and contentment she had finally achieved through Comfort's teachings." Art historian Michael Kelley described her symbolist paintings as being "staged in a distant idyllic world where. . . . dreams have become reality."

In 1941 Alvarez had a solo show at the Los Angeles Museum, and many more one-person exhibitions followed. In 1995 several of her earlier paintings and portraits were shown in Los Angeles as part of Autry Museum of Western Heritage's groundbreaking exhibition of women painters in the American West. Four years later, a retrospective show tracing Alvarez's career traveled throughout Southern California, to museums such as the Orange County Museum of Art.

Mabel Alvarez, a modern California master who dared to explore spirituality and symbolism in her luminous and technically proficient work, died on March 13, 1985, in Los Angeles.

Further Reading

Fort, Ilene Susan. "The Adventuresome, the Eccentrics, and the Dreamers: Women Modernists of Southern California." In *Independent Spirits: Women Painters of the American West, 1890–1945,* edited by Patricia Trenton, 86, 89–90, 99. Berkeley: University of California Press, 1995.

Kovinick, Phil. *The Woman Artist in the American West, 1860–1960.* Fullerton, Calif.: Muckenthaler Cultural Center, 1976.

— C. K.

ARBUS, DIANE (Diane Nemerov)
(1923–1971)   *Photographer*

During her brief, controversial career, Diane Arbus had a profound influence on contemporary American documentary photography. Capturing hidden truths behind public exteriors, she was renowned for her unsettling photographs of "freaks," nonconformists, and disfigured people living on the edge of society. She was also praised for her affecting celebrity portraits and fashion photography. After her death by suicide in 1971, Arbus became a popular cult figure.

Born Diane Nemerov on May 14, 1923, in Manhattan, she was raised in a wealthy, assimilated Jewish family. Her parents, owners of a fashionable women's clothing store called Russeks, emphasized artistic achievement. A tall, slender, exceedingly shy child, Diane was close to her older brother, Howard, who would become a distinguished poet, but she had more distant relationships with her parents and younger sister.

Nemerov excelled in painting and sculpting classes at Ethical Culture and Fieldston, the progressive private schools she attended. One of her teachers, Victor D'Amico, commented on the burgeoning artist's "visual talent and imagination," which seemed to compel her to live in a state of "internal crisis, of excitement." At times those internal crises led to recklessness. For example, as an adolescent she would stand on the window ledge of her parents' 11th-story apartment, gazing at the trees in Central Park and the skyscrapers, until her frightened mother pulled her back indoors. Arbus was consumed by a sense of unreality and, like her mother, suffered from clinical depression. She admired the "freaks" she would later photograph for being "aristocrats" who had "already passed their test in life" by courageously refusing to play by society's rules.

On April 10, 1941, 18-year-old Nemerov married Allan Arbus, whom she had known and loved since she was 14. During World War II, while serving in the Army Signal Corps, Allan attended photography school, and then he taught his young bride everything he had learned. After he returned from his post in Burma, in 1944, the couple set up a successful fashion photography studio, with Diane styling the shoots and Allan taking the pictures. They worked for prestigious magazines such as *Vogue, Glamour,* and *Harper's Bazaar.*

In 1945 Arbus had a daughter, Doon, and nine years later she gave birth to second child, Amy. In 1951 the Arbuses spent a year in Europe to escape the pressures of the high-powered fashion photography industry. "All her impressions . . . noises, colors, textures, shapes, expressions, whirled around in her head," wrote Patricia Bosworth in her 1984 biography of the photographer.

With her husband's encouragement and his technical assistance, in 1954 Arbus left the studio to try her luck as an independent photographer; years earlier she had attended classes taught by the noteworthy photographer BERENICE ABBOTT, and she had also enrolled for a short time in Alexey Brodovitch's Design Laboratory. Arbus described her new avocation as "contemporary anthropology," because she saw photography as a way to document society, especially its nonconformists. With her first camera in hand, a 35-millimeter Speed Graphic, she delved into the medium and discovered its potential: "A photograph was a secret about a secret. The more it tells you, the less you know."

In the mid-1950s, Arbus began studying with the Austrian-born documentary photographer

Lisette Model at the New School in Manhattan. Model, who became Arbus's mentor and friend, helped her focus on taking direct, incisive photographs of "forbidden" people and places. As critic Peter Bunnell said of Arbus's work, she learned to capture the "isolation of the human figure" and "mirror the essential aspects of society."

Another important influence on Arbus was Marvin Israel, art director of *Harper's Bazaar.* He introduced her to people who could help further her career. He also encouraged her to take more risks. Using a deceptively simple, confrontational style, enhanced by a flash or frontal lighting and a large, square snapshot format that became her trademark, most of her subjects looked directly at the camera and seemed to reveal themselves to her without reserve. Arbus took pictures that were sometimes grotesque but always imbued with dignity. Her subjects included drug addicts, the homeless, small-town circus performers, prostitutes, twins, midgets, and transvestites. There were memorable portraits of a Jewish giant with his parents, a man in hair curlers, and overweight teenagers. She also visited gay nightclubs, tattoo parlors, wax museums, nudist camps, and a Times Square freak show. Arbus, wrote critic A. D. Coleman in *The Village Voice,* documented "the freakishness of normalcy and the normalcy of freakishness."

At home, Arbus's marriage was failing, even though for years she and Allan had been accepting of each other's numerous extramarital affairs. In 1959 the Arbuses separated; they would divorce 10 years later, but even after he remarried Allan remained a close personal and professional friend.

In 1960 *Esquire* magazine published Arbus's first photographic essay, "The Vertical Journey," which chronicled the lives of six New Yorkers. The following year *Harper's Bazaar* printed "The Full Circle"—portraits of Arbus's eccentric subjects with accompanying captions. She continued to be fascinated, as she described it, by "singular people who appear like metaphors somewhere further out than we do."

To supplement her income, Arbus took celebrity portraits of such luminaries as writers

W. H. Auden and Marianne Moore. She also photographed models and movie stars, noting that "beauty itself is an aberration, a burden, a mystery." All told, she would publish more than 250 pictures in more than 70 magazine articles, including, in 1966, a children's fashion spread for the Sunday *New York Times* that was more provocative than the more commonplace family-oriented photographs of young fashion models.

Arbus was awarded two Guggenheim Fellowships—in 1963 and 1966—that enabled her to travel across the country photographing what she called "the considerable ceremonies of our present." Her sometimes macabre choice of subjects included twin fetuses in a bottle of formaldehyde and a headless man dressed in a business suit.

In spite of the critical attention her work received, Arbus remained insecure. Approaching her subjects was a painful task. But, according to Bosworth, "her terror aroused her and made her *feel;* shattered her listlessness, her depression. Conquering her fears helped her develop the courage she felt her mother had failed to teach her." Arbus was also financially insecure and in the 1960s and 1970s accepted teaching positions at institutions such as the Rhode Island School of Design in Providence and at Westbeth, the artists' cooperative in Greenwich Village where she would spend the final years of her life.

In 1967 Arbus was invited to participate in *New Documents,* a three-person exhibition at New York's Museum of Modern Art, along with the influential photographers Gary Winogrand and Lee Friedlander. The show received mostly positive reviews, although one critic was disgusted by Arbus's "repulsive" work and called her "The Wizard of Odds." Others, however, called her a "modernist heroine," praising her radical documentary style and her refusal to distance herself from her subject. "When we have met the gaze of a midget or a female impersonator, a transaction takes place between the photograph and the viewer. In a kind of healing process, we are cured of our criminal urgency by having dared to look," asserted the reviewer for *Arts* magazine.

In the early 1970s Arbus visited an institution for mentally handicapped adults in New Jersey, where she took photographs of her subjects outdoors, in action. The powerful and compassionate pictures, known as the Unititled series, were more fluid than her earlier work, although they seemed to Arbus to be "out of control." In 1970 she was named the recipient of the Robert Leavitt Award from the American Society of Magazine Photographers for outstanding achievement, and she produced the first of a series of limited editions of her work. Nonetheless, she became increasingly depressed. Her work, she said, was not enough.

On July 26, 1971, 48-year-old Diane Arbus committed suicide in her apartment in Westbeth, having written the words "last supper" in her journal entry for that day. "Nothing about her life, her photographs, or her death was accidental or ordinary," said photographer and friend Richard Avedon. "They were mysterious and decisive and unimaginable, except to her. Which is the way it is with genius."

A year after she died, the Museum of Modern Art in New York held a major retrospective of Arbus's work; viewed by millions of people, it traveled throughout North America and later to Japan, Europe, and the Western Pacific. Also in 1972, Aperture published the first of two well-received monographs of her best-known photographs, and Arbus became the first American photographer invited to exhibit her work at the prestigious Venice Biennale. Ten large blowups of her sensational photographs of society's misfits were exhibited to much acclaim. But Arbus, whose photographs continue to appear posthumously in solo and group shows worldwide, had said that she did not want to be known as the voyeuristic photographer of freaks. She hoped that her pictures would suggest the secret experiences that are locked within all people and that they would grapple with larger issues such as identity versus illusion. "In the end the great humanity of Diane Arbus's art is to sanctify that privacy which she seemed at first to have violated," noted Marion Magid in *Arts* magazine.

Further Reading

Arbus, Diane. *Diane Arbus.* Exhibition Catalogue. New York: Museum of Modern Art, 1972.

———. *Diane Arbus: Magazine Work,* with texts by Doon Arbus and Marvin Israel. Millerton, N.Y.: Aperture, 1984.

Bosworth, Patricia. *Diane Arbus: A Biography.* New York: Alfred A. Knopf, 1984.

Coleman, A. D. *The Grotesque in Photography.* New York: Summit Books, 1977.

Livingston, Jane. *The New York School: Photographs 1936–1963.* New York: Stewart, Tabori and Chang, 1992.

— C. K.

ASAWA, RUTH
(1926–) *Sculptor*

Ruth Asawa has many talents in the art world. She is a sculptor whose woven forms are made of wire. She also works in dough. She has been acclaimed for her public art commissions, most notably fountains she constructed in San Francisco and northern California. And she is an outspoken art educator and activist.

Born on January 24, 1926, in Norwalk, California, Ruth helped her impoverished Japanese immigrant parents and six siblings tend a vegetable farm in southern California. As a young child, she worked long hours but dreamed of becoming an artist.

During World War II, in response to the Japanese bombing of Pearl Harbor, the U.S. government forced more than 120,000 Americans of Japanese descent living on the West Coast to leave their homes and enter internment camps. Ruth was separated from her father for four years. Along with the remaining members of her family, she was sent to a camp set up at California's Santa Anita racetrack. Also interned there were three artists who had worked at Walt Disney Studios. They gave art lessons to the displaced children. Ruth spent several hours a day drawing. "No other sixteen-year-old Americans were receiving (and still aren't) such training—many hours of instruction and practice with professional artists," she later recalled.

Her family was sent to a relocation center in Arkansas, where she graduated from high school in 1943. She was then permitted to study at Milwaukee State Teacher's College (now the University of Wisconsin at Milwaukee) for the next three years. Because of widespread distrust of Japanese Americans, Asawa dropped the idea of becoming an art teacher. From 1946 to 1949, she studied at Black Mountain College, an experimental school in North Carolina. Her teachers included such influential figures as Buckminister Fuller and Josef Albers. "It [Black Mountain] provided enough inspiration . . . to last for the rest of my life," she said. Asawa found more inspiration at a Quaker workshop she attended in Mexico in the summer of 1947. There she learned a folk art method of making baskets that involved crocheting wire. That technique was the precursor of the wire sculptures that would become her trademark.

In 1949 Asawa married Albert Lanier, an architectural student whom she had met at Black Mountain. They settled in San Francisco and had six children. Lanier became a respected architect, while Asawa began to exhibit her sculptures, beginning with a solo show in 1956 at the Peridot Gallery in New York.

In 1962 museum director Gerald Nordland lauded Asawa for creating sculptures that "turned inside into outside and . . . made no distinction between interior and exterior [so that] a free flow of form and space was produced."

Asawa's airy, seemingly transparent pieces were well received and were shown in New York City at the Whitney Museum in 1958 and the Museum of Modern Art in 1959. In 1973, the San Francisco Museum of Art (now the San Francisco Museum of Modern Art) held a retrospective of her work. Asawa invited the public to join her in a "dough-in." Using baker's clay—a mixture of flour, salt, and water—more than 1,000 mostly young participants collectively created a piece. In 1973 Asawa used this medium to sculpt a fountain which was eventually cast in bronze, and placed it in front of a hotel near San Francisco's landmark Union Square.

Asawa has also received several important public art commissions, including five fountains in San Francisco, the earliest of which is *Mermaid Fountain* (1968), a whimsical bronze structure in Ghiradelli Square made up of mermaids, turtles, and frogs. Another fountain, which Asawa constructed in 1976 in Japantown, is based on origami, the Japanese art of paper folding. In 1994 she installed a bronze bas-relief work entitled *Japanese-American Internment Memorial Sculpture* that was commissioned for the city of San Jose.

In addition to continually developing her sculpture, Asawa has been an active civic leader in San Francisco and a fervent advocate of art-centered education in the public schools. "I would like to recapture the times when cathedrals were built and the whole village worked together," she once explained. Asawa helped established the School of the Arts in San Francisco, cofounded a workshop that brings professional artists like herself into the city's schools, and has collaborated with artists who work in other mediums because, she explains, "it is enriching all of us."

In 1966 Asawa was the first recipient of the Dymaxion Award for artist/scientist, and in 1974 she received the fine arts gold medal from the American Institute of Architects. In recognition of Asawa's civic and artistic contributions, the mayor of San Francisco proclaimed February 12, 1982, as Ruth Asawa Day. In 1996 she won an arts education award from the National Education Association, and that same year garnered the Japanese American Lifetime Achievement Award. Well into her seventies, Asawa continues to draw and works closely with her neighborhood elementary school. She is also a proud grandmother.

Further Reading

Hamilton, Mildred. "A Tour of Ruth Asawa's San Francisco," *San Francisco Examiner,* September 19, 1976, Arts Section, 1.

Sculptor Ruth Asawa works with bronze, wire, and dough.
(Photo by Irene Poon, 1996)

Nordland, Gerald. *Ruth Asawa: A Retrospective View.* San Francisco: San Francisco Museum of Art, 1973.
Rubinstein, Charlotte Streifer. *American Women Sculptors.* Boston: G. K. Hall, 1990.

— C. K.

AYCOCK, ALICE
(1946–) *Sculptor, Installation Artist, Illustrator*

Alice Aycock is an internationally known sculptor who combines metaphysics and mysticism with science and technology in her complex, often unnerving large-scale installations. Influences on her formidable body of work include classical history and architecture; the impact of industrialization on modernity; and her own childhood fears, dreams, and fantasies.

Born on November 20, 1946, in Harrisburg, Pennsylvania, Alice Aycock attended Douglass College (Rutgers University) in New Brunswick, New Jersey. There she received a bachelor's degree in studio art and art history in 1968. In 1971 she earned a master's degree from Hunter College in New York City, having studied with the preeminent sculptor Robert Morris. A year later she created her first site-specific sculpture, a work that coexists with and is defined by a particular environment or landscape. *Maze* was a 12-sided circular outdoor installation comprised of five concentric wooden rings. Viewers could easily enter the sculpture through one of three openings but encountered difficulty when trying to exit the labyrinth. Aycock's intention, she said in a 1982 interview, was to fabricate a moment of "absolute panic—when the only thing that mattered was to get out."

Another early work, from 1973, the half-sunken, tomblike *Low Building with Dirt Roof (for Mary),* purposely encouraged viewers to face their fear of entrapment. This piece was constructed on a Pennsylvania farm site with the help of her mother and was inspired by Aycock's visit to Greek tombs in Mycenae. In *Contemporary Women Artists* (1999), Dorothy Valakos describes the impact of Aycock's provocative site-specific pieces: "Based on an almost encyclopedic array of historical, scientific, occult, and literary sources, [her] astounding confabulations of intellect and curiosity push at the limits of human understanding to border on the irrational, the perverse, and the dangerous."

In 1977 Aycock held her first major solo exhibition at New York City's prestigious Museum of Modern Art. The following year she had an individual exhibition at New York's John Weber Gallery, which represents her work to this day. During the late 1970s and early 1980s, Aycock became more interested in metaphysical and spiritual issues and switched from building forms that invited viewer participation to non-sited sculptures that were meant to be observed. These works, using materials such as steel, glass, and batteries, often resembled scientific experiments or theatrical stage sets, with props, cranks, and pulleys. For example, a series entitled *How to Catch and Manufacture Ghosts* (1979) was described by Aycock as "an attempt to mix science and magic." It was comprised of a live dove in a glass jar wrapped in wires attached to a battery made out of a lemon. While Aycock's intentions are serious, she has a lighter, mischievous side—illustrated by her use o a piece of fruit as a battery. Like many of her other sculptures, *Ghosts* had substantive notes accompanying it. Often these texts make references to archaeology, mysticism, or history. In this case, they were the hallucinatory writings of a schizophrenic who felt he could transcend ordinary space and time, which is something the artist attempts to do in her quest for a "transrational state of consciousness."

Having constructed more than 70 arresting installations worldwide, Aycock uses industrial materials such as graphite, welded metal, and fluorescent lights, as well as organic materials such as dirt, to create underground wells, dungeons, towering ramps, Ferris wheels, and carousels in her increasingly theatrical presentations. In 1982 she began using motorized metal blades, which were by turn mysterious and frightening, benign and destructive. In a catalog that accompanied Aycock's 1981 one-person exhibition at Philadelphia's Institute of Contemporary Art, Kay Larson noted that "Aycock's machines are her private version of the philosopher's stone, a device that allows anything to be converted into anything else, through the action of self on matter." In a piece titled *The Solar Wind* (1983), rotating metal scimitar blades seemed to threaten to slice the viewer, emotionally as well as physically.

Aycock has had two major retrospective exhibitions, the first of which originated in 1983 in Stuttgart, Germany, and traveled to several European cities. Solo exhibitions have ranged from the Tel Aviv Museum in Israel (1986) to the Storm King Art Center in Mountainville, New York (1990). The latter featured both her large-scale sculptures and her drawings on Mylar, which resemble architectural plans. Her work can also be found in permanent collections at New York City's

Alice Aycock combines mysticism and science in her
large-scale installations.
(Portrait by Timothy Greenfield-Sanders)

addition, Aycock has garnered three National
Endowment for the Arts Fellowships (1975, 1980,
1986) and has taught at Princeton and Yale Uni-
versities, Rhode Island School of Design, Hunter
College, and the School of Visual Arts in New
York. She lives in Manhattan's Soho area with her
son: "A child is something I very much wanted,"
Aycock said. "It's like going back to the earth."

Her recent work, exemplified by a three-
dimensional piece called *Some Night Action*
(1993), in which marbles become random clusters
of constellations according to the laws of physics
and chance, deals with "creation and preservation," as the artist explains it. Increasingly Alice
Aycock weds architecture and technology, the past
and the present. Her art, asserts Dorothy Valakos,
focuses on the "endless process of reconfiguration"
and "the very magic and strange beauty of these
[incomprehensible] constructs that allows us to
glimpse our true nature."

Further Reading

Price, Aimee Brown. "Artist's Dialogue: A Conversation
with Alice Aycock." *Architectural Digest,* April 1983,
54, 58, 60.

Robins, Corinne. *The Pluralist Era: American Art
1968–1981,* 104–106. New York: Harper and Row,
1984.

Valakos, Dorothy, "Alice Aycock." In *Contemporary Women
Artists,* 39–42. Detroit: St. James Press, 1999.

Watson-Jones, Virginia. "Alice Aycock." In *Contemporary
American Women Sculptors,* 28–29. Phoenix, Ariz.:
Oryx Press, 1986.

— C. K.

Museum of Modern Art, Guggenheim, and Whitney Museums as well as at the Hirshhorn Museum
in Washington, D.C. She has been part of groundbreaking Biennial shows in Venice, Italy (1978),
and at the Whitney Museum (1979, 2000). In

B

BACA, JUDITH FRANCISCA
(1946–)   *Muralist, Painter*

A fervent advocate of community-based art and a prominent Latina muralist, Judith Baca is best known for *The Great Wall of Los Angeles* (1976–83), a large-scale urban mural depicting and celebrating the history of California's diverse population. To assist her in its implementation, Baca hired young people from a variety of cultural and ethnic backgrounds.

Raised in a strong female household in Angeles, where she was born in 1946, Judith Francisca Baca earned a bachelor's degree in studio art in 1969 from California State University at Northridge. While teaching art at a Catholic high school in Los Angeles, she assigned students to work collaboratively on a mural, so that they not only would learn to paint, but they would also talk about each other's neighborhoods, backgrounds, and lifestyles. A few years later, while a resident artist for the Los Angeles Recreation and Parks Department, Baca convinced street gang members in East Los Angeles to participate in "muralist brigades," encouraging them to use paintbrushes instead of weapons.

In 1974 Baca was named director of a citywide mural project in Los Angeles. Under her leader-ship, close to 1,000 apprentice artists and crew members created more than 250 public murals that were displayed throughout Los Angeles over a 10-year period. Meanwhile, Baca and her assistants painted colorful murals at a California state prison for women and at a convalescent home for indigent residents. Also in 1974, she accepted a contract from the U.S. Army Corps of Engineers to design a mural for a segment of the Tujunga Wash Flood Control Channel, in the San Fernando Valley, that would reflect the history of Los Angeles's diverse population. In 1976 Baca named the project *The Great Wall of Los Angeles*. At 2,435 feet, it is the longest mural in America.

The Great Wall of Los Angeles, which took 700 gallons of paint and five summers to complete (1976 to 1981, and 1983), employed hundreds of young people from mostly lower-income neighborhoods, as well as art assistants, historians, and support staff. *The Great Wall* is an impressive object d'art and an example of how art can help break down social barriers. Some of the young participants were hired through the Los Angeles juvenile justice system, while others opted to work on the mural instead of being sent to reform school. One of the mural makers, 16-year-old Sergio Moreno, explained: "When I started working here,

I did it for the money. Then I began to take pride in the mural and in the Chicano section in particular. . . . I hope that when people see this mural they forget all their prejudices and try to live with all people, no matter what race, in peace."

In spite of flash floods and pollution, *The Great Wall* has survived and, notes art critic Carrie Rickey in *Art in America,* is considered a "monumentally scaled history painting depicting the panorama of events that contributed to Los Angeles' distinctive profile [by] showing the significance of various indigenous and immigrant ethnic groups."

In order to organize such a massive undertaking, in 1976 Baca helped found, and since 1981 has served as the artistic director of, the Social and Public Art Resource Center (SPARC), a multicultural public arts center in Venice, California, where Baca lives. Baca prepared artistically for *The Great Wall* by attending an intensive workshop in Cuernavaca, Mexico, where she immersed herself in mural painting. Her role models were premier Chicano muralists Diego Rivera and David Alfaro Siqueiros. In 1979 she completed a master of fine arts degree at California State University at Northridge.

During the mid-1980s Baca worked on a mural for the Olympics; two billboards, *Be Skeptical of the Spectacle* (1985) and *Represent Your Perspective* (1985), both of which invited viewers to question the veracity of media-induced images; and an enormous portable mural whose theme is worldwide peace. *The World Wall: A Vision of the Future Without Fear* (1987) traveled to Finland and the Soviet Union, with artists from different countries contributing to it.

Based on the success of *The Great Wall,* which she refers to as "both inclusive of other artistic expressions and a people's retelling of their own history," in 1988 Baca was asked by Los Angeles mayor Tom Bradley to create a new citywide mural project. Great Walls Unlimited: Neighborhood Pride Program has already produced more than 70 murals throughout Los Angeles. In 1990 she developed a series of murals in Guadalupe, California, that poignantly present the plight of migrant farmworkers in America.

Baca has taught at the University of California at Irvine and at California State University at Monterey Bay. Her more recent work includes murals commissioned for the University of Southern California and the Denver International Airport as well as two murals that provide information for homeless people who live on Skid Row in Los Angeles. She has had one-person shows in New York City, Chicago, and several western states. Her priority, however, has never wavered: to use art as a means of providing expression for the "pariah community in America," a phrase coined by Nobel laureate Toni Morrison. In a slide narrative that accompanied *The Great Wall of Los Angeles,* Judith Baca contends that the mural is the story, often overlooked in classroom textbooks, of California's ethnic groups, "their contributions and their struggles to overcome obstacles."

Further Reading

Baca, Judith Francisca. "Our People Are the Internal Exiles." Interview by Diane Neumaier in *Cultures in Contention,* edited by Douglas Kahn and Diane Neumaier. Seattle, Wash.: Real Comet Press, 1985.

Hernández, Luciano. "Judith Baca." Available online. URL: http://www.sscnet.ucla.edu/chavez/jb_bio.html. Posted on April 22, 1998.

Levick, Melba. *Murals of Los Angeles: The Big Picture.* Boston: Little, Brown and Company, 1988.

Rickey, Carrie. "The Writing on the Wall." *Art in America* (May 1981): 54–57.

— C. K.

BACON, PEGGY (Margaret Frances Brook)
(1895–1987)   *Caricaturist, Printmaker, Painter, Illustrator*

Peggy Bacon, a prominent author, printmaker, illustrator, and painter, was best known as a satirical caricaturist who depicted everyday urban scenes and cultural icons of the 1930s and 1940s. She also wrote and illustrated more than 50 books for children and adults; contributed stories, poems, and drawings to prestigious magazines; and penned a prizewinning mystery novel.

Born Margaret Frances Bacon on May 1, 1895, in Ridgefield, Connecticut, to two professional artists, Peggy, as she was known, grew up surrounded by palettes and paintbrushes, and she was drawing by the time she was a toddler. Her parents had met at the Art Students League in New York City, where Bacon would meet her future husband. In 1913 she graduated from a private boarding school in New Jersey. That same year, her father committed suicide, apparently because he felt he had failed as a painter. Nonetheless, 18-year-old Bacon was determined to become an artist. She enrolled at New York's School of Applied Arts for Women and, assisted by her landscape teacher, Jonas Lie—who in 1915 held a solo show of her work in his New York City studio—was able to sell her early illustrations and thereby finance her art education.

For the next five years, Bacon studied at the Art Students League, showing a natural aptitude for painting and printmaking. She admired the realism of her noteworthy painting and lithography teachers, John Sloan and George Bellows, and the biting social commentary of French caricaturist Honoré Daumier. In 1917 she taught herself, and soon excelled at, drypoint, a method of engraving in which a hard steel needle is used like a pen to carve lines in a softer metal plate, usually copper, to create a print. Bacon used drypoint technique to illustrate the first book she wrote, *The True Philosopher and Other Cat Tales* (1919). That same year, her prints were shown at exhibitions of the Society of Independent Artists and the Painter-Gravers of America.

In 1920 Bacon married painter Alexander Brook, a fellow student, and within two years had two children. The family settled in Rock City, near the avant-garde art colony of Woodstock, New York, where they and other young modernists were known as the "Rock City Rebels" because they distanced themselves from more traditional artists such as Bacon's former teachers Sloan and Bellows. After a few years, Bacon and Brook moved to Greenwich Village, a bohemian neighborhood in New York City, but they spent their summers in art enclaves in Cape Cod, Massachusetts, and Maine.

Bacon became a highly regarded printmaker and illustrator, but she stopped painting. The reason, according to her biographer Roberta Tarbell, was that she felt inferior to her husband, who was highly critical of his wife's paintings. Nonetheless the couple sometimes exhibited together, for example at the Joseph Brummer Gallery in New York City. Promoted by the Whitney Studio Club, which eventually evolved into New York's Whitney Museum of American Art, Brook and Bacon were considered successful artists whose work sold well.

In the late 1920s Bacon began to explore lithography, etching, and pastel, but drypoint remained her favored medium, and characters involved in quotidian life continued to be her favorite subject. Although she contributed satirical drawings to the *New Masses,* a Marxist magazine that was popular during the 1920s, she was more interested in capturing personalities on paper than in politics. In 1928 the influential photographer Alfred Stieglitz held a one-person exhibition of Bacon's work at New York's Intimate Gallery that was well received by artists such as Charles Demuth. She also began, in 1935, a long teaching stint at the Art Students League. In later years she taught at a variety of colleges and institutions, including the Corcoran School of Art in Washington, D.C.

In 1942 the Association of American Artists held a major retrospective of Bacon's work. She had solo exhibitions at several important venues in New York City, including four shows, from 1953 to 1972, at the Kraushaar Gallery. Assisted by a Guggenheim Foundation fellowship in 1934, Bacon produced *Off with Their Heads,* a commercially successful book comprised of detailed, stylized black-and-white satirical portraits accompanied by humorous vignettes that lambasted 40 art world luminaries, including GEORGIA O'KEEFFE. Bacon also contributed satirical drawings to national periodicals such as the *New Republic, The New Yorker, Vanity Fair,* and *Town and Country.* But by 1940 she had stopped producing them, noting that she may have inadvertently hurt the feelings of her friends, even though her drypoints were meant to be good-natured, witty commentaries on American people and places. Instead, she turned to landscape and genre scenes, especially while summering in Maine.

In 1940 she and her husband were divorced, which freed Bacon to return to oils. No longer feeling inadequate, she experimented by combining watercolor, gouache, and ink. In 1953 she wrote a prizewinning mystery novel, *The Inward Eye,* which the Mystery Writers of America honored with an Edgar Allen Poe Mystery Award for best novel of the year. In 1961 she moved to Maine and settled near her son Alexander, a newspaper publisher, in a cottage situated over a cove at Cape Porpoise. She continued to write and illustrate books such as *The Ghost of Opalina* (1967) and *The Magic Touch* (1968), and to paint, always adding a touch of fantasy to her colorful canvases.

In 1975 Bacon became the first living woman artist accorded a retrospective at the National Musuem of American Art, and in 1980 she received a gold medal from the American Academy and Institute of Arts and Letters for outstanding work in the graphic arts; other eminent contenders for the award included Jasper Johns and Robert Rauschenberg. She worked well into her 80s, with the help of a magnifying glass attached to her easel, since she was nearly blind. After a long and fruitful career in the arts, Peggy Bacon died on January 4, 1987, at the age of 92, in Kennebunk, Maine.

Further Reading

Bacon, Peggy. *Off with Their Heads.* New York: Robert M. McBridge & Company, 1934.

Dunford, Penny. *A Biographical Dictionary of Women Artists in Europe and America Since 1850,* 15–16. Philadelphia: University of Pennsylvania Press, 1989.

Hellen, Jules, and Nancy G. Hellen. *North American Women Artists of the 20th Century.* New York: Garland Publishing, 1995.

Tarbell, Roberta. *Peggy Bacon: Personalities and Places.* Washington, D.C.: National Collection of Fine Arts, Smithsonian Institution Press, 1975.

— C. K.

BARTLETT, JENNIFER LOSCH
(1941–   ) *Mixed Media Artist, Painter, Sculptor, Printmaker*

In 1976 Jennifer Bartlett's groundbreaking Rhapsody series of paintings took the American art world by storm. The huge multipart installation featured repetitive motifs on square steel plates that covered the walls of a New York City gallery. *Village Voice* critic Jerry Saltz asserted that it "echoed artists and styles that hadn't even happened yet." Since that time, Bartlett's work has continued to demand respect and attention.

Born on March 14, 1941, in Long Beach, California, Jennifer Losch spent most of her childhood in suburbia, which she described as "depressing and oppressive." But she was captivated by the nearby ocean: "Waves would dash across the boardwalk, and there were secret places to play underneath it. . . . I adored that." (Water, as represented by floods, waterfalls, and oceans, would figure prominently in her paintings.)

Early on, Bartlett was convinced that she would be a successful artist and live in New York City. She did not want to end up like her mother, a fashion illustrator who gave up her career to raise her four children. Bartlett attended Mills College in Oakland, California, where in her senior year she befriended ELIZABETH MURRAY, who like Bartlett would become a high-profile abstract painter. Initially Bartlett dabbled with landscape and figure painting, but she was drawn to the less restrictive quality of abstract shapes. "It was exciting. I was allowed to go on my own way," she said in *Originals: American Women Artists* (2000).

Bartlett graduated from Mills College in 1963 and two years later received a master of fine arts degree from Yale University School of Art and Architecture. Her teachers included premier abstract expressionist Jack Tworkov and pop artist Jim Dine. Although she admired and was influenced by their work, she wanted a form that would enable her to go beyond the "old way of painting" and "always be open." She discovered grid paper as a way to structure and clarify, simply, her complex ideas. She explained that she wanted to create everyday, related objects and combine them with organic body shapes.

In 1964, having married Edward Bartlett, a medical student, she lived in New Haven, Connecticut, and in a loft in Soho, an area of New York City then populated by factories and young artists like herself. Inspired by the steel station signs she observed while riding the New York subway, Bartlett experimented with flat steel plates. She covered them with Testor's enamel paint—the kind found in model airplane kits—and overlaid them with a grid. A controlled and disciplined craftsperson, Bartlett managed to imbue her cool work with passion and mystery.

After her divorce in 1972, Bartlett lived full-time in Soho. She taught at the School of Visual Arts in New York and in 1975 began working on her magnum opus, the Rhapsody series. A year later, in what was her third one-person show, Rhapsody was exhibited at the Paula Cooper Gallery. The colorful multipart gridded painting filled the entire space. In her introduction to *Rhapsody* (1985), a book about the monumental project, Roberta Smith called the work "an extended portable mural . . . a process-installation painting built to last . . . a complex conceptual narrative conducted from multiple viewpoints . . . that announced [Bartlett's] artistic coming of age." The series of 987 square steel plates—baked with white enamel and then silk-screened with quarter-inch grids stippled with points, dots, or dashes shaped into imagery—was arranged in 142 vertical rows of approximately seven plates each. It featured four archetypal images (house, mountain, tree, and ocean), and repetitive theme modules that varied from childlike drawings to sophisticated abstract forms.

New York magazine applauded Bartlett as one of the two strongest painters (the other being her former classmate Elizabeth Murray) of the post-minimal generation. *New York Times* art critic John Russell called Rhapsody the "most ambitious single work of new art that has come my way since I started to live in New York." Bartlett herself described the work as a "conversation, where you start a thought, bring in another idea to explain it, and then drop it." At 35, she had fulfilled her childhood dream of becoming a recognized professional artist living in New York City. After the show at the Paula Cooper Gallery closed, a collector bought Rhapsody and for two years it traveled to 10 American museums, including the landmark 1978 exhibition, *New Image Painting,* at the Whitney. (Bartlett was also invited to participate in the coveted Whitney Biennial exhibition in 1981.) She had solo shows that ranged from the Tate Gallery in London to the Contemporary Art Gallery in Seibu, Japan, and more than 15 at New York's Paula Cooper Gallery. A retrospective of her work originated in 1993 at Florida's Orlando Museum of Art and toured throughout the country.

Bartlett was commissioned to create a number of public and corporate works such as *In the Garden* (1979–80), a huge multipart construction that combined drawings, paint on canvas, glass, wooden screens, and mirrors. It was based on views of a garden and adjacent cracked swimming pool, from the dining room of a villa in Nice, France, where Bartlett had spent a winter. In 1979, in the lobby of the federal court building in Atlanta, Georgia, Bartlett produced a large-scale, multimedia mural entitled *Swimmers: Atlanta.* Versatile and industrious, she also built three-dimensional sculptural works by pairing paintings with actual objects, such as a canvas depicting a table, with a functional wooden table placed in front of it. In addition, she was asked to design urban gardens in New York and the sets and costumes for an opera that was staged in Paris.

In 1999, after a decade-long hiatus, Rhapsody was installed at the Robert Miller Gallery in New York. In 2000, the Lawrence Rubin Greenberg Van Doren studio held a show of 15 of Bartlett's signature enamel-and-steel paintings. In April 2000, *New York Times* journalist Grace Glueck praised Bartlett's "vivacious . . . quirky abstractions" as her "best and brightest" and noted that a new image has been added to the artist's more

Jennifer Bartlett, an innovative mixed-media painter,
sculptor, and printmaker
(Portrait by Timothy Greenfield-Sanders)

familiar iconography of houses, trees, and domestic rites: playful monsters.

The recipient of the 1983 American Academy and Institute of Arts and Letters Award and the 1986 American Institute of Architects Award, Bartlett is represented in prestigious permanent collections such as New York's Metropolitan Museum of Art and the Philadelphia Museum of Art.

Art critic Jerry Saltz has described Bartlett as ambitious, brash, "out there," and worldly. When asked why she paints, Bartlett, who is married to Mathieu Carriere and lives in New York and Paris, replied: "I want to move people. . . . I'd like to be a strong, heartbreaking artist."

Further Reading

Bartlett, Jennifer. *Rhapsody*, with an introduction by Roberta Smith and notes by the artist. New York: Harry N. Abrams, 1985.

Goldwater, Marge, Roberta Smith, and Calvin Tomkins. *Jennifer Bartlett*. New York: Abbeville Press, 1990.

Munro, Eleanor. *Originals: American Women Artists*. New York: Simon and Schuster, 2000.

Russell, John. *Jennifer Bartlett: In the Garden*. New York: Harry N. Abrams, 1982.

Saltz, Jerry. "The Way We Were." *Village Voice*, February 17–23, 1999, pp. 7–8.

— C. K.

BASCOM, RUTH HENSHAW MILES
(Aunt Ruth)
(1772–1848)   *Pastel Crayon Portraitist, Folk Artist*

The pastel portraits created by Ruth Henshaw Bascom, an early 19th-century folk artist who hailed from New England, are valued for their simplicity, sensitivity, and directness. She combined her domestic duties and responsibilities as a pastor's wife with her creative abilities as a portraitist.

Ruth Henshaw was born December 15, 1772, in Leicester, Massachusetts. The eldest of 10 children, she spent her formative years in nearby Worcester. Her father, Colonel William Henshaw, participated both in the French and Indian War and the American Revolution. After attending Leicester Academy, Ruth, like most girls in the late 1700s, was largely self-taught. When she was 17, she started keeping a diary and continued to do so for 57 years. Her entries were mostly about daily familial or social events, but on occasion they were spirited and even lyrical: "Spun and sang songs all day until night approached," she wrote as a teenager. In a later entry, she described a painting technique for making her living-room floor look as if it had been carpeted: "I finished painting my floor at 6 p.m. Striped with red, green, blue, yellow and purple— carpet like." Colors and shapes were of particular interest to her, both in her needlepoint work and her profile portraits.

In 1804 Henshaw married a professor at Dartmouth College, Dr. Asa Miles, who died in 1806. That same year she became the wife of Reverend Ezekiel Lysander Bascom and traveled with him from pastorate to pastorate, living mostly in Gill,

Massachusetts. The couple also resided in Deer-field and Ashby, Massachusetts, and in Fitzwilliam, New Hampshire. Although childless, as a pastor's wife Bascom kept busy by planning and hosting social and religious events. Nonetheless she found time, beginning around the 1820s, for "taking profiles" of her friends, neighbors, and relatives. As Beatrix T. Rumford points out in *American Folk Portraits,* Bascom developed a gentle "abstract, simple form of portraiture that undoubtedly suited her abilities and ambitions."

The majority of Bascom's pastel crayon portraits were executed during the 1830s, while living in Gill, when she was close to 60 years old. The full-sized or nearly full-sized profiles of children and adults were described by Charlotte Streifer Rubinstein in *American Women Artists: From Early Indian Times to the Present* (1982) as having "calm strength of characterization combined with a sensitive feeling for shape, color, and texture." In keeping with the tradition of most artists of the colonial period, especially women, Bascom rarely signed her work. And she never accepted payment for it.

"Aunt Ruth," as Bascom was frequently called, created profile portraits by "taking a shadow." The sitter cast a shadow upon a piece of paper, and Bascom traced it in pencil. She then used pastel crayons for color, for example, applying a trace of red on the cheeks. She also added her own unique decorative touches such as cutting out and pasting the face on a different-colored background or pasting on gold paper beads or shiny pieces of tinfoil to create ornamental eyeglasses or jewelry. To further enliven the silhouettes of her subjects, Bascom would occasionally include a bucolic landscape in the background, instead of the more common-place pale backdrop.

Examples of Bascom's work include her *Self-Portrait* (1830), one of many, comprised of a soft-ened image set off by a sharply defined facial outline. *Edwin Davis* (1838), a full-sized work of a young boy, features a stylized head and upper torso placed against a light blue background; the boy's dark blue coat sports brass-colored buttons. Bascom's pastel portraits are represented in collections held at Boston's Museum of Fine Arts, Old Sturbridge Village (Massachusetts), the Museum of American Folk Art in New York City, and the American Museum in Britain.

Like other late 18th- and early 19th-century primitive female folk artists who had little or no professional training, Ruth Henshaw Bascom was an affluent amateur hobbyist who was both prolific and talented. She died in 1848 at the age of 76 in Ashby. Most of her portraits were discovered in Franklin County, Massachusetts, and they date from the 1830s. Her unpublished journals, important for their record of quotidian colonial life from a woman's point of view, are housed at the American Antiquarian Society in Worcester, Massachusetts.

Further Reading

Dewhurst, G. Kurt, Betty MacDowell, and Marsha MacDowell. *Artists in Aprons: Folk Art by American Women.* New York: E. P. Dutton and the Museum of American Folk Art, 1979.

Dods, Agnes M. "Ruth Henshaw Bascom." In *Primitive Painters in America,* by Jean Lipman and Alice Winchester, 31–38. New York: Dodd, Mead, 1950.

Rumford, Beatrix T. *American Folk Portraits.* Boston: New York Graphic Society, 1981.

Weatherford, Doris. *American Women's History.* New York: Prentice Hall, 1994.

— C. K.

BEAUX, CECILIA
(1855–1942) *Painter, Portraitist*

One of the most popular and distinguished female painters of the late 19th and early 20th centuries, Cecilia Beaux was an award-winning portraitist recognized for her masterful painterly style and sensuous brushwork, as well as her ability to capture character traits and physical likenesses. Her straightforward early portraits evolved, over time, into more complex, insightful works.

Cecilia Beaux was born in 1855 in Philadelphia, Pennsylvania. Her mother—who was from New England and from whom Beaux said she inherited her "steadfastness of purpose"—died shortly thereafter. Her despairing father, from whom she claimed her poetic, sensual side, returned to his native France, leaving maternal relatives to raise Cecilia and her sister. Like most upper-class young ladies in the mid-1800s, Cecilia was tutored at home. She cultivated an interest in European culture, especially the fine arts, and later recalled that her Aunt Eliza, a musician and amateur watercolorist, always carried a sketchbook and pencil with her. It was from her aunt that Cecilia learned how to copy lithographs. (Years later Beaux would copy paintings by the old masters in Paris and Venice).

At 16, after dabbling with oils "quite a little but without advice," Cecilia took drawing lessons from Catharine Anne Drinker, a distant relative and respected painter who helped Cecilia discover, as she put it, "the wonders of light." She also studied at the prestigious Philadelphia Academy of Fine Arts and participated in a women's painting class led by the German-trained portraitist William Sartain, who traveled from New York City to teach the enthusiastic group of amateurs. In addition, Beaux was influenced by the flamboyant painter James Whistler, who believed that "art should be independent of all claptrap," and by the controversial realist Thomas Eakins, who was soundly criticized for his radical teaching methods at the Philadelphia Academy of Fine Arts, particularly his use of a nude male model in a mixed class. From Eakins, Beaux learned to paint with brio.

Beaux soon made her own controversial decision: not to marry or have children. Instead she opted to devote herself to her craft. Industrious and ambitious, she never complained about toiling for days, and sometimes for months, over a canvas in order to achieve exactly the effect that she desired. For example, *The Dancing Lesson* (1898) took her a year to complete, and she produced it in an unheated barn in the summer home of the parents of her two young models. When it poured, for weeks at a time, she wore boots and slogged through the puddles so she could continue painting. She even built a wooden platform to keep her sitters dry.

To support herself, Beaux drew lithographs of fossils for an American geological survey and then worked for a commercial manufacturer producing overglaze paintings of children on china plates; these sentimental mementos sold very well. But for Beaux, what mattered was that one of her early profile paintings, *Les Derniers Jours d'Enfance* (1883)—a tender, well-executed composition of mother and child for which her sister and nephew served as full-length, life-sized models—was an immediate success. Exhibited at the Pennsylvania Academy of Fine Arts (where Beaux would become the first female full-time instructor), *Les Derniers Jours d'Enfance* received the academy's Mary Smith Prize for "the best painting by a resident woman artist." Beaux went on to win the Mary Smith Prize four times. The painting was also shown at the Paris Salon of 1887 and launched Beaux's career as an internationally respected portraitist.

Using as models first family and friends, then more notable figures, Beaux refined her portraits, often selecting unusual points of view and tonal contrasts to underscore the character of her subject. "She was always very selective in whom she chose to paint, and frequently turned down lucrative commissions when confronted with a face she didn't judge strong," commented Frank H. Goodyear Jr. in his introduction to *Cecilia Beaux: Portrait of an Artist*. Beaux tended toward realism, especially in her earlier works, but she rarely flattered her sitters. Like the artist John Singer Sargent, with whom she has been favorably compared, Beaux believed that what counted most was not the subject per se, but rather the manipulation of design and color in imaginative ways. And like Sargent, she was influenced by modern European impressionists as well as by traditionalists such as Rubens, Titian, and Rembrandt.

In 1888 Beaux traveled to Paris where she enrolled in a women's drawing class at the Académie Julian; painting was not an option for women. She spent an impressionable summer on the coast of Brittany, where she studied with plein air (outdoors rather than in a studio) painters. The luminous light and sensuous colors she was introduced to in the small French villages profoundly affected her work, and she discarded the drab, or what she called "brown sauce," colors of her earlier paintings for lusher tones.

Beaux made many sojourns to Europe, including a trip to France in 1896 during which six of her portraits were exhibited at the Paris Salon. Soon thereafter she was elected to the Société Nationale des Beaux-Arts. Meanwhile, back in America, in 1897 she had her first major exhibition at the St. Botolph Club in Boston; it would be followed by 14 one-woman shows.

By the turn of the century, Beaux's paintings became increasingly more impressionistic, featuring sun-drenched rooms, dashing figures, and expressive brushwork and content. For example, in *Sita and Sarita* (1893–94), Beaux placed a woman dressed dramatically in white with her black cat perched on her shoulder. In the 1898 portrait *Man with the Cat (Henry Sturgis Drinker),* which was purchased by the National Museum of American Art, Beaux's brother-in-law donned a white suit as he posed with his tabby cat near a window. That same year, a double portrait of two women standing in long evening cloaks entitled *Mother and Daughter* garnered Beaux more prizes than any other work. At the awards ceremony for the Carnegie Institute gold medal, Beaux was described as "not only the greatest living painter, but the best that has ever lived." In 1900 she received another gold medal, at the noteworthy Paris Exposition.

After 1900 Beaux divided her time between a studio in Washington Square in New York City and an oceanside resort she had purchased north of Boston. However, she is considered primarily a Philadelphia painter, for it was in that city that she was born, raised, trained, and taught for 20 years. Beaux's mature works, such as *After the Meeting* (1914), are more animated, complex, and ambitious. In *Women Artists: An Illustrated History,* Nancy Heller points out how the abstract shapes and complicated series of spatial planes in *After the Meeting* create a "lively, intimate quality of a candid photograph that catches the subject in mid-action."

Beaux's roster of sitters included prominent social, political, and artistic figures such as art collector Isabella Stewart Gardner, the Italian actress

Preeminent American portraitist Cecilia Beaux, early 1920s
(Courtesy of the Pennsylvania Academy of the Fine Arts, Philadelphia. Archives. Gift of Cecilia Saltonstall through Tara Leigh Tappert.)

Eleanora Duse, and both Mrs. Theodore Roosevelt and Mrs. Andrew Carnegie. Socially, Beaux hobnobbed with and sometimes painted portraits of the writer Henry James and the musician Frédéric Chopin. "It doesn't pay to paint everybody," she once wryly observed. While some art historians admired her work, others paid scant attention to a female society painter. However, she believed, as did the artist Vincent van Gogh, that portraits were the highest form of painting. Beaux was, in fact, recognized during her lifetime with a bevy of accolades and awards, including honorary degrees from the University of Pennsylvania (1908) and Yale University (1912). In the 1920s she received two important gold medals: from the Art Institute of Chicago and the American Academy of Arts and

Letters. She was also the first American woman invited by the Uffizi in Florence to paint a self-portrait for the Medici Gallery of prominent artists.

Unfortunately, in 1924 Beaux broke her hip, and because it never healed properly, her ability to paint was severely limited. Never one to remain inactive, in 1930 she published her autobiography, *Background with Figures.* Five years later the American Academy of Arts and Letters, to which she had been elected a member, sponsored the largest exhibition of her work during her lifetime.

Ranked by some critics as one of the most outstanding woman painters in America, Beaux undoubtedly would have been better known today had she been a male. On the other hand, she did not like being labeled a "woman artist" and considered herself simply "an artist." Cecilia Beaux died in 1942 in Gloucester, Massachusetts, at her beloved summer home. "Art is not born," she wrote in her autobiography. "It is born of life—and in one form or another, vigorous, developed life always turns toward beauty." In 1974, a retrospective of her impressive body of work, executed during a lengthy and productive career, was held at the Pennsylvania Academy of the Fine Arts.

Further Reading

Beaux, Cecilia. *Background with Figures.* Boston: Houghton Mifflin, 1930.

Goodyear, Frank H., Jr., and Elizabeth Baily. *Cecilia Beaux: Portrait of an Artist.* Philadelphia: Pennsylvania Academy of Fine Arts, 1974.

Tappert, Tara Leigh. *Cecilia Beaux and the Art of Portraiture.* Washington, D.C.: Smithsonian Institution Press, 1995.

Tufts, Eleanor. "Cecilia Beaux." In *North American Women Artists of the Twentieth Century,* edited by Jules Heller and Nancy Heller, 55–56. New York: Garland Press, 1995.

— C. K.

BISHOP, ISABEL WOLFF
(1902–1988)   *Painter, Printmaker*

Isabel Bishop's realistic yet luminous paintings and drawings of ordinary city dwellers and their every-day urban activities display a mastery of draftsmanship and form. For more than 60 years, she produced beautifully crafted, insightful renderings of the human figure and astute observations of working-class life in New York City.

Born on March 3, 1902, in Cincinnati, Ohio, Isabel Bishop spent most of her childhood in Detroit, Michigan, where her father was principal of a public high school. Isabel grew up in a working-class neighborhood, but because her father considered himself intellectually superior to the neighbors, he discouraged his six children from having anything to do with them. "I wasn't supposed to play with the children on my block, but I wanted to," Bishop wrote. "I thought, they have a warmer life than we do—they all see each other, and we are isolated." The youngest of her siblings by 13 years, Isabel felt further estranged by her mother—a feminist who hated housework and acted as if she did not enjoy spending time with her children; her mother's indifference deeply hurt young, lonely Isabel.

Fortunately, at an early age Bishop had a natural aptitude for drawing, claiming it was the only thing that she could do well; she looked forward to weekend art classes, at which she focused on the human figure: "It was a shock to walk into class and find a great fat nude woman posing," she later recalled. At 16, having graduated from high school, and with financial backing from a wealthy relative, Bishop moved to New York City and enrolled in the illustration program at the School of Applied Design for Women. A few years later she switched to the less structured and more avant-garde Art Students League, where for four years she studied with Kenneth Hayes Miller, one of the most influential painting teachers of that generation. Many of his students would become notable painters, including Reginald Marsh and brothers Raphael and Moses Soyer. Miller became Bishop's mentor and encouraged her to commit herself wholeheartedly to perfecting classical form, and then to adapting those techniques to contemporary subjects—namely everyday life in lower Manhattan, where she lived and worked. Bishop happily complied. She was, she explained, prepared to do anything to keep herself painting.

Bishop also studied with and befriended Guy Pene du Bois, a more urbane, satirical painter who reminded her that "to be an artist was to say something for oneself." Bishop had to find her own voice, but first she steeped herself in the works of European old masters such as Peter Paul Rubens and Rembrandt; it was from them that she learned to imbue her canvases with an inner glow. Her early style displayed "the momentary suspension of movement in figures caught between poses," wrote an art critic in *Encounter* magazine.

Bishop also excelled at works on paper. Edward Lucie-Smith, in *American Realism* (1994), described her drawings as among the strongest in 20th-century American art. But Bishop saw herself as a "painter's painter," and her drawings and etchings as preparatory stages for the final product: paintings. In 1927, at 25, Bishop completed the first in a series of modest self-portraits that were, according to Helen Yglesias, author of *Isabel Bishop* (1989), "intensely honest probings of the self . . . and revelatory in [their] humanity and clarity of emotion." Bishop would continue to paint self-portraits until shortly before she died, in her mid-80s. "In these masterpieces," noted Yglesias, "as in the female nudes, Bishop was unique among American women painters, working within a vision closer to the Europeans."

For Bishop, it was essential to capture on canvas life's ever-changing mobility and human vitality through composition and form. In an ambitious, haunting early "Union Square" painting entitled *Virgil and Dante in Union Square* (1932), the literary figures Dante and Virgil appear as robed visitors among a crowd of contemporary New Yorkers, all of whom seem to be on their way somewhere. Bishop, in a 1989 interview, placed importance on representing the "multiplicity of souls," rather than on ideology: "I felt like I was saying some small thing which was true of American life—apart from politics and economics."

The young New York painters who lived or worked in the Union Square neighborhood of lower Manhattan in the late 1920s and early 1930s

became known as the Fourteenth Street School. In 1931 Bishop and several other members of the group visited Europe to study the Renaissance and baroque painters, and to apply the old masters' sense of color and muted tonality to 20th-century subjects. At last Bishop had close friends and colleagues, something she had longed for since childhood.

For more than 40 years, from the mid-1930s to the late 1970s, Bishop painstakingly recorded, at the rate of three or four paintings a year, scenes of ordinary life in New York City. She seemed to have had an instinctive understanding of the working-class women she observed in her neighborhood or on the subways, and sometimes in her studio. With an almost classical respect for the human figure, Bishop drew or painted these young women chatting together amicably or rushing around during their lunch breaks. Often light moved across or through Bishop's female figures. "Although not consciously working from a feminist point of view, the vigor and strength of Bishop's vision is revealed in her women," commented Ann Sutherland Harris and Linda Nochlin in *Women Artists: 1550–1950*. Bishop was never condescending toward her female subjects; the nudes were beautiful but not idealized, the secretaries were dignified but down-to-earth. John Russell, *New York Times* art critic, wrote that Bishop had a "novelist's eye for idiosyncracies of anatomy, dress and social behavior."

In 1933 she gave her first solo exhibition at Midtown Galleries in New York. Over a 55-year period, she would have a dozen more individual shows at that venue. She also participated in numerous group exhibitions ranging from the Whitney Museum of American Art's 1936 Biennial to the 1940 New York World's Fair. Bishop's paintings and drawings are represented in the permanent collections of more than 70 prestigious museums, including New York's Metropolitan Museum of Art. There have also been two major retrospectives of her work: at the University of Arizona Museum of Art in 1974 and, a year later, at the Whitney Museum in New York.

Bishop married the prominent and highly cultured neurologist Harold G. Wolff in 1934 and

Painter and printmaker Isabel Bishop recorded scenes of ordinary urban life.
(AP/Wide World Photos)

moved with him to Riverdale, a suburb of New York City, where six years later she had a son named Remsen. Wolff supported his wife's profession and her need to commute on a daily basis to her studio in downtown Union Square. Although by all accounts Wolff could also be demanding, the couple seemed to enjoy a loving, compatible relationship until Wolff's death in 1962.

Bishop's later works became more abstract and less representational, and her figures more veiled and transparent, with dots and dashes creating a rich, almost mystical finish to the surface of her multilayered paintings.

Bishop was the recipient of an impressive array of awards and honors. In 1943 she won the American Academy of Arts and Letters Award. Three years later she became the first female officer of the National Institute of Arts and Letters. She also taught at New York's Art Students League and at Yale University School of Fine Arts, and she received several honorary doctorates. In 1979, President Jimmy Carter presented her with the Outstanding Achievement in the Arts Award. Eight years later she garnered the Gold Medal for Painting from the American Academy and Institute of Arts and Letters.

Isabel Bishop died in the Bronx, New York, on February 19, 1988, at the age of 86.

Further Reading

Harris, Ann Sutherland, and Linda Nochlin. *Women Artists: 1550–1950*. New York: Alfred A. Knopf and Los Angeles County Museum of Art, 1976.

Lucie-Smith, Edward. *American Realism*. New York: Harry N. Abrams, 1994.

Lunde, Karl. *Isabel Bishop*. New York: Harry N. Abrams, 1975.

Nemser, Cindy. "Conversations with Isabel Bishop." *Feminist Art Journal* 5: 1 (spring 1976): 14–20.

Yglesias, Helen. *Isabel Bishop*, with a foreword by John Russell. New York: Rizzoli, 1989.

— C. K.

BLAINE, NELL
(1922–1996) *Painter, Graphic Artist*

Dubbed by critics "the priestess of light" and the "Queen of Unpolluted Color," during her 50-year exemplary career Nell Blaine switched from geometric abstract art to beautifully executed figurative oils and works on paper. In her exuberant landscapes and flower-filled still lifes, Blaine was concerned primarily with tapping into the "rhythm inside" and "the life of forms as revealed by light."

Nell Blaine was nearly blind when she was born in Richmond, Virginia, on July 10, 1922. When she was given special eyeglasses as a toddler, the world suddenly opened up for her. Nell's discovery of light and color seemed to propel a lifelong interest in the visual arts. At 16 she enrolled at the School of Art of the Richmond Professional Institute. She was trained in the strict academic realist tradition, but one of her instructors, surrealist Worden Day, encouraged her to think about art "in a whole new way" and to move to New York City.

In 1942 Blaine left the South and her conservative, austere roots, where she had never felt comfortable. She arrived in New York "full of wild enthusiasm for art in all its forms . . . like a bird out of a cage." She was taken under the wing of her renowned modernist teacher, Hans Hofmann,

whose credo was that "work is an extension of blood and body; it has the rhythm of nature." Blaine was also influenced by notable abstract artists Piet Mondrian and Fernand Leger.

During her leisure time, Blaine immersed herself in jazz. One of her more arresting abstract paintings, *Lester Leaps* (1944), currently part the collection of the Metropolitan Museum of Art in New York City, was named for a Lester Young jazz recording. In 1943 Blaine married French-horn player Robert Bass; she herself was an amateur jazz drummer. "I think handling the drumsticks affected to this day the way I use paintbrushes," she once quipped. She also befriended unconventional poets such as John Ashbery and Kenneth Koch and collaborated with them on avant-garde verse/design projects.

At 22, Blaine became the youngest member of the American Abstract Artists, an organization comprised of artists who believed in abstract, as opposed to representational (also known as figurative), modes of painting. In 1944 Blaine joined Jane Street Gallery, a pioneering cooperative gallery where she met fledgling artists such as Larry Rivers, a saxophone player who later became her art student. Rivers credited Blaine with profoundly affecting his work. "In a way," he said, "everything is through Nell."

In 1945 Blaine held her first solo exhibition at Jane Street Gallery. Although she was known as an inveterate abstract artist, she insisted that her strongest initial impressions were from nature. "My work," she explained, "has always had light in it." According to art historian Martica Sawin, in *Nell Blaine: Life and Art* (1998), during the late 1940s and early 1950s Blaine "fused the fundamental principles used in her nonobjective work with her new absorption of physical phenomena." *Sketching the Model* (1948–49), for example, exemplifies Blaine's transition period, during which she moved from geometric shapes into "freer movements of color." Blaine began spending her summers in Gloucester, a picturesque seaside town north of Boston frequented by artists. There, among the beach grass and brilliantly hued flowers, she delighted in the luminosity and color that imbued her best-known still lifes.

In 1948 Blaine's marriage to Bass was annulled. From that point on she had long-term relationships with women, including the modern dancer Midi Garth, for whom she had designed costumes, and in later years the painter Carolyn Harris. In 1950 she traveled to Paris, where she studied the works of old masters such as Eugene Delacroix and Gustave Courbet. In a document she wrote in 1970, *Art: A Woman's Sensibility*, she noted: "I respect those grand traditions of composition (or structure) which many feminists regard as *man*-made and, at their finest, I regard as purely human." While in Paris, she began to paint outdoors. "It was like opening a window," she later recalled. "Suddenly a lot of sunlight came in. So I decided to let myself go and become a kind of hedonist, to enjoy painting again, loose painting. Even too loose." Blaine experienced that same sense of excitement when she came in contact with natural light in Mexico, the Caribbean islands, and Greece.

Increasingly Blaine's work was becoming more figurative. In 1954 art critics described her as an "abstract impressionist." Her subjects—floral bouquets, rooftops, and sun-drenched interiors—were considered unusual choices for a modernist, who was supposed to discard anything too conventional or pretty. Blaine defended her choice of subjects, her heightened sense of color, and her profusion of brush strokes by explaining, in a 1958 interview in *Art News,* "For me the word 'pretty' is not a bad word."

In 1959, having been recognized as one of the leading new "painterly realists," Blaine had several well-received solo shows at New York's Poindexter Gallery. But that same year, while painting in Greece, she contracted polio and had to return to New York; she was hospitalized for several months and nearly died. Nonetheless Blaine retrained herself to paint with her left hand, from a wheelchair, for the rest of her life. "Don't make much of it," she said in a 1978 interview. "I don't." To help defray her considerable medical expenses, the art community held a special benefit exhibition at which 80 artists, including Willem de Kooning and Milton Avery, exhibited their work. In 1960 Blaine moved to an apartment on Riverside Drive, overlooking the Hudson River. A few years later she purchased a cottage on Cape Ann in East Gloucester, Massachusetts, and split her time between the beach cottage and her apartment in Manhattan. In 1964, having garnered a third Yaddo fellowship, she felt strong enough to travel to Europe and then to Saint Lucia in the British West Indies, where she lived on a banana plantation. Blaine painted *Dorset Garden 2* (1964), the first in a series of lush paintings of gardens that she would continue for the next 30 years.

Blaine received numerous accolades, including two Guggenheim Fellowships, and honorary doctorate degrees. In 1979 she was the recipient of the first Governor's Award for the Arts in Richmond, Virginia. That same year she held her first solo show at the Fischbach Gallery in New York City, which would represent her for the remainder of her career. She also has participated in pivotal national and international group exhibitions, from the Museum of Modern Art in Rome to the Museum of Modern Art in New York. In 1990 she received the Louise Nevelson Award in Art from the American Academy and Institute of Arts and Letters. Six years later, the Muscarelle Museum of Art in Williamsburg, Virginia, held a retrospective of her impressive body of work.

Blaine, an artist who unabashedly rejoiced in nature and in taking risks, said that each new painting begins in "the body of the artist," in the sensation of "a physical oneness with pain, a hedonist delight," and the pleasure of "connecting with the outside." Nell Blaine continued to exhibit her work regularly until a year before she died in New York on November 14, 1996.

Further Reading

Cochane, Diane. "Nell Blaine and High Wire Painting." *American Artist,* August 1973, 20–25.

Gussow, Alan. *A Sense of Place: The Artist and the American Land.* New York: Friends of the Earth and Seabury Press, 1971.

Munro, Eleanor. *Originals: American Women Artists*. New York: Da Capo Press, 2000.

Sawin, Martica. *Nell Blaine: Her Art and Life*. New York: Hudson Hills Press, 1998.

— C. K.

BOURGEOIS, LOUISE

(1911–)   *Painter, Printmaker, Multimedia Sculptor*

In a career that has spanned more than 60 years, Louise Bourgeois began as a painter and engraver before achieving prominence as a sculptor. She worked in a variety of mediums that ranged from marble, bronze, and wood to wax, plaster, and latex. Much of her pioneering, controversial, and highly personal work combines aspects of love, eroticism, rejection, alienation, fear, and rage that she sees as permeating the complex world of male-female relationships.

Louise Bourgeois was born on December 25, 1911, in Paris, three years before the outbreak of World War I. By the age of 10, Louise was using her natural artistic abilities to help restore old tapestries—the family business—by providing designs for parts that had been damaged over the centuries. Her childhood labors provided her with a view of art as being related to everyday life. As she put it, "Art was real work, not elitist or luxury. Later I felt no guilt about being an artist. It was serious work for me."

Bourgeois's view of art was also shaped by her relationship with her father. His 10-year affair with his children's youthful English tutor left young Louise, a middle child, with deep feelings of jealousy, anger, and rejection. Added to these intense emotions was sympathy for her mother, who, notwithstanding her feminist beliefs, suffered but forgave her husband's multiple marital indiscretions. Bourgeois's conflicting emotions ultimately found their way into her work, as did other traumas she experienced early in her life. "Everything I create comes from something personal; some memory or emotional experience," she once stated.

Bourgeois did not initially intend to become an artist. As a university student at the Sorbonne, she studied mathematics. The precision of mathematics—in particular solid geometry—eased her anxieties and provided her with a sense of order. The quest to feel safe and protected continued when Bourgeois abandoned mathematics for art and enrolled at the École des Beaux-Arts in Paris, where she studied from 1936 to 1938. Many years later she told an interviewer, "I didn't have the security of any kind of religion. So in the end, that is how I became an artist—to find a mode of survival."

In 1938 Bourgeois married Robert Goldwater, an American art historian who had come to Paris to complete his doctoral dissertation. The couple came to the United States, settled in New York City, and eventually had three sons. The marriage, Bourgeois recalled, enabled her to feel safe enough to transform her "old anxiety" into "manageable loneliness." She did not let raising three sons get in the way of her burgeoning career as an artist. But Bourgeois found satisfaction in motherhood, even though the role involved a "fantastic amount of physical work"; she commented that her reaction to women who told her they didn't want children was, "I just don't believe it."

Shortly after settling in New York, Bourgeois began studying at the avant-garde Art Students League. Her circle of friends included artists such as the abstract expressionists Willem de Kooning and Jackson Pollock, as well as a number of refugees who had fled Europe after the outbreak of World War II, among them the French-born surrealist Marcel Duchamp. During most of the 1940s, Bourgeois focused on painting, drawing, and printmaking and was a respected member of what was called the New York School of art. In 1943 some of Bourgeois's drawings were shown at the Museum of Modern Art. Feminist themes soon appeared in her work, most notably in a series of paintings in 1947 called *Femme Maison* ("House Woman"), which featured the lower portion of female bodies attached to houses that served as their torsos and heads.

By the end of the decade, Bourgeois had moved from painting to sculpture. Most of her early work was in wood, but by the 1960s she turned to new materials, including bronze, plaster, and latex. She

Louise Bourgeois produces highly
personal sculptures.
(Portrait by Timothy Greenfield-Sanders)

used latex, plaster, and other materials to produce a series of semi-abstract sculptures entitled Lairs. By the 1970s her work was receiving increased critical attention as the growing feminist movement took an interest in her depiction of sexuality and the relationship between the sexes. In 1974 she exhibited one of her signature works, *The Destruction of the Father*, an Oedipal and personally cathartic latex sculpture that suggest a man being murdered and eaten by his children. In 1982, the Museum of Modern Art in New York City, in recognition of her achievement, gave Bourgeois a retrospective exhibition, something rarely accorded a living artist.

Bourgeois's idiosyncratic work has received numerous awards and honors, among them honorary doctorates from Yale University (1977) and the New School for Social Research (1987). At Yale, she was lauded for her courage: "You have

offered us powerful symbols of our experience and of the relations between men and women. You have not been afraid to disturb our complacency." In 2000 Bourgeois was the subject of a stage portrait—*Louise Bourgeois: I Do, I Undo, I Redo*—written and performed by the Brazilian actress Denise Stoklos, in New York City. The text was drawn solely from Bourgeois's works. The artist, at age 88, designed the set herself. In 2001, *New York Times* art critic Ken Johnson wrote: "Ms. Bourgeois remains, even at her most abstract, a maker of metaphorically resonant images."

Further Reading

Johnson, Ken. "Louise Bourgeois and Yayoi Kusama," *New York Times*, June 22, 2001, B31.

Kuspit, Donald. *Bourgeois: An Interview with Louise Bourgeois by Donald Kuspit*. New York: Vintage Books, 1982.

Munro, Eleanor, "Louise Bourgeois." In *Originals: American Women Artists*, 154–169. New York: Da Capo Press, 2000.

Wye, Deborah. *Louise Bourgeois*. New York: The Museum of Modern Art, 1982.

— C. K.

BOURKE-WHITE, MARGARET
(1904–1971)   *Photojournalist*

As one of the pioneers of the field of photojournalism, Margaret Bourke-White enjoyed great success and notoriety. In a career that took her to four continents and featured an impressive number of "firsts"—both for women in her profession and for photographers in general—Bourke-White produced a gripping pictorial record of many of the key events of her time.

Margaret White—she became Bourke-White when she affixed her mother's maiden name to her own last name in 1927—was born on June 14, 1904, in New York City, the second of three children of Joseph and Minnie (Bourke) White. Her father, a successful engineer and inventor, was also an avid amatuer photographer who introduced his daughter both to the craft of photography and to the world of machines. Machinery would become her first major subject when she began her professional career. Her mother provided a role model by ignoring the traditional rules governing how women should behave: Minnie Bourke took up bicycling before the start of the 20th century, when it was considered a sport for men only. She also gave Margaret her first camera, a $20 second-hand ICA Reflex with a cracked lens.

Bourke-White used the camera her mother gave her to take photos to help defray expenses while she was a student at Cornell University. By then her father had died, and Bourke-White's first marriage, which lasted only two years, had ended in divorce. After graduating from Cornell in 1927, Bourke-White moved to Cleveland, Ohio, to embark on a career as a freelance professional photographer. Her fascination with modern technology led to a series of remarkable photographs of architecture and industrial machinery that caught the eye of *Time* publisher Henry Luce, who in 1929 hired Bourke-White for *Fortune,* his new business magazine. Bourke-White's outstanding work for Luce's successful new venture enhanced her reputation, as she photographed industrial enterprises in the United States, Canada, and Europe. While on assignment for *Fortune* in Europe, in 1930, she became the first foreigner allowed to photograph the industrialization drive going on in the Soviet Union. That and a subsequent visit there resulted in two books and a series of articles for the *New York Times Magazine.* Bourke-White later wrote that in the early 1930s "no one could have known less about Russia politically than I knew." Her photographs showcased the enormous industrial growth taking place, while also focusing on a variety of human interest stories, but, as critic Theodore M. Brown noted, recorded no evidence "of the labor camps, the suffering, and the terror that was also a part of Stalinist Russia."

Bourke-White's career took a quantum leap forward in the mid-1930s. In 1936 she collaborated with *Tobacco Road* author Erskine Caldwell (whom she would marry in 1939) on a book documenting the dreadful living conditions of sharecroppers and tenant farmers in the South. *You Have Seen Their Faces* (1937), unlike Bourke-

White's volumes on Russia, carried an unmistakable political and social message about the need for reform. The book was highly praised and remains a classic of photorealism; some critics consider it the single best piece of work of Bourke-White's career. She and Caldwell collaborated on two other successful books, *North of the Danube* (1939), a chronicle of life in Czechoslovakia on the eve of the Nazi takeover, and *Say, This Is the USA* (1941), a survey of the United States immediately before it entered World War II. Although they worked well together, Bourke-White's marriage to Caldwell ended in divorce in 1942.

In 1936 Bourke-White became one of four photographers whom Henry Luce hired for his new magazine venture, *Life,* the mission of which was "to eyewitness great events." Luce planned to achieve his goal by using photographs to "bring people the news." Bourke-White's first assignment was to photograph the construction of the Fort Peck Dam in Montana—part of a chain of New Deal dams in the Columbia River basin. Bourke-White photographed the dam in dramatic fashion by showing the enormous concrete structure towering over workers who looked like tiny specks at its base. But she also used her camera to record the daily lives of workers and their families living in the shanty towns surrounding the construction site. A photograph of the dam became *Life*'s first cover on November 23, 1936, and *Life*'s editors wove Bourke-White's photographs of the dam's builders and the text that accompanied them into a lead article for the premiere issue. This marked a major step in the development of a new journalistic form that had been evolving during the 1930s: the photo essay. Some critics consider Bourke-White's Fort Peck Dam article to be the first fully developed example of that genre.

Over the next 20 years, Bourke-White completed more than 280 assignments for *Life,* a highly popular periodical that represented one of the greatest success stories in American journalistic history. Bourke-White's reputation flourished along with the magazine and reached new heights during World War II. Her picture of British prime minister Winston Churchill appeared on *Life*'s cover in April 1940. She was in the Soviet Union when it was attacked by Nazi Germany in June 1941 and was the only foreign photographer present to cover the first German bombing attack on Moscow in July; she got her pictures by ignoring orders to go a basement air-raid shelter in her hotel, instead climbing to the roof. Bourke-White's photographs taken during this period filled another well-received book, *Shooting the Russian War* (1942).

Bourke-White's work in Russia was only a prelude to her achievements during World War II. She was the first woman accredited as a war photographer and the first, and only, woman to fly on a combat mission. The latter episode, in which Bourke-White photographed a raid on a German airfield in North Africa, made her a celebrity when *Life* ran a story in March 1943 called "Life's Bourke-White Goes Bombing," complete with a picture of the photographer, a propeller behind her left shoulder, dressed in full flying regalia. Bourke-White also photographed the terrible fighting that took place in Italy, providing *Life* with some of its most poignant wartime images. Many of her most memorable photographs came in the last days of the war when, traveling with General George Patton's Third Army, she recorded the horrors of the Buchenwald concentration camp.

After World War II, Bourke-White covered the grim conditions and violence that gave birth to the nations of India and Pakistan. Her most celebrated image from that period, however, was a peaceful one: *Mahatma Gandhi at his Spinning Wheel* (1946). Another notable achievement was her coverage in 1949 and 1950 of diamond and gold miners in South Africa, who labored for pennies a day under suffocating conditions thousands of feet underground. In one instance, Bourke-White had to be lowered 2,000 feet in a basket to get the shots she wanted.

In 1952, while returning home from covering the Korean War, Bourke-White noticed a dull ache in her left arm and leg. She was experiencing the first signs of Parkinson's disease, which by the late 1950s,

The pioneering photographer Margaret Bourke-White was known especially for her pictures in *Life* magazine.
(AP/Wide World Photos)

despite experimental surgery, forced her to give up photography. Her valiant struggle against the disease was the subject of a movie, *The Margaret Bourke-White Story*, starring Eli Wallach and Teresa Wright.

In her autobiography, *Portrait of Myself* (1963), Bourke-White wrote, "I don't repeat myself well. I want and need the stimulus of walking forward from one new world to another." She did exactly that in a remarkable and courageous career during which she searched continually for "discoveries waiting to be made." Those discoveries earned her many honors, including the Achievement Award from *U.S. Camera* in 1963 and the Honor Roll award from the American Society of Magazine Photographers in 1964. Margaret Bourke-White died of Parkinson's disease in Stamford, Connecticut, on August 27, 1971.

Further Reading

Bourke-White, Margaret. *Portrait of Myself.* New York: Simon and Schuster, 1963.

Brown, Theodore M. *Margaret Bourke-White: Photojournalist.* Ithaca, N.Y.: Andrew Dickson White Museum, 1972.

Goldberg, Vicki. *Margaret Bourke-White: A Biography.* New York: Harper and Row, 1986.

Online Photography at Filmpicken.com. "Photography Greats: Margaret Bourke White." Available online. URL: http://www.filmpicken.com/greats/white.htm. Updated on September 5, 2000.

Rubin, Susan Goldman. *Margaret Bourke-White: Her Pictures Were Her Life,* with photographs by Margaret Bourke-White. New York: Harry N. Abrams, 1999.

— C. K.

BRIDGES, FIDELIA
(1834–1923)   *Painter, Illustrator*

Fidelia Bridges is best remembered for her precise and delicate renderings of nature, especially birds and flowers. Her detailed work, wrote Frederic Sharf in *Notable American Women, 1906–1950,* "combined the temper of romanticism with the technique of a scientist." Bridges, whose watercolors were exhibited widely during and after her lifetime, was also a successful commercial illustrator of books and greeting cards.

Born on May 19, 1834, in Salem, Massachusetts, Fidelia Bridges was the youngest daughter of four surviving children of a sea captain, Henry Gardner Bridges, and his wife, Eliza (Chadwick) Bridges, both of whom perished in 1849, when Fidelia was a teenager. In 1854 Eliza, the eldest sister, who was a teacher, moved the family from New England to Brooklyn, New York, where she opened a school. When Eliza died only two years later, Fidelia became a mother's helper and teacher for William Augustus Brown, a wealthy seafaring Quaker, and his family. She tried administering and teaching at her sister's school but decided instead to follow her artistic bent by taking drawing lessons.

In 1860 Bridges moved to Philadelphia, Pennsylvania, to study with William Trost Richards, a marine and landscape painter who was influenced by the English Pre-Raphaelites such as Dante Gabriel Rossetti. This artistic and literary movement originated in relation to the Pre-Raphaelite Brotherhood, a group of mid-19th-century avant-garde painters. He taught Bridges to capture and document on canvas minute details of nature, from a withering single leaf on a tree to a bird's downy feather. Acting as both mentor and friend, Richards introduced and recommended Bridges to his wealthy patrons as well as to museum curators. By 1862 Bridges had established her own studio in Philadelphia and was exhibiting her highly detailed botanical paintings at the Pennsylvania Academy of Fine Arts.

In 1865 Bridges returned to Brooklyn, where she opened a studio in the Brown home. She befriended Anne Whitney, a sculptor from New England who encouraged Bridges to find her own style, and Whitney's companion, Boston painter Adeline Manning. In 1867 the threesome spent a year in Rome, Italy, where they painted, studied, lived, and traveled together. Although Bridges— who was described as handsome, tall, stately, and refined—lost both parents at 15 and never married, she surrounded herself with friends and enduring professional and personal relationships. Writer Mark Twain was one of her patrons and friends; she had been for many years a governess of his three young daughters.

After returning from Europe, Bridges turned to vibrantly colored watercolors rather than oils and increasingly concentrated on studies of birds, flowers, and meadowlands. In 1868, having established a studio in New York City, she exhibited her work at the National Academy of Design; six years later she was elected an associate of the academy. In 1871 Bridges began spending her summers in bucolic Stratford, Connecticut. There she delighted in the wildlife, wildflowers, and salt grass that lined the banks of the nearby Housatonic River, where she would sit for hours in a boat, shielded from the sun by an umbrella, sketching the flora and fauna. Watercolors such as *Daisies and Clover* (1871) and *Thrush in Wild Flowers* (1874) demonstrate Bridges's artistic maturity as well as a sense of poetry and subtlety of design. "Her works were like little lyric poems, and she dwelled with loving touches on each of her birds," commented landscape painter John Frederick Kensett, an important figure in the American art scene at that time, in *Art Journal* (1875).

In 1876 Bridges began a long and successful association with Boston publisher and lithographer Louis Prang. Recognizing Bridges's talent, he reproduced many of her prints and paintings on his popular holiday greeting cards and calendars, and he selected her as one of his permanent designers. She was also invited to show three of her paintings at the Philadelphia Centennial Exposition of 1876. That same year her illustrations appeared in a book of verse by Celia Thaxter and in *Scribner's Monthly* and *St. Nicholas,* two popular periodicals. She was further honored in 1879, while visiting her brother in England, when she was invited to exhibit at the Royal Academy. Critics commented on her asymmetrical designs, simplified backgrounds, and an oriental influence that was more apparent than in her botanically correct early work.

Bridges left Brooklyn and the Browns' home and moved in 1892 to Canaan, a relatively rural small town in Connecticut, where she sketched and enjoyed picnics and afternoon teas with her bevy of friends. She continued to show her work at the Pennsylvania Academy, the National Academy of Design, and the American Society of Painters in Watercolors.

Fidelia Bridges died in 1923. A small bird sanctuary was erected in her memory by the citizens of Canaan. In 1984, one of her watercolors was included in *Reflections of Nature,* an exhibit at the Whitney Museum of American Art in New York. Her memorable, finely crafted paintings of nature were also represented in the 1985 exhibition *The New Path, Ruskin and the American Pre-Raphaelites* at the Brooklyn Museum in New York and are in the permanent collection at the Smithsonian Institution in Washington, D.C.

Further Reading

Dunford, Penny, editor. *Women Artists in Europe and America Since 1850.* Philadelphia: University of Pennsylvania Press, 1989.

Falk, Peter H., editor. *Who Was Who in American Art: 1564–1975.* Madison, Conn.: South View Press, 1999.

Hill, May Brawley. *Fidelia Bridges: American Pre-Raphaelite.* New Britain, Conn.: Museum of American Art, 1981.

Sharf, Frederic A. "Fidelia Bridges." In *Notable American Women, 1607–1950,* 122–123. Cambridge, Mass.: The Belknap Press of Harvard University Press, 1971.

Tufts, Eleanor. *American Women Artists, 1830–1930.* Washington, D.C.: National Museum of Women in the Arts, 1987.

— C. K.

BROOKS, ROMAINE (Beatrice Romaine Goddard)
(1874–1970)   *Painter, Portraitist*

Romaine Brooks was a skilled and perceptive portraitist whose ability to reveal the inner reality hidden beneath the outward appearances of her subjects led one critic to label her the "thief of souls." An American who spent most of her life as an expatriate in Europe, Brooks was not well known in American until after her death in 1970, when there was a resurgence of interest in her provocative drawings and oil paintings.

Beatrice Romaine Goddard (known as Romaine) was born in a hotel room in Rome, Italy, on May 1, 1874, the third and youngest surviving child of Harry and Ella Goddard. By 1874, her parents' marriage had disintegrated and was in its final stages. Ella Godddard came from a wealthy Pennsylvania family and was therefore financially secure when her husband deserted her and the children shortly after Romaine's birth. She was, however, mentally unstable and obsessed with finding a cure for her beloved only son, who at an early age showed signs of mental disturbance; she searched for a cure by traveling throughout Europe to consult physicians, with Romaine serving as her brother's special keeper. Brooks later provided a concise assessment of her painful childhood by calling her memoir *No Pleasant Memories.*

At the age of 21, Brooks finally achieved a modicum of independence when her mother agreed to provide her with a small monthly stipend. She then studied painting in Rome and Paris for several years before moving to the island of Capri. Her deranged brother died in 1901. When her mother died a year later, Brooks inherited a considerable fortune. Financially independent, she was free to live as she wanted for the remainder of her life.

Before striking out on her own, she was married briefly to John Ellingham Brooks, an English dilettante. Her reasons for wedding him are not entirely clear. It seems to have been a marriage of convenience: John Brooks was a homosexual and, notwithstanding a few affairs with men, Romaine Brooks was a lesbian. In any event, the odd marriage was over by 1904. The real love of Romaine Brooks's life was Natalie Clifford Barney, an American expatriate writer who ran a literary salon and was well regarded in Parisian artistic and lesbian circles when Brooks met her in 1915. The intense relationship endured, in spite of infidelities by both partners, for 50 years.

After her marriage ended, Brooks went to England to study the paintings of James McNeill Whistler. The renowned artist's influence can be seen in the subtle shadings of gray, white, and black that became a signature of Brooks's portraits. By 1908 Brooks had settled in Paris, adopted a flamboyant, masculine style of dress, and decorated her apartment dramatically, with an emphasis on black. In fact, she became a popular interior decorator as well as an up-and-coming portraitist.

By 1910, when Brooks had a successful solo exhibition of her portraits at a prestigious gallery in Paris, two other important people had entered her life: Gabriele D'Annunzio, the Italian poet and nationalist, and Ida Rubinstein, a Russian ballerina whose extraordinarily wan and delicate features captivated men and women alike. D'Annunzio became Brooks's close friend and, for a while, her lover. Rubinstein also became her lover, but more significantly she became Brooks's model for several

of her most famous paintings, including nudes such as *Asalées Blanches* ("White Azaleas," 1910) and *Le Trajet* ("The Crossing," 1911). Both works exemplify the emaciated-looking, sexually androgynous female figure that appears in all of Brooks's nudes of women. Brooks also did a noteworthy portrait of D'Annunzio entitled *Le Poète en Exil* ("The Poet in Exile," 1912). It is suggestive of her view of herself as being isolated and an outcast that can also be seen in her *Self Portrait* of 1923.

Brooks enjoyed her greatest popularity in the 1920s. Aside from her *Self Portrait,* her paintings from that period include several portraits of women in masculine attire, among them a remarkable and unflattering portrait of the popular lesbian writer Lady Una Troubridge. In 1925 her works were exhibited in major galleries in Paris, London, and New York City.

By the 1930s interest in Brooks had waned, and she gave up painting in favor of drawing. While working on her memoirs, Brooks produced more than 100 surrealist drawings that expressed the inner turmoil and pain she had felt during her traumatic childhood. Critic Adelyn Breeskin has called the abstract series of works on paper "the most exciting original aspect of her art." Brooks came to the United States in 1935 for a show of her drawings at the Arts Club of Chicago, Illinois. She then went to New York City, where she remained until returning to Europe in 1936.

Brooks spent World War II living with Natalie Barney in Italy, a choice of residence that reflected Brooks's right-wing leanings. (According to George Wickes, the journal that Brooks wrote during the war shows that she was sympathetic toward Fascism and hoped the Germans would defeat the Russians.) She continued to live in Italy until 1967. Brooks then moved to the southern French resort town of Nice, where she became increasingly reclusive.

The "Thief of Souls," as Robert de Montesquiou had dubbed her, died on December 7, 1970, at 96. Interest in her work revived shortly thereafter. In 1971 an exhibition of Brooks's works opened at the National Collection of Fine Arts in Washington, D.C., and then moved to the Whitney Museum of

American Art in New York City. The National Collection of Fine Arts (now the National Museum of American Art), which has more than 60 of her paintings and drawings in its permanent collection, staged subsequent exhibitions of her works in 1980 and in 1986. A major retrospective—*Amazons in the Drawing Room: The Art of Romaine Brooks*—was presented by the National Museum of Women in the Arts, in Washington, D.C., in 2000.

Further Reading

Bailey Brooke. *The Remarkable Lives of 100 Women Artists.* Holbrook, Mass.: Bob Adams, 1991.

Breeskin, Adelyn D. *Romaine Brooks, "Thief of Souls."* Washington, D.C.: Smithsonian Institution Press, 1971.

Secrest, Meryle. *Between Me and Life: A Biography of Romaine Brooks.* New York: Doubleday, 1974.

Women in American History by Encyclopaedia Britannica. "Romaine Goddard Brooks," Encyclopedia Britannica, Inc. Available online. URL: http://www.women.eb.com/women/articles/Brooks_Romaine.htm. Downloaded on July 6, 2000.

— C. K.

BROWNSCOMBE, JENNIE AUGUSTA
(1850–1936)   *Genre Painter, Printmaker*

A popular genre artist who specialized in American historical paintings, Jennie Brownscombe is best known for *The First Thanksgiving,* a tourist attraction at the Museum of Pilgrim Treasures in Plymouth, Massachusetts, where it is permanently exhibited. Many of Brownscombe's prints and paintings were reproduced commercially during the late 19th century.

Jennie Augusta Brownscombe was born in a log cabin near Honesdale, Pennsylvania, on December 10, 1850. Her father, who was from Devonshire, England, died while Jennie was an adolescent. Her mother, Elvira (Kennedy) Brownscombe, hailed from a family of very early New England settlers; Jennie would become a dedicated member of the Mayflower Descendants and the Daughters of the American Revolution. Having herself dabbled in

poetry, Jennie's mother encouraged her only child to develop an interest in literature and art, especially because young Jennie demonstrated an aptitude for writing and drawing. While attending high school in Honesdale, Jennie exhibited paintings at the Wayne County Fair that earned her prizes.

Once Brownscombe decided to pursue a career in art, she moved to New York City and enrolled at the School of Design for Women of the Cooper Union (now known as Cooper Union). After graduating in 1871, she studied for four years at the National Academy of Design, where she won first prize for her work. She exhibited annually at the National Academy from 1874 to 1887, and she later was named an associate. Eleanor Tufts, author of a book about early American women artists, noted that Brownscombe had a "penchant for narrative painting rendered with realism." Her subjects were frequently genre based—nostalgically depicting scenes from daily life, such as a one-room schoolhouse in rural Pennsylvania, which in fact was very similar to the one Brownscombe attended. An art critic in the New York *Evening Post* described the first major painting that Brownscombe sold, *Grandmother's Treasures,* as a "large and cleverly painted interior . . . with figures." It was part of a show at the National Academy of Design in 1876.

Brownscombe was also a founder of the progressive Art Students League of New York. In order to help pay for expenses, she taught classes at the league. Beginning in 1882, to further supplement her income, Brownscombe sold more than 100 paintings to magazines such as *Scribner's Magazine* and *Harper's Weekly* and to publishers of greeting cards and calendars. Her illustrations were widely reproduced and were therefore familiar to scores of Americans.

In 1882 Brownscombe traveled to France to study in Paris and Brittany with Henry Mosler, an established American genre painter. After returning to America, she was invited to exhibit one of her portraits, *Brittany Peasant Girl,* at the National Academy of Design. She suffered an eye injury and had to give up painting for a year but in 1884 returned to her New York City studio. Beginning in 1886, she spent her winters in Rome.

Some of Brownscombe's paintings were executed in the impressionistic style that was popular in Europe. In *Apple Orchards in May* (1885), Brownscombe applied dots of white and green to give the impression of the wispy, lovely bloom of apple trees in springtime. But she was foremost a genre painter of Americana, as exemplified by *A Love's Young Dream* (1887), a sentimentalized portrait of a lovestruck young woman turning away from her parents and their farm, toward the vast landscape, in order to capture a glimpse of her beloved. It is considered one of her most memorable works. Another romantic but more sophisticated painting, *In Anticipation of the Invitation* (1888), depicts a vain young woman looking at herself in a hand mirror, while contemplating a nearby envelope that may contain the "invitation" alluded to in the oil painting's title.

As her stature grew, Brownscombe became a member of the American Artists' Professional League and the New York Women Painters Society. In 1900 her paintings were exhibited at the venerable Royal Academy in London and the Water Color Society in Rome. While in Rome she met George Henry Hall, an admired American still-life specialist. Hall deeply influenced Brownscombe's sense of style, color, and craftsmanship. Until Hall's death in 1913, he and Brownscombe shared a summer studio in the Catskill Mountains of New York. Brownscombe continued to summer in the Catskills, while spending her winters in New York and in Bayside, Long Island.

During the 1890s, she initiated a series of early American historical figure paintings that focused on colonial and revolutionary scenes, especially those involving George Washington. *The Peace Ball* (1895–97), which hangs at the Newark Museum in New Jersey, shows General Washington introducing Rochambeau and Lafayette to his mother after the victory in Yorktown. *The First Thanksgiving* (1914) is seen annually by busloads of tourists visiting Plymouth, Massachusetts—the historic pilgrim town in New England. At 76,

Brownscombe illustrated the text of Pauline Bouve's *Tales of the Mayflower Children*. A year later, in spite of a stroke, she painted *Children Playing in an Orchard* (1932) for a school in her Pennsylvania hometown. Reserved and industrious, with large brown eyes and a pronounced dimpled chin, Brownscombe relished her career. She lived alone, simply and contentedly, proud of her artistic technique and her American heritage. She called her art and the research it entailed "great fun" and showed no interest in changing her precise, traditional style. Her work is represented in the permanent collections of several notable museums, including the National Museum of Women in the Arts in Washington, D.C.

A journalist for *The Wayne Independent* reported that at 84, Brownscombe was still painting in her studio in Bayside and had been commissioned to paint portraits of judges, doctors, and military officers. Jennie Augusta Brownscombe died on August 5, 1936, and was buried, as per her request, next to her parents in Honesdale, Pennsylvania.

Further Reading

Artist Profiles. "Jennie Augusta Brownscombe." Available online. URL: http://www.nmwa.org/legacy/bios/browrose.htm. Downloaded on July 6, 2000.

Hazzard, Florence W. "Jennie Augusta Brownscombe." In *Notable American Women, 1607–1950,* 259. Cambridge, Mass.: Belknap Press of Harvard University Press, 1971.

Jette, Edith K., and Ellerton M. Jette, editors. *American Painters of the Impressionist Period Rediscovered.* Waterville, Maine: Colby College Press, 1975.

Tufts, Eleanor. *American Women Artists, 1830–1930.* Washington, D.C.: National Museum of Women in the Arts, 1987.

— C. K.

BURKE, SELMA HORTENSE
(1900–1995) *Sculptor, Art Educator*

Many readers of this book have seen an example of Selma Burke's work: the image of President Franklin D. Roosevelt, taken from Burke's bronze relief of the president, that appears on the United States dime. The Roosevelt plaque, while Burke's most famous work, is only one of many accomplishments in a career as a distinguished figurative sculptor and a dedicated art educator that spanned most of the 20th century.

Selma Hortense Burke was born on December 31, 1900, in Morresville, North Carolina, the seventh of 10 children of Neil and Mary Colfield Burke. Neil Burke was a Methodist minister who supplemented the family income by working for a railroad. Notwithstanding her family's modest economic status, Selma Burke grew up in a home with a rich artistic heritage: Her father was an art collector, her maternal grandmother was a painter, and both her parents encouraged her to develop the artistic talent she demonstrated at an early age. As a young girl, Selma began making models out of clay that she took from a riverbed near her home. However, when it was time for Selma to choose a profession, her mother vetoed an art career—"You can't make a living at that," she told her daughter. Selma instead earned a degree as a registered nurse.

Burke's medical career turned out to be short-lived. A wealthy heiress in New York City for whom Burke worked as a private nurse in the 1920s supported her interest in art and became her patron. Burke became acquainted with many of the black artists who had gathered in the Harlem section of New York City and were part of the Harlem Renaissance movement that promoted African-American art, literature, and music. During the 1930s she garnered scholarships that enabled her to study in Europe. After studying ceramics in Austria, she traveled to France to study with the modernist sculptor Aristide Maillol, whose style—one that combined classical and modern forms—greatly influenced her. While in Paris she also had the opportunity to meet the painter Henri Matisse, who praised her work.

After returning to the United States, and again with the assistance of scholarships, Burke earned a master of fine arts degree from Columbia University in 1941, the same year she had her first solo exhibition in New York City. Around that time,

she taught at the Harlem Community Art Center and worked on the New Deal Federal Art Project. In 1943 Burke won the competition to do a bronze relief portrait of President Roosevelt. He posed for the portrait in 1944, but died before it was unveiled. It was left to President Harry S. Truman, in 1945, to preside over the unveiling. Today the bronze plaque is on display at the Recorder of Deeds Building in Washington, D.C. Burke's design was later adapted for the image of Roosevelt that appears on the U.S. dime.

Burke aspired to be what she called a "people's sculptor," an artist who creates works that can be appreciated by most people, including those lacking a formal art education. Some of the distinguished works that exemplified that goal are *Despair* (1951), a kneeling figure with head in hands; *Fallen Angel* (1958), a neoclassical bronze that portrays an angel expelled from heaven; and *Together* (1975), a five-foot-high bronze relief whose theme is familial love. Burke believed that another way of reaching the "people" was by educating them about art. She taught at several schools, colleges, and universities and served as a consultant to major arts foundations. She also founded the Selma Burke School of Sculpture in New York City and the Selma Burke Art Center in Pittsburgh, Pennsylvania, where thousands of children benefited from her passionate commitment to art education. In 1970, at the age of 70, she earned a doctoral degree from Livingston College in North Carolina. During that same decade, she had solo exhibitions at Princeton University and the Carnegie Museum in New York, among other venues.

While the portrait of Roosevelt is Burke's most famous work, she also executed portraits of eminent African Americans such as Booker T. Washington, Duke Ellington, and Martin Luther King Jr. She was honored during her lifetime with several honorary doctorates in fine arts. Governor Milton Shapp proclaimed July 20, 1975, as Selma Burke Day in Pennsylvania. And in 1979, President Jimmy Carter presented Burke with the Women's Caucus for Art's Outstanding Achievement Award. The Metropolitan Museum of Art and the Whitney Museum of American Art in New York City and the Philadelphia Art Museum are among the premier institutions that hold her works in their permanent collections. In 1983 the Selma Burke Gallery, the first fine arts gallery named in honor of a black woman artist, opened at Winston-Salem State University in North Carolina. Its collection included more than 50 of Burke's sculptures as well as works by other African-American artists from Burke's private collection.

Burke married twice, both times briefly. Her first marriage, to acclaimed Harlem Renaissance writer Claude McKay, ended in divorce; her second marriage, to architect Herman Kobbe, lasted until his death in the early 1950s. At age 94, on August 19, 1995, Selma Burke died in the artists' community of New Hope, Pennsylvania. A well-regarded sculptor, she believed strongly in art and art appreciation for everyone. In a statement that appeared in *Artnews* (now *ARTnews*) in 1944, she elegantly expressed that vision: "Art didn't start black or white, it just started. There have been too many labels in this world: Nigger, Negro, Colored, Black, African-American. . . . Why do we still label people with everything except 'children of God'"?

Further Reading

Gangewere, Robert J. "An Interview with Selma Burke." *Carnegie Magazine* 49 (January 1975): 6–12.

Hedgepeth, Chester M., Jr., editor. *Twentieth Century African American Writers and Artists.* Chicago: American Library Association, 1991.

Schlegel, Sharon. "Selma Burke: The Artist Is Honored," *Trenton Times,* October 9, 1983, 21.

— C. K.

CASSATT, MARY STEVENSON
(1844–1926)   *Painter, Graphic Artist*

One of America's foremost female painters, Mary Cassatt spent most of her long and influential career in France. Best known for her memorable paintings of mothers and children, she was also a skillful printmaker. Cassatt is considered by many critics to have been the greatest American impressionist.

Mary Stevenson Cassatt was born in Allegheny City, a suburb of Pittsburgh, Pennsylvania, on May 22, 1844, into a prominent middle-class family. By the time she was 16, she knew she wanted to become an artist. Her father—a successful banker and local politician who had little interest in the arts—vehemently opposed his daughter's decision. "I would almost rather see you dead," he reportedly said. In 1851 the Cassatts moved to Europe and remained there for four years. During that time Mary became enamored of French culture, especially its art treasures.

Once she returned to the United States, Cassatt enrolled at the Pennsylvania Academy of the Fine Arts and graduated from the prestigious institution in 1865. However, she had felt restricted by the academy's conservative style of teaching. Attractive, independent, and self-

assured, Cassatt told a friend that one day she would paint better than the old masters (eminent artists from the 15th to 18th centuries), whose works she greatly admired. At 22 Cassatt returned to Europe to study painting, and in 1866 she settled in Paris. She worked diligently and steadily to improve her technique and sense of artistry.

In 1868 Cassatt was honored when her painting, *A Mandolin Player,* was selected as part of the illustrious Paris Salon, where it was displayed prominently. Other works, including *On the Balcony During the Carnival* (1872), were accepted by the salon for five successive years. However, with the onset of the Franco-Prussian War (1870–71), Cassatt was forced to return to America. She missed "seeing a good picture," as she wrote to a friend, and returned to Europe as soon as possible. By 1873, with the Paris Salon exhibiting another of her paintings, *Torrero and Young Girl,* Cassatt had established a name for herself and opened a studio in Paris. One of her earliest visitors, May Alcott, sister of the American writer Louisa May Alcott and herself a young artist, described Cassatt as "a woman of real genius . . . whose paintings are handled in a masterly way." In 1876 Cassatt exhibited her first painting in America at New York City's Society of American Artists; later her work would appear at the National Academy of Design in New York. But during her lifetime Cassatt remained relatively unknown in the United States, unlike her female contemporaries CECELIA BEAUX and FIDELIA BRIDGES.

When the Paris Salon rejected one of her paintings, insisting that she tone down the vivid colors to make the work more acceptable to the judges, Cassatt reacted angrily. She was therefore very enthusiastic when she was approached by the modernist French painter Edgar Degas in 1879. He had seen her work at the Salon in 1877, and he invited her to join a breakaway group of independent artists, which became known as the impressionists. Cassatt had already incorporated some elements of their new style into her work, including a lighter, brighter palette and vigorous brush strokes. The early impressionists included French artists Berthe Morisot and Claude Monet, as well as Degas.

Like Cassatt, Degas was highly opinionated, cultivated, and passionate. He admired Cassatt's bold, masterfully controlled work. "I will not admit that a woman can draw like that,"he purportedly said. Both artists strove to realistically convey ordinary people involved in everyday activities, as exemplified by Cassatt's disarmingly unflattering buck-toothed *Girl Arranging Her Hair* (1886). Cassatt favored domestic scenes of women at the theater, reading in a garden, sewing, or having tea together. There is no doubt that Cassatt was greatly influenced by Degas. She once remarked that "the first sight of his [Degas's] pictures was the turning point of my artistic life." However, according to Adam Gopnik in the March 22, 1999, edition of *The New Yorker,* she was not an imitator and retained her own style throughout her evolving career. "Cassatt turned his [Degas's] essentially cold, analytic, beautifully classical gaze into something engaged," wrote Gopnik. "She turned a dry, cold style into a dry, warm style."

Cassatt remained an active and respected impressionist for seven years, beginning in 1879 when she was represented at the exhibition by 10 paintings, and ending with the eighth and final impressionist

exhibition in 1886. When she was not painting, Cassatt helped wealthy family and friends, particularly her brother Alexander and her friend Louise Havemeyer, select art for their formidable American collections. She encouraged and persuaded them to purchase works by Manet, Monet, Morisot, Renoir, Pissarro, and Degas. Art historian Frederick Sweet asserted that Cassatt "not only furthered [but] in fact almost created an interest in French impressionism" in America. Although she was the only American among the impressionists, and had lived and painted in France for most of her life, Cassatt never gave up her American citizenship or her native accent. Her parents and elder sister, Lydia, moved to Paris in 1877 to live with her and often served as her models. Her mother finally recognized her daughter's ambition and need to paint: "Mary is at work again, intent on fame and money she says," wrote her mother to another relative. "After all, a woman who is not married is lucky if she has a decided love for work of any kind and the more absorbing it is the better."

Cassatt worked painstakingly on each canvas, sometimes spending eight hours a day imbuing each painting with lyricism and luminosity. She turned down many awards, including a Lippincott Prize, explaining that as a member of the impressionist circle she had agreed not to accept medals or awards. "At last," she told a biographer, "I could work with absolute independence without considering the opinion of a jury. I had already recognized who were my true masters. I admired Manet, Courbet and Degas. I hated conventional art—I began to live."

In addition to painting, Cassatt excelled at pastel drawings. In fact, in *American Impressionism,* William H. Gerdts called her "one of the great pastellists of the 19th century." She was also a renowned printmaker of etchings and drypoints, known especially for a series of 10 intensely colored aquatints, including one of her earliest mother-and-child works on paper, *The Bath* (1891). Her colors became clearer and more boldly defined. She was influenced—like many other impressionists—by Japanese woodcuts she had seen on display at an

Mary Cassatt, considered the greatest American impressionist, circa 1872
(Library of Congress)

exhibition in Paris. Cassatt created more than 220 prints during her lifetime and, very much a risk taker, experimented with many forms of printmaking. In the 1890s she had two solo shows in Paris celebrating her paintings, pastels, and prints.

Although she did not consider herself an ardent feminist, Cassatt cared about women's causes. She was commissioned to paint a large mural for the Woman's Building of the 1893 World's Columbian Exposition, which was held in Chicago. Several years later she would send her paintings to a benefit exhibition for woman's suffrage in New York City. A critic in *Art Journal* noted in 1976 that Cassatt was "the only artist of her period to depict a woman driving a buggy." Unfortunately she had to spend years as a caretaking nurse, first for her ailing parents, then for her sick sister, who died of kidney disease. Therefore, unlike her male counterparts, she was unable to devote herself full time to her craft.

During the early 1900s, Cassatt abandoned impressionist brushwork and color, opting instead for solid form and design. She focused mostly on poignant portraits of mothers and children. "It is the isolation of the mother and child that marks Cassatt's new images, and the bond that brings together mother and child seems less one of instinct than one of shared emotion," asserted Gopnik in *The New Yorker.* Cassatt never married or had children, and her objective studies of mother and child were rendered tenderly but without a trace of sentimentality. Her respect for children was apparent: "Almost all of my pictures with children have the mother holding them, would you could hear them talk, their philosophy would astonish you," she once explained. She was, according to Gopnik, the first to grasp the modern condition of mother and child. "She discovered, or recorded, a new emotion in the world: the nearly adulterous, exhausting love with which middle-class women have come to address their babies."

In 1904 the French government awarded Cassatt the Legion of Honor, a rare achievement for a woman. She became blind, and by 1914 was forced to give up painting. She died of diabetes at her summer country home near Paris on June 14, 1926, at 82, and was buried in France. Her work can be seen in many public collections, including the Museum of Modern Art in New York City. Noted art critic Robert Hughes, in *American Vision: The Epic History of Art in America* (1977), praised Cassatt for her "insights as an artist, her originality of mind and temperament . . . and her steely rigor of design that undergirded her scenes of domesticity and pleasure."

Six years before her death, Mary Cassatt, her own worst critic, had written to a friend: "I have not done what I wanted to but I tried to make a good fight." In 1999 a retrospective of her work and her life entitled *Mary Cassatt: Modern Woman* traveled from the Art Institute of Chicago to Boston and Washington, D.C. A reviewer of the retrospective noted that Cassatt's art and her life, seen close up, were not only more moving than one might expect but far more courageous.

Further Reading

Gerdts, William H. *American Impressionism.* Seattle: Henry Art Gallery, University of Washington, 1980.

Gopnik, Adam. "Cassatt's Children." *The New Yorker,* March 22, 1999, 114–120.

National Museum of Women in the Arts. "Selected Bibliography: Mary Cassatt." Available online. URL: http://www.nmwa.org/library/bibs/cassatt.htm. Downloaded on July 30, 2000.

Peterson, Karen, and J. J. Wilson. "After All, Give Me France—Mary Cassatt." In *Women Artists,* 87–90. New York: Harper & Row, 1976.

Sills, Leslie. *Visions: Stories About Women Artists.* Morton Grove, Ill.: Albert Whitman and Company, 1993.

Tufts, Eleanor. *American Women Artists 1830–1930.* Washington, D.C.: National Museum of Women in the Arts, 1987.

— C. K.

CHASE-RIBOUD, BARBARA
(1939–)   *Multimedia Sculptor, Writer*

A talented artist and writer, Barbara Chase-Riboud first gained critical acclaim as a sculptor creating large-scale works from unusual combinations of contrasting materials, in particular metals such as bronze and steel and fibers such as silk, wool, or hemp. When she subsequently focused on writing in addition to sculpture, she became a best-selling author of historical fiction and a respected poet.

Barbara Chase was born in Philadelphia, Pennsylvania, on June 26, 1939. The only child of black middle-class parents, she later described herself as "one of those theatrical brats, bred for the arts." By seven she was taking lessons at Philadelphia's Fletcher Memorial Art School; a year later she won her first sculpture prize, a small Greek vase. By then she was also studying piano and ballet, and she had begun to write poetry. While in high school, Barbara received a *Seventeen* magazine prize for one of her woodcuts and sold her woodcut print *Reba* to New York City's Museum of Modern Art. After graduat-

ing summa cum laude from the Philadelphia High School for Girls, Barbara was offered seven college scholarships: she chose to attend Temple University's Tyler School of Fine Arts, where she earned a bachelor of fine arts degree in 1957. That same year, she was awarded a John Hay Whitney Fellowship to study at the American Academy in Rome.

Chase began to cast in bronze, using the direct-wax method and materials such as plants and bones to create her own unique sculpting style. While in Europe, an impromptu trip to Egypt turned into a three-month stay that exposed Chase for the first time to non-Western art. Deeply impressed by Egyptian art's "sheer magnificence" and "timelessness," she never again would be satisfied working within the confines of Western art. Instead, she searched for inspiration from non-Western cultures, especially African traditions.

After returning to the United States, Chase studied design and architecture at Yale University, where in 1960 she received a master of fine arts degree. She then returned to Europe, where she has lived ever since. In 1961 she met and married photojournalist Marc Riboud and changed her name to Barbara Chase-Riboud. The couple had two sons. Chase-Riboud spent several years traveling and raising her children before resuming her art career in 1967. (She would divorce Riboud in 1980 and marry publisher and art expert Sergio Tosi in 1981.)

When Chase-Riboud returned to sculpting, her work had changed dramatically. Having been influenced by the civil rights movement and her travels in Asia and Africa, she wrote: "I felt great pressure to fuse these [non-Western] influences with my Western image." She was especially impressed by African tribal dancing masks that, due to their construction process, had their structure concealed, thereby imbuing them with a "magical presence." Working with bronze and a variety of fibers to create nonrepresentational rather than figural sculptures, Chase-Riboud developed and refined techniques for making the bronze appear soft or free-flowing, while the fibers appeared solid or static—the fiber thus seemed to be the strong element that was holding up the bronze.

Her goal, she noted, was to create art that "united opposing forces—male/female, negative/positive, black/white." She further commented: "I seek to create an art based on classicism, emotion, engagement with the public, and reconciliation with our past—whether Western, Eastern, or African."

Chase-Riboud's first one-woman exhibition in the United States was held in 1970 at the Massachusetts Institute of Technology's Hayden Gallery in Cambridge, Massachusetts, and included four memorial sculptures in honor of Malcolm X. Among her lauded later works are *Cape* (1973), a six-foot-high multicolored sculpture of cast bronze with hemp cord on a welded aluminum and steel support; *Cleopatra's Door* (1983), in which she combines small bronze pieces with beams of wood in the shape of a doorway; and *Tantra* (1995), a work of gold, silk, and bronze that reflects Hindu influences.

In 1995 Chase-Riboud was one of several artists commissioned to produce works to honor the 18th-century African-American burial ground that had been unearthed in 1991 during construction of a federal office building in the Wall Street section of Manhattan. The result was the monumental 20-foot-tall bronze sculpture *Africa Rising*, which has been called her masterpiece. The top part of the three-level work consists of an abstracted African-American female figure who, as art historian Peter Selz observed, "appears to forge ahead toward light, and some unseen objective, with a compelling sense of triumph in which the physical sweep is lifted into a transcendental realm." In 1999 *Africa Rising*, which was installed in the lobby of the Federal Building in lower Manhattan, received a Design Award from the General Services Administration as the best public art for the period covering 1993 to 1998.

Chase-Riboud's impressive list of solo exhibitions ranges from the Musée d'Art Moderne de la Ville de Paris in 1974 to New York's Metropolitan Museum of Art in 1999. The Metropolitan Museum of Art in New York and the Centre Pompidou in Paris are among the permanent collections in which her works are represented. Chase-Riboud's powerful writing has also received

Barbara Chase-Riboud, a critically acclaimed sculptor and writer
(AP/Wide World Photos)

accolades. For example, *Sally Hemings,* a novel about Thomas Jefferson's black slave mistress, won the Janet Heidinger Kafka Prize for the best novel by an American woman in 1979.

In *Barbara Chase-Riboud: Sculptor,* art historian Anthony Janson asserts that while Chase-Riboud participates in the mainstream of Western art and "consistently adheres to a mode of abstraction that is as exacting as it is personal," her work nonetheless "stands apart as a result of her interest in other cultures and civilizations."

Further Reading

Chase-Riboud, Barbara. *Sally Hemings.* New York: Viking Press, 1979.

King-Hammond, Leslic, ed. *Gumbo Ya Ya: Anthology of Contemporary African–American Women Artists,* 53–55. New York: Midmarch Arts Press, 1995.

Munro, Eleanor. *Originals: American Woman Artists.* New York: Da Capo Press, 2000.

Seltz, Peter Howard and Anthony F. Janson. *Barbara Chase-Riboud: Sculptor.* New York: Harry N. Abrams, 1999.

— C. K.

CHICAGO, JUDY COHEN
(1939–) *Painter, Sculptor, Installation Artist*

A controversial artist and outspoken feminist, Judy Chicago has been criticized and praised for her provocative, politicized multimedia installations, especially *The Dinner Party* (1974–79), which she described as a "symbolic history of women's achievements and struggles." Chicago's goal has been to visually represent feminist concerns and to reverse the way women are seen in our culture. "It is power, not justice," asserts Chicago, "which determines the nature of the world and, therefore, the definition of art."

Judy Chicago—the name she adopted in 1970 in order to avoid using her father's or her three husbands' surnames—was born Judy Cohen on July 20, 1939, in Chicago, Illinois. Displaying a talent for drawing and painting at an early age, she began taking art lessons at the Art Institute of Chicago when she was eight. In the 1950s she moved to Los Angeles, California, where she received a bachelor's degree in 1962, followed by a master of fine arts degree in 1964, from the University of California (UCLA). She taught sculpture and painting at various branches of the University of California.

While a student at UCLA, Chicago married writer Jerry Gerowitz, but he was killed in a car accident in 1963, only two years after the couple had wed. Around that time, Chicago completed one of her first spray-painted works, *Car Hood.* She had learned the art of spray painting by working at an auto body shop, just like "one of the boys," as she put it. She also taught herself carpentry and became increasingly interested in machinery and pyrotechnics (fireworks). Chicago believed that women could and should master "male skills" and incorporate those techniques into their art.

In her early work, Chicago mixed minimalist and pop art techniques and used colors to portray female emotions, especially expressions of sexual pleasure. She moved easily from painting to sculpture, and her work became more abstract and personal in the late 1960s. In 1966 she held her first solo show at the Rolf Nelson Gallery in Los Angeles. During the next 35 years, she would have individual exhibitions in American and European cities ranging from Santa Fe, New Mexico, to Frankfurt am Main, Germany. In 1969 Chicago married sculptor Lloyd Hamrol, but the couple was divorced. A year later, during an exhibition in Fullerton, California, that included Chicago's *Pasadena Lifesavers,* a series of large paintings that used color to portray the sensations of female orgasm, Chicago—then known as Judy Gerowitz—announced that she would "freely choose her own name." She would also challenge sex discrimination, which she believed to be rampant in the male-dominated art world. In a later artist's statement, she recalled: "I [with artist MIRIAM SCHAPIRO] organized the first feminist art program in America in 1970 [the Fresno Feminist Art Program at California State University, which became the California Institute of Arts in Valencia]. I am a feminist artist, interested in making the female experience stand for an aspect of the human condition which has been shrouded in mythology and fantasy."

As a faculty member at the California Institute of Arts, Chicago taught the history of women artists and encouraged her students to use autobiographical journal writing as a source of inspiration for their art. The result was what is considered America's first feminist exhibition, *Womanhouse* (1972), a renovated space comprised of rooms exhibiting mixed-media installations by women artists that commented on women's issues and societal roles. The collaborative effort included Chicago's graphic work *Menstruation Bathroom,* a garbage can filled with used tampons. During the early 1970s Chicago also completed a series of flower petal paintings. With their bright circular centers and vaginal imagery, they were highly evocative. She was moving away from pure abstraction in order, she said, "to make my work openly subject-matter oriented (while still being abstract) and to try reveal intimate emotional material through my forms."

In 1974 Chicago began a sculptural installation entitled *The Dinner Party.* Assisted by an industrial designer and hundreds of volunteer artisans and researchers (some of whom complained about being exploited by Chicago, who was known to be difficult to work for), the five-year fine arts and crafts project commemorated the history of women in Western civilization. The format was a series of 39 place settings of hand-painted china plates designed by Chicago. Each plate, in the shape of a butterfly-vagina, represented and celebrated an important female. The project included 999 other notable women, whose names were inscribed in gold on a tiled floor where the enormous table supporting the place settings rested. "Women have never had a 'Last Supper' but they have had dinner parties," Chicago observed. The project afforded them an opportunity to show off and share their achievements, instead of "facilitating conversations and nourishing their guests."

The Dinner Party—with its room-sized sculpture, videotapes, films, and photographs—was installed at the San Francisco Museum of Modern Art in 1979 and subsequently at 13 other settings in the United States, Canada, and Europe. While a few critics praised it as a monument of early feminism and an empowering aesthetic experience for women, many reviewers considered *The Dinner Party* crude propaganda rather than art. Even some feminist critics did not like the way in which women were represented by their genitals. Nonetheless, the multimedia work raised important questions about the role of politics and gender in relationship to art. "I wanted to wed my skills to my real ideas and to aspire to the making of art that could clearly reveal my values and point of view as a woman," wrote Chicago in her influential autobiography *Through the Flower* (1975).

Feminist artist Judy Chicago, in 1979, portrays what she calls "images that change consciousness." (AP/Wide World Photos)

By the time Chicago completed *The Dinner Party* in 1979, she had designed almost 50 other works in various textile mediums. She was also the recipient of several awards and grants, including an honorary doctorate in fine arts from Russell Sage College in New York. In 1980 she began another collaborative five-year project, *The Birth Project,* made up of quilts, weavings, macrame, and needlework. The idea, Chicago said, was to "represent different aspects of this universal experience—the mythical, celebratory, and the painful." The project was followed by Powerplay, a series of drawings, paintings, textiles, and sculptures that explored male definitions of power and how men viewed their world.

Chicago and her third husband, photographer David Woodman, began working in 1993 on *The Holocaust Project,* a massive undertaking comprised of paintings and photographs that grew out of a 1987 trip the couple—both assimilated Jews—had taken during which they had visited concentration camp sites. Chicago also studied the Holocaust for two years and came to the conclusion that "a people's identity and pride are largely determined by an understanding of their roots." As Joyce Antler points out in *The Journey Home: Jewish Women and the American Century* (1997),

Chicago connected the experience of women to that of Jews by highlighting the "sexual exploitation of women [including the rape of women prisoners] and homosexuals in the camps." For the artist, it was a journey from the "darkness of the Holocaust" and patriarchal values to the "light" of the human spirit. Many critics, however, felt that Chicago was trivializing the Holocaust. Christine Temen, art critic for the *Boston Globe,* described Chicago's *Holocaust Project* as "execrable, self-serving, and starring Chicago rather than the 6 million dead."

Chicago's feminist art is represented in distinguished collections such as the Museum of Modern Art in New York and the National Museum of Women in the Arts in Washington, D.C. "I am committed to expanding the perspective of my world through breaking the historical silence of women," Chicago has written. "I am trying to make art that relates to the deepest and most mythic concerns of human kind and I believe that, at this moment of history, feminism is humanism."

Further Reading

Chicago, Judy. *Beyond the Flower: The Autobiography of a Feminist Artist.* New York: Penguin Books, 1996.

———. *The Birth Project.* New York: Doubleday and Company, 1985.

———. *Holocaust Project: From Darkness into Light.* New York: Viking Penguin, 1993.

———. *Through the Flower: My Struggle as a Woman Artist.* New York: Anchor, 1975.

Jones, Amelia, editor. *Sexual Politics: Judy Chicago's Dinner Party in Feminist Art History.* Berkeley, Calif.: University of California Press, 1996.

Lippard, Lucy. "Judy Chicago's 'Dinner Party.'" *Art in America* 68:4 (April 1980): 114–126.

— C. K.

CHRYSSA (Chryssa Vardea)
(1933–) *Sculptor*

A sculptor who unites art and technology in her work, Chryssa is best known for her striking works of neon-light tubing. When she began creating neon in 1961, she became, according to art historian Sam Hunter, the "first American artist to use emitted electric light and neon rather than projected or screened light."

Chryssa Vardea (she later dropped her last name) was born in Athens, Greece, on December 31, 1933. As a young schoolgirl, she covered miles of roadway between her home and school with chalk graffiti. But as an idealistic young woman confronting her country's suffering during World War II and its subsequent civil war, she was drawn to a career in social work. However, Chryssa became disillusioned after being sent by the Greek ministry of social welfare to assist earthquake victims on the island of Zante in the Ionian Sea. There she discovered that the government had money to restore damaged monasteries but not to help children left homeless by the disaster. Chryssa abandoned social work, returned to Athens, and began studying painting with the abstract artist Anghelos Prokopion.

In 1953 Chryssa moved to Paris, where she studied briefly at the Académie de la Grande Chaumière and met leading surrealists such as André Breton, Max Ernst, and Edgard Varèse. The following year she moved to the United States. After a brief interlude studying at the California School of Fine Arts in San Francisco, she settled in New York City in 1955.

Aside from her experiences in Greece during and immediately after World War II, it is America—where she became a naturalized citizen—rather than Europe, that provided Chryssa with her most immediate sources of inspiration. She does not consider the early abstract paintings she produced while living in Athens important, and she was less impressed by French surrealism than by the work of American abstract expressionist Jackson Pollock, which she encountered for the first time while in San Francisco. Above all else, it was America's glittering modern urban landscape, and especially the neon-sign vistas of New York City, that most affected her development as an emerging artist. "America is very stimulating, intoxicating for me," she said in 1968. "Believe me, when I say there is wisdom, indeed, in the flashing lights of Times Square. The boldness of America as seen in the lights of Time Square is poetic, extremely poetic. . . . In Times Square, the sky is like the gold background of Byzantine mosaics of icons."

After working in a variety of materials during the 1950s, Chryssa produced her first sculpture using neon in *Times Square Sky,* a work comprised of neon tubing, aluminum, and steel. In 1964 she began *Gates of Times Square,* a massive 10-foot cube of welded stainless steel, cast aluminum, Plexiglas, and neon tubing that some critics have called her masterpiece. The work took two years to complete and was a highly consuming project. After its completion, Chryssa recalled, "For two years I did not want to see anyone." Over the next several years, Chryssa created a series of pieces elaborating on various elements of *Gates of Times Square* that she called Studies for the Gates. They included *Clytemnestra* (1967), a sculpture inspired by Greek actress Irene Pappas's performance in the Euripides tragedy *Iphigenia in Aulis,* which is a protest against human injustice and the taking of life. Chryssa was praised for *Clytemnestra II,* the second version of this work, executed in 1968 on a much larger scale: 15 feet high versus the original's 51 inches. The colorful, sensational piece was purchased by the National Gallery of West Berlin, Germany.

The success of *Clytemnestra II* led to a commission for a group of large murals to be erected in a German castle owned by Count Peter Wolf Metternich; it kept Chryssa busy during much of the 1970s. During a visit to New York City's Chinatown, she was inspired to create several paintings based on Chinese calligraphy. By the early 1980s these, in turn, led to Chinese Cityscapes, a series of wall reliefs that included *Mott Street #1* (1981), a massive abstract landscape almost 12 feet long made of aluminum and metallic paint, and *Chinatown* (1981), a similarly sized piece that combined aluminum, metallic paint, and fluorescent light.

Since the 1960s, Chryssa—one of the pioneers of electrified art—has had individual exhibitions at many respected museums and galleries around the world, including New York City's Guggenheim Museum, Whitney Museum of American Art, and Museum of Modern Art; the Musée d'Art Moderne de la Ville de Paris; the Albright-Knox Art Gallery in Buffalo, New York; and, in 1988 and 1991, the Leo Castelli Gallery in New York City. Her work is also housed in permanent collections at New York's Guggenheim and Museum of Modern Art, the Tate Gallery in London, and the Corcoran Gallery of Art in Washington, D.C., among others.

Chryssa, who was the recipient of a Guggenheim Fellowship in 1973, lives and works in New York City. As critic Douglas Schultz has observed, "[She] continues to create art that embodies her own 'reality' and that serves as icons or symbols of the urban world."

Further Reading

Hunter, Sam. *Chryssa.* New York: Harry N. Abrams, 1974.

Restany, Pierre. *Chryssa.* New York: Harry N. Abrams, 1977.

Schultz, Douglas. *Chryssa: Cityscapes.* London: Thames and Hudson, 1990.

Spaulding, Karen Lee, editor. *Albright-Knox Art Gallery: The Painting and Sculpture Collection, Acquisitions Since 1972.* New York: Hudson Hills Press, 1987.

Williams, Sheldon. "Chryssa." In *Contemporary Women Artists,* edited by Laurie C. Hillstrom and Kevin Hillstrom, 138–190. Farmington Hills, Mich.: St. James Press, 1999.

— C. K.

COMAN, CHARLOTTE BUELL
(1833–1924) *Painter*

Notwithstanding her late start—she was nearly 40 years old when she began her painting career—Charlotte Buell Coman became one of America's preeminent female landscape painters of the late 19th and early 20th centuries. Longevity helped compensate for having started her artistic career in midlife: Coman worked from the 1870s through the early 1920s, and according to some critics she did some of her best work after the age of 80.

Charlotte Buell Coman was born in 1833 in Waterville, New York, where her father owned a tannery and shoe factory. As a young woman, she married and moved to the then-frontier town of Iowa City, Iowa, enduring the arduous life of a pioneer. After her husband died, she returned to Waterville. Meanwhile, Coman's hearing was failing; she was almost totally deaf before she turned to the visual arts as a way of expressing herself. She took her disability in stride, once commenting wryly that "Everything in life has its compensations, even my deafness. Critics never make such caustic criticisms through an ear trumpet as they do in ordinary conversation."

Coman began her serious study of painting about 1870 in New York City. Her first teacher was James R. Brevoort, a successful landscape painter. She also studied in France with Emile Vernier and Harry Thompson, and then spent several years living and studying in Holland. Coman was strongly influenced by the works of esteemed French landscape painters Jean-Baptiste-Camille Corot and Charles-François Daubigny. They belonged to the Barbizon school, a group of artists whose work reflected a romantic reverence for and idealization of nature. One of Coman's landscapes from that era, *A French Village,* was praised at the Centennial Exposition in Philadelphia in 1876. Another landscape, *Near Fountainbleau,* was exhibited at the Paris Exposition in 1878.

Coman returned to the United States in the early 1880s, establishing her own studio in New York City and subsequently working in several other locations. Her spiritual and misty landscapes showed the influence of tonalism, a trend related to American impressionism that had developed out of Barbizon style. The art critic H. Vance Swope, praising Coman's work in 1924 in *Artnews* (now *ARTnews*), wrote that her "coloring was unusually quiet, but of a subtle delicacy, and all of her pictures are pervaded with a fine poetical feeling."

Coman won many awards during her lifetime, including a bronze medal at the Midwinter Exposition in San Francisco in 1904, the Shaw Memorial Prize at the exhibition of American Artists in 1905, second prize at the exhibition of the Society of Washington Artists in 1906, and the Burgess Prize from the New York Women's Art Club in 1907. She was elected an associate member of New York City's National Academy of Design in 1910. Her *Well-Worn Path* was selected one of the "best pictures from current shows" by the Detroit Museum's exhibition of 100 representative American artists. Known for her witty and intelligent conversation, when offered the faint praise that she painted almost as well as a man, Coman quipped back: "Well, I should hope I paint better than most of them."

Coman's works are represented in distinguished permanent collections such as the Metropolitan Museum of Art in New York (*Clearing Off,* 1912), the National Gallery in Washington, D.C. (*Early Summer,* 1907), and the Hoyt Institute of Fine Arts (*A Farmer's Cottage, Picardy, France,* 1884). Charlotte Buell Coman, praised for her beautiful, tenderly executed landscapes, continued to paint well into her 90s; she died on November 11, 1924, in a rest home in Yonkers, New York. Her work, which she often signed as "C. B. Cowman," was rediscovered during the 1970s, and she was represented at an exhibition in 1976 entitled *Nineteenth Century American Women Artists,* at the downtown branch of the Whitney Museum of American Art.

Further Reading

AskART. "Artist Summary: Coman, Charlotte Buell." Available online. URL: http://askart.com/theartist. asp?id=23692. Downloaded on August 9, 2000.

Rubinstein, Charlotte Streifer. *American Women Artists from Early Indian Times to the Present.* New York: Avon Books, 1982.

— C. K.

CUNNINGHAM, IMOGEN
(1883–1976) *Photographer*

A pioneer in the development of photography as an art form, Imogen Cunningham's distinguished career stretched from the turn of the 20th century to the mid-1970s. She was lauded for her remarkable close-ups of flowers and plants and for her realistic portraiture, the subjects of which often were contemporary celebrities and luminaries such as Spencer Tracy, Cary Grant, Gertrude Stein, and Alfred Stieglitz.

Imogen Cunningham was born in Portland, Oregon, on April 12, 1883, the first of six children born to Isaac and Susan Cunningham. Her father, an individualistic, self-educated, well-read eccentric, encouraged his favorite child's intellectual development by teaching Imogen himself, at home, a curriculum that included the Bible, Shakespeare, and Dante's *Inferno*. When she began public school at the age of eight, he provided her with private art lessons on weekends and during vacations. That was not easy to do because he was struggling to support 10 children. (Isaac and Susan, both widowed, each had four children from previous marriages.) Along with her academic and artistic studies, young Imogen was forced to learn lessons about self-reliance, which she readily passed on to others. While in her 80s, she told a class of eager students: "Everyone has to find his own way in photography. If you want help in photography, don't go to famous photographers."

While Cunningham's interest in photography dated from high school, she detoured from that goal and majored in chemistry at the University of Washington in Seattle. Still, she bought her first camera while in college and began snapping shots of the campus, as well as a nude, out-of-doors self-portrait. Upon graduation, Cunningham worked in the Seattle portrait studio of Edward S. Curtis, who was compiling his renowned multivolume study of the vanishing culture of the North American Indians. It was there that she learned how to retouch negatives and print with platinum paper. In 1909 she received a scholarship to study photographic chemistry in Dresden, Germany, returning to Seattle a year later to establish her own portrait studio.

Her first solo shows were held in 1914 at the Brooklyn Institute of Arts and Sciences and at the Portland Art Museum in Oregon. The following year, Cunningham married printmaker Roi Partridge; the couple had three sons before divorcing in 1934. Also in 1915, Cunningham defied accepted convention by photographing a series of nudes of her

Influential photographer Imogen Cunningham poses with a camera in 1967.
(AP/Wide World Photos)

husband posing on a pond on Washington's Mt. Rainier. All of the pictures were back views shot with a soft focus lens—producing a hazy image—characteristically used by pictoralist photographers such as Alfred Stieglitz and GERTRUDE KÄSEBIER, who were committed to the concept of photography as a distinct art form rather than merely a technical craft. The publication of the series of nudes, which included *The Bather* (1916)—a romantic pose of Partridge observing his reflection in the pond, which was published in the Seattle's *Town Crier*—caused a scandal and led Cunningham to withdraw the negatives for many years.

By the 1920s, Cunningham had moved to northern California and was among a group of notable photographers that included Edward Weston and Ansel Adams, who abandoned the hazy focus of pictorialism and turned to realistic photography to convey their artistic visions. A hallmark of Cunningham's new direction was *Magnolia Blossom* (1925), a remarkable close-up that takes the viewer inside the flowing curtain formed by the petals of a single flower. Soon Cunningham was commissioned to shoot portraits of celebrities; another of her signature photographs, *Martha Graham 44,* appeared in the December 1931 edition of *Vanity Fair,* the most important fashion magazine of that era.

In the early 1930s, Cunningham joined with Weston, Adams, Willard Van Dyke, John Paul Edwards, Sonia Noskowiak, and other photographers based in California to found the informal Group f/64, which was organized to promote realistic photography. The name of the group was derived from the lens setting on a large-format camera that gives the sharpest possible image with the greatest detail. During the mid-1930s, Cunningham experimented for the first time with double exposures and photomontage. She also focused on portraiture, often photographing celebrities for *Vanity Fair,* and she opened her own studio in San Francisco. Although she also did documentary work recording the impact of the depression, Cunningham always was more interested in the individuality of her subjects than in portraying American society. For her, photography was primarily a means of creating art, not a vehicle for social commentary. As she put it: "I have no ambition, never did have any ambition, to be a reporter. . . . I still feel that my interest in photography has something to do with the aesthetic, and that there should be a little beauty in everything."

Cunningham's focus on celebrity portraiture continued for three decades. During the 1960s, in the wake of the youth counterculture movement and the domestic turmoil over the Vietnam War, San Francisco provided Cunningham with a turbulent setting for documentary street photography. In the last years of her long life, she turned to photographing her peers; the result was a book entitled *After Ninety* (1977).

Cunningham's dossier of individual exhibitions encompasses a long list of prominent museums and art galleries, including the San Francisco Museum of Art, the Metropolitan Museum of Art in New York City, and the Galleria-Libreria Pan in Rome. Aside from the collection of the Imogen Cunningham Trust in Berkeley, California, her work is represented in many permanent collections. She was also the recipient of numerous awards and honors, including a Guggenheim Fellowship and an honorary doctor of fine arts degree from the California College of Arts and Crafts.

Imogen Cunningham died on June 24, 1976, in San Francisco, at the age of 93. She was still actively working until she entered a hospital a week before her death. In 1993 Richard Lorenz, an expert on Cunningham and her work, wrote: "Her fearless explorations, through several generations, were always relevant to photographic developments of the time, and she accumulated a multitude of hard-won achievements, all the while indefatigably protesting that her best photograph might yet be made tomorrow."

Further Reading

Cunningham, Imogen. *After Ninety.* Seattle: University of Washington Press, 1977.

Dater, Judy. *Imogen Cunningham: A Portrait.* Boston: New York Graphic Society, 1979.

Lorenz, Richard. *Imogen Cunningham, Ideas without End: A Life of Photographs.* San Francisco: Chronicle Books, 1993.

Rule, Amy, editor. *Imogen Cunningham: Selected Texts and Bibliography.* Boston: G.K. Hall, 1992.

— C. K.

D

 DE KOONING, ELAINE MARIE CATHERINE FRIED (E de K)
(1920–1989)   *Painter, Graphic Artist, Art Critic*

A renowned New York–school abstract expressionist who excelled at figurative art, Elaine de Kooning was also a well-regarded art critic and teacher. Her landscapes, portraits, and studies of male athletes were especially acclaimed for their boldness and verve.

Born Elaine Marie Catherine Fried on March 12, 1920, into a large, middle-class, Irish-German family in New York City, de Kooning grew up surrounded by reproductions of famous paintings, many of which were by female artists. Her favorite childhood activities were visiting Manhattan's plethora of art museums and galleries, examining her mother's impressive collection of art books, dancing, and sketching. By the time she was 10, her friends referred to her as "the artist."

After graduating from Erasmus Hall High School in Brooklyn, New York, where she majored in art, Fried attended Hunter College for a short period of time. She enrolled at the American Artists School and at the Leonardo da Vinci Art School, both in New York City, and immersed herself in sculpting, etching, and watercolor. While at Leonardo da Vinci, she was introduced to a group of social realists and abstract painters that included her future husband, Willem de Kooning. He would become a leading exponent of abstract expressionism, a form of nonrepresentational modern art that took hold in America in the late 1940s and 1950s.

Fried became de Kooning's private student, model, and inspiration. Under his strict tutelage she worked on still lifes and modern spatial concepts. Her style was quick and self-assured, while his was painstakingly slow. Both artists, however, adhered to the expressionistic "gestural" style that featured slashing brush strokes and a reliance on intuition. The couple shared a small studio in lower Manhattan and married in 1943. They became pivotal figures—both socially and professionally—in a group of aspiring, politically radical artists who rejected conventional figurative art. Like the other struggling expressionists, the de Koonings could barely pay their rent: When they could not afford to purchase new canvases, they painted on top of used ones.

For many years Elaine de Kooning, who signed her work "E de K," was better known as an art critic than as an artist. In 1948 she began writing for *Artnews* (now *ARTnews*). Her insightful, witty reviews focused on contemporary artists such as Josef Albers, Franz Kline, and Arshile Gorky. In addition to her husband, she credited Gorky with having the most profound influence on her work.

In 1952 de Kooning's first solo exhibition was held at the Stable Gallery in Manhattan. She had many individual shows, and her work can be found in the permanent collections of New York City's Guggenheim Museum and the Museum of Modern Art.

As her artistry developed, it became apparent that "E de K" was more interested in character that "comes out of the work" than in style. "Style is something I've always tried to avoid," she once said. Although she usually painted with explosive energy on huge canvases, like the other abstract expressionists, she never completely abandoned realism. Her materials varied widely, from charcoal and pastels to oils and acrylics.

During the 1950s, de Kooning wrote two influential articles for *Artnews*. The first, entitled "Subject: What, How or Who?," asserted that the artist had only "partial control" in choosing his or her subject or styles; the second, "Pure Paints a Picture," focused on technique. In 1956 the de Koonings separated, although they never divorced and remained mostly on friendly terms. Elaine de Kooning left New York City to teach at the University of New Mexico in Albuquerque. She would hold visiting professorships in art at numerous universities such as Yale, Carnegie-Mellon, and the University of Pennsylvania. She also led workshops at museum schools throughout the country, received several honorary doctorates, and was named a fellow of Rhode Island School of Design in Providence.

While living in Albuquerque, de Kooning made forays into Juárez, Mexico, to watch the bullfights and in 1957 began a celebrated series of paintings based on bullfighting. "The color experiences of New Mexico," she wrote, after returning to New York, "convinced me that the 'feeling' was the thing." Critic Lawrence Campbell noted in *Artnews* (1960) that "her style changed from compressed vertical forms to expansive, horizontal area . . . from hidden to shouting color, although the content remained the same."

De Kooning was an unabashed admirer of masculinity and virility, and her subjects were almost always males, whether faceless or sports figures in action. "I was interested in the gesture of the [male] body—the expression of character through the structure of clothing," she said in an interview in *Originals: American Women Artists.*

Even while working furiously on abstract paintings, de Kooning returned to and excelled at portraiture. In 1962 she was invited to Palm Beach, Florida, to execute a commissioned portrait of President John F. Kennedy. "He was incandescent, golden. And bigger than life," she wrote. De Kooning created hundreds of drawings and more than two dozen paintings in her quest to create "a composite image" of the nation's handsome, vivacious leader. Although one of her studies hangs in the Truman Library in Independence, Missouri, and another in the John F. Kennedy Library in Boston, she was never able to complete to her satisfaction a final painting of Kennedy because, as she put it, "the assassin dropped my brush."

Traumatized by the murder of the president and her own personal sense of failure, de Kooning stopped painting altogether and turned to sculpture. In one year she cast 14 bronzes, including a bust of Kennedy. She described how it felt to work in a three-dimensional medium: "I was tearing, bending sheets of wax, tacking them together with a torch. It was as if all the drawing and painting I'd done in my life was preparing me for this." But de Kooning returned to painting, and in 1973 a retrospective of her portraits was held at the Montclair Art Museum in New Jersey.

In 1976, deeply moved by a bronze statue of Bacchus she had come upon in the Luxembourg Gardens in Paris, de Kooning undertook a series of large lithographs she described as "frozen motion—the limbs pouring over one another, as in those paintings of athletes." Admittedly "obsessed" by Bacchus's image, over several years she executed 50 brightly colored abstract acrylic sketches of the

Elaine de Kooning, next to her portrait
of President Kennedy, in 1964
(AP/Wide World Photos)

means of spontaneous brushwork from the rough, accidental surfaces of the cave walls." When asked to describe the nature of abstract expressionism, de Kooning replied: "The main difference . . . between abstract and nonabstract art is that the abstract artist does not have to choose a subject. But whether or not he chooses, he always ends up with one."

New York Times art critic John Canady referred to de Kooning as abstract expressionism's "mascot, sibyl and recording secretary." After a versatile and prolific career as artist, writer, and art teacher, Elaine de Kooning died of lung cancer on February 1, 1989, near her home in East Hampton, Long Island, New York, at the age of 68.

Further Reading

Campbell, Lawrence. "Elaine de Kooning Paints a Picture." *Artnews* 59:8 (December 1960): 40–44.
De Kooning, Elaine. *The Spirit of Abstract Expressionism: Selected Writings.* New York: George Braziller, 1994.
Munro, Eleanor. *Originals: American Women Artists.* New York: Da Capo Press, 2000.
Slivka, Rose. *E de K: Elaine de Kooning.* Athens: University of Georgia Press, 1992.

— C. K.

ancient god of wine. They were shown to much acclaim at a gallery in New York City in 1982, the same year she was named Avery Professor at Bard College in New York.

Next, de Kooning turned to Time of the Bison (1983–88), a series of etchings based on Paleolithic cave paintings she had visited in southern France and northern Spain. She was captivated by the primitive, lifelike appearance of the animals, especially the bison. In fact, the image of the bison recalls the bulls of de Kooning's earlier series, although the bison seem to represent life rather than death. The etchings were critically well received when they appeared in a solo show at New York's Fischbach Gallery in 1988. In the *New York Times,* Grace Glueck described how the "graffiti-like images of horses, deer, antelope, bison and bulls appeared in flowing panorama, seeming to emerge—as they do in the caves themselves—by

DEWING, MARIA OAKEY
(1845–1927) *Painter*

A successful author, consummate gardener, and amateur botanist, as well as a gifted artist, Maria Oakey Dewing was recognized as one of the most distinguished flower painters of the late 19th and early 20th centuries. "Her flowers," wrote an art critic in the *New York Herald Tribune,* "have made for themselves a place apart in American painting. She gives us their character, their special texture, their special droop. She paints, literally, their portraits."

Maria Oakey was born in New York City on October 27, 1845, the fifth of 10 siblings, into the prosperous and cultured household of William Francis and Mary (Sullivan) Oakey. Maria's father, a successful businessman, enjoyed talking with his young daughter about "everything artistic." Her mother, a proper Bostonian whose family lineage included a Massachusetts governor and a revolutionary war general, was an established writer whose circle of friends included artistic and literary luminaries.

Although in her early years Maria was more interested in writing than in painting, she ultimately opted to concentrate on the visual arts. She studied in New York City at the Cooper Union School of Design for Women from 1866 to 1870 and at the Antique School of National Academy of Fine Arts from 1871 to 1875. During those years she also studied with the eminent flower painter and devotee of Japanese aesthetics John La Farge, who probably had the single greatest influence on her art; Oakey insisted that she and many other artists "owed (him) an unpayable debt" and called La Farge's work "the most beautiful in all the world."

Oakey was fortunate to have two other notable teachers of landscape painting: Boston's William Morris Hunt (in 1875) and Thomas Couture (in 1876), the Paris-based artist whose pupils included French painter Édouard Manet. She already had established a solid reputation in figure painting and portraiture when in 1881 she married fellow artist Thomas Wilmer Dewing, six years her junior. The couple had two children, a son who died in infancy and a daughter, Elizabeth, born in 1885.

While Dewing's interest in flower painting dated from the early 1860s, it was only after her marriage that it became the central focus of her work. One important reason why Dewing switched from figure to flower painting was that the latter was more compatible with the demands of motherhood and household tasks. Another reason, according to some critics, was that it enabled Dewing to avoid competing with her husband, who emerged as one of the finest figure painters of that era. Dewing collaborated with her husband by providing floral backgrounds to several of his paintings, among them *Hyman* (1886), the only work signed by both artists.

Critic William H. Gerdts observed in 1982 that Dewing's "flower paintings combine a poetic sensibility derived from her teacher, John La Farge,

with a thorough knowledge of botany nourished and enhanced by the cultivation of her own garden." Dewing considered the knowledge she gained from her devotion to that garden—which was located in an artists' colony in Cornish, New Hampshire, where the Dewings summered for almost 20 years—as essential to her art. She maintained that to paint nature well an artist required a "long apprenticeship in the garden." For Dewing, who subscribed to the doctrine of aestheticism (art for art's sake, with no ulterior social or political purpose), the point of her work was to create something captivating and appealing. As she expressed it, "The flower offers a removed beauty that exists only for beauty, more abstract than it can be in a human being, even more exquisite."

Some of Dewing's best-known paintings include *Garden in May* (1895), *Iris at Dawn* (1899), and *Bed of Poppies* (1909). During her lifetime, her works won bronze medals at the 1893 Columbian Exposition in Chicago and at the 1901 Pan American Exposition in Buffalo, New York. Among the permanent collections where her works are represented are the National Museum of American Art in Washington, D.C., the Hood Museum of Art in Hanover, New Hampshire, and the Addison Gallery of American Art in Andover, Massachusetts. Dewing returned to figure painting late in her life, but it was the paintings of flowers that gave her enduring distinction. As critic Arthur Edwin Bye wrote in 1921, "These remarkable works are absolutely unique. There is nothing like them in the field of flower painting."

Maria Oakey Dewing, praised for her originality, technical skills, and profound sense of beauty, died on December 13, 1927, in New York City.

Further Reading

Doumato, Lamia. "Maria Oakey Dewing." In *Dictionary of Women Artists,* edited by Delia Gaze, 454–456. Chicago, Ill.: Fitzroy Dearborn Publications, 1997.

Martin, Jennifer. "Portraits of Flowers: The Out-of-Door Still-Life Paintings of Maria Oakey Dewing." *American Art Review* VI: 3 (December 1977): 48–55, 114–118.

"Hood Museum of Art Acquires Rare Outdoor Still Life by Maria Oakey Dewing." Available online. URL: http://www.tfaoi.com/aa/laa/laa29.htm. Downloaded on August 26, 2000.

— C. K.

DREIER, KATHERINE SOPHIE
(1877–1952)   *Painter, Art Patron*

An accomplished painter whose works were exhibited throughout the United States and in Europe during her lifetime, Katherine Dreier was better known as a longtime, tireless advocate and promoter of modern art in America. She was an associate of the dadaist French painter Marcel Duchamp, who for 35 years was Dreier's close friend and collaborator in furthering the modern art movement to which they were both passionately committed.

Katherine Sophie Dreier was born on September 10, 1877, in Brooklyn, New York, the youngest of five children—four daughters and a son—of Theodor and Dorothea Dreier, immigrants from Germany. Her father became a very successful businessman, and the family prospered. Katherine's parents transmitted to their children their love of German culture along with their confirmed democratic beliefs, which included giving their daughters the same opportunities as were afforded to their son. Katherine, who attended an exclusive private school and began art lessons at the age of 12, grew up with an appreciation of art and a strong commitment to social reform. As a young woman she was involved in several civic and charitable organizations, as well as in the suffrage movement; she was a delegate to the Sixth Convention of the International Woman Suffrage Alliance.

After enrolling at the Brooklyn Art School and studying there from 1895 to 1897, Dreier attended the Pratt Institute in 1900 and then, during 1902 and 1903, traveled and studied in Europe. In 1903 she returned to New York and studied privately with Walter Shirlaw, a painter who specialized in nudes and who had an enormous influence on her career. Although Shirlaw's own work was fairly conventional, he encouraged individuality in his students and therefore, Dreier later recalled, laid the basis for her appreciation and understanding of modern art. As she put it, "without the training which Shirlaw gave me in Beauty—Vitality—Rhythm—and Design or Organization—I could never have taken the step or leap into this new great expression in art, based as it is fundamentally on these manifestations."

Upon returning to Europe, where she had two solo exhibitions (1911 in London; 1912 in Frankfurt), Dreier for the first time encountered modernism, which deeply impressed her. Europe's avant-garde painters, she discovered, "were not slavish followers, imitators . . . but men who were doing vigorous, original work." She went back to New York City and totally embraced modern abstract painting after viewing the famed but, for the most part, poorly received 1913 Armory Show, which included two of her works (*Blue Bowl* and *The Avenue, Holland*). The show's controversial centerpiece was Marcel Duchamp's *Nude Descending a Staircase*.

Dreier and Duchamp soon became friends. In 1918 her painting *Abstract Portrait of Marcel Duchamp* exemplified his influence, as well as that of Wassily Kandinsky, on her work. Two years later, along with Man Ray, a prominent American dadaist and surrealist, she and Duchamp cofounded the Société Anonyme. Among the many leading European and American figures of modern art whose work the Société Anonyme championed or introduced to American audiences were Kandinsky, Kasimir Malevich, Paul Klee, Fernand Léger, Heinrich Campendonk, Stanton Macdonald-Wright, David Burliuk, and Joan Miró. Dreier provided the critical energy and a large share of the funding for the organization. The Société also sponsored traveling exhibitions and lectures and published a large variety of books and pamphlets. Its permanent collection of paintings in effect turned the Société into America's first museum of modern art. (The New York Museum of Modern Art was founded in 1929.) By the time the Société Anonyme donated its collection to Yale University in 1941, it held more than 800 works by 175 artists.

Dreier wrote several books on modern art, including *Western Art in the New Era* (1923). In that volume she maintained that "art is constantly in the making, as fluid as the development of any force existing in man. . . . The function of art is to free the spirit of man and to invigorate and enlarge his vision." Her own work was the subject of a retrospective in 1933 at New York's Academy of Allied Arts. In 1948 she delivered the Trowbridge Lecture at Yale University on a topic close to her heart: "Intrinsic Significance of Modern Art." By then Dreier already was seriously ill, although she continued to write and lecture. In 1951, the Société Anonyme dissolved itself.

Katherine Sophie Dreier died of nonalcoholic cirrhosis of the liver in Milford, Connecticut, on March 29, 1952. A few years later, art critic Aline Saarinen wrote: "She believed in reincarnation, but it would seem that her soul has not yet found its new lodging. Modern art has known no other so fervent a propagandist."

Further Reading

Bailey, Brooke. "Katherine Sophie Dreier." In *The Remarkable Lives of 100 Women Artists,* 44–45. Holbrook, Mass.: Bob Adams, 1994.

Bohan, Ruth. "Katherine Sophie Dreier and New York Dada," *Arts Magazine* 51 (May 1977): 97–101.

Bohan, Ruth. *The Société Anonyme's Brooklyn Exhibition: Katherine Dreier and Modernism in America.* Ann Arbor, Mich.: UMI Research Press, 1982.

Saarinen, Aline B. *The Proud Possessors: The Lives, Times, and Tastes of Some Adventurous American Art Collectors.* New York: Random House, 1958.

— C. K.

DWIGHT, MABEL JACQUE WILLIAMSON

(1875–1955)   *Printmaker, Painter, Illustrator*

Although early in her career Mabel Dwight enjoyed minor success as a painter and illustrator in New York, she was past 50 when, in the mid-1920s, she established a reputation as one of America's best lithographers. Her popular yet insightful work chronicled, often with a touch of humor, the people and eccentricities of New York City's urban landscape.

Mabel Dwight was born Mabel Jacque Williamson on January 31, 1875, in Cincinnati, Ohio, the only child of Paul Houston and Adelaide Jacque Williamson. The Williamsons moved to New Orleans, Louisiana, when Mabel was a young girl and then, in the early 1890s, to San Francisco, California, where she finished her secondary education. She subsequently studied at San Francisco's Mark Hopkins Institute of Art and became a member, and ultimately a director, of the Sketch Club, California's first organization solely for women artists. It was during her stay in San Francisco that Williamson's political views were shaped: she was introduced to socialistic ideas which, she later recalled, was like "getting religion."

After leaving California, Williamson traveled to Egypt, Ceylon (now Sri Lanka), India, and Java (Indonesia). By 1903 she had settled in New York City's Greenwich Village, a gathering place for emerging artists, writers, and young people attracted to socialism and other radical causes. She married fellow socialist and artist George Higgins in 1906; their childless union ended in divorce a decade later.

During the mid-1920s Dwight abandoned her married name, although why she chose the surname Dwight is unclear. Her marriage was followed by a lengthy and often painful love affair with a friend named Roderick Seidenberg, an architectural draftsman and militant socialist who was 14 years Dwight's junior. Their relationship ended by 1929, when Seidenberg left New York for a temporary job on a construction project in the Soviet Union. During his return trip, he met another woman, whom he eventually married. Dwight's years with both Higgins and Seidenberg were marked by emotional hardship and poverty. Along with her political beliefs, her own experiences help explain Dwight's fundamental conviction that "poverty is the great evil—a form of black plague inexcusable in a scientific age."

The major turning point in Dwight's career came in 1926 when she traveled to Paris and took up lithography, working with the French printer Édouard Duchatel. She returned to New York in 1927, where the well-known print dealer Carl Zigrosser, her friend since 1913, was promoting her work. Dwight chronicled New York City life with a wryly satiric, as opposed to a tough cynical, eye. She began with *In the Subway* (1927) and continued with classics such as *Ferry Boat* (1930), *Derelicts* (1931)—a grim depiction of depression-era outcasts along the East River—and *Queer Fish* (1936), described by Dwight as a confrontation she witnessed at the New York Aquarium that featured "a huge Grouper fish and a fat man trying to outstare each other."

In "Satire in Art," as essay written during the late 1930s, Dwight observed that "satire may play lightly with man's foibles–in kindly, ironic vein portray him not as such a bad fellow after all, but at times a rather absurd one." She rejected excessive distortion, dismissing it as a "noisy show rather than a subtle suggestion," and adding that the artist "has only to look at . . . people with sympathy and translate them into art just as tragic and humorous as he may wish."

In 1933 one of her watercolors was included in the influential First Biennial Exhibition of Contemporary American Sculpture, Watercolors, and Prints at the Whitney Museum of American Art in New York. Between 1934 and 1939 Dwight worked for two arts projects sponsored by the federal Works Project Administration, one of the New Deal agencies established during the Roosevelt administration. Her initial job, which Seidenberg helped her get, rescued her from dire economic straits. As the depression wore on, Dwight's political views became increasingly radical, and she became associated with a variety of left-wing causes and groups. At the same time, her artistic reputation burgeoned. Her prints were widely shown, and she had two one-woman shows, in 1932 and 1938, at New York's Weyhe Gallery. In 1939, art critic Thomas Craven's *Treasury of American Prints* cited her as one of the "foremost living American artists." She was praised for her keen wit and artistry.

Dwight's health declined rapidly in the 1940s, and by the end of the decade she was confined to convalescent homes. She died, following a stroke, on September 4, 1955, in Colmat, Pennsylvania. Today her works are in the collections of New York's Museum of Modern Art, the Boston Museum of Fine Arts, London's Victoria and Albert Museum, and the Tamarind Institute of Albuquerque, New Mexico.

In 1949, her lifelong friend and curator of prints at the Philadelphia Museum of Art Carl Zigrosser provided an apt evaluation of Mabel Dwight's body of work. He wrote in *American Artist* that she was a master of the *comédie humaine,* by which he meant an artist whose work "probes into the depths" of the drama of everyday human life, "ever imbued with pity and compassion, a sense of irony, and an understanding that comes from profound experience."

Further Reading

Dwight, Mabel. "Satire in Art." In *Art for the Millions: Essays From the 1930s by Artists and Administrators of the WPA Federal Art Project,* edited by Francis V. O'Connor, 151–154. Boston: New York Graphic Society, 1975.

Henkes, Robert. *American Women Painting of the 1930s and 1940s: The Lives and Work of Ten Artists.* Jefferson, N.C.: McFarland, 1991.

Robinson, Susan Barnes, and John Pirog. *Mabel Dwight: A Catalogue Raisonné of the Lithographs.* Washington, D.C.: Smithsonian Institution Press, 1997.

Zigrosser, Carl. "Mabel Dwight: Master of Comédie Humaine." *Artnews* 6:126 (June 1949): 42–45.

— C. K.

E

EAKINS, SUSAN HANNAH MACDOWELL

(1851–1938)   *Painter, Printmaker, Photographer*

Award-winning Susan Macdowell Eakins was considered one of the foremost female artists of her time, although her work was not deemed worthy of a solo exhibition until 35 years after her death. Eakins's interests varied from traditional portraits and still lifes to contemporary photographs.

The fifth of eight children, Susan Hannah Macdowell was born in Philadelphia, Pennsylvania, on September 21, 1851. Her father, a highly regarded engraver, emphasized the importance of artistic achievement. He provided his daughter, who at an early age was already an accomplished pianist, with her own attic studio in order to develop her talent. Both Susan and her younger sister Elizabeth became noteworthy artists.

Like MARY CASSATT and CECILIA BEAUX, Macdowell enrolled at the Pennsylvania Academy of Fine Arts, which in the late 19th century was considered the best art school in the country. In 1876 Macdowell first viewed Thomas Eakins's *The Gross Clinic* at the Hazeltine Gallery. She was so impressed by the painting, which was thought to

be far too realistic and graphic at the time but is now considered a masterpiece, that she decided she had to study with the artist—then a teacher at the Philadelphia Academy. During her six years at the academy, Macdowell was able to participate in a limited number of classes; others were open only to male students. Her teachers included Christian Schussele and Eakins, her future husband and one of America's most illustrious artists.

During her years at the Pennsylvania Academy, Macdowell's work, for the most part, reflected Eakins's adherence to realism and his quest to "peer deeper into the heart of American life." Macdowell painted portraits and domestic scenes using family members as models. In her first year as a student at the Academy, one of her paintings was shown at the annual exhibition and was sold. She was elected class secretary, and as a leader of the student body, she insisted that the school offer a life-drawing class, from nude models, for its female students.

In 1879 Macdowell became the Pennsylvania Academy's first recipient of the Mary Smith Prize for the best picture submitted by a female artist residing in Philadelphia. Three years later, in recognition of the most accurately executed drawing, she won the Charles Toppan Prize. Macdowell also continued to develop an early interest in photography: she was among the first members of the Philadelphia Photographic Society. One of her most acclaimed photographs, *Child with Doll,* was exhibited at the Philadelphia Salon of Photography. Macdowell also excelled at watercolors. Her subjects were often beautifully rendered, solitary, introspective figures of women engaged in such domestic chores as knitting. Her oil paintings, including *Portrait of a Gentleman and Dog* (1878–79) and *Portrait of a Lady* (1880), reflected her "firm handling and solid anatomical construction blended with generally dark tonalities," according to art historian Susan Casteras.

After Macdowell married Eakins in 1884, the couple worked in separate studios in their Philadelphia home—a lively abode frequented by visiting artists, relatives, and a variety of pets, including a monkey. The 32-year-old bride devoted most of her time to keeping house and helping her husband further his burgeoning and sometimes tempestuous career: Thomas Eakins insisted on using nude models and was therefore frowned upon by the wealthy, conservative establishment, which refused to buy his risqué paintings.

In her spare time, Eakins held informal piano recitals and continued to paint portraits, paying special attention to draftsmanship and to the character of her sitters as revealed through their facial features and expressions. Her portraiture was praised and respected by other artists, including by Thomas Eakins, who considered his wife "as good a woman painter as he had ever seen." He also once said that she knew more about color than he did.

After Thomas Eakins died in 1916, Susan Macdowell Eakins painted almost every day for the remainder of her life. Her body of work during the 1920s and 1930s was impressive. Art historian Susan Casteras describes Eakins's brighter, looser late style as "a weakening solidity of three-dimensional form and more acid, higher-keyed colors, both indicating movement away from a purely Eakinesque practice and palette." One of Eakins's best known portraits was of her husband, the posthumously executed *Thomas Eakins* (ca. 1920–25).

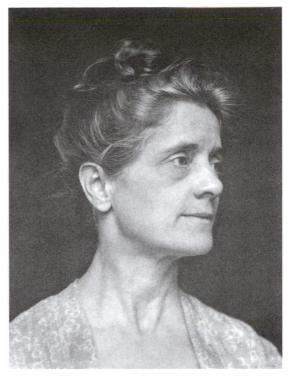

Award-winning painter Susan Macdowell Eakins, *circa* 1900
(Courtesy of the Pennsylvania Academy of the Fine Arts, Philadelphia. Charles Bregler's Thomas Eakins Collection. Purchased with the partial support of the Pew Memorial Trust)

Eakins's finely crafted still lifes and portraits endure because they are, wrote art critic Lucy Lippard, "incisive and adventurous, full of both life and thought." In 1936 Eakins helped organize a show at the Philadelphia Art Club, which featured paintings by her late husband and her sister Elizabeth, as well as 20 of her own works.

Susan Macdowell Eakins died at her home in Philadelphia on December 27, 1938, at age 86. Until the 1970s she was relatively unknown, other than as the wife of Thomas Eakins. Thanks to a renewed interest in female artists, Eakins's portraits and photographs were rediscovered. The first comprehensive show of more than 50 of her paintings and drawings was held in 1973, fittingly at the

Pennsylvania Academy. Her work was also included in *Nineteenth Century Women Artists,* an exhibition at the Whitney Museum of American Art in 1976.

Further Reading

Casteras, Susan P. "Mr. and Mrs. Eakins: Two Painters, One Reputation," *Harper's,* October 1977, p. 69–71.

Casteras, Susan P., and Seymour Adelman. *Susan Macdow-ell Eakins, 1851–1938.* Exhibition Catalog. Philadelphia: Pennsylvania Academy of Fine Arts, 1973.

Heller, Jules, and Nancy G. Heller, editors. *North American Women Artists of the 20th Century.* New York: Garland Publishing, 1995.

Lippard, Lucy. "19th Century Women Artists." *Art in America,* September–October 1976, p. 113.

— C. K.

EBERLE, MARY ABASTENIA ST. LEGER
(1878–1942) *Sculptor*

Abastenia St. Leger Eberle's prizewinning, exuberant, and realistic small bronze sculptures reflected her passionate concern for the immigrants who lived on New York City's Lower East Side during the early 1900s. Eberle often focused on the daily life of immigrant women and children and claimed that her material was rooted in the "work-a-day world with all its commonplaces."

Mary Abastenia St. Leger Eberle was born to Canadian parents on April 6, 1876, in Webster City, Iowa, and grew up in Canton, Ohio. As a young child, Abastenia (she was known by her middle name) demonstrated a gift for modeling images in clay, wax, and mud. An accomplished young violinist, she was confident that she would become an equally accomplished sculptor. "I knew it was my work," she said. Abastenia's parents encouraged her artistry by enrolling her in a clay modeling class taught by a local sculptor.

When Eberle was 20, she moved with her family to Puerto Rico, where her father, a physician, was posted as an army surgeon. Eberle built a small art studio for herself. She enjoyed observing local people at work and at play and used them as her

models, casting their colorful images in bronze. Eberle moved to New York City in 1899 to attend, as a scholarship student, the highly regarded Art Students League. She studied with the eminent sculptor George Grey Barnard. When Barnard traveled, he put Eberle in charge of his class.

From 1903 to 1906, Eberle shared an apartment and studio with ANNA VAUGHN HYATT HUNTINGTON, a well-known animal sculptor. The two friends collaborated on several sculptures, including *Men and Bull,* which won a bronze medal at the 1904 Louisiana Purchase Exposition in St. Louis. The piece was acclaimed by a leading American sculptor, Augustus Saint-Gaudens, and represented the first of several awards Eberle would garner at museum shows in New York and San Francisco and at international expositions in Venice, Rome, and Paris.

Eberle's technically competent, graceful sculptures poignantly expressed the immigrant experience, without sentimentalizing it. *Roller Skating* (1906), a bronze figure of a shabbily dressed young immigrant girl who clearly enjoyed escaping by skating against the wind, was typical of the artist's work: she accorded her subjects respect and dignity. In 1907 Eberle traveled to Italy to study neoclassicism. Her works were cast in bronze at a foundry in Naples, much to the surprise of the foundry workers, who were not used to dealing with female sculptors.

Beginning in 1907, and for six consecutive years, Eberle's pieces were exhibited at the Macbeth Gallery in Manhattan. However, her work did not sell well, and she supported herself by selling bronze tobacco jars and bookends. A few years after returning to America from Italy, Eberle moved from a comfortable apartment and studio in New York's Greenwich Village to the heart of the crowded Lower East Side, where her models worked and lived. "When I landed in New York," she wrote, "I began again to sense the modern spirit. . . . I made little journeys over the East Side . . . and smelt its pungent odors and saw its children playing in the streets. And I learned something about another side of the great city, the

Sculptor Mary Abastenia St. Leger Eberle was concerned with urban immigrant life in New York City.
(Courtesy David's Gallery, Webster City, Iowa)

underworld with its crimes and prostitutions and awfulness. Then my awakening came."

Eberle rejected what she called the "archaic" classical and allegorical art in favor of the Ashcan school's style of depicting the grittiness of everyday urban life. Increasingly her works captured the poverty and brutal social conditions of immigrant women, as exemplified by *Woman Picking Up Coal* in 1907 and *Ragpicker* in 1911. She set up a playroom adjoining her studio so she could observe the neighborhood children, and then she cast them in action. Eberle was influenced by the writings of social reformer Jane Addams and wrote that the artist "must see for the people—reveal them to themselves and to each other."

In 1908 Eberle exhibited four contemporary pieces at the National Academy of Design. Two years later the academy awarded her the Helen Foster Barnett Prize for one of her best-known pieces, *Windy Doorstep,* a bronze portrait of a farm woman in the act of sweeping. The compassion and admiration she felt for her working-class subjects were abundantly clear in *Windy Doorstep.* Her most controversial work was entitled *White Slave* (1913), a plastic sculpture of a leering old man auctioning off a young, naked immigrant girl whose hands are bound and who hangs her head in shame. A photograph of *White Slave* appeared on the cover of a magazine called *The Survey* and caused a scandal. It was also shown at the Armory Show in New York in 1913, the first great modern art show in America, along with another more conventional, lyrical piece entitled *Girls Wading,* which was comprised of three bronze figures unified on a single base.

A suffragist, Eberle participated in shows by women sculptors in 1912 and 1915. In 1920, she exhibited 21 sculptures at the Montclair Art Museum in New Jersey. A year later, a solo exhibit of her work was held at the Macbeth Gallery in New York. Sadly, while in her thirties Eberle was stricken with heart disease and had to stop working. She continued to live alone in her New York studio until city life became too difficult, and then moved to a farmhouse in Westport, Connecticut, which she had restored and winterized.

In 1932 Eberle won the Lindsey Morris Sterling Memorial Prize from the Allied Artists of America, and one of her sculptures was selected in 1940 for an exhibition at New York's Whitney Museum of American Art. Mary Abastenia St. Leger Eberle died on February 26, 1942, at the home of a friend in New York City, at age 63. She donated her works, many of which were considered overly polemical or graphic, to the Kendall Young Library in Webster City, Iowa. In recent years, Eberle's affecting studies of immigrant life in New York have been recognized for their originality and draftsmanship. Among the institutions that own her work are New York's Metropolitan Museum of Art and the Whitney Museum of American Art, and the Art Institute of Chicago.

Further Reading

Conner, Janis, and Joel Rosenkranz. *Rediscoveries in American Sculpture: Studio Works, 1893–1939.* Austin: University of Texas Press, 1989.

Noun, Louise R. *Abastenia St. Leger Eberle, Sculptor (1878–1942).* Exhibition Catalog. Des Moines, Iowa: Des Moines Art Center, 1980.

"Statues to Sculpture: 1890–1930." In *200 Years of American Sculpture,* edited by Tom Armstrong, 133–138. New York: Whitney Museum of American Art and David R. Godine, 1976.

Rubinstein, Charlotte Streifen. *American Women Sculptors.* Boston: G. K. Hall, 1990.

— C. K.

F

 FINE, PERLE
(1908–1988)   *Painter, Printmaker,*
Art Teacher

An abstract expressionist known for her geometric paintings, Perle Fine also excelled at printmaking. In *Artnews* (April 1963; now *ARTnews*), her work was praised by critic John Russel for its "quality of lyricism . . . and its life affirming idealistic feelings [achieved] through the construction of ordered color spaces. The force of relationships and quiet eloquence of [Fine's] colors triumph."

Born in Boston, Massachusetts, on May 1, 1908, Perle Fine was raised on a dairy farm outside of Boston and knew early on that she wanted to become an artist. When her family moved to New York City, she enrolled at the Art Students League, at that time considered the country's most important art school, and studied drawing with Kimon Nicolaides. She befriended a fellow student, Maurice Berezov, whom she would later marry. Like Fine, Berezov became a prizewinning abstract artist. However, the couple maintained separate identities; unlike many female artists, such as ELAINE DE KOONING, Fine kept her own last name.

In 1939 Fine began studying with Hans Hofmann, a well-regarded abstract painter, first at the Art Students League, and then at his Eighth Street School in New York City's Greenwich Village, not far from her studio. Although Hofmann is considered among the greatest art teachers of the 20th century, and Fine greatly admired him, she disagreed with his theory that line should be subordinated to color and with his manic style of expressionism. Fine also became interested in printmaking and in 1944 signed up for Stanley William Hayter's graphic arts workshop. The illustrious British engraver emphasized experimentation and openness. Fine's early prints, such as *Deep of the Night* and *Complete Abandon,* reflected her growing reliance on automatism, a method in which the artist suppresses conscious control over the movements of the hand, allowing the subconscious mind to take over. Increasingly she turned to geometric curves, vivid colors, and flowing shapes to express her unconscious feelings.

In the 1940s, Fine met Baroness Hilla Rebay, director of the Guggenheim Foundation. Rebay supported Fine's abstract art by obtaining funds for her and promoting her work at the Guggenheim Museum. Fine met Jackson Pollock, who at that time was working as a security guard at the museum. After viewing his work, she became one of his earliest supporters and proposed him for membership in a newly formed group of American abstract artists. But most members were purists who favored geometric abstraction and cubism over expressionism, and they rejected Fine's proposal. Pollock would go on to become the most famous American abstract expressionist painter.

Fine's first solo exhibition was held in 1945 at Manhattan's Marian Willard Gallery. She had two more well-received individual shows at other New York galleries. A critic in *Artnews* described one of Fine's paintings during that period, entitled *Polyphonic,* as an "immobilized" Alexander Calder mobile, with its Calderesque sense of harmony and wiry black lines. (Calder was an American sculptor known for mobiles and wire works.) While Fine used various printmaking techniques such as lithography to express herself, she believed that only through abstract painting could she convey a sense of, as she put it, the "universal and ideal." She employed numerous forms—from triangles to biomorphic elements—in some of her best-known paintings, notably *Form and Line* (1946) and *Taurus* (1946), and she was flattered when the distinguished architect Frank Lloyd Wright, known to generally dislike paintings, purchased one of her works.

In 1954 Fine and Berezov moved to The Springs, an art colony near East Hampton, Long Island, New York, where several up-and-coming American abstract expressionists resided and worked. Around that same time, Fine began exhibiting her paintings and prints at the Betty Parsons Gallery in New York City. "Her canvases," writes art historian Charlotte Streifer Rubinstein, "grew larger, looser, and almost cloud-like in imagery." Fine also accepted a position as associate professor at Hofstra University in New York and taught there for 12 years. She described the process of teaching as a "creative commitment" that had to be taken "very seriously." In 1955 Fine received a Purchase Award from the Brooklyn Museum for her color woodcut *Wide to the Wind* (1955).

When she stopped teaching in the late 1960s due to illness, Fine tried her hand at minimalist collages and succeeded admirably. Her most highly

Perle Fine, a first-generation abstract expressionist
(Portrait by Timothy Greenfield-Sanders)

regarded series, Accordment, combined collages comprised of wood pieces and painted grids. The paintings that were part of the Accordment series, including *Gently Cascading, The Dawn's Wind,* and *A Woven Warmth,* came closest to achieving her goal: to bring luminosity, balance, and harmony to her canvases.

Perle Fine's work is represented in permanent collections of major museums including the Smithsonian Institution in Washington, D.C., New York's Guggenheim Museum of Art and Whitney Museum of American Art, the Brooklyn Museum, and the Los Angeles Museum of Art. Along with LEE KRASNER and Elaine de Kooning, Fine was one of the first generation of abstract expressionist women artists. She painted until she was in her late seventies and died at her home in Long Island, New York, in 1988, at the age of 80.

Further Reading

Bailey, Brooke."Perle Fine." In *The Remarkable Lives of 100 Artists,* 56–57. Holbrook, Mass.: Bob Adams, 1994.

Deichter, David. *Perle Fine: Major Works, 1954–1978 (A Selection of Drawings, Paintings and Collages).* East Hampton, N.Y.: Guild of East Hampton, 1978.

Russell, John. "Reviews and Previews," *Artnews,* April 1963.

Rubinstein, Charlotte Streifer. *American Women Artists: From Early Indian Times to the Present.* New York: Avon Books, 1982.

Art in Context. "Perle Fine (1908–1988) Works on Papers." Available online. URL: http//www.artincontext.org/listings/pages/exhit/o/fkmxOg20/press.htm. Downloaded on December 9, 2000.

— C. K.

FISH, JANET
(1938–) *Painter*

Janet Fish is a realist who specializes in bold, lyrical still lifes. She is particularly fond of painting commonplace objects, such as teacups and glass vessels, focusing on their shapes and the way light reflects from their surfaces. "You see things differently all the time depending on the light," said Fish during an interview in 1975.

Born in Boston, Massachusetts, on May 18, 1938, Janet Fish was raised in a family that included an American impressionist (her grandfather), two sculptors (her mother and uncle), and a photographer (her sister). Early on, Janet knew she wanted to be an artist. As an adult she recalled that the windows of her childhood home were filled with glass bottles—subjects of some of her most arresting paintings in later years. Janet went to school in Bermuda, having moved there from Connecticut at the age of 10. She was allowed to use her mother's kiln, discovered she was good at ceramics, and decided to become a sculptor. At Smith College, in Northampton, Massachusetts, she studied sculpture and printmaking with Leonard Baskin. After graduating, in 1960, she attended Yale University of Art and Architecture, where she received bachelor and master of fine arts degrees (1961–63).

Although Fish repudiated the abstract, geometric Bauhaus style of painting favored by most of her teachers at Yale, there were aspects of abstract expressionism—a style that was very much in vogue during the 1960s—that she incorporated into her figurative paintings: working on a large scale, infusing canvases with boldness, and importing fluidity to the brush strokes. Nonetheless Fish felt "totally disconnected" from abstraction and preferred the "physical presence of objects."

After completing a summer session at Maine's Skowhegan Art School, in 1961 Fish turned to landscapes. She was pressured by her peers not to become a realist, but she braved their criticism. Art writer Nancy Heller described Fish's early paintings as combining "the sensuous, active surface quality of abstract expressionism with specific, recognizable subject matter." Fish carefully assembled commonplace objects according to the way light refracted from them, attempting, she said, to "paint things at their most exciting."

Fish was married twice, briefly, and believed that her marriages failed, in part, because she was too ambitious and refused to become a "good conventional housewife." Her first solo exhibition, in 1967 at Fairleigh Dickinson University in Rutherford, New Jersey, featured lustrous close-up views of fruits and vegetables. Two years later she had her first show in New York. She was working on still lifes of supermarket items wrapped tautly in cellophane packages. "The plastic wrap," she explained, "catches the light and creates fascinating reflections." Next she began to paint transparent glassware—jars, bottles, goblets, and glasses half-filled with water, vinegar, or liquor. Her luminous works of ordinary household objects, such as *Vinegar Bottles* (1972), *Glass Garden* (1974), *Tequila* (1974), and *Eight Water Glasses Under Fluorescent Light* (1974), demonstrated the artist's technical command and became her trademark.

Beginning in 1971 and continuing throughout the 1980s and 1990s, Fish had one-person shows in Manhattan at the Jill Kornblee, Robert Miller, Grace Bogenicht, and D. C. Moore galleries. In an introduction to the catalog from Fish's 1980 exhi-

Realist Janet Fish vividly depicts
commonplace objects.
(Photograph © www.StewartStewart.com 1996)

bition at the Robert Miller Gallery, Barry Yourgrau
noted that the artist "chooses and assembles these
objects [plastic and glass] for their activity in the
light, and not for any cultural commentary or alle-
gory." Increasingly Fish painted detailed, contem-
plative still lifes of transparent containers, such as
glass teacups infused with light, or containers
holding lush, colorful fruit or flowers in vases, such
as *Red Vase, Yellow Tulips* (1980). Sometimes, as in
Raspberries and Goldfish (1981), she would add
goldfish or seashells. She also included the human
figure, as in *Barry* (1982). Another canvas, *Charles,
Drummer, Lorna, Roxanne and Jonathan* (1986)
showcases people, pets, and vegetables, and com-

bines landscape, portraiture, and still life in one
painting. Intense or diffused light always remained
central to the artist's compositions.

Fish, who resides in New York City and rural
Vermont, is the recipient of three MacDowell
Colony Fellowships (1968, 1969, and 1972). In
1974 she won the Harris Award at the Chicago
Biennial. In 1993 she received the American Artist
Achievement Award in Oils, followed a year later
by the American Academy of Arts and Letters
Award in Art. Fish has taught at New York's School
of Visual Arts and Parsons School of Design, Syra-
cuse University, and the University of Chicago.
Her work is represented in permanent collections
at notable museums such as the Whitney Museum
of American Art and the Metropolitan Museum of
Art in New York, the Museum of Fine Arts in
Boston, and the Museum of Victoria in Australia.

Janet Fish's masterly paintings, wrote art critic
Eleanor Tufts, are both realistic and poetic. "She is
an artist whose skill keeps growing."

Further Reading

Henry, Gerrit. *Janet Fish*. New York: Burton and Skira,
1987.
Nemser, Cindy. *Art Talk: Conversations with 15 Women
Artists*. New York: HarperCollins, 1975; Icon Editions,
1995.
Steiner, Elaine. "Gardens: Janet Fish, the Artist, Cultivates
her Palette on a Vermont Hillside." *Architectural Digest*
(August 1997), 64–68.
Yourgrau, Barry. *Janet Fish: Exhibition Catalog*, introduc-
tion. New York: Robert Miller Gallery, 1980.
— C. K.

FLACK, AUDREY
(1931–) *Painter, Sculptor*

A major figure of the photorealist movement in
painting from its inception in the mid-1960s,
Audrey Flack successfully began a second career as
a sculptor during the 1980s. As both a painter and
a sculptor, Flack has established a reputation for
originality and independence. She defies accepted

canons and boldly moves in new and different directions to express her creative impulses.

Audrey Flack was born in the Washington Heights neighborhood of New York City on May 30, 1931. Although her parents objected, she was determined to be an artist from the time she was young. Her first attempt to realize that ambition occurred at age seven, when she asked a man who she saw drawing in a park to give her art lessons; not surprisingly, her parents vetoed the idea. The setback was temporary, however, as Flack's undeniable talent enabled her to attend New York City's renowned Music and Art High School, where she won its coveted Saint-Gaudens Art Medal. After high school Flack enrolled at Cooper Union and upon graduation in 1951 was awarded a scholarship to Yale University. She was one of a group of outstanding students recruited by the distinguished abstract artist Josef Albers, a German émigré who had recently been named chairman of Yale's School of Art and Architecture. However, while at Yale, Flack clashed with Albers because he wanted his students to follow his geometric abstract style and become, as she recalled years later, "square" painters. (Albers's format at the time consisted of squares contained within squares.) Flack's rebellion against abstractionism raised tensions to the point where student and teacher were no longer on speaking terms when Flack graduated in 1952.

Flack's difficulties at Yale grew out of her desire to produce realistic work. As she told Cindy Nemser in *Art Talk* in 1974:

> I always wanted to draw realistically. For me art is a continuous discovery into reality, an exploration of visual data which has been going on for centuries, each artist contributing to the next generation's advancement. I wanted to go a step further and extend the boundaries. I believe people have a deep need to understand their world and that art clarifies reality for them.

Although Flack had demonstrated her ability to produce abstract expressionist compositions while at Cooper Union and Yale, she recognized that she lacked the technique to become a representational artist. She therefore decided to study anatomy with Robert Beverly Hale at the Art Students League in New York City.

During the 1950s, Flack's work became increasingly representational. When her paintings were exhibited in group shows, they often were the only figurative works on display. At New York's Sable Gallery, Flack's painting—the sole representational painting in the show—was hung upstairs and hidden in the back, a virtual pariah. As Flack later recalled, "It was heretical then to do any figurative realistic art."

A major turning point in Flack's career occurred in the early 1960s when she began using photographs to create her paintings. Deeply affected by the assassination of President John F. Kennedy, she used a color photograph—previously she had used only black-and-white shots—to paint *Kennedy Motorcade, November 22, 1963* (1964), which is considered her first photorealist painting. Five years later, Flack was commissioned to do a family portrait of museum director Oriole Farb. In order to paint it, Flack projected a slide directly on to her canvas and used that image to apply her color. That technique, she wrote in *Audrey Flack on Painting* (1981), "opened up a new way of seeing and working. . . . It allowed me a greater freedom and a direct contact with the canvas."

The 1970s were a productive and prolific period for Flack. She discovered and was inspired by the work of the 17th-century Spanish female sculptor Louisa Roldan. Flack's paintings from that period, including *Macarena Esperanza* (1971) and *Lady Madonna* (1972), were part of a series in which Flack focused on spiritual and feminist themes. She also produced still lifes, such as her monumental *Vanitas,* which art critic Thalia Gouma-Peterson observed, "created her most ambitious and modern versions of still life and pushed this ancient genre to new limits." Numerous critics pointed out that Flack's work differed from that of other leading photorealist artists such as Chuck Close and Don Eddy because their works tended to be cool and impersonal, while hers reflected a strong emotional commitment,

Audrey Flack is a well-known
photorealist painter.
(Photo by Joyce Ravid. Courtesy Louis Meisel Gallery)

often informed by a concern for social and femi-nist issues. Flack herself commented that she pre-ferred to be called a "Super Realist" because she often exaggerated reality, "bringing it into sharp focus at some points and blurring it in others. An apple is never red enough, nor a sky blue enough."

During the early 1980s, Flack turned to sculpture. She explained why in her book *Art and Soul* (1986):

> And why sculpture after a lifetime of painting?
> . . . The art world and the world outside of it
> seems to be going haywire—out of control, struc-
> tureless, oversized, and temporary. I needed the
> substance of sculpture, the compactness of scale
> reduction in the form of a recognizable human

figure—something solid, real, tangible. Some-thing to hold and to hold on to.

Much of her work dating from the 1980s and 1990s was inspired by Greco-Roman and Renais-sance art as well as Victorian-era sculpture. These striking bronze heroic women and goddess figures include *The Art Muse* (1988), *Receiver of the Sun* (1989–90), and *Egyptian Rocket Goddess* (1990).

Among Flack's commissions was the gateway for the city of Rock Hill, South Carolina, entitled *Civitas: Four Visions (Gateway to the City of Rock Hill)* (1990–91). A patinated and gilded bronze with a black grange base consisting of four female bronze figures, each standing 22 feet high, it won the 1996 Design for Transportation National

Award. Flack's other awards include an honorary doctorate from Cooper Union (1977) and the Artist of the Year Award (1985) from the New York City Art Teachers Association. In 1992 she won an international competition to build a monument to Catherine of Braganza, a Portuguese princess who became an English queen and who is the namesake for New York City's borough of Queens. If completed, the nine-story sculpture would be second in size only to New York's historic Statue of Liberty.

Audrey Flack's works are held in numerous distinguished collections, including New York's Museum of Modern Art, Metropolitan Museum of Art, and Whitney Museum of American Art, the National Museum of Women in the Arts in Washington, D.C., and the San Francisco Museum of Modern Art.

Further Reading

Flack, Audrey. *Art and Soul: Notes on Creating.* New York: E. P. Dutton, 1986.
———. *Audrey Flack on Painting.* New York: Harry N. Abrams, 1981.
Gouma-Peterson, Thalia, editor. *Breaking the Rules: Audrey Flack, A Retrospective, 1950–1990.* New York: Harry N. Abrams, 1992.
Nemser, Cindy. *Art Talk: Conversations with 15 Women Artists.* New York: Icon Editions, 1995.

— C. K.

FRANK, MARY LOCKSPEISER
(1933–   )   *Sculptor, Painter, Graphic Artist*

Primarily known as a sculptor working in clay, during the 1990s Mary Frank achieved recognition for her oeuvre in a variety of other mediums. That work includes drawings in charcoal, ink, and pastel; oil paint on glass, metal, and paper; and, as described in 1991 by Robert G. Edelman (*ARTnews*), "just about anything else that suits her purpose."

Mary Lockspeiser was born in London, England, on February 4, 1939, the only child of Eleanor, an American-born painter, and Edward, a prominent musicologist and critic. In 1939, after the start of World War II, Mary was one of thousands of children evacuated from London because of German bombing attacks on the British capital. The next year she moved with her mother to New York City and resided with Eleanor Lockspeiser's parents in Brooklyn. After her parents divorced four years later, Mary rarely saw her father.

In the United States, as it had been while living in England, art was the center of Mary's home life. At the age of 13 she enrolled in New York City's prestigious Music and Art High School and also spent two years majoring in dance at New York's Professional Children's School. During five years of formal dance training, Lockspeiser studied with master dancer Martha Graham and several other notable teachers.

Although Lockspeiser ultimately gave up dancing for sculpture and painting, dance and movement remained central to her work. As critic Hayden Herrera pointed out in his 1990 book about Frank:

> Mary incorporated her dance training into her sculpture. Her passion has always been to catch movement in all its potential for continuous unfolding. . . . Mary's figures move as if propelled by a force spreading outward from their center. With her deep kinesthetic understanding of gesture, Mary . . . choreographs her figures so that each posture seems charged with an intensity than can border on the portentous.

As she herself put it, "Certain elemental gestures interest me a lot, like a standing, walking, or running figure, a figure crouching, kneeling, or lying down."

In 1950, at the age of 17, Mary Lockspeiser married Swiss photographer Robert Frank. The couple had two children, a son born in 1951 and a daughter in 1954, before separating in 1969 and later divorcing. During the 1950s, Frank briefly studied wood carving with Alfred van Loen and drawing with Max Beckmann and Hans Hofmann. Her first solo exhibit, of wood sculptures and drawings, was held in 1961 at the Stephen

Reich Gallery in New York City. During the mid-1960s, she began concentrating on modeling in plaster, and by the end of the decade had started working with clay. Many of the clay pieces that won her high praise were female figures fired in sections in a kiln and then reassembled. These works, such as *Landscape Woman* (1973–74), *Chant* (1984), and *Persephone* (1985), conveyed a wide range of intense emotion, from loss and rage to love and sensuality. At the same time, one of her signature pieces, *Horse and Rider* (1982), a gripping study of panic and despair, depicts a male rider made of clay desperately straddling two galloping horses as he looks back over his shoulder at something or someone presumably chasing him.

During the second half of the 1980s, Frank moved from sculpture to painting on materials such as plaster, glass, metal, and paper. She has focused increasingly on monoprints, in which an image painted on a metal or glass plate is transferred to paper by using a press or manually pressing the paper on top of the plate. In praising Frank's paintings and drawings in *ARTnews* in 1996, critic Margaret Moorman wrote, "With these works, Frank takes us to the line between life and death, love and longing, painting and knowledge."

Mary Frank has had solo exhibitions in the United States and Europe. Her awards include election to the American Academy and Institute of Arts and Letters in 1984 and two Guggenheim Fellowships (1973 and 1983). Her works are represented in many prominent collections, including Boston's Museum of Fine Arts, the Metropolitan Museum of Art and the Whitney Museum of American Art, both in New York, and the Pennsylvania Academy of Fine Arts in Philadelphia. In 2000, her work was the subject of a retrospective at the D. C. Moore Gallery in New York City and the Neuberger Museum in Purchase, New York. "Experience and expression mix in vivid and instructive ways," wrote Eleanor Munro in the *New York Times* (October 8, 2000) about Frank's improvisational paintings on view during the two retrospectives.

Further Reading

Herrera, Hayden. *Mary Frank*. New York: Harry N. Abrams, 1990.

Moorman, Margaret. "Mary Frank," *ARTnews,* June 1996, 85.

Munro, Eleanor. *Originals: American Women Artists*. New York: Da Capo Press, 2000.

— C. K.

FRANKENTHALER, HELEN
(1928–) *Painter*

Helen Frankenthaler is one of the most prominent 20th-century American abstract expressionist artists, as well as the originator of a painting technique that became the basis of what is known as color field art: the result of thin paint poured onto unprimed canvas. Frankenthaler achieved recognition and success while still in her twenties, and since the early 1950s her diverse and often unpredicatable body of work has made her one of the most celebrated American female artists in modern times.

Helen Frankenthaler was born in New York City on December 14, 1928, the youngest of three daughters of Alfred Frankenthaler, a respected and wealthy New York State Supreme Court judge, and Martha Lowenstein Frankenthaler, who had a gift for painting but was never afforded the opportunity to develop it. Helen and her two older sisters grew up near Manhattan's Museum of Modern Art and many of the city's leading art galleries. They enjoyed a progressive and privileged upbringing that included exclusive private schools. However, tragedy struck in 1940 when Helen's beloved father died, a loss that profoundly affected the 12-year-old.

After several lonely and difficult years, Helen enrolled at the Dalton School, where she took art classes taught by the Mexican painter Rufino Tamayo. She then attended avant-garde Bennington College in Vermont, studying under the abstract painter Paul Feely, head of the art department. His focus on cubism was reflected in Frankenthaler's early still lifes. After graduating from Bennington in 1949, she briefly studied art history at Columbia University before turning full time to painting. A major turning point in Frankenthaler's career as an artist occurred when she met the influential New York art critic Clement Greenberg, and through him leading abstract expressionists, including Arshile Gorky, Willem and ELAINE DE KOONING, Jackson Pollock, and LEE KRASNER.

After following Greenberg's advice and studying with Hans Hofmann, the influential German-born painter and teacher, during the summer of 1950, Frankenthaler accompanied Greenberg to an exhibition of Pollock's paintings at Manhattan's Betty Parsons Gallery in November of that year. The large scale and intensity of Pollock's work had an enormous impact on the young artist; she later recalled that she felt as though she was in the center ring of Madison Square Garden. While influenced by other major abstract expressionists, Frankenthaler found Pollack's work the most inspiring, and she changed her own method of painting after watching him work in his studio. As she told critic Henry Geldzahler in *Artforum* (1965):

> I looked at and was influenced by both Pollock and de Kooning and eventually felt there were more possibilities for me out of the Pollock vocabulary. De Kooning made enclosed linear shapes and "applied" the brush. Pollock used shoulder and ropes and ignored the edges and corners. I felt I could stretch more in the Pollock framework. . . . You could become a de Kooning disciple or satellite or mirror, but you could *depart* from Pollock.

By the early 1950s, Frankenthaler was beginning to make her mark on the New York City art scene. She was the youngest exhibitor in the acclaimed *Ninth Street Show,* which showcased works by some of the younger generation—the so-called second generation—of abstract expressionist painters. In 1951 Frankenthaler had her first solo exhibition at Tibor de Nagy Gallery. However, it was a year later, after a trip to Nova Scotia, Canada, with the completion

Critically acclaimed contemporary American artist
Helen Frankenthaler
(Portrait by Timothy Greenfield-Sanders)

of the seven-by-10-foot *Mountains and Sea* (1952), that she became a major abstract expressionist. In the painting, which is still considered her most famous work, Frankenthaler used Pollock's technique of directly dripping or pouring paint on unprimed canvases, but she added a crucial innovation of her own. She diluted oil paints to the thickness of watercolors on her untreated canvas, thereby creating what became known as "stain painting." That technique enabled Frankenthaler to create the characteristic brilliant colors that became a hallmark of her work. The next year, in 1953, about two months after *Mountains and Sea* was shown for the first time to a lukewarm reception from most critics and the general public, two artists, Morris Louis and Kenneth Noland, traveled from Washington, D.C., to New York to view the painting. They saw Frankenthaler's technique as a breakthrough. Louis called her work "a bridge between Pollock and what was possible" and, along with Frankenthaler, used stain painting to found what became known as color field painting—a variant of the broader abstract expressionist school. The term evokes a large canvas seen as a field of luminous color.

By the end of the 1950s, Frankenthaler was well established. In 1959, a year after her marriage to Robert Motherwell, a leading abstract expressionist of the Pollock generation (the marriage ended in divorce in 1971), Frankenthaler's *Jacob's Ladder* (1957) won first prize at the 1959 Paris Biennale. During the late 1960s and 1970s, as her painting became increasingly abstract, she continued to win kudos from critics and the public. In 1969, a retrospective exhibition of her works opened at New York's Whitney Museum of Modern Art.

In the 1970s Frankenthaler expanded her activity to new areas including printmaking (with woodcuts and lithographs), sculpture in clay, and tapestry design. She garnered numerous awards and honors, among them the New York Mayor's Award of Honor (1986), the Connecticut Arts Award (1989), and the Distinguished Artist Award for Lifetime Achievement from New York's College Art Association (1994). Her work is in many of the world's most distinguished collections, including New York's Metropolitan Museum of Art, Museum of Modern Art, Solomon R. Guggenheim Museum, and the Whitney Museum of American Art; the Art Institute of Chicago; the Museum of Fine Arts, Boston; and the National Gallery of Art in Washington, D.C. In 1985 the Guggenheim held a retrospective of 35 years of her works on paper. That exhibition, curated by art historian Karen Wilkin—who called Frankenthaler's works on paper "vibrant, intimate, and masterful"—traveled throughout the United States.

Throughout her illustrious career, Frankenthaler has refused to let herself be bound by restrictions. In 1984 she observed that "the only rule is that there are no rules. Anything is possible. . . . It's all about risks, deliberate risks. The picture unfolds, leads, unravels as I push ahead. . . . I must be ready to work with what is insisting on emerging and use it and take it from there."

Further Reading

Carmean, E. A., Jr. *Helen Frankenthaler: A Painting Retrospective.* New York: Harry N. Abrams, 1989.

Elderfield, John. *Frankenthaler.* New York: Harry N. Abrams, 1989.

Munro, Eleanor. *Originals: American Women Artists.* New York: Da Capo Press, 2000.

Wilkin, Karen. *Frankenthaler: Works on Paper, 1949–1984.* New York: George Braziller, 1984.

— C. K.

FREILICHER, JANE NIEDERHOFFER
(1924–) *Painter*

An artist who uses abstract expressionist technique to create representational paintings, Jane Freilicher is known for her fluid and poetic landscapes, cityscapes, and still lifes. In assimilating, blending, and reinterpreting these different traditions, Freilicher has produced what art writer Linda L. Cathcart calls "work of singular unity, and great verity and modernity."

Jane Niederhoffer was born on November 19, 1924, in Brooklyn, New York, to Martin and Bertha Niederhoffer, who excelled, respectively, in linguistics and music. In a conversation with art critic Eleanor Munro, the artist recalled that she enjoyed painting and drawing from an early age and, while not convinced she had any specialized talent, noted: "I thought I might do something in art, not for fame or achievement, but out of a romantic inclination to beautiful things. A free-floating feeling that something was creative *in me.*"

After graduating from high school at 17, Jane eloped with jazz musician Jack Freilicher. The marriage was annulled, but Jane kept her ex-husband's name and through him gained entrance to a circle of artists and musicians that included painters Larry Rivers and NELL BLAINE, and which would have a major influence on her work. Having decided on art as a career, Freilicher earned a bachelor's degree in art from Brooklyn College in 1947, studied at the Hans Hofmann School of Fine Arts in New York City and Provincetown, Massachusetts, and then earned a master's degree from Columbia University's Teachers College, where she studied with renowned art historian Meyer Schapiro. She married painter Joseph Hazan in 1957; the couple have a daughter, Elizabeth, who is also a painter.

Along with numerous other outstanding painters of her generation, Freilicher was deeply influenced by Hans Hofmann, a renowned painting and composition teacher. "His magnetism," Freilicher recalled, "made you aware of how great art could be." Although himself an abstract expressionist, Hofmann did not dogmatically impose his style on his students. Thus, while Freilicher experimented with abstraction and absorbed abstract expressionist techniques such as rapid brushwork and the use of color in place of line, her commitment was to realistic rather than abstract art. It was, she once explained, a matter of where she discovered her inspiration: "I had to have something to refer to besides myself. I felt that otherwise my paintings would be thin."

For most of her career, Freilicher has painted from two locations: a studio in New York City with an expansive view of lower Manhattan and a second studio in the bucolic town of Water Mill on eastern Long Island. Many of her works, such as *Flowers and Mirror before a Landscape* (1983) or *12th Street and Beyond* (1976), are a combination landscape or cityscape with a still life foreground, as viewed from one of her studio windows. She has also painted many landscapes and a lesser number of cityscapes, such as *Bluish Horizon* (1984) and *A City Winter* (1984), without the still life foreground. Freilicher's still lifes reflect her fusion of abstract expressionism and realism. *Still Life with Calendulas* (1955) seems almost abstract, while works such as *Boned Striped Bass* (1973) are far more realistic. Art scholar Linda L. Cathcart wrote that Freilicher's still lifes "mix observation and invention, skill and feeling in order to relate both the real and the ideal. She achieves a marriage of expression and deliberation."

Freilicher had her first solo exhibition in 1952 at the Tibor de Nagy Gallery in New York City and has had more than 25 individual exhibitions since then. Her awards include an American Association of University Women Fellowship (1974), a National Endowment of the Arts Grant (1976), the Saltus Gold Medal from the National Academy of Design (1987), and the Academy of the Arts Lifetime Achievement Award (1996). Her works are in many prominent collections, including the Metropolitan Museum of Art, the Museum of Modern Art, the Whitney Museum, the Brooklyn Museum, the National Academy of Design (all in New York City), the Cleveland Museum of Art, and the Hirshhorn Museum and Sculpture Garden in Washington, D.C.

Critic and art instructor John Yau has pointed out that Freilicher "both responds to her subjects and examines the way they are looked at." Freilicher offers her own description of her painting process in the 1989 *Current Biography Yearbook:*

> When I start painting, it's with this rush of feeling—an emotional reaction to something I find beautiful in the subject, which provides the energy, the impetus to paint. Then, as the process evolves, other things enter into it—a discovery of what it is I think I'm seeing.

Jane Freilicher, who follows her own path as an American realist, insists that she always seeks "a new beginning, even if the subject matter remains much the same."

Further Reading

AskART. "Jane Freilicher." Available online. URL: http://askart.com/Bibliography.asp. Downloaded on December 24, 2000.

Doty, Robert, editor. *Jane Freilicher: Paintings.* New York: Taplinger Publishing Company, 1986.

Mathews, Margaret. "Jane Freilicher." *American Artist,* March 1983, 32–37.

Munro, Eleanor. "Women of the Second Wave: Mavericks at Midway." In *Originals: American Women Artists,* 204–205. New York: De Capo Press, 2000.

Porter, Fairfield. "Jane Freilicher Paints a Picture." *Artnews,* September 1956, 77–79.

— C. K.

FULLER, META VAUX WARRICK
(1877–1968) *Sculptor*

A forerunner of the Harlem Renaissance movement that promoted African-American art during the 1920s and 1930s, Meta Vaux Warrick Fuller was a Victorian-era artist whose Rodinesque bronze sculptures were rooted in African art, history, and culture. Her pioneering works reflected her belief in the importance of black consciousness and her reaction to the devastating effects of slavery.

A native of Philadelphia, Pennsylvania, Meta Vaux Warrick, the great-granddaughter of an Ethiopian princess brought to America as a slave, was born on January 9, 1877, and grew up in a middle-class family. Meta was encouraged by her parents to develop her artistic interests, and they provided her with drawing lessons at an early age. In 1894 she won a scholarship to the Pennsylvania School of Industrial Arts (now the Philadelphia College of Art); she was one of the few black students to attend the school. Upon graduating with honors in 1899, Warrick received the Crozer Prize for Sculpture and a postgraduate fellowship to study in Paris, France, which at the turn of the century was considered the art center of the world for sculpture.

Warrick was welcomed in Paris by other artists, although she experienced racism firsthand when she was turned away from a hotel because she was black. She studied sculpture at the Académie Colarossi and drawing at the École des Beaux-Arts. Premier sculptor Auguste Rodin admired Warrick's realistic and expressionistic work, and after looking at *Secret Sorrow (Man Eating His Heart),* he asserted that she was a "born sculptor" with a powerful sense of form. Rodin sponsored private shows of her works and encouraged her to be even more daring. Warrick also befriended beaux-arts American sculptor Augustus Saint-Gaudens and Samuel Bing, the director of the avant-garde L'Art Nouveau Gallery, where in 1902 she had her first solo exhibition. Among the 22 works displayed at the gallery were *The Wretched, Man Carrying a Dead Comrade,* and *The Thief on the Cross.* These pieces reflected her obsession with death and suffering and earned her the title "sculptor of horrors" by contemporary critics. Her works were included in the Paris Salon in 1903, the same year she returned to America and her family in Philadelphia.

Although she had been successful in Paris, where her sculptures had sold well, most American art dealers and gallery owners ignored her because—Warrick believed—she was black. Nonetheless, beginning in 1906 she exhibited her works at the Pennsylvania Academy of Fine Arts, along with MARY CASSATT and other notable artists. In 1907, Warrick's *The Press of the Negro in North America,* a 15-piece work about the creation and history of the African-American community of Jamestown in 1607, won a gold medal at Virginia's Jamestown Tercentennial Exposition.

In 1909 Warrick married Liberian physician Solomon C. Fuller, America's first black psychiatrist. The Fullers moved to Framingham, Massachusetts, a suburb of Boston, where they were one of the first black families in the middle-class white neighborhood. Fuller gave birth to and raised three sons and increasingly devoted herself to motherhood. But, using her own money and without telling her husband, she built a small art studio near their home and sculpted busts of black Americans whose values she admired, such as Frederick Douglass and Sojourner Truth.

Tragically, a fire in 1910 destroyed a Philadelphia warehouse that held most of Fuller's sculptures. However, that did not stop her from continuing to sculpt: she turned to smaller pieces and used African Americans as her models. In 1913 W. E. B. DuBois, the distinguished civil rights activist, commissioned Fuller to create a piece for the 50th anniversary of the Emancipation Proclamation festivities in New York City. Fuller described *Emancipation Proclamation* (1913) as representing her ethnicity through a male and female figure standing under a tree, "the branches of which are the fingers of Fate grasping at them to draw them back into the fateful clutches of hatred."

Ethiopia Awakening (1914) is perhaps Fuller's best-known work. The evocative bronze sculpture of a shrouded, proud female figure mixes ancient Egyptian and modern African elements and calls upon the viewer to awaken to the evils of slavery. The piece stands firmly in the African tradition of ancient Egyptian–centered art by black female sculptors including EDMONIA LEWIS and BARBARA CHASE-RIBOUD. In *Black Art and Culture in the 20th Century*, critic Richard J. Powell wrote that *Ethiopia Awakening*, which was widely exhibited, reflected a major step in the history of African-American art, because it represented one of the first examples of ethnic African consciousness.

Fuller continued to accept public commissions, the subjects of which ranged from the ruthlessness of war to *Mary Turner: A Silent Protest Against Mob Violence* (1919), a powerful sculpture based on the lynching in Georgia of Mary Turner, a black woman accused of planning to murder a white man, and the silent parade of 10,000 black workers in New York City who protested that heinous act of violence. One of Fuller's major works, the Rodinesque *Talking Skull* (1937), expressively portrays a nude African male kneeling in front of a skull that is resting on the ground. He appears to be gazing sadly at the skull, perhaps communicating to it his terrible ordeals and fears.

In 1940 Fuller completed *Refugee,* another sculpture that realistically reflected human despair, this time that of a Jewish refugee, ravaged by war, leaning on a walking stick. Fuller also explored Christian themes in her work.

In 1957, four years after her husband died, Fuller was commissioned by the National Council of Negro Women to sculpt 10 dolls representing historically important black females, one of her favorite themes. Fuller's figurative sculptures—mostly bronze and plaster—were shown at exhibitions at the Boston Public Library, the Art Institute of Chicago, the Harmon Foundation in New York City, and at Chicago's *American Negro Exposition.*

Meta Vaux Warrick Fuller died in Framingham, Massachusetts, on March 13, 1968. In 1973 a retrospective of her work was held at the Danforth Museum of Art in Framingham. In 1998, her work was featured in *Rhapsodies in Black: Art of the Harlem Renaissance,* a show at San Francisco's Legion of Honor; Fuller, one of only a few academically trained African-American artists who studied both in America and in Europe at the turn of the century, is frequently recognized as a precursor of the Harlem Renaissance. Her work is housed in collections at the Museum of Afro-American History in Boston, Yale University, and the Smithsonian Institution in Washington, D.C.

"Art must be the quintessence of meaning," Fuller said during an interview in 1966. "Creative art means you create for yourself. Inspirations can come from most anything. Tell the world how you feel . . . take the chances . . . try, try!"

Further Reading

Dannett, Sylvia G. I. "Meta Warrick Fuller." In *Profiles of Negro Womanhood,* volume 2, 46. Yonkers, N.Y.: Educational Heritage, 1966.

Farris, Phoebe. editor. *Women Artists of Color: A Bio-Critical Sourcebook of 20th Century Artists in America,* 267–273. Westport, Conn.: Greenwood Press, 1999.

Kennedy, Harriet Forte. *An Independent Woman: The Life and Art of Meta Warrick Fuller (1877–1968)*. Framingham, Mass.: Danforth Museum, 1985.

Lewis, Samella S. *African-American Art and Artists*. Berkeley, Calif: University of California Press, 1990.

Rubinstein, Charlotte Streifer. *American Women Sculptors*. Boston: G. K. Hall, 1990.

— C. K.

FULLER, SUE (Caroline Susan Fuller)
(1914–) *Sculptor, Printmaker*

A passionate devotee of modern art, Sue Fuller began her professional career as a printmaker and subsequently used some of the techniques she experimented with for that medium to develop an original form of sculpture. Fuller's marriage of modern technology with the aesthetics of modern art has earned her wide critical acclaim as a sculptor. In addition, she earned a United States government patent for one of the processes she developed to create her art.

Caroline Susan Fuller (who is known as Sue) was born on August 11, 1914, in Pittsburgh, Pennsylvania, into a cultured and well-to-do home. Thread and glass, and the beauty associated with them, were among her earliest childhood memories. Her father, a construction engineer who helped design bridges, also made model bridges out of thread and string. Fuller's mother was an expert at knitting, sewing, and crocheting, and the designs and textures of her work fascinated young Sue, as did the family home's sunporch, "with windows of beautiful prismatic leaded glass. Every day that area was iridescent." Sue frequently accompanied her parents to exhibitions at Pittsburgh's Carnegie Institute of Technology, where she was impressed by contemporary art from around the world. As she later recalled, "I was taught indirectly by the great contemporary artists of modern persuasion." All of these factors had an influence on the work that Fuller would produce as a mature artist.

While a high school student, Fuller spent a summer studying painting at the Ernest Thurn School of Art in Gloucester, Massachusetts; it was there that she encountered her first books on modern art. In 1932 Fuller enrolled in the art program at the Carnegie Institute of Technology, where she won prizes for her American scene (realistic recordings of aspects of American life) watercolors. During the summer of 1934, she returned to the Thurn School and had the opportunity to study with Hans Hofmann, who has been described as "one of the giants of modern art." Fuller proudly noted that Hofmann "repeatedly chose [her] work as examples for his class." In 1937, a year after earning her bachelor's degree, Fuller traveled to Germany and saw the "antithesis" of the Carnegie Institute's exhibitions—the Nazi show of "Degenerate Art" designed to attack German modern artists. To Fuller, the exhibition was a profound example of the importance of the constitutional guarantee of freedom of expression.

After returning from Germany, Fuller earned a master's degree in art education from Columbia University's Teachers College in New York City. By then printmaking had become her principal artistic focus. In 1943 she enrolled at the New School for Social Research, where Stanley William Hayter, a British artist who had left Paris for New York in 1940, had set up the Atelier 17 print workshop. Among the outstanding modern artists (many of whom were European refugees) who made prints at Atelier 17 during the 1940s were Joan Miró, Roberto Matta, and Jacques Lipshitz. During the two exciting years Fuller spent at the New School, she "was being taught directly by modern artists."

In 1944 Fuller attended an eight-session workshop run by Josef Albers at the Camera Club in New York. She was introduced by Albers, a German-born abstract painter and rectilinear designer, to the Bauhaus techniques of weaving and collage. She described those modernist techniques as the "keystone resolving the direction of my work." In 1945 Fuller produced her best-known print, a semiabstract soft-ground etching entitled *The Hen*. Another inspiration was a 1946 exhibition at New York's Museum of Modern Art that featured the purely geometric abstract constructivist sculptors Naum Gabo and Antoine Pevsner, brothers whose directive was "to construct" art. The exhibition had an important influence on Fuller's career as she moved from printmaking to sculpture, increasingly producing what she called "string compositions" using wood, thread, and dyes.

One of Fuller's new three-dimensional works, *String Composition No. 11* (1950), was included in the Museum of Modern Art's *Abstract Art in America* exhibition in 1951. In 1955, New York's Whitney Museum of American Art and the Metropolitan Museum of Art both purchased string compositions for their collections. However, there was a problem: the materials Fuller used to create her works were delicate and easily deteriorated. It took her a year to discover materials and techniques to make her sculptures more durable. She was helped by the development of plastics, and by the 1960s she was embedding threads and microfilaments in transparent plastic. Her constructivist sculpture was described by art critic John Gruen of the *New York Herald Tribune* as "a kind of 21st-century weaving." A reviewer in the *Boston Globe* wrote that Fuller's ability to encase her "threaded wonders" in Plexiglas was like "capturing a snowflake and preserving it for all time." Meanwhile, Fuller continued to perfect the encasement process, and in 1967 she received a patent on it.

Fuller has had numerous solo exhibitions, ranging from the Elaine Benson Gallery in New York to the Corcoran Gallery of Art in Washington, D.C. Among the many awards she has received are a Tiffany Foundation Fellowship (1947), a grant from the National Institute of Arts and Letters (1950), the Carnegie Mellon University Alumni Merit Award (1974), and the Women's Caucus Art Award (1986). Her works are in several permanent collections, including those of the Museum of Modern Art, the Whitney Museum of American Art, the Solomon R. Guggenheim Museum (all in New York City), and the Tate Gallery in London.

Although she was born at the beginning of the 20th century and began her career in its third decade, Sue Fuller's work often seems to have pointed forward to the 21st century. As she commented in 1965, after an exhibt of her string compositions at a gallery in Boston:

> The path of a trajectory to the moon, or in orbit around Mars is a line drawing. Translucency, balance, and precision are the aesthetics associated with such graphics. My work in terms of linear geometric progression is visual poetry of infinity in the space age.

Further Reading

Actow, David. *A Spectrum of Innovation: Color in American Printmaking.* New York: Norton, 1990.

Browne, Rosalind. "Sue Fuller." *Art International* 16 (January 1972): 37–40.

Fuller, Sue, and Maurice Amar. *String Composition* (VHS) 1974.

Rubinstein, Charlotte Streifer. *American Women Sculptors.* Boston: G. K. Hall, 1990.

— C. K.

G

GARZA, CARMEN LOMAS

See LOMAS GARZA, CARMEN

GOLDIN, NAN (Nancy Goldin)
(1953–) *Photographer*

Contemporary photographer Nan Goldin's magnum opus, the 800-image multimedia slide presentation *The Ballad of Sexual Dependency* (1972–92), is typical of her controversial but compelling oeuvre: the photographic documentary graphically captures, over many years, the gritty world of sex and drugs in New York City's East Village, and the subjects are mostly Goldin and her friends.

Born on September 12, 1953, in Washington, D.C., Nancy (Nan) Goldin dropped out of high school when she was 14 and opted for what she called a "free hippie school." Her real education, she later asserted, came from going to movies and museums. She also attended Tufts University in Medford, Massachusetts (1977), and the School of the Museum of Fine Arts, Boston (1977–78). She began taking photographs, mostly portraits, when she was 18, having received a camera as a gift.

Goldin repudiated the carefully crafted, black-and-white nature prints that were popular in fine art photography in the 1970s. Instead, she took pictures—often tawdry ones—of herself, her family, and her friends, thereby transforming documentary photography from, as Harvard University reporter Scott Rothkopf described it, "a detached stare to diaristic narrative, warmly embracing subjects once condemned to clinical study or voyeuristic objectification." Goldin returned—sometimes over a 25-year period—to the same subjects, taking their pictures mostly with flash and in bedrooms. Goldin had been profoundly affected by the suicide of her sister in 1965 and was determined to keep a pictorial record of people she loved. In the "anthropological" tradition of documentary photographers such as DIANE ARBUS, Goldin used the traditional family photo album approach in order to, as she describes it, "trace histories of lives and offer visual drawings which others can read."

Goldin's first solo exhibition of what she called "social portraits" took place in 1973 at Project Inc., in Cambridge, Massachusetts. By the mid-1970s, *The Ballad of Sexual Dependency* (the title was taken from a Kurt Weill song), with its emphasis on sexuality and gender relationships, in all forms, and the use and abuse of power, was being discussed seriously by art critics: Some considered her work provocative and groundbreaking, while others denounced it as flawed and artless. *Village Voice* critic J. Hoberman labeled *Ballad* a "diary" and a "soap opera." The enormous project, in the form of 35mm color slides and accompanied by a musical soundtrack, intimately chronicled "young, punkish people engaged with one another in scenes of desire and frustration," wrote Max Kozloff in *Art in America* in 1987.

By the 1980s, Goldin, who was living in New York City, had switched from black-and-white snapshots to color and had combined her photographs with music. Increasingly her works were being shown at mainstream art institutions such as New York's Museum of Modern Art and the Whitney Museum of American Art, and at galleries around the country and in Europe. Meanwhile, Goldin was attempting to cope with a disastrous relationship. In 1984 she was badly beaten by a former boyfriend; she documented the horrific experience in a self-portrait entitled *Nan one month after being battered.*

Goldin began to spend more time in Europe, especially in Berlin, where her work was critically and publicly accepted. But her evocative photographs were also being noticed in America. In 1985 *The Ballad of Sexual Dependency* was included in the highly competitive biennial show at the Whitney Museum. (Twenty-two color prints from other series were included at the 1993 Whitney Biennial.) *Ballad* also traveled to museums in Amsterdam and Madrid, and excerpts from the multimedia piece were published in book form in 1986, with reprints in 1993 and 2000. In 1988 Goldin admitted that she was drug addicted and entered a rehabilitation clinic in the Boston area. Once again she documented, in her typical brutally honest fashion, the laborious process of recovering from drug abuse.

Among other kudos, Goldin received the Mother Jones Documentary Photography Award in 1990 and the Louis Comfort Tiffany Foundation Award in 1991. Her numerous individual exhibitions have ranged from the Galerie du Jeu de Paume in Paris and the Christminister Gallery in New York to the Galerie Barbara Weiss in Berlin.

A retrospective of Nan Goldin's photography was held at the Whitney Museum in New York in 1996. (Portrait by Timothy Greenfield-Sanders)

All by Myself, a major series of self-portraits taken while Goldin was attempting to recover from drug abuse, was completed in 1994. Goldin also documented communities of drag queens, transsexuals, and transvestites in America, Europe, and Asia, and she compassionately chronicled the lives of two friends dying from AIDS. In 1995 Goldin produced a film called *I'll Be Your Mirror* for the British Broadcasting Company; it explored issues that are central to her growing body of work, including sexual identity, the power of addiction, and the effects of AIDS on individuals and society. Goldin described the film as a "mediation on the medium of photography and nature of memory, as well as a document of one artist's work."

A 25-year retrospective of Nan Goldin's work, also titled *I'll Be Your Mirror,* was held at New

York's Whitney Museum in 1996. "My photography has served as a way to feel grounded in chaos, to pay homage to the beauty of my friends, and to keep the memory of the people I loved," Goldin wrote in that same year. Also in 1996, a solo multimedia presentation was mounted by the Tate Gallery in London. In the mid-1990s, Goldin, by then well-known for the snapshot quality of her work, turned to fashion shoots and advertising campaigns that appeared in the *New York Times Magazine* and other periodicals. In 1999 the largely self-educated artist taught photography at Harvard University. But she wanted her work to be "accessible to the people." In 1999 Goldin commented that her art is more about the human condition than about documenting the lives of people who live on the edge of society in cities such as New York and Tokyo.

In November 2001 a retrospective took place at the Centre Pompidou in Paris. It included Goldin's new slide show documentary, *Heart Beat,* of four couples having sex. "It's a prayer for lovers based on a heartbeat," said Goldin.

Further Reading

Armstrong, David, and Walter Keller, editors. *The Other Side.* Introduction by Nan Goldin. New York and Zurich: Scalo, 2000.

Goldin, Nan. *The Ballad of Sexual Dependency.* New York: Aperture, 1996.

Kozloff, Max. "The Family of Nan." *Art in America* 75:11 (November 1987): 38–43.

Rothkopf, Scott. "Interview with Nan Goldin," Harvard Advocate. Available online. URL: http:/hcs.harvard.edu/~advocate/spring99/interview.html. Downloaded on June 4, 2001.

— C. K.

GOODRIDGE, SARAH
(1788–1853)   *Painter*

In spite of having received minimal art instruction, Sarah Goodridge still managed to become one of the most distinguished and prolific 19th-century American miniaturist painters. Her subjects, produced on ivory, included many notables of her day, from the legendary senator Daniel Webster to the influential portrait painter Gilbert Stuart.

Sarah Goodridge was born in Templeton, Massachusetts, on February 5, 1788, the sixth of nine children of farmer and mechanic Ebenezer and his wife Beulah (Childs) Goodridge. Sarah was raised on a farm and attended local district schools, where she drew portraits of her friends. Since paper was scarce and expensive, her early pictures generally were done with a pin on birch bark or a stick on a sanded floor. The only examples from which she could learn technique and artistry were poorly executed, low-quality woodcuts.

When she was 17, Goodridge moved in with her eldest brother, William, first living in Milton, Massachusetts, and then in Boston, where William relocated for a job in his brother-in-law's organ-building business. During those years Goodridge managed to take a few drawing lessons, but she was mainly self-taught; the bulk of her knowledge about painting on ivory came from a booklet she had read on miniature portrait painting. After teaching school for two summers, Goodridge spent a summer selling portraits. Her fees were five cents for a life-size crayon drawing and $1.50 for a watercolor sketch. In 1812 she returned to Boston to keep house for another brother, while continuing in her spare time to paint in oils. Goodridge also managed to study painting on ivory with a miniaturist from Hartford, Connecticut, and in 1820, having moved in permanently with her sister and brother-in-law, Beulah and Thomas Appleton, she opened her own studio in Boston.

Goodridge's break as an artist came when she was introduced to the preeminent American portrait painter Gilbert Stuart. He took an interest in her work and visited her studio. He also advised her to attend a local drawing school, invited her to bring her pictures to him to critique, and over the next several years offered her instruction that dramatically improved her skills. In 1825, apparently with the words "Goode, I intend to let you paint me," Stuart requested that Goodridge paint a miniature of him. The result was a perceptive and realistic portrait that many considered unflattering, but which Stuart—whose assessment of an earlier portrait done by a New York artist was that it made him look "like a fool"—considered the finest of any portrait of himself. He had it preserved in a bracelet along with locks of his own and his wife's hair. Half a century later, Stuart's daughter Jane wrote in *Scribner's Monthly* magazine that Goodridge's portrait of her father was "the most lifelike of anything ever painted of him in this country, although the expression is a little exaggerated." Goodridge subsequently made two copies of her most famous miniature: one is in New York's Metropolitan Museum of Art and the other is one of 20 portraits by Goodridge owned by Boston's Museum of Fine Arts. In addition, Asher Brown Durand, the noted engraver and Hudson River school landscape painter, made an engraving of the miniature for the National Portrait Gallery in Washington, D.C.

After painting Stuart, Goodridge continued to work as an artist for a quarter of a century. Her reputation brought her commissions to paint many well-known clients, including General Henry Lee and U.S. senator Daniel Webster; she painted almost a dozen portraits—watercolors on ivory— of the flamboyant senator and orator. Between 1827 and 1835, five exhibitions of her miniatures were featured at the gallery of the Boston Athenaeum. Eight of her portraits are in the National Museum of American Art in Washington, D.C., while others are represented in the Yale Art Gallery, the New-York Historical Society, and many private collections. According to art history professor Eleanor Tufts, Goodridge's miniature bust portraits, most of which were rectangular in format, display a "photographic technique for detail."

Goodridge worked steadily, and her income enabled her to support her mother, care for an ill brother, raise an orphaned niece, and in 1851, a year after her failing eyesight forced her to retire, realize a lifelong wish: to buy her own cottage in Reading, Massachusetts. Sarah Goodridge, who in her prime—between 1820 and 1850—painted up to three miniatures a week, died of "paralysis" while on a Christmas visit to Boston on December 28, 1853.

Further Reading

Commine, Anne, editor. "Sarah Goodridge." In *Women in World History: A Biographical Encyclopedia,*. Volume 6, 379. Detroit, Mich.: Yorkin Publications, 2000.

Dods, Agnes M. "Sarah Goodridge," *Antiques,* May 1947.

Morgan, John Hill. *Gilbert Stuart and His Pupils.* New York: Da Capo Press, 1969.

Petteys, Chris. *An International Dictionary of Women Artists Before 1900.* Boston, Mass. G. K. Hall, 1985.

Wehle, Harry B., and Theodore Bolton. *American Miniatures.* Garden City, N.Y.: Doubleday, Page, and Company, 1927.

— C. K.

GOODY, JOAN EDELMAN
(1935–)   *Architect*

A native New Yorker, Joan Goody has spent most of her career as an architect working in New England. She is known for designs that provide spaces for people to congregate as well as her commitment to having new construction blend with and add to an existing urban landscape, rather than obliterate it.

Born Joan Edelman in New York City on December 1, 1935, she was encouraged by her parents "to feel I could do whatever I wanted to do." While a preadolescent student at the Ethical Culture School, Joan was helped by her father, an industrial engineer, to build a drafting table and was introduced to the use of a T square. "There was no suggestion," she told Barbaralee Diamonstein in a 1985 interview in *American Architecture Now II,* "that I should be playing with dollhouses instead of designing houses."

Notwithstanding her interest in design and drawing, Edelman majored in history as an undergraduate at Cornell University, graduating in 1956. However, during her junior year of study abroad at the University of Paris, she took a trip to Spain and visited the Alhambra, the famous citadel in Granada built by Spain's Moorish kings between 1248 and 1354, and she was deeply impressed by its design and use of space. The Alhambra's plan, she said, "recalled the character of the space, which confirmed the feeling that I wanted to work with three-dimensional design." When she returned to

Architect Joan Goody considers the urban landscape in her prizewinning designs.
(Courtesy Joan E. Goody, FAIA Principal, Goody, Clancy Associates, Boston, Mass.)

Cornell for her senior year, Edelman challenged herself by registering in the architects' first-year design course. It turned out to be one of the most satisfying courses in her academic career and set her on the path to becoming an architect.

Edelman entered Harvard University's Graduate School of Design, where she earned a master's degree in architecture in 1960, the same year she married architect Marvin E. Goody. In 1956 he had cofounded an architectural firm, and Joan Goody joined the firm as an employee in the six-person office. Working alongside her husband proved to be beneficial to the young architect:

> I developed strengths of my own, and Marvin and John [John Clancy, who had recently become a partner in the firm] were respectful of those things I did well. I found that Marvin and I complemented each other more than we competed with

each other. Quite early on he felt he could turn to me for advice on certain issues, and I knew that there were things about which I would go to him for his opinion. Right through our joint careers, that seemed to be of particular value. That mutual system was beneficial to both of us, an extra boost that most architects don't have.

Goody's early work often involved the renovation of older buildings, which made her realize that she was "adding to buildings that had a past life and adjusting them to current needs." This in turn spurred an interest in historic preservation and ultimately more than a decade of service, beginning in 1976, on the Boston Landmarks Commission. Because of the enormous and growing scale of modern construction, one of Goody's major concerns was and remains that society—as she described it in *Contemporary Architects* (1994)—is "in danger of overwhelming, if not obliterating our past." Believing in the importance of "visible history," Goody is convinced that architects and city planners should build projects that "enhance those parts of an environment that have a distinctive quality, make an effort to reuse them, and build the new in a scale, and with materials and forms that are sensitive to the past."

One of Goody's favorite urban environments is the Beacon Hill neighborhood of Boston, where she lives. It boasts narrow, neighbor-friendly streets, alleys ending in dead-end mews that create shared courts and gardens, and other quaint features that both bring people together and encourage them to enhance the general environment through individual modifications, such as adding window boxes or planting flowers around a tree. Goody calls her vision the "village in the city," by which she means "the cohesive spirit of that small town in a large city."

Goody's concern for scale melds perfectly with her commitment to projects that bring together the residents or workers to help establish a sense of community. One of the best-known buildings designed by her Boston firm is the eight-story Massachusetts Department of Transportation Building in Boston, completed in 1983. Its concave brick exterior matches those of neighboring buildings, retail space on the ground floor was included to increase street traffic and revitalize the neighborhood, and an atrium was designed to allow community meetings and cultural events. Goody also included energy-saving features such as solar panels that provide the building with more than 80 percent of its hot water needs. Other notable works by Goody include Summer Street Housing for the Elderly in Hyde Park, Massachusetts, and the Biology Building of the Massachusetts Institute of Technology in Cambridge.

Goody has been the recipient of many honors, including awards from the Boston Society of Architects, the American Institute of Architects, the American Planning Association, and the Urban Land Institute. She has taught at the Harvard Graduate School of Design and since 1961 has been a principal in the firm of Goody, Clancy, and Associates. (Marvin Goody died in 1980; Joan Goody remarried, to Peter Davison, in 1984.) "Our task," wrote Goody in 1994, "is to [create] innovative designs that . . . reflect our era, but also enrich the existing cityscape."

Further Reading

Diamonstein, Barbaralee. *American Architecture Now II.* New York: Rizzoli, 1985.

Emanuel, Muriel, editor. *Contemporary Architects.* Farmington Hills, Mich.: St. James Press, 1994.

Goody, Joan. *New Architecture in Boston.* Cambridge, Mass.: Harvard University Press, 1965.

Torre, Susana, editor. *Women in American Architecture: A Historic and Contemporary Perspective.* New York: Whitney Library of Design, 1977.

— C. K.

GRAVES, NANCY STEVENSON
(1940–1995)   *Sculptor, Painter*

Originally trained as a painter, Nancy Graves is best known for the bronze sculptures she produced during the last two decades of her life. Whatever the medium, Graves's diverse work frequently combined art and natural science, while being at once abstract and representational. She is generally considered a constructivist sculptor.

Nancy Stevenson Graves was born in Pittsfield, Massachusetts, on December 23, 1940, the daughter of Walter L. Graves, an assistant to the director of the Berkshire Museum of Art and Natural History as well as an amateur painter and wood-carver, and Mary B. Graves, a secretary and volunteer worker whose artistic inclinations were reflected in her flower arrangements. Graves later recalled that she had decided to become an artist by the age of 12. Young Nancy spent a lot of time exploring the Berkshire Museum's art and natural history exhibits, which in turn led her "to think of art and natural history as one, in a way that never would have happened in a bigger town. When I was growing up those stuffed animals were Michelangelo and Bernini rolled into one."

Having received her primary and secondary education in private schools, Graves earned a bachelor of arts degree in English literature from Vassar College in 1961. She then won a scholarship to the Yale Summer School and subsequently enrolled in Yale's highly regarded School of Art and Architecture, where she was influenced by the tenets of abstract expressionism and pop art. She earned a combined bachelor's and master's of fine arts degree in 1964. Among her fellow students at Yale was sculptor Richard Serra, whom Graves married in 1965; the marriage ended in divorce five years later.

Graves spent 1965 in Paris on a Fulbright-Hayes Fellowship. The next year she and Serra lived in Florence, Italy, where while visiting the natural history museum, Graves encountered and was inspired by the remarkable life-size wax casts of human beings and animals created by the 18th-century anatomist Clemente Susini. Notwithstanding their ultrarealistic qualities, the casts also had artistic and surreal characteristics, suggesting to Graves how she could combine her interests in both natural history and art. Graves chose sculpture as the medium for achieving this goal; initially her subject matter was the two-humped camel, because, as she told art critic Thomas Padon, "the

As a sculptor, Nancy Graves combined art
and natural science.
(Portrait by Timothy Greenfield-Sanders)

camel is relatively *unfamiliar* in Western culture, so the camel gave me the freedom to explore an image without reference to art history."

Graves began creating camel sculptures in Italy and continued constructing them after moving to New York City in 1966. Two individual shows, the first in 1968 at Manhattan's Graham Gallery and the second at the Whitney Museum of American Art, featured three of her life-sized camel sculptures. While critical reviews of the exhibitions were mixed, Graves's massive, realistic-looking sculptures did get her noticed as an important new, albeit representational, artist at a time when minimalism was the dominant mode in sculpture. Graves, however, did not see her works as purely realistic. As she put it, "The degree of surface incident articulated in my camels has a different dimension from the camels in the real world."

Between 1969 and 1971 Graves reinforced that point by producing paleontological sculptures of animal bones, made of materials such as steel, wax, marble dust, and latex, which she grouped into various patterns (*Fossils,* 1970). She also produced abstract works that suggested the rituals of ancient or disappearing primitive cultures (*Totem,* 1970). She made three short films about her camel sculptures in 1970 and 1971 but then abandoned sculpture as a medium, devoting the next four years to abstract painting. Her works during this period, which met with mixed reviews, included paintings of animals executed with a pointillist technique and others based on maps of the ocean floor and satellite photographs of lunar topography.

After 1976 Graves returned to sculpture. She received a commission from the Ludwig Museum of Modern Art in Cologne, West Germany, for a bronze version of one of her earlier camel bone pieces (*Ceridwen, out of Fossils,* 1969–77). Graves continued to work in bronze, at first using the conventional lost-wax technique but then switching to what is called direct casting, a process in which the form to be cast is encased in a ceramic mold that burns away during firing. Working in bronze placed Graves within a broad trend among sculptors of her generation, but she became the most committed practitioner of direct casting, and between 1980 and 1995 she produced almost 200 bronze sculptures using that technique. Graves completed these works by welding cast objects together and then coloring them with chemical patinas and polyurethane paints. Among the best-known of these works is *Zaga* (1983), which reflects the influence of cubist Pablo Picasso and, even more so, the renowned 20th-century American sculptor David Smith. In 1986 she collaborated with choreographer Trisha Brown on the set and costumes for a dance entitled *Lateral Pass,* which earned Graves a New York Dance and Performance Bessie Award.

Graves received many honors, including a National Endowment for the Arts Grant (1972), the Yale Arts Award for Distinguished Achievement (1985), Vassar College's Distinguished Visitor Award (1986), the Award of American Art from the

Pennsylvania Academy of Fine Arts (1987), and honorary doctor of fine arts degrees from the University of Maryland and Yale University (1992). Among the prominent collections where her works can be found are the Whitney Museum of American Art, the Museum of Modern Art, the Metropolitan Museum of Art (all in New York City), and the National Gallery of Canada in Ottawa.

Nancy Graves died of cancer in New York City on October 24, 1995. She was 55 years old. About her diverse, complex work, art critic Robert Hughes wrote: "[It is] wonderfully inclusive; formally rigorous, it spreads a wider fan of poetic association than does any sculptor's of her generation."

Further Reading

Carmean, E. A., Jr. "Nancy (Stevenson) Graves." In *Dictionary of Women Artists,* edited by Nelia Gaze, 606–608. Chicago, Ill.: Fitzroy Dearborn Publications, 1997.

_____, et al. *The Sculpture of Nancy Graves: A Catalogue Raisonné.* New York: Hudson Hills Press, 1987.

Nadelman, Cynthia. "Nancy Graves: The Missing Link." *ARTnews,* September 1996, p. 82.

Pardon, Thomas. *Nancy Graves: Excavations in Print.* New York: Harry N. Abrams, 1996.

GREENWOOD, MARION
(1909–1970)   *Muralist, Painter, Printmaker*

During a career that spanned 40 years, Marion Greenwood depicted the lives and struggles of the oppressed and underprivileged in addition to promoting social reform. From the massive murals she was commissioned to paint, first in Mexico and subsequently for various New Deal agencies in the United States, to the small easel paintings and prints she produced independently after 1940, Greenwood's commitment to social justice was the motivating force behind her life and her work.

Marion Greenwood was born in Brooklyn, New York, on April 6, 1909. Considered a child prodigy, she left high school at 15 after winning a scholarship to study at New York's Art Students League, which at that time was one of the most important and progressive art schools in America. One of her teachers at the league, and a major

influence on Greenwood, was John Sloan, a socialist whose paintings of city scenes reflected his belief that daily life should inspire works of art. Greenwood also spent time at the Yaddo artists' colony in Saratoga Springs, New York, which provided funding for writers, artists, and composers, enabling them to focus on their creative work. She painted portraits of a number of luminaries in residence, among them the composer Aaron Copland, and she took advantage of Yaddo's stimulating atmosphere to broaden her intellectual horizons. In addition, Greenwood became an outspoken advocate of artistic freedom.

After several years at the Art Students League, Greenwood was able to study in Paris at the Académie Colarossi—thanks to the proceeds from a portrait she had painted of a wealthy financier. By 1930 she was back in New York earning money as a portraitist and by selling sketches to the *New York Times.* From New York, Greenwood traveled to the Southwest to study and to paint pictures of the local Native Americans. From there, in 1932, she went to Mexico, where she began to paint murals depicting Mexican life. Diego Rivera, head of the Mexican government's mural program, noticed her work and hired her and her elder sister Grace to work on a massive mural project in the center of Mexico City. Greenwood's section of that mural, a militant depiction of the exploitation of rural agricultural workers, was widely admired throughout Mexico, and she became something of a local icon. The reaction to her work led the great Mexican muralist David Alfaro Siqueiros—who along with Rivera and José Clemente Orozco were known as the *Tres Grandes* (the Three Great Ones) of Mexican art in the 1930s—to exclaim that Greenwood "could have been the queen of Mexico."

The Mexico City mural also brought Greenwood to the attention of American architect Oscar Stonorov. Greenwood and her sister were hired by the Treasury Relief Art Project to execute wall paintings (since painted over) for a housing project being built in Camden, New Jersey. Other New Deal commissions followed, among them a mural for a post office in Crossville, Tennessee, that

Social reformer Marion Greenwood with
one of her paintings, 1942
(AP/Wide World Photos)

endorsed the Tennessee Valley Authority, and *Blueprint for Living* (1940), frescos (since painted over) for a housing project in Brooklyn, New York.

During World War II, Greenwood was one of two females (the other was Anne Poor) appointed by the government to be war artist-correspondents. Poor and Greenwood executed a series of paintings that depicted the rehabilitation of wounded soldiers. After the war, Greenwood largely abandoned murals for easel painting, but her themes remained the same. As she explained in a *New York World Telegram* article in November 1944, her interest was not in "fussing with cute and fancy nudes and pretty-pretty things," but rather in depicting "the life of America, whether it be industry, farming or just plain people." Greenwood did paint two murals after the war: the first, honoring Tennessee music, was executed in 1954 while Greenwood served as a

visiting professor of fine arts at the University of Tennessee in Knoxville; the second, *Tribute to Women* (1965), created at Syracuse University, was dedicated to women throughout the world.

Greenwood's work earned her many honors and awards, including second prize at the Carnegie Institute exhibition of 1944 for the painting *Mississippi Girl* (1943); the National Association of Women Artists Grumbacker Prize (1959); and election to the National Academy of Design (1959). She spent the last decades of her life primarily in New York City and at an art colony in Woodstock, New York. Marion Greenwood, an American whose works were legendary in Mexico, died in 1970 from injuries suffered in an automobile accident.

Further Reading

Ask ART. "Artist Summary: Greenwood, Marion." Available online. URL: http://askart.com/Biography.asp. Downloaded on December 31, 2001.

Henkes, Robert. *American Women Painters of the 1930s and 1940s: The Lives and Work of Ten Artists.* Jefferson, N.C.: McFarland, 1991.

Marling, Karal Ann. *7 American Women: The Depression Decade.* Poughkeepsie, N.Y.: Vassar College Art Gallery, 1976.

Salpeter, Henry. "Marion Greenwood: An American Artist of Originality and Power." *American Artist,* January 1948, 14–19.

— C. K.

GRIFFIN, MARION LUCY MAHONY
(1871–1961) *Architect*

A pioneering female architect, Marion Mahony Griffin played a significant role in architecture as an indispensable assistant to Frank Lloyd Wright, one of the giants in the field. Her later work with her husband, architect Walter Burley Griffin, resulted in projects on three continents that were based on an environmentally sensitive approach to architecture now considered well ahead of its time.

Marion Lucy Mahony was born on February 14, 1871, in Chicago, Illinois, the second of five children. After her father—a poet, journalist, and educator—died in 1882, her mother supported the family as a school principal. Marion attended public schools and, with financial assistance from a Chicago civic leader, enrolled at the Massachusetts Institute of Technology (MIT), receiving her degree in architecture in 1894, only the second woman to do so in the distinguished engineering school's history. Returning to Chicago, Griffin became the first woman licensed to practice architecture in Illinois. She worked briefly for an older cousin and architect in Chicago, who also had attended MIT.

In 1895 Mahony began her 14-year tenure with Frank Lloyd Wright at his famous Oak Park, Illinois, studio. Mahony is best known for the work she did while a member of Wright's staff when he was the leading practitioner of the prairie school of architecture. This style originated among architects in the Midwest and stressed both the adaptation of design to function and a close relationship between building and landscape. Mahony's special talent was in delineation, or rendering, which is the creation of architectural drawings, known as "presentation drawings," that indicate what a project will look like when it is completed. Delineation, therefore, represents a point where architecture and art meet.

Aside from being what a fellow member of Wright's studio called "the most talented member of Frank Lloyd Wright's staff," Mahony also was, according to critic Reyner Banham, in a 1973 *Architectural Review* article, "the greatest architectural delineator of her generation." Wright and Mahony were two of the prime contributors (out of a group of five) to the Wasmuth Drawings, a portfolio of design plans published in Berlin in 1910 that played a crucial role in spreading Wright's reputation from America to Europe. In addition, Mahony was responsible for designing in impeccable detail the interior furnishings, leaded glass, mosaics, and other features that were part of Wright's celebrated houses.

In 1909, when Wright suddenly abandoned his practice and family and moved to Europe, Mahony refused his offer to take over his firm. She did, however, agree to stay on as the designer with the new head of the firm, Hermann Von Holst, who greatly admired Mahony's work. During the next two years, she was responsible for designing

several houses for which Wright had received commissions before he left for Europe. Another architect who worked with Von Holst during that period was Walter Burley Griffin. When Marion Mahony, at the age of 40, married Griffin in 1911, she went to work in his office, and the couple soon became a distinguished architectural team.

The Griffin partnership achieved its most memorable triumph almost immediately, when in 1912 Walter Griffin won the competition to design Canberra, a new capital city planned for Australia. A key factor in winning that commission was Marion Griffin's remarkable perspective renderings of her husband's concepts. They were on a gigantic scale, eight feet wide and 30 feet long, and unfolded like Japanese screens. (Frank Lloyd Wright was an expert on Japanese prints and greatly influenced Marion Griffin's work.) Particularly noteworthy was a drawing depicting the view from the summit of Mt. Ainslie, near Canberra, which is all the more remarkable since neither Walter nor Marion Griffin had been to Australia. In the end, the Canberra project would prove to be a disappointment, as most of the Griffin designs were never executed. However, the couple did spend 20 years in Australia, where they created designs for several towns, suburban estates, civic and commercial buildings, low-cost housing, and landscapes—270 projects in all.

In 1935 the Griffins moved to India, where within two years they were responsible for designing more than 40 projects. When Walter Griffin died in 1937, Marion returned to the United States. During her marriage, she had taken no credit for the work she had executed with her husband. That has been rectified in recent years, and she has received the recognition due to her. Architectural historian Mark Lyons Pleisch described the Griffin partnership as a "complete merging of personalities and ideals, an artistic union so perfect that to distinguish or separate their later careers becomes virtually impossible."

After returning to America at age 66, Griffin set up her own practice and focused on city planning, working well into her 80s. She died in Chicago on

August 10, 1961, and was buried in Graceland Cemetery next to America's greatest architects. In 1998 a book was published in Australia entitled *The Griffins in Australia and India*. In the words of one reviewer, it finally provided the definitive study of "the intertwined lives of Walter and Marion Griffin . . . two of the great figures in architecture and landscape design in the twentieth century,"

Further Reading

Berkon, Susan Fondiler. "Marion Mahony Griffin." In *Women in American Architecture: A Historic and Contemporary Perspective,* edited by Susana Torre, 75–78. New York: Whitney Library of Design, 1977.

Brooks, H. Allen. *Frank Lloyd Wright and the Prairie School.* New York: George Braziller, 1984.

"Frank Lloyd Wright and the Wasmuth Drawings." *Art Bulletin* 48 (June 1966): 193–202.

Turnbull, Jeff, and Peter Y. Navaretti. *The Griffins in Australia and India: The Complete Works and Projects of Walter Burley Griffin and Marion Mahony Griffin.* Melbourne, Australia: Melbourne University Press, 1998.

— C. K.

GROSSMAN, NANCY
(1940–)   *Sculptor, Painter, Illustrator*

After a decade-long career of figurative painting and drawing as well as semiabstract collages, Grossman earned recognition and notoriety with her two- and three-dimensional leather-bound sculptures of sexually charged figures and heads, in addition to her anguished, angry drawings of men.

Born in New York City on April 28, 1940, Nancy Grossman was the eldest of five siblings and often served as their caretaker, because both her parents worked. A rebellious, unhappy child, she wanted to be her own person, "rather than a property, my father's or my mother's." Nancy grew up on a dairy farm in rural upstate New York, in an extended family that included 16 children and combined her mother's Italian and her father's Jewish heritage. The atmosphere was often volatile: "I was smacked around a lot," she recalled in a 1975 interview.

As soon as she could get away, Grossman left for New York City. She decided to become an artist, because as a young child she had loved drawing— "on walls, on books, on scrap paper." She enrolled at New York's Pratt Institute in 1958, where she was influenced by Richard Linder, who was painting exaggerated and constricted body parts that appeared isolated through the use of abstract shapes of color. In order to pay for tuition at Pratt (she defied her father's orders and refused to return home), she got a job and won a scholarship. Grossman graduated from Pratt in 1962 with a bachelor of fine arts degree, and two year later, she had a solo exhibition of her early drawings and lithographs at New York's Oscar Krasner Gallery. Her hard-edged works on paper, points out art historian Charlotte Streifer Rubinstein, already revealed a "disturbing, visceral quality" while showing the "failure of communication between men and women."

In 1966 Grossman received a Guggenheim Foundation Fellowship. She began to draw intestine-like coils, cogs, and wheels, a series that seemingly recorded the inner workings of anthropomorphized machines. She also constructed sexually charged collages made from found objects such as tubing, rusty cans, laces, metal, and leather. Grossman called some of these abstract expressionistic works, such as *The Bride* (1966), "women landscapes," in which sexual imagery, both vaginal and phallic, is prominent. According to Rubinstein, these collages often had a "ruptured, violated quality, like torn-open viscera." Grossman has professed that "anyone who does anything great in art and culture is out of control."

After earning a living as a children's book illustrator, Grossman returned to her studio and changed her artistic direction. Beginning in the late 1960s, she moved from abstract collages to three-dimensional sculptures comprised of leather-bound, zipped-up, neuter figures, with either decapitated or covered heads. In 1968 Grossman exhibited her work at New York's Whitney Museum of American Art and was praised by most mainstream art critics. Increasingly, her neuter figures were becoming males in bondage. The heads became closed up, covered by leather as if by a second layer of skin, and carved in wood. According to Grossman, these rageful, surreal, sadomasochistic forms that she had stitched up in plaster and leather, and which are considered the artist's signature image, came out of her subconscious and frightened her.

In 1974 Grossman won an American Academy and Institute of Arts and Letters Award for her provocative head sculptures and drawings. Grossman was pleased at the critical acclaim she was receiving but felt "self-conscious" because her work was also highly controversial, especially her drawings of aggressive, tied-up males with guns in place of penises. In 1985 Grossman taught sculpture at the Museum School of Fine Arts, Boston, and was the recipient of a National Endowment for the Arts sculpture award. That same year she completed a relatively serene, ritualistic sculpture entitled *Eldridge Ram* (1985), which was made from carved wood, ram's horns, leather, and nickel hardware. Amazingly, Grossman had found authentic ram's horns in a shop on Eldridge Street near her studio in New York City. She also worked on iconoclastic bronze sculptures, some of which were on view in 1991 as part of three retrospective exhibitions of her work: at the Exit Gallery and the Sculpture Center in New York City, and at Hillwood Art Gallery at Long Island University.

While Grossman is a feminist who believes that "to be a woman and not to be able to experience your power, your aggression, or your passivity, is not to be alive," she is not, writes Cindy Nemser in *Art Talk,* "a man-hater." "Her exquisite portrayal of the male body, along with her empathetic treatment of the male as both victim and victimizer, can be interpreted as an outcry transcending sexual bounds against all forms of human degradation."

Grossman's sculptures, paintings, and drawings are in collections at New York City's Whitney Museum and Metropolitan Museum of Art, the University Art Museum in Berkeley, the Israel Museum in Jerusalem, the Museum of Fine Arts in Dallas, and other distinguished museums. "My work is my evidence of having existed, had feelings and intelligence—evidence of my choice of how I spent my life," wrote Nancy Grossman in an artist's statement in 1986. "My work addresses both the philosophical and the physical. It is the Skeleton and Structure of my attempt to find my own meanings."

Nancy Grossman creates affecting, controversial sculptures and drawings.
(Portrait by Timothy Greenfield-Sanders)

Further Reading

Blau, Douglas, "Nancy Grossman." *Arts Magazine* 55:6 (February 1981): p. 3.

Diamondstein, Barbaralee. *Open Secrets: Ninety-Four Women in Touch with Our Time.* New York: Viking Press, 1970.

Genauer, Emily. "Art and the Artist: Nancy Grossman," *New York Post,* December 4, 1971.

Nemser, Cindy. "Nancy Grossman." In *Art Talk: Conversations with 12 Women Artists,* 327–333. New York: Charles Scribner's Sons, 1975.

Rubinstein, Charlotte Streifer. *American Women Artists from Early Indian Times to the Present.* Boston: G. K. Hall, 1982.

Turmer, Jane, editor. "Nancy Grossman." *The Dictionary of Art,* 698. New York: Macmillan, 1996.

Vine, Richard. "Nancy Grossman at LedisFlan." *Art in America,* November 1994, p. 152.

— C. K.

HALL, ANNE
(1792–1863)   *Painter*

A prominent painter of miniatures, Anne Hall achieved both critical acclaim and commercial success, gaining her the distinction of being the first woman elected to membership in the National Academy of Design and enabling her to earn a living painting portraits of wealthy New York families.

Anne Hall was born in Pomfret, Connecticut, on May 26, 1792, the sixth of 11 children of Dr. Jonathan Hall, an eminent physician who was interested in and supported the arts, and Bathsheba (Mumford) Hall. Anne displayed artistic talent at a young age and was encouraged by her parents, and also by a family friend who gave her a gift of watercolors and pencils, to develop her skills. Unlike SARAH GOODRIDGE, another highly regarded painter of miniatures, Hall was the beneficiary of formal instruction. Her first teacher, Samuel King, taught her the technique of painting on ivory; several of his students became notable artists. Another instructor, Alexander Robertson, was a landscape painter and miniaturist; Hall studied oil painting with him. In addition, her older brother Charles, a businessman who lived in Europe for several years,

sent his sister oil paintings and miniatures as samples of what was being done abroad.

Having made the decision to specialize as a miniaturist, Hall exhibited some of her works at New York City's Academy of Fine Arts in 1817 and 1818. By the mid-1820s she had moved to New York and established herself there. She was elected an artist of the National Academy of Design in 1827, an associate member in 1828, and a full member in 1833, the only female to achieve that honor until 1900. Hall exhibited her miniatures at the academy's annual exhibitions from 1828 to 1852. Probably her best-known painting was *Garafilia Mahalbi, a Greek Girl of Ipsera, Died at Boston, March 17, 1830, Age 13*, a portrait of a Greek girl captured by the Turks during Greece's war of independence. That work was later reproduced as an engraving. The subjects of many of her other miniatures were members of her large extended family—her brothers and sisters and their children.

As a professional portrait painter specializing in women, children, or mothers and children, Hall reportedly earned her commissions of up to $500 from wealthy New York patrons. At the same time, most of Hall's contemporary critics enthusiastically praised her paintings. Historian William

Dunlap, in his 1834 volume *A History of the Rise and Progress of the Arts of Design in the United States,* wrote: "Her later portraits in miniature are of the first order. I have seen groups of children composed with the taste and skill of a master, and the delicacy which the female character can infuse into works of beauty beyond the reach of man."

A reviewer of the Academy of Design's 1835 exhibition observed that Hall's *Full Length Miniature of a Child* "is one of the best, although we do and ever must exclaim against the excessive warmth of her flesh tints." Today, Hall's works are considered excessively sentimental.

Ann Hall never married. She died at the age of 71 in New York City on December 11, 1863. Her "dainty and lovable little confections," as one writer described her portraits, reflected the American art scene in the early 1800s.

Further Reading

Gerdts, William H. "Hall, Anne." In *Notable American Women 1607–1950*. Volume 2, 117–118, edited by James T. Edwards, et al. Cambridge, Mass.: Harvard University Press, Belknap Press, 1971.
———. *Art Across America.* Vol. 1. New York: Abbeville Press, 1990.
Wehle, Harry B., and Theodore Bolton. *American Miniatures, 1730–1850.* Garden City: Doubleday, Page, and Company, 1927.

— C. K.

HARTIGAN, GRACE
(1922–)   *Painter*

A fundamentally abstract artist who has also included figurative elements in her work, Grace Hartigan became a leading member of the New York school of abstract expressionist painters during the early 1950s and was one of the first female artists to earn an international reputation. While her work received less attention during the 1960s and 1970s, the 1980s marked a revival of interest in her painting that has continued until the present time.

Grace Hartigan was born in Newark, New Jersey, on March 28, 1922, the eldest of four children. Her mother was a real estate agent whose lineage entitled her to membership in the Daughters of the American Revolution. During Grace's childhood in the industrial city of Bayonne, New Jersey, she was exposed to considerable friction between her parents and, once the Great Depression began, to financial hardship. Grace was much closer to her father than to her mother, and it was he, she recalled, who "told me I could do anything I wanted to do." After Grace recovered from a serious bout with pneumonia when she was five, the Hartigans moved to suburban Milburn, New Jersey. Shortly after graduating from high school in 1940, 17-year-old Grace married Robert Jachens, "an idealistic New Jersey boy" two years her senior; the couple moved to California, where "nine months and two weeks" after their marriage a son was born.

Encouraged by her husband, Hartigan started painting. In 1941 Jachens was drafted into the army, and Grace returned to Newark, where she worked as a mechanical draftsperson in an airplane engine factory. She attended evening drawing classes and studied painting with local artist Isaac Lane Muse. Shortly after the war ended, her marriage to Jachens also ended. It was the first of four marriages, the second of which was annulled. She gave her son to her husband's parents (a few years later, she sent the boy to her remarried ex-husband in California and never saw him again), moved to New York City's Lower East Side, and "dedicated herself to being an artist."

Hartigan soon met first-generation abstract expressionists Jackson Pollock and Willem de Kooning, as well as other artists and avant-garde literary figures, among them poet Frank O'Hara. The major influences on Hartigan's work during her early years in New York were Pollock, whose drip paintings she first saw at an exhibition in January 1948, and de Kooning. By 1950 she was an integral part of the New York school of abstract expressionists. That same year she experienced a major breakthrough when one of her paintings, *Secuda Esa Bruja* (1949), was selected by art critics Clement Greenberg and Meyer Schapiro to be included in what became a landmark exhibition, the so-called *New Talent* show at New York's Koontz Gallery. The next year, the newly opened Tibor de Nagy Gallery, which would become a showplace for abstract expressionist art, featured Hartigan's works in the gallery's first solo show. Further recognition came in 1953, when the illustrious Museum of Modern Art in New York purchased Hartigan's *Persian Jacket* (1952).

In the early 1950s Hartigan's work became more figurative, a phase that would last for about five years. Her move away from abstract expressionism was motivated by a search for her own authentic "form." As she recalled to critic Irving Sandler, she had felt "guilty" borrowing from Pollock and de Kooning "without having gone through their struggle. . . . I decided I had no right to that form—I hadn't found it myself—and that I had to paint my way through art history." The result was a series of paintings based on the works of Rubens, Velázquez, Goya, and other old masters (eminent artists from the 15th to the 18th centuries).

However, Hartigan soon returned to her own themes. In 1954 she painted *Grand Street Brides,* a study of mannequins of brides in a Lower East Side store window, where, as she put it, "wedding gowns are on display in a strange rivalry of ugliness and hope." Another major work, more abstract than *Grand Street Brides,* was *City Life* (1956), a response to the urban scene Hartigan saw from her studio window. It was one of her "boldest paintings of the 1950s," according to critic Robert Saltonstall Mattison. In 1956 Hartigan's work was included in the *Twelve Americans* exhibition at the Museum of Modern Art. A year later, *Life* magazine, in an article entitled "Women Artists in Ascendence" that focused on a number of rising stars including HELEN FRANKENTHALER and NELL BLAINE, called Hartigan "the most celebrated of the young American women painters." And in 1958, she was the only female artist included by the Museum of Modern Art in its *New American Painting* show, which toured eight European countries to much acclaim.

Hartigan's move to Long Island, New York, in 1957 also marked a return to abstractionism, in particular the applied action or gestural abstraction style of de Kooning. In 1960 she married a scientist, Dr. Winston Price. He turned out to be, as Hartigan wrote at the time, "the man of my life." Hartigan moved to Baltimore, Maryland, where Price was a medical research scientist at Johns Hopkins University, and the two remained devoted to each other until his death in 1981. However, the move to Baltimore removed and distanced Hartigan from the New York art scene, which perhaps was a factor in the reduced interest in her work. Still, she continued to paint and in 1967 began teaching at the Maryland Institute College of Art, where she also served as director of its Hoffberger Graduate School of Painting.

After a difficult period in the 1970s, during which Hartigan struggled with health problems and alcoholism, her life got back on track. By the 1980s, there was renewed interest in her work, beginning with *Grace Hartigan: Twenty-Five Years of Collage,* a traveling exhibit initiated by the Baltimore Museum of Art, and a 30-year retrospective in 1981 at the Fort Wayne Museum of Art in Texas. Hartigan, meanwhile, continued her habitual practice of incorporating new styles without necessarily abandoning old ones, so that, as critic Terence Diggory observed, "all remain simultaneously available for the artist to call upon in response to the demands of a particular painting." Hartigan's most recent retrospective was held in the spring of 2000 at the Susquehanna Art Museum in Harrisburg, Pennsylvania.

Grace Hartigan's works are part of many prominent collections, including the Museum of Modern Art, the Metropolitan Museum of Art, and the Whitney Museum of American Art (all in New York), the Albright-Knox Gallery in Buffalo, the Baltimore Museum of Art, and the Carnegie Institute Museum of Art in Pittsburgh. In terms of her artistry, she continues to look forward. As she told interviewer Cindy Nemser, "It doesn't interest me to think of myself in a retrospective way. One doesn't want to be one's own history. I just think about the next painting."

Further Reading

Diggory, Terence. *Grace Hartigan and the Poets: Paintings and Prints.* Saratoga Springs, N.Y.: Skidmore College, 1993.

Hartigan, Grace. "An Artist Speaks." *Carnegie Magazine,* February 1961.

Westfall, Stephen. "Then and Now: Six of the New York School Painting Look Back: Grace Hantigan." *Art in America,* June 1985, 118–20.

Mattison, Robert Saltonstall. *Grace Hartigan: A Painter's World.* New York: Hudson Hills Press, 1990.

Nemser, Cindy. *Art Talk: Conversations with 15 Women Artists.* New York: HarperCollins, 1995.

— C. K.

 ## HESSE, EVA
(1936–1970) *Sculptor, Painter, Graphic Artist*

In spite of a highly promising career cut short by her untimely death at the age of 34, Eva Hesse is nonetheless considered a major postmodern artist. In the works on paper and sculptures, she experimented with both material and form and was, according to art critic Lucy Lippard, remarkably successful at fusing "formal and emotional intensity."

Eva Hesse was born into a Jewish family in Hamburg, Germany, on January 11, 1936. When she was two years old, she and her sister were sent to Holland to escape from Nazi persecution. They arrived safely but were separated, and Eva was placed in foster care with a Catholic family. A year later the Hesses located their daughters and immigrated with them to the United States. However, once they settled in New York City, her parents were soon divorced. In 1946, a year after she became an American citizen, Hesse's mother, who was manic-depressive, committed suicide. The tragic event had a profound effect on Hesse. "Everything for me is glossed with anxiety," she once explained to a friend.

Hesse knew early on that she wanted to become an artist. A restless and rebellious child, she needed to express herself and had a talent for painting and drawing. As an adolescent, she started keeping journals and continued to do so throughout her life. The diaries reveal a great deal about her personal and artistic development. After graduating from Manhattan's High School of Industrial Arts in 1952, Hesse enrolled in a two-year advertising design course at Pratt Institute in New York. She studied for two years at New York's Art Students League, and from 1954 (the same year *Seventeen* magazine printed her illustrations in a competition award) to 1957, she attended Cooper Union.

After winning a scholarship, Hesse entered Yale School of Art and Architecture, earning a bachelor of fine arts degree from the prestigious institution in 1959. While there, Hesse studied abstract painting with Rico Lebrun, Bernard Chaet, and color theorist Josef Albers. Albers introduced her to abstract geometric patterns similar to the squares that would dominate her drawings. Although she was considered gifted by her teachers, Hesse had little confidence in her painting ability and was caught in the conflict between the reductive, cool style of minimalist artists and the more emotional, passionate mode of the early abstract expressionists. She preferred minimalism, with its repetition and deceptively simple forms, but she also gravitated toward a more personal and involved, yet still abstract, style of art.

After leaving Yale, Hesse turned to drawing, especially ink, wash, and gouache drawings of repeated circles or squares with lines descending from them. She moved back to New York and began to sell her watercolors and drawings. In 1961 she married Tom Doyle, an established sculptor. Two years later, at the Allan Stone Gallery in New York, Hesse had her first solo show of drawings, which ranged from abstractions to boxes and circles. In 1964 Hesse and Doyle moved to Kettwig-am-Ruhr, West Germany, where Doyle had received a 15-month commission from a wealthy art collector. For Hesse, returning to her homeland, from which she had been forced to flee as a child, was a traumatic experience. In addition, she felt like the "artist's wife," with no self-identity or purpose. Forcing herself to work, it was—ironically—

Postmodernist Eva Hesse died at the age of 34.
(Reproduced with the permission of the Estate of Eva Hesse.
Courtesy Galerie Hauser & Wirth, Zurich)

in Germany that she developed her own form of artistic expression, first through biomorphic and erotic line drawings, and then by creating relief forms that evolved into sculptures. She described her drawings of squares, rectangles, and grids, such as *And He Sat in a Box* (1964), as "boxes and windows." She wrote to her friend and supporter, conceptual artist Sol LeWitt, that her drawings were "crazy like machines . . . larger, bolder. . . . [I] have been really discovering my weird humor."

Then Hesse turned to sculptures using string from the weavings she found lying around the empty warehouse where she and Doyle were living. She combined the string with plaster and other found objects. In both her drawings and relief forms, she used recurring leitmotifs, or what she called "repetition in an unrepetitive way," and experimented freely with plastics and synthetic fibers. Hesse's goal, wrote Cindy Nemser in an *Art Talk* interview with the artist, was to "move the figure off the canvas into actual space in order to dissolve the boundaries between drawing, painting, and sculpture. [She wished to] temper the geometric with the organic,

the ordered with the chaotic, the logical with the absurd, the detached with the engaged."

Hesse returned to New York in 1965 with a cache of abstract drawings and wood-and-masonite painted reliefs, including *Ringaround Arosie* (1965)—her first sculpture. She and Doyle separated in 1966, and a year later her works were included in what is considered the first conceptual art show, held at New York's Museum of Normal Art. In her pieces, Hesse continued using industrial materials and "stringy" components such as latex, rope, fiberglass, wire mesh, and polyester resin, and she experimented with techniques such as layering, wrapping, puncturing, and gluing. Although she could be self-absorbed and used her work for self-analysis, Hesse had a sense of humor. For example, she liked her sculpture *Hang-Up* (1965–66), a wooden piece wrapped in a painted rope with a gigantic metal rod protruding from it, because it was "the most ridiculous structure . . . I ever made." Hesse valued the random, absurd, and mysterious. About her 1968 solo show at Manhattan's Fischbach Gallery, Hesse said of her "anti-form" sculptures, "I would like the work to be non-work. This means that it would find its way beyond my preconceptions."

By 1969, the year the Whitney Museum of American Art held an individual exhibition of her work entitled *Anti-Illusion: Procedures/Materials,* Hesse had been diagnosed with a brain tumor and was suffering its effects. She attended the Whitney show in a wheelchair. Even while she was hospitalized, she directed the construction of latex, wire, and fiberglass pieces that are considered among her most compelling work. In 1999, art critic John Roberts described her sculptures as "dream-objects, a collection of personal and cultural effects . . . in many ways a revisitation of childhood itself."

After a prolific decade that began in 1960, Eva Hesse died of cancer on May 29, 1970, in New York City. Her large and impressive body of drawings and sculptures have secured her a place in America's canon as a pivotal sculptor. Hesse's work was shown posthumously in numerous solo exhibitions, including in New York City at the Fishbach Gallery (1970), the School of Visual Arts (1971), and the Kolbert Gallery; and at the Whitechapel Arts Gallery in London. She was the first female artist to have a retrospective at New York's Solomon R. Guggenheim Museum (1972). Twenty years later, a second traveling retrospective of Hesse's work originated at Yale University Art Gallery.

Hesse's work is also represented in the collections of prestigious museums in New York such as the Guggenheim, Whitney, and Museum of Modern Art, as well as in the Tate Gallery in London and the National Gallery of Australia in Canberra. A critic in the *New Yorker* magazine asserted that Hesse's works have not "lost their potency; on the contrary, they now appear seminal."

Further Reading

Lippard, Lucy. *Eva Hesse.* New York: New York University Press, 1976.

Nemser, Cindy. *Art Talk: Conversations with 12 Women Artists.* New York: Scribner's, 1975.

Pincus-Witten, Robert. "Eva Hesse: Last Words," *Artforum,* November 1972, 74–76.

Wagner, Anne M. *Three Artists: Modernism and the Art of Hesse, Krasner and O'Keeffe.* Berkeley: University of California Press, 1996.

— C. K.

HOFFMAN, MALVINA CORNELL
(1885–1966) *Sculptor*

Renowned for her finely crafted sculptures of luminaries and ordinary people from diverse ethnic backgrounds, Malvina Hoffman produced several major sculptural projects during her prolific career. "Probing for what lies beneath the surface has been the search of my whole life," she once wrote. Hoffman, who has been dubbed "America's Rodin," studied with the French master in Paris.

Malvina Cornell Hoffman, born on June 15, 1885, in New York City, was brought up in "the lurid atmosphere of Broadway and Forty-third Street," recalled the artist about her youth. Her family nurtured and encouraged her artistic expression, especially her father, a distinguished concert pianist who had performed with the New York Philharmonic. Her mother, too, was a pianist, and the Hoffman household was filled with artists and musicians. While attending private school in New York City, Malvina took art lessons and later studied painting at the Women's School of Applied Design, the Art Students League, and the Veltin School. However, she decided to become a sculptor because she liked understanding how things work and felt the three-dimensional medium would allow her more artistic freedom.

In 1909, at 24, Hoffman created her first important sculpture, a clay portrait of her beloved but ailing father. The highly regarded sculptor Gutzon Borglum, who was one of her teachers, encouraged her to carve her father's bust in marble. "My child. . . . Above all, you must *be* an artist; after that you may create art," said Hoffman's father; he died two weeks after his daughter had completed his portrait, which was accepted by the National Academy of Design for its 1910 exhibition. That same year, Hoffman won honorable mention at the Paris Salon for a bust of Samuel Bonarios Grimson, a family friend and violinist whom Hoffman would marry in 1924 and divorce in 1936.

In 1910 Hoffman and her mother, traveling on a limited budget and with two of Hoffman's marble busts and a letter of introduction to the illustrious sculptor Auguste Rodin, moved to Paris. Although Rodin was reluctant to meet the young American, Hoffman was determined to meet him. She repudiated his rebukes and, after five futile attempts, caught Rodin's attention by quoting from memory a sonnet by Alfred de Musset that the sculptor had been attempting to remember. She then convinced Rodin to look at the marble heads she had brought from America. Rodin quickly recognized Hoffman's potential as a sculptor and invited her to study with him. For 16 months, he was her teacher and mentor, greatly influencing her style and form; Rodin and Hoffman remained friends until his death.

After returning to New York, Hoffman studied anatomy at Columbia University Medical School. She returned to Paris for two summers, during which time she visited bronze foundries in order to understand the craft of sculpting—how metal worked and how it could be manipulated. She became a skilled master founder, casting her own bronzes instead of depending on others to do the heavy lifting for her. (In 1939 she would publish a technical textbook on bronze casting entitled *Sculpture: Inside and Out*.) In Paris and New York, Hoffman befriended, among other cultural icons, writer Gertrude Stein, sculptor ROMAINE BROOKS, and Russian ballet dancer Anna Pavlova. The world-famous ballerina would sometimes pose for Hoffman, who attempted to capture "that new kind of freedom in the dance" in bronze. Hoffman's pieces *Povlowa Gavotte* and *Bacchanale Russe,* produced between 1915 and 1920, earned her critical international acclaim.

During the 1920s, Hoffman worked on several large monuments, including *The Sacrifice* (1922), an affecting war monument commissioned by Harvard University, and a larger-than-life-sized bronze portrait of Yugoslavian sculptor Ivan Mestrovic, with whom she had studied. In 1929 she had her first major solo exhibition at Manhattan's Grand Central Art Gallery. It featured 105 sculptures that Hoffman had created from a variety of materials. A year later she was commissioned by Chicago's Field Museum of National History to create her masterwork, *The Races of Man,* for the museum's Hall of Man. Originally intended as five sculptures, the demanding project was comprised of more than 100 life-sized figures upon completion, the majority of which were cast in bronze and the remaining in marble or stone. In *Heads and Tales* (1936), the first of two memoirs, Hoffman described the museum's new hall: "The heroic-sized bronze group representing the three main divisions of the human race (White, Yellow, and Black) and surmounted by a globe, is the central point of interest in the octagonal room. Flanked on both sides of the galleries are 34 full-length figures. . . . In the alcoves are heads and busts repre-

senting the subdivisions of the main races which are shown in full-length figures."

The Races of Man took Hoffman five years to complete and was ready for the 1933 World's Fair. At the time, it was the largest sculptural commission awarded to a woman. The goal of the project was to represent peoples of various nationalities and ethnicities and required enormous research and observation. Hoffman and Grimson traveled for two years to faraway places such as Bali, East India, and Africa. "Her adventures with bushmen, head hunters, and the Hairy Ainu of Japan . . . made excellent tabloid journals in the 1930s," reported the *New York Times.*

Some art critics called *The Races of Man* "one of the most popular exhibitions in the world," while others considered it more an anthropological study than a work of art. Hoffman viewed it as both: "To understand the submerged passion that burns in the human eye, to read the hieroglyphs of suffering etched in the lines of a human face . . . to watch the gesture of a hand or listen for the false notes and the truth in a human voice, these are the mysteries that I found I must delve into and try to unravel when I made a portrait," she explained in *Heads and Tales.*

Although she excelled at spirited monumental works, Hoffman was best known for her smaller, naturalistic portrait sculptures. Subjects who sat for her ranged from family members and friends to conservationist John Muir and politician Wendell Willkie. She also created a facade of 13 bas-relief panels depicting the evolution of medicine for the Joslin Clinic in Boston; the World War II American Battle Monument at Epinal, France; and a bronze piece, *Mongolian Archer,* which won a gold medal of honor in 1962 from the Allied Artists of America.

Hoffman retired in 1963, having produced an enormous oeuvre. At 81 she died of a heart attack on July 10, 1966, in her Manhattan studio, where she had happily resided for more than 45 years and where her parties and costume balls were reported in New York's social columns. In a front-page *New York Times* obituary, Hoffman was referred to as "one of the few women to reach first rank as a sculptor." An industrious, ambitious classicist, she described the "mass of [contemporary] abstract sculpture" as "not excellent." However, she also believed that "it is exciting to be alive in an age of experiment and pioneering. . . . Nothing is more deadly than the apathy of indifference or self-satisfaction."

Hoffman's works can be found in permanent collections in premier museums in America and in Europe, including New York's American Museum of Natural History and the Metropolitan Museum of Art. She was the recipient of five honorary doctorates and many awards, including the National Academy of Design's gold medal (1924) and the National Sculpture Society's gold medal of honor (1964). First and foremost, Malvina Hoffman stood by her work, noting: "For better or for worse, [my work] expresses my thoughts, my ideals, in brief, my way of meeting life and people who are so rich a part of life."

Further Reading

Encyclopedia Britannica. "Hoffman, Malvina," Women in American History. Available online. URL: http://women. eb.com/women/articles/Hoffman_Malvina.html. Encyclopedia Britannica, Inc. Downloaded on June 4, 2001.

Hill, May Brawley. *The Woman Sculptor: Malvina Hoffman and Her Contemporaries.* New York: Berry-Hill Galleries, 1984.

Hoffman, Malvina. *Heads and Tales.* New York: Scribner's, 1936.

———. *Yesterday is Tomorrow: A Personal History.* New York: Crown, 1965.

Metro Active Features. "Refuse To Be Typecast: Malvina Hoffman, Sculptor, 1885–1966." Available online. URL: http://www.metroactive.com/papers/gvz/03.10.99/women2-9910.htr. Posted on March 10, 1999.

New York Times, Obituary, "Malvina Hoffman Dead at Age of 81," July 11, 1966, 1.

— C. K.

HOKINSON, HELEN ELNA
(1893–1949) *Cartoonist, Illustrator*

Helen Hokinson began her career as a fashion illustrator but attained fame in the 1930s and 1940s as a cartoonist for *The New Yorker,* an esteemed literary magazine. Hokinson's cartoons, which gently poked fun at the privileged upper-middle class, became one of the most popular features of the periodical and, as drama critic John Mason Brown has observed, "a comic pattern cherished and admired by all Americans, including those from whom it was derived."

Helen Elna Hokinson was born in Mendota, Illinois, on June 29, 1893, the only child of her father, a farm machinery salesman, and her mother, a business college graduate who at her commencement gave an address defending the right of women to participate in "practical business." While in high school, Helen enjoyed sketching her classmates and local townspeople. After graduating in 1913, she enrolled at the Academy of Fine Arts in Chicago where for the next five years she studied cartooning and illustrating, while earning money by doing fashion sketches for several major Chicago department stores.

In 1920 Hokinson moved to New York City. She continued to work, with notable success, as a fashion illustrator for department stores. She and a friend created a comic strip, "Sylvia in the Big City," for the newly established *New York Daily Mirror,* but their job at the newspaper was short-lived. Hokinson also studied painting at the New York School of Fine and Applied Art under Howard Giles, an advocate of a design principle known as "dynamic symmetry."

Hokinson's big break came in 1925 when some of her fellow art students convinced her to send her drawings to Harold Ross and Raoul Fleischmann, founders of a fledgling magazine they were calling *The New Yorker.* One of her drawings was accepted, and two weeks later, after delivering a second sketch, Hokinson was astonished to learn that the magazine's editors wanted her to submit drawings for consideration on a regular basis. Hokinson's first *New Yorker* drawings did not contain captions, but the editors began to add them to the cartoons, as well as suggesting ideas to Hokinson for new drawings.

In 1931 writer and fellow *New Yorker* contributor James Reid Parker found out that Hokinson lived around the corner from him in New York's Gramercy Park neighborhood. He admired her work, so he arranged to meet with her. That meeting was the start of an extraordinarily successful professional partnership and friendship that lasted throughout Hokinson's life. In effect, Parker and Hokinson collaborated in creating *New Yorker* cartoons, with Hokinson responsible for the drawings and Parker providing the captions; sometimes he also suggested situations for Hokinson to draw. The two of them often toured Manhattan together, with Parker taking notes while Hokinson, as he recalled, was "forever sketching people in parks, in restaurants, in the lobbies of hotels and business buildings, during theater intermissions, at special events held in Madison Square Garden and Grand Central Palace, and in fact wherever we went." Hokinson produced about 1,700 cartoons for the *New Yorker*, as well as covers—often landscapes, which she painted in watercolor.

During her lifetime, Hokinson published three collections of cartoons: *So You're Going to Buy a Book!* (1931), *My Best Girls* (1941), and *When Were You Built?* (1948). Three more volumes of her cartoons were published posthumously. While Hokinson's cartoons were satirical, they were never cruel. Her characters were made to look foolish, but never meanspirited. As John Mason Brown pointed out in *The Hokinson Festival* (1956):

> Hers was the rarest of satiric gifts. She had no contempt for human failings. She approached foibles with affection. She could ridicule without wounding. She could give fun by making fun, and in the process make no enemies.

Helen Hokinson was killed on November 1, 1949, when the aircraft on which she was flying was involved in a midair collision as it was about to land in Washington, D.C. All 55 passengers died in one of the worst civil aviation disasters at that time. Hokinson was buried in her hometown of Mendota. In a tribute to her, John Mason Brown wrote that Hokinson had become "a living part of our vocabulary."

Further Reading

Brown, John Mason. "Helen E. Hokinson." In *The Hokinson Festival,* with a memoir by James Reid Parker and an appreciation by John Mason Brown. New York: Dutton, 1956.

———. *The Ladies, God Bless 'Em!.* New York: Dutton, 1950.

James, Edward T., editor. *Notable American Women, 1607–1950: A Biographical Dictionary.* Cambridge, Mass.: Belknap Press of Harvard University Press, 1971.

Lorenz, Lee. *The Art of the New Yorker: 1925–1995.* New York: Knopf, 1995.

— C. K.

HOLZER, JENNY
(1950–)   *Mixed Media Artist, Installation Artist*

Committed to using art and language to elicit responses from as many audiences as possible, Jenny Holzer works in a zone where art, politics, and technology meet and meld. Since the late 1970s, she has been disseminating written messages using media that ranges from notices printed on white paper to T-shirts, from metal plaques and stone benches to computerized light-emitting signs displayed in venues as varied as major art galleries and city streets.

Jenny Holzer was born on July 29, 1950, in Gallipolis, Ohio, the eldest of three children. Her father was an automobile dealer, and her mother, a riding teacher in college, was active in community affairs. Interested in art as a child, Holzer recalled that she "drew wildly" until she was eight, when she became "self-conscious about it" and stopped. She attended high school in Lancaster, Ohio, where the family lived, but completed her secondary education at Pine Crest Preparatory School in Fort Lauderdale, Florida. Holzer attended Duke University and the University of Chicago before earning a bachelor of fine arts degree at Ohio University in 1972. She found the atmosphere at Ohio University congenial because, as she put it, "the teachers were challenging, but very accepting of experimentation, which is perfect for artists."

Installation artist Jenny Holzer incorporates language in her mixed-media work.
(Portrait by Timothy Greenfield-Sanders)

Holzer received a master of fine arts degree from the Rhode Island School of Design in 1977. There, she was an abstract painter influenced by color field painters such as Morris Louis. She then received a fellowship in the Whitney Museum of American Art's Independent Study Program in New York City, where she lived until the mid-1980s. Holzer was deeply impressed by the Whitney's "wonderful reading list," which introduced her to a broad range of ideas that she determined to "translate . . . into a language that was accessible" to a broad audience through her work. She turned from abstract imagery to "the pure writing" of language. In 1983 she married fellow artist Mike Glier and moved to Hoosick Falls, New York, where the couple's daughter, Lili, was born in 1988.

Holzer's original vehicle for engaging people in her art was posters that she had placed on public buildings and surroundings in New York City. She began with two series of messages: Truisms (1978) and Inflammatory Essays (1979–82). They consisted of a diverse collection of provocative one-line slogans printed in capital letters, such as "MURDER HAS ITS SEXUAL SIDE," "MONEY CREATES TASTE," and "STERIL-IZATION IS OFTEN JUSTIFIED." A third series, Living (1981–82), which dealt with every-day news and events and consisted of bronze and hand-lettered wall plaques, was created in collabo-ration with the artist Peter Nadin, whose paintings accompanied Holzer's texts. Beginning in 1982, Holzer used electronic signboards, including the Spectacolor Board in Times Square in Manhattan, and LED signs—matrices of computer-activated, light-emitting diode lamps displaying traveling texts and graphics. In 1986 she began engraving texts into granite benches and sarcophagi and dis-playing them along with electronic messages.

Art critics and writers have characterized Holzer's controversial work as everything from pro-found to superficial. But most of them agree that her work evokes strong reactions. Diane Waldman, who curated Holzer's solo exhibition at New York's Guggenheim Museum in 1989, wrote: "Holzer is one of the most visible artists on the contemporary scene: much of her work is by definition presented in public surroundings. Couched in accessible lan-guage, it seeks public response. . . . Holzer's art can be both site-specific and self-sufficient, a party of a public arena and an entity unto itself."

Holzer's honors include being selected to repre-sent the United States at the 1990 Venice Bien-nale—the first woman to represent America in the prestigious international exhibition. Her works are housed in permanent collections of the Museum of Modern Art and the Whitney Museum of American Art in New York, the Tate Gallery in London, and the Musée d'Art Moderne in Paris. Holzer defines herself as "strange . . . I don't even basically think of myself as an artist." On the other hand, by taking her visual investigation of language to the streets, she suggests that she just might be a "universal voice." Diane Waldman, taking the

99

approach of an art historian, views Jenny Holzer as "heir to a twentieth-century artistic tradition that began with Cubist collage and has figured prominently in many of the major movements of our time."

Further Reading

Casey, Mary Alice. "Jenny Holzer: Creating Art for the Mind," *Ohio University Today.* Available online. URL: http://www.ohiou.edu/ohiotoday/fall_winter98/interest/holzer.htm. Downloaded on January 11, 2001.

Ferguson, Bruce. "Wordsmith: An Interview with Jenny Holzer," *Art in America,* December 1986, 109–114.

Siegel, Jeanne. "Jenny Holzer's Language Games." *Arts Magazine,* December 1985, 64–68.

Waldman, Diane. *Jenny Holzer.* New York: The Solomon R. Guggenheim Foundation in association with Harry N. Abrams, 1989.

— C. K.

HOSMER, HARRIET GOODHUE
(1830–1908) *Sculptor*

The most successful American woman sculptor of her generation, Harriet Hosmer earned an international reputation for her neoclassical sculptures during the second half of the 19th century. Both as an artist making her way in a world dominated by men and as a single woman living an independent lifestyle, she was a pioneer who set an example for other women to follow.

Harriet Goodhue Hosmer was born in Watertown, Massachusetts, on October 9, 1830, the second of four children of a physician and his wife. In the tragic wake of the deaths of three of his children (two in infancy), and his wife from tuberculosis, Dr. Hosmer was determined to reinforce the health of his remaining child, Harriet, through a vigorous regimen of outdoor life and exercise that included riding, swimming, skating, and shooting. Harriet became robust and independent. When not creating clay models of animals and human figures, she often broke rules and conventions—behavior that got her expelled from three schools. Her father responded by sending her to the pro-gressive Charles Sedgwick's School for Girls in Lenox, Massachusetts, where she thrived. Harriet had the opportunity to meet a number of literati who visited the school, including Ralph Waldo Emerson and Nathaniel Hawthorne, as well as the British actress Fanny Kemble, who encouraged her to become a sculptor. Harriet also was fortunate to have as a roommate Cornelia Crow, who later would become her biographer, and whose wealthy father, Wayman Crow, played a vital role as a patron in supporting and furthering Hosmer's career as a sculptor.

Hosmer completed her secondary schooling in 1849 and returned home, where she set up a studio and practiced drawing and modeling. She also began studying with Boston sculptor Paul Stephenson. However, her attempt to study anatomy, essential to becoming a serious sculptor, was thwarted because she was a woman. When her father was unable to convince any nearby medical school to admit her, Wayman Crow stepped in and convinced Dr. Joseph McDowell of the Missouri Medical College to allow Hosmer to take an anatomy class at the medical college; she received a diploma for the course.

After returning home, Hosmer worked 10 hours a day to produce a marble bust titled *Hesper, the Evening Star* (1852). She also met Charlotte Cushman, a well-known British actress living in Rome, who encouraged her to travel to Rome to pursue her studies. After some hesitation, Dr. Hosmer agreed, and he accompanied his daughter to Rome, where the noted British sculptor and leading neoclassicist John Gibson, impressed with Harriet Hosmer's daguerreotype photographs of *Hesper,* violated his practice of not accepting students and invited her to become his only pupil. The elderly British gentleman and the irrepressible young American woman proved to be an excellent match: Gibson gave Hosmer a workroom in his studio and took great pride in her progress, while Hosmer—who was "convinced Heaven smiled most benignantly upon me when it sent me to him"—became a devoted admirer of Gibson and helped the aging sculptor manage his affairs.

Hosmer's progress became apparent in two busts produced in 1853, *Daphne* and *Medusa.* She also became a fixture in Rome's expatriate art colony, which included British poets Robert and Elizabeth Browning. Hosmer's friendship with the Brownings resulted in the praiseworthy bronze, *Clasped Hands of Elizabeth and Robert Browning* (1853). Elizabeth Browning's admiration of Hosmer extended from the sculptor's work to her lifestyle, as she indicated in a letter to a friend in 1854: "Miss Hosmer . . . the young American sculptress, who is a great pet of mine and Robert's and who emancipates the eccentric life of a perfectly 'emancipated female' from all shadow of blame by the purity of hers." However, that same year Hosmer faced a crisis when her father informed her that because of his own monetary losses, he could no longer support her work in Rome. Hosmer was able to remain in Rome by cutting expenses (including selling her horse) and by turning to Wayman Crow for financial help, which he generously provided.

In 1855 Hosmer completed her first life-size figure in marble, *Oenone,* the wife Paris deserted to pursue Helen of Troy. The work, which depicts a despondent Oenone staring at the ground, reflected a theme already evident in Hosmer's earlier sculptures and which would continue to reappear: the difficulties faced by women in a man's world. Meanwhile, she took a major step in overcoming at least one set of difficulties—supporting herself—with a piece entitled *Puck* (1856), a statue of the mischievous sprite in Shakespeare's *A Midsummer Night's Dream.* It became an instant critical and financial success, especially after the Prince of Wales bought a marble replica. Almost 50 more were sold at $1,000 each, making Hosmer financially self-sufficient. Several commissions followed, including one in 1860, facilitated by Wayman Crow, from the state of Missouri for a huge bronze of its five-time senator, Thomas Hart Benton. *Thomas Hart Benton* (1868), the first public monument in St. Louis, stands in that city's Lafayette Park, where it was dedicated in 1868.

Hosmer's career peaked between the late 1850s and late 1860s. During that time, her most impres-

Harriet Hosmer was a popular early neoclassical sculptor.
(Library of Congress)

sive work was *Zenobia* (1859), a seven-foot-high statue of an ancient queen who was defeated by the Romans and was marched through the streets of their city in chains. Although she was defeated, Zenobia, as depicted by Hosmer, was stately and majestic, and therefore a restatement of Hosmer's views of women dominated by men. In writer Nathaniel Hawthorne's words, "she (Zenobia) is decked with ornaments; but the chains of her captivity hang from wrist to wrist, and her deportment indicating soul so much above her misfortune, yet not insensible to the weight of it, makes those chains a richer decoration than all other jewels." The statue soon became a feminist symbol for Hosmer in a more direct sense. It was a critical success, first at the London International Exhibition in 1862 and then in Boston, New York, and Chicago.

However, in 1863 two London magazines printed stories alleging that *Zenobia* was not really Hosmer's sculpture but was produced by her assistants—male Italian artisans. She defended herself with a libel suit and an article, "The Process of Sculpture," which appeared in the *Atlantic Monthly* in December 1864, and she eventually received retractions from both London publications.

Although she continued to work, often fulfilling commissions from wealthy English aristocrats, by 1870 Hosmer's most creative years were behind her. By the 1880s neoclassicism was out of vogue, and Hosmer's standing as an artist was diminished. However, in her later years Hosmer became identified with the women's suffrage movement, and she executed a life-size statue entitled *Queen Isabella I* (1893), for a Chicago suffragist organization. It was exhibited at the World's Columbian Exposition in Chicago in 1893 and proved to be her last major project.

In 1900 Harriet Hosmer, one of the foremost American female sculptors of the 19th century, returned to her birthplace, Watertown, Massachusetts. She died of a lung ailment on February 21, 1908. Today, examples of her work are in many prominent permanent collections, including those of the Metropolitan Museum of Art in New York, the National Museum of American Art of the Smithsonian Institution in Washington, D.C., and the Wadsworth Atheneum in Hartford, Connecticut.

Further Reading

Gerdts, William H. *The White Marmorean Flock: Nineteenth-Century American Women Neoclassical Sculptors.* Exhibition Catalog. Poughkeepsie, N.Y.: Vassar College Art Gallery, 1972.

Rubinstein, Charlotte. *American Women Sculptors: A History of Women Working in Three Dimensions.* Boston: G.K. Hall, 1990.

Sherwood, Dolly. *Harriet Hosmer: American Sculptor, 1830–1908.* Columbia: University of Missouri Press, 1991.

Tufts, Eleanor. *American Women Artists, 1830–1930.* Washington, D.C.: National Museum of Women in the Arts, 1987.

— C. K.

HUNTER, CLEMENTINE
(ca. 1886–1988)   *Painter, Folk Artist*

A self-taught painter who labored in southern plantation cotton fields or kitchens from childhood until she retired, Clementine Hunter did not touch a paintbrush until she was more than 50 years old. Yet the woman who has been called "the black GRANDMA MOSES" produced about 5,000 paintings and is widely considered one of this country's outstanding folk artists.

Clementine Hunter, born in either December 1886 or January 1887 on the Hidden Hill plantation just south of Cloutierville, Louisiana, was the first of seven children of Antoinette Adams and Janvier Reuben. Clementine's heritage reflected the Creole mixture of Louisiana's population: her father, she recalled, was "a pure Frenchman," while her mother had both African-American and Native American ancestors. As Hunter told James L. Wilson, author of *Clementine Hunter* (1988):

> All my people were Creoles. They say us Creoles got more different kinds of blood than any other people. When I was growing up all the folks on the lower Cane River were Creoles . . . spoke nothing but French.

In fact, Hunter spoke a Creole dialect into adulthood, when her second husband taught her English.

When Clementine was about five, her family moved to Cloutierville, where she briefly attended a Catholic elementary school but never learned to read or write. When she was a teenager ("not a little girl, not old enough to marry") she ended up on Melrose Plantation, near the town of Natchitoches, where Hunter worked in the cotton fields. She was married twice. The first, a common-law marriage, was to Charlie Dupree, a mechanical wizard who reportedly built a piano without ever having seen one; the couple had two children. Hunter lived as a single mother for 10 years after Dupree's death in 1924 and eventually married Emanuel Hunter, "a good Christian husband," in January 1924. She and Emanuel had five children, two of whom were stillborn. In

1979, when Hunter was interviewed for the Black Women Oral History Project of the Schlesinger Library of Harvard University, only one of her children was still alive.

Melrose Plantation was a special place. It was owned by John Hampton Henry and his wife Carmelita Garrett Henry, an art collector with a deep interest in the arts and crafts of Louisiana. Melrose became a destination for many artists and art devotees, among them François Mignon, who in 1938 took a job at Melrose as Carmelita Henry's literary assistant. He remained there until his death 30 years later. It was Mignon who discovered Clementine Hunter, encouraged her to paint, and provided her with materials. Her first "canvas" was an old window shade, but she would also paint on cardboard boxes, paper bags, lumber scraps, cartons, and anything else she could find. Hunter stretched her painting supply by thinning it, often with turpentine. Therefore, many of her early oils, which Mignon thought were her best, looked somewhat like watercolors.

After a full day's work as a cook and maid—in addition to caring for her ailing second husband, who died in 1944—Hunter would paint. She favored exuberant colors and focused on everyday activities, later seen in such works as *Pickin' Cotton* (1973) and *Wedding* (1976). She needed money to continue to paint, and financial assistance came from another visitor at Melrose, writer and artist James Register, who in 1945 helped her obtain a foundation grant. Mignon and Register both publicized Hunter's work, and in 1949 the New Orleans Arts and Crafts Show displayed a selection of her paintings.

Hunter's reputation rapidly grew. In 1953 she was included in a group of folk artists whose works were reviewed in *Look* magazine, then one of America's most popular magazines. Two years later, two important Louisiana galleries exhibited her paintings. At one of them, the Delgado Museum (today called the New Orleans Museum of Art), Hunter's show was the first ever by a black artist. Meanwhile, Northwestern State College in Natchitoches also was exhibiting her

work. However, because segregation was still enforced in the South, Hunter was unable to publicly attend her own show. Fortunately a teacher at the college sneaked her in through the back door on a Sunday when the gallery was locked. Ironically, in 1986, more than 30 years after she had been turned away from Northwestern State College's gallery, the institution awarded her an honorary doctor of fine arts degree.

Hunter, who would paint for more than half a century, is thought to have done her best work between 1940 and 1950. While she was recognized by many art critics—Robert Bishop, director of the American Museum of Folk Art in New York City, called her "perhaps one of the most celebrated contemporary Southern painters"—others noted unevenness in her art and contended that it was at times created for commercial purposes. None of this deterred Hunter, who continued to paint until a few weeks before her death on January 1, 1988. She was 101 years old. "Hunter," wrote James L. Wilson, "did not consider herself an artist, nor, as some have said, a genius. If anything, she considered herself merely as one who lived a life—largely a happy one."

Today, pictures by the untrained folk artist who once gave her works away or sold them for as little as a quarter sell for $3,000 and more in prestigious art galleries. As for Clementine Hunter, the success and fame she enjoyed in the second half of her long life did not seem to go to her head. She once commented, "God puts those pictures in my head and I just puts them on the canvas, just like he wants me to."

Further Reading

Hill, Ruth Edmonds, editor. *The Black Women Oral History Project.* Volume 6. Westport, Conn.: Meckler Publishing, 1991.

Smith, Jessie Carey. *Notable Black American Women.* Detroit: Gale Research, 1992.

Wilson, James L. *Clementine Hunter: American Folk Artist.* Gretna, La.: Pelican Publishing Company, 1988.

— C. K.

HUNTINGTON, ANNA VAUGHN HYATT

(1876–1973) *Sculptor*

Anna Hyatt Huntington was one of the America's finest animal sculptors. "Animals have many moods and to represent them is my joy," she once said. Best known for her monumental and heroic equestrian statues, Huntington was a prolific academic sculptor whose career spanned 70 years and whose realistic works were characterized by meticulous craftsmanship and detail.

Born in Cambridge, Massachusetts, on March 10, 1876, Anna Vaughn Hyatt was influenced by her father, a paleontologist and zoology professor at the Massachusetts Institute of Technology, as well as an amateur painter, and by her mother, who illustrated her husband's textbooks and encouraged her three children to develop their creative abilities. Anna became fascinated with animal anatomy and behavior, as well as with drawing and music (she was a talented violinist). Although mostly self-taught in sculpture (she had successfully modeled the family's Great Dane), during the 1890s she and her sister briefly studied with Henry Hudson Kitson, a well-known Boston sculptor.

Hyatt had her first solo exhibit in 1900 at the Boston Arts Club, when she was 24. It included 40 animal sculptures and was praised by local art critics. She moved to New York City and studied for a short time with George Grey Barnard at the Art Students League. However, nature was her primary teacher: she observed animal life by visiting zoos and circuses, where she often modeled her subjects. In New York she befriended and lived with the sculptor MARY ABASTENIA ST. LEGER EBERLE and collaborated with her on *Men and Bull* (1904), a prizewinning sculpture at the Louisiana Purchase Exposition. Hyatt sculpted the bull, while Eberle crafted the men. In 1906 Hyatt traveled to France and Italy, exhibiting a pair of life-sized, ominous-looking jaguar sculptures at the 1908 Paris Salon.

In 1909 Hyatt won a competition for her first equestrian commission, a huge rendition of Joan of Arc. She conducted research for the demanding project in France, studying in detail the period during which Joan of Arc had lived. The first heroic equestrian statue by a woman, Hyatt's *Joan of Arc* featured a bronze Saint Joan garbed in armor and astride her steed, with her sword outstretched. It was placed on Riverside Drive in New York City and has been frequently casted and reproduced in other cities in America and abroad. Hyatt concentrated on the Maid of Orleans's spiritual intensity, commenting: "It was only her mental attitude, only her religious fervor, that could have enabled her to endure so much physically." Art writer Charlotte Rubinstein contends that Hyatt's own "mental attitude" resembled that of her heroine. *Joan of Arc* is considered a landmark in the history of women sculptors. France bestowed upon Hyatt the Chevalier of the Legion of Honor. In addition, the Spanish government decorated her with the Grand Cross of Alfonso the Twelfth for her focus on Spanish subjects, including *El Cid Campeador* (1927), which was erected to much acclaim in Seville, Spain.

Hyatt's works sold well and were exhibited widely. She was feted with honors, including gold medals for distinction from the Pennsylvania Academy and the American Academy of Arts and Letters; she had been the first woman sculptor admitted to the Academy. At age 47, Anna Hyatt—by all accounts handsome, witty, and dignified—married, in her art studio, a wealthy Hispanic poet and scholar, Archer Milton Huntington, the adopted son of a railroad magnate. The couple became important philanthropists and supported wildlife preservation and protection as well as cultural institutions. In 1932 they purchased Brookgreen Gardens in South Carolina, and created an outdoor sculpture museum set among 10,000 bucolic acres of protected indigenous flora and fauna. In the sculpture park and museum, Huntington showed her work—mostly bronze pieces but also some sculpted figures from aluminum; she was one of the first American sculptors to use the lightweight metal. She also commissioned pieces by other sculptors, many of whom were unemployed during the Great

Depression. The Huntingtons founded 14 museums and funded four wildlife preserves.

Four years after a 1936 retrospective exhibition of 171 of her sculptures, sponsored by the American Academy of Arts and Letters, the Huntingtons moved to Stanerigg Farm, an estate in rural Connecticut. There Huntington could continue to sculpt large animal figures and equestrian statues, practice organic farming, raise Scottish deerhounds, ride (she was an expert horsewoman), protect her bird sanctuary, and invite the intelligentsia for Sunday tea.

A prolific and energetic artist, Huntington created figurative sculptures of nymphs and children, portrait busts, and intimate studies of domestic and wild animals, as well as her massive pieces. Over time she scaled down the decorative, over-life-size sculptures, like *Diana of the Chase* (1922), which had earned her a Saltus Gold Medal, and turned to smaller, more delicate garden statuary. Nonetheless, at 90 she completed *General Israel Putnam,* an homage to the Revolutionary War hero, the last of seven large heroic equestrian monuments. She never wavered from her realistic and anatomically accurate approach to sculpture and considerd modern art "a tasteless machine" and "an overwhelming flood of degenerate trash drowning sincere and conservative workers in all the arts."

Anna Hyatt Huntington, a popular and admired American animal sculptor and patron of the arts, died at Stanerigg on October 4, 1973, at age 97. Her works, especially her portrayals of animals, are represented in more than 200 museums worldwide, as well as in parks and gardens.

Further Reading

Evans, Cerinda W. *Anna Hyatt Huntington.* Newport News, Va.: Mariners Museum, 1965.

Mellon, Eleanor M. *Anna Hyatt Huntington.* American Sculptor Series 3. New York: W. W. Norton, 1947.

Proske, Beatrice Gilman. "Anna Hyatt Huntington." *Brookgreen Bulletin* (fall 1973): 1–15.

Rubinstein, Charlotte Streifer. *American Women Sculptors.* Boston, Mass.: G.K. Hall, 1990.

— C. K.

ITAMI, MICHI
(1938–) *Printmaker, Painter,
Digital Media Artist, Potter*

For Michi Itami, art and family history are, as she explains, "inextricably intertwined." Itami uses her art to "tell the story visually" of her Japanese-American background and familial experiences and to delineate her strongly held beliefs about the importance of multiculturalism.

Born in Los Angeles, California, on May 6, 1938, Michi Itami had a difficult start. During World War II, she and her family were sent to Manzanar, one of the largest internment camps for West Coast residents of Japanese ancestry. Itami's parents were *Kibei-Nisei*—born in the United States but raised in Japan. After a couple of terrifying years in the relocation camp, in order to get his family out of Manzanar, Itami's father volunteered for the U.S. Army. He taught Japanese at an army language school in Savage, Minnesota, which is where Michi spent her childhood. After being awarded the Legion of Merit, the highest noncombat medal, for his work on Japanese materials in Washington, D.C., he was appointed head interpreter of the Tokyo War Crimes Trials. In 1947, Itami's mother was among the first American dependents permitted to join their spouses in Japan, and Michi accompanied her. "My memories of Japan at that time have fueled much of my work," wrote Itami years later in *Voices of Color.*

Itami attended the University of California in Los Angeles, where she earned a bachelor's degree in English literature in 1959. She moved to New York City to study Japanese and English language and literature at Columbia University. Before returning to the West Coast, where she obtained a master of fine arts degree in ceramic design at the University of California, Berkeley, in 1971, Itami was an apprentice with ceramist Kimpei Nakumura in Japan.

Itami then turned from ceramic design to printmaking, which she taught for 12 years at the San Francisco Art Institute in California and at California State University in Hayward. Itami evolved from an abstract artist to a representational one as she saw the need to "have [her personal ethnic] history both enhance the multicultural dimensions of our society and serve as an agent for social change," according to art critic Phoebe Farris in *Women Artists of Color* (1999).

Itami has had numerous national and international shows in venues ranging from San Francisco and New York City to London, Kyoto, and Seoul. Her first individual exhibition in New York City took place at the A.I.R. Gallery (the first women artists' cooperative in America) in 1991; her most recent solo show was at the Atelier 221 Gallery in New Delhi, India, in 1999.

In 1989 Itami became involved with computers. One of her major works, *The Irony of Being American* (1994), a prizewinning computer-generated digital photo collage, reflects her willingness to experiment with new technology, while it also is a reference to her past. Itami's father had left her a "treasure trove of photographs" of him and his family, which were taken in Japan and America. She incorporated images from her father's photographs into her work through photo-etching processes. Computer-generated images, she explained in *Women Artists of Color,* enabled her to "enhance both the size and scope" of her work and "proved to be an expression not only of her father's history but of her own as well." Itami's collage photograph is comprised of three images of her father at varying stages of life, superiposed over a photograph taken by renowned photographer Ansel Adams of the relocation camp where her father had been sequestered. Furthermore, money to purchase the high-end computer used to create *The Irony of Being American* came in part from the reparation payment Itami received for having been interned in Manzanar. (The letter from President George H. W. Bush accompanying the reparation payment is placed next to the multimedia work.)

Among the awards and fellowships she received, Itami won printmaking grants from the National Endowment for the Arts (1981) and the New York Foundation for the Arts (1995). A committed social activist, Itami chaired the College Art Association's Committee on Cultural Diversity and served as the association's vice president. She is also active in several Asian groups, among then Godzilla: The Asian American Art Network.

Itami, who is divorced and has two daughters, an opera singer and a writer, lives with architect William B. Hess in Manhattan and Sag Harbor,

Photomontagist Michi Itami experiments with digital technology in her work.
(Photo: W. B. Hess)

New York. She is a professor of art at the City University of New York (CUNY), which Itami calls "perhaps the most culturally diverse university in the United States," and where she also directs the master of fine arts program. Her work is represented in distinguished permanent collections such as San Francisco's Legion of Honor Museum, the Brooklyn Museum in New York, and the National Museum of Modern Art in Kyoto, Japan. "All of us have a story to tell, and understanding and empathy are increased when we share our stories," Itami once wrote. She has chosen to tell her stories through her art.

Further Reading

Farris, Phoebe, ed. "Asian Pacific American Women Artists." In *Women Artists of Color: A Bio-Critical Sourcebook of 20th Century Artists in the Americas,* 388–394. Westport, Conn.: Greenwood Press, 1999.

Harrison, Helen A. "Some Luminous Surfaces and Two Asian Survey Shows," *New York Times,* Long Island edition, October 12, 1997.

Itami, Michi. "The Irony of Being American." In *Voices of Color: Art and Society in the Americas,* edited by Phoebe Farris-Dufrene, 20–28. Atlantic Highlands, N.J.: Humanities Press International, 1997.

Trenton, Patricia, ed. *Independent Spirits: Women Paintings of the American West.* Berkeley: University of California Press, 1995.

— C. K.

JOHNSON, ADELAIDE
(Sarah Adeline Johnson)
(1859–1955) *Sculptor*

Adelaide Johnson's claim to fame, *Memorial to the Pioneers of the Women's Suffrage Movement* (1921), is a marble sculpture, erected in the U.S. Capitol and composed of portrait busts of three American suffrage leaders. Johnson, who dedicated her life to memorializing in stone the early women's rights movement, believed that feminism was "the mightiest thing in the evolution of humanity."

The early feminist sculptor was born Sarah Adeline Johnson on September 26, 1859, in rural Plymouth, Illinois, where she played with stepsiblings from her parents' previous two marriages as well as with farm animals. Displaying an early interest in art, as a teenager Sarah lived with an older half brother so she could take classes at Missouri's St. Louis School of Design. In 1877, at age 18, she won the two top prizes at a state exhibition in which she competed against professional woodcarvers. A year later she changed her name to Adelaide—which in her view had more flair—and took off for Chicago. She supported herself by wood carving and interior decorating, but while at a concert at Chicago's Central Music Hall, she fell

down an elevator shaft and broke her hip. The mishap turned out to be a blessing in disguise: Johnson used the $15,000 insurance award to finance a trip to Europe to study art.

After taking painting courses in Germany, Johnson settled in Rome, Italy, in 1884. There she studied sculpture for 11 years with Giulio Monteverde, the highly accomplished Italian sculptor. Although she often returned to America, she maintained a studio in Rome for 25 years. At various points in her life, she also rented studios in New York City, Chicago, London, and Carrara, Italy, where she reveled in the city's elegant marble. In 1886 Johnson started work on a marble bust of Susan B. Anthony, one of her heroines. The sculpture was featured at the 1887 Woman Suffrage Convention in Washington, D.C., although she continued to modify it until she was pleased with the likeness. (A believer in the occult, Johnson claimed that while she was in Carrara, the model of Anthony shattered and then regrouped itself.)

Anthony suggested to Johnson that she sculpt portrait busts of two other important suffragists, Elizabeth Cady Stanton and Lucretia Mott. Johnson agreed, and in 1893, in the Woman's Building at the World's Columbian Exposition in Chicago, the three portrait busts, plus one of physician

Caroline B. Winslow, were prominently displayed. Three years later, Johnson married Alexander Frederick Jenkins, an English businessman. The ceremony was most unusual for that time: It was conducted by a female minister in Johnson's studio, and Johnson was surrounded by her "bridesmaids," the busts of Susan B. Anthony and Elizabeth Cady Stanton. Because Johnson wanted to appear younger than her 25-year-old husband, the marriage certificate stated that she was 24, instead of 36. Jenkins, who like his bride was an ardent vegetarian and occultist, took his wife's last name as "the tribute love pays to genius." (Twelve years later the couple went through a bitter divorce.)

Johnson's fervent dream was to build a museum to chronicle the achievements of the women's movement. When she was unable to raise the necessary funds, she offered her home studio in Washington, D.C., replete with her own sculptures, as the venue for a feminist museum. When no one seemed willing to back that idea, she asked the National American Woman Suffrage Association (NAWSA) to pay the expenses for a group monument that she would build to honor the suffrage movement. But in 1904, Johnson had a disagreement with Susan B. Anthony, president of the NAWSA, about where the historic sculpture should be placed: Anthony felt it belonged in the Library of Congress, while Johnson wanted it erected in the U.S. Capitol. Eventually, Alva Belmont and the National Woman's Party, a rival organization of the NAWSA, financed the project.

Johnson's 14,000-pound white Carrara marble masterwork, *Memorial to the Pioneers of the Women's Suffrage Movement,* featured striking portrait busts of Anthony, Stanton, and Mott. It was unveiled on February 15, 1921—the 101st anniversary of Susan B. Anthony's birth. In 1936, Johnson's portrait of Anthony was used as the model for a postage stamp commemorating the 16th anniversary of suffrage for women. Meanwhile, Johnson increasingly faced financial difficulties. Proud and stubborn, she refused to sell her sculptures for anything less than what she felt they were worth. In 1939, when she was about to be

Sculptor and early feminist Adelaide Johnson
in her studio in 1939
(AP/Wide World Photos)

evicted from her home in Washington, D.C., the eccentric artist called a press conference and invited reporters to watch her mutilate some of her work. Congressman Sol Bloom of New York, moved by her plight, came to Johnson's rescue and blocked her eviction. The publicity stunt had worked, and Johnson was able to keep her home until 1947, when she was forced to give it up and live with friends. She appeared on television quiz programs with the intention of using the prize money to help repurchase the house, but she did not win enough to keep her home. Looking once again for sympathy, she reversed her earlier statement about her age and declared herself 12 years older than she really was.

Adelaide Johnson died in Washington, D.C, on November 10, 1955, at the impressive age of 96 (not 108, as reported in newspapers). Her works are housed in permanent collections in prominent museums such as the Metropolitan Museum of Art in New York and the Smithsonian Institution in Washington, D.C. Although she never lived to see her dream come true—a museum dedicated to feminist history—her sculpture in the Capitol remains the only national monument to the pioneers of America's suffrage movement.

Further Reading

A Woman a Week Archives. "Adelaide Johnson." Radcliffe College. Available online. URL: http://members.aol.com/taylorteri/johnson.htm. Downloaded on January 16, 2001.

Bailey, Brooke. "Adelaide Johnson." In *The Remarkable Lives of 100 Women Artists,* 96–97. Holbrook, Mass.: Bob Adams, 1994.

Mayo, Edith. "Adelaide Johnson." In *Notable American Women.* Cambridge, Mass.: Belknap Press of Harvard University Press, 1971.

Rubinstein, Charlotte Streifer. *American Women Sculptors.* Boston: G.K. Hall, 1990.

— C. K.

JOHNSTON, HENRIETTA DEERING
(1670–ca. 1728)   *Pastellist, Portraitist*

There is little information about the life of colonial artist Henrietta Johnston, but what is available is enough to credit her with two "firsts" in the history of American art: Johnston probably was the first professional American woman artist and, according to critic Homer Eaton Keyes, "the first American artist of either sex to work in pastel."

Henrietta Deering was born in Ireland, most likely in 1670. She was married to Reverend Gideon Johnston, a Church of England minister, in Dublin, Ireland, on April 11, 1705. Reverend Johnston had two sons and two daughters by a previous marriage and a pile of debts that would keep the family in perpetually dire monetary straits. It was the reverend's financial crisis that in 1707 motivated him to try to improve his fortunes by taking the post of rector of St. Philip's Church in Charles Town (today, Charleston), South Car-

olina, at that time part of Great Britain's colonies in distant North America. That move, it turned out, did nothing to improve the family's finances; instead, it ruined Reverend Johnston's health and left his wife with the multiple burdens of nursing her husband and helping support the family in addition to performing domestic chores.

Out of necessity, Henrietta Johnston turned to portraiture to earn money. She ended up drawing portraits of many of Charles Town's prominent citizens. She did not have professional training, although according to art historian Anna Wells Rutledge, Johnston may have been a pupil of Simon Digby, the bishop of Elphin in Ireland, who was an amateur portraitist, and she may have studied with Edward Lutterell, a painter in London and Dublin. In any event, Johnston did her work in pastels, a relatively new technique developed by her European contemporary, the Italian painter Rosalba Carriera (1675–1757). According to Reverend Johnston, Henrietta's income was vital to the family's survival. He wrote to a superior in England in 1790 that without his wife's contribution, "I shou'd not have been able to live."

Art historian and Johnston biographer Margaret Simons Middleton has observed that Johnston's technique was "not perfect," but that she was able to achieve "good likenesses" in which "each individual stands out—himself or herself, and not other." At the same time, "certain details of drawing eluded her," among them "her inability to draw arms and legs well." Anna Wells Rutledge, whose evaluation of Johnston's work generally parallels Middleton's, called Johnston's likenesses "uncompromising and direct." Her skills were certainly in demand with Charles Town's elite, as she executed more than 40 portraits of them on 9-by-12-inch sheets of paper and then placed the paintings in wooden frames that she signed. Most were completed between 1707 and 1720, but several portraits done in New York City as late as 1725 are attributed to Johnston.

Johnston's life in Charles Town, which was little more than a frontier settlement frequently under threat from Indians or from French and Spanish privateers, was extremely difficult. Besides her duties as a stepmother, housewife, and minister's wife, she suffered the loss of her own son, who died in early childhood. Johnston returned to England briefly during 1711–12, apparently for health reasons and to represent her husband's interests to church officials. She also used that opportunity to replenish her stock of art supplies, notably pastels, which were unavailable in the British colonies.

In 1716 Johnston's husband drowned in a boating accident in Charles Town harbor, and she was left on her own. There is little record of her subsequent life, other than the surviving portraits in New York that are dated 1725 and attributed to her. It remains uncertain when she died, but she was buried in Charles Town, according to the register of St. Philip's Church, on "March 7, 1728/9." Most of Johnston's portraits are in private collections. Several, however, are in museums, including the Gibbs Museum of Art in Charleston, Boston's Museum of Fine Arts, and New York's Metropolitan Museum of Art. Henrietta Johnston was a pioneer and possibly America's first female professional artist who, as Middleton observes, "brought a touch of beauty to the barren [North American] wilderness of the early 1700s."

Further Reading

Middleton, Margaret Simons. *Henrietta Johnston of Charles Town, South Carolina: America's First Pastellist.* Columbia: University of South Carolina Press, 1966.

Rutledge, Anna Wells. "Henrietta Johnston." In *Notable American Women, 1607–1950,* edited by Edward T. James, 281–282. Cambridge, Mass: Belknap Press of Harvard University Press, 1971.

Turner, Janet, editor. "Henrietta Johnston." In *The Dictionary of American Art,* 626. New York: Macmillan, 1996.

— C. K.

K

KÄSEBIER, GERTRUDE STANTON
(1852–1934) *Photographer*

Gertrude Käsebier, who did not begin her professional career until she was 45 years old, was described by the venerated photographer Alfred Stieglitz as "beyond dispute, the leading portrait photographer in the country." Käsebier was a popular, prominent photographer whose body of work and artistry reflected the impressionistic, painterly style that flourished at the turn of the 20th century.

Born in Des Moines, Iowa, on May 18, 1852, Gertrude Stanton grew up in Leadville, Colorado, a frontier mining town. After her father died, four-year-old Gertrude and her mother moved to Brooklyn, New York, and after attending Moravian Seminary for Girls in Bethlehem, Pennsylvania, she helped her mother run a boardinghouse in Brooklyn. In 1874 she married Eduard Käsebier, a prosperous shellac importer from Germany who had been a tenant in the boardinghouse. The couple lived in suburban New Jersey and had three children. Käsebier spent her time keeping house and taking care of her family until her children were teenagers. Then she applied to Cooper Union, a leading art school in New York. Her application was rejected, but she remained determined to become an artist.

In 1888, having convinced her husband to move back to Brooklyn, 36-year-old Käsebier enrolled at the Pratt Institute to study portrait painting. She was only moderately successful, and she recognized that painting was not the right medium for her, although her formal training in painting would greatly influence her photography. In 1892 Käsebier won a $50 prize in *The Monthly Illustrator* for a photography contest, and a year later, while chaperoning a group of art students to France, she picked up a camera and discovered her true vocation as a photographer. Käsebier did not have access to a darkroom, so she worked late at night, carrying the wet plates to a stream to be washed and developing the pictures in the dead of night. She then apprenticed herself to a German scientist in order to learn the technical basis of photography and, upon returning to Brooklyn, worked under Samuel H. Lifshey, a portrait photographer, to learn the business of running a studio.

Käsebier's first solo exhibition was in 1896 at the Boston Camera Club. A year later she opened her own portrait studio in New York City, followed in 1899 by a second studio in Newport, Rhode

Photographer Gertrude Käsebier was
a prominent pictorialist.
(Library of Congress)

Island. In only a few years—and in spite of her husband's vocal disapproval of his wife having a time-consuming career—45-year-old Kasebier had become a commercial and critical success as a portrait photographer. In 1897, the Pratt Institute exhibited 150 of Käsebier's photographs. The following year, 10 of her photographs were shown at the prestigious Philadelphia Photographic Salon, where her carefully composed, luminous pictures were praised by critics and viewers. According to art historian Naomi Rosenblum, Käsebier credited her art education as the most important factor in her ability to determine pose, lighting, and expression.

Käsebier was an early and ardent advocate of pictorialism, a movement that emphasized photography as having aesthetic merit and not merely a medium for documentation. (The pictorialists began in England in the 1890s and viewed photography as being equal to the other visual arts.) As a pictorialist, Käsebier used a painterly, artistic approach to photography. Her pictures were bathed in soft light and the details were often fuzzy and blurred, purposely evoking paintings by the old masters. She was one of only two women elected to The Linked Ring, a society that began in England and promoted pictorial photography as a form of fine art. In 1899, one of her best-known platinum prints, *The Manger,* which depicted a symbolic Madonna in a stable holding a swaddled infant, commanded $100, at that time the highest price ever fetched for a photograph. Also in 1899, Käsebier served, along with her friend and colleague Frances Benjamin Johnston, as juror for the Philadelphia Photographic Salon. That same year, Alfred Stieglitz, who enthusiastically promoted her work, gave Käsebier a solo exhibition at the Camera Club of New York. British pictorial photographer F. Holland Day invited her to show her photos in the *New American Photography* exhibition in London in 1900 and in Paris in 1901.

Käsebier was known for her evocative, gently nostalgic, impressionistic mother-and-daughter photographs, such as *Mother and Child* (ca. 1900). "A woman never reaches her fullest development until she's a mother," Käsebier once said. In 1902, along with Alfred Stieglitz, Edward Steichen, and two other influential photographers, Käsebier helped found the Photo-Secession, whose goal was to advance pictorial photography and elevate the medium to fine art. In 1903, Stieglitz devoted the first issue of his magazine *Camera Work* to Käsebier's photographs. Her work was also reproduced in *American Pictorial Photography* magazine and popular journals such as *McClure's.*

In 1910 the *International Exhibition of Pictorial Photography* exhibited 22 of Käsebier's photographs at the Albright-Knox Art Gallery in Buffalo, New York, which purchased *The Manger* for its permanent collection. Käsebier, a radical who in 1915 called herself the "dean of the 'new' photography," was also a highly successful portrait photographer and businesswoman. Mark

Twain, Booker T. Washington, and Rose O'Neill, inventor of the Kewpie doll, were among the bevy of notables who sat for her and paid her top dollar. Prolific and ambitious, in 1907 she took a series of pictures of sculptor Auguste Rodin in his Paris studio. She also did a memorable series of photographs of Sioux Indians who worked in Buffalo Bill's Wild West Show, as well as compassionately rendered individual portraits of Native Americans.

In 1912 Käsebier resigned from the Photo-Secession and broke with her mentor, Alfred Stieglitz, who had abandoned pictorialism because he increasingly favored harder-edged, less intimate, more realistic prints. Four years later Käsebier and photographer Clarence H. White cofounded the Pictorial Photographers of America, a rival organization. She also became cofounder of the Women's Federation of the Photographers' Association of America. Käsebier's pictorial style of photography was out of favor by the early 1920s, but exhibitions of her work at the Museum of Modern Art in New York (1992) and at the Philadelphia Museum of Art (1993) helped rejuvenate her reputation. "Whether of Indians or society belles, children or fellow artists, her portraits are all stunningly organized and emotionally complex," wrote *Mirabella's* art critic in 1992.

Gertrude Käsebier died in New York on October 12, 1934, at age 82. She had achieved her self-stated goal: "to make likenesses that are biographies, to put into each photograph . . . temperament, soul, humanity." "Käsebier is one of the leading pictorial photographers of her generation and certainly among the most prominent," wrote William I. Homer, a professor of art history at the University of Delaware.

Further Reading

Hail, Michael W. "The Gertrude Käsebier Collection," Messenger. Available online. URL: http://www.udel.edu/PR/Messenger/94/1/42.htm. Downloaded on June 6, 2001.

Homer, William I. *A Pictorial Heritage: The Photographs of Gertrude Käsebier.* Wilmington: Delaware Art Museum, 1979.

Michaels, Barbara L. *Gertrude Käsebier: The Photographer and Her Photographs.* New York: Harry N. Abrams, 1992.

Rosenblum, Naomi. *A History of Women Photographers.* New York: Abbeville Press, 1994.

— C. K.

KATZEN, LILA PELL
(1932–1998) *Sculptor, Painter, Mixed Media Artist*

Lila Katzen's large-scale sculptures are characterized by grace, fluidity, and originality. She experimented with a variety of innovative materials to create floating forms in space, including large environments constructed out of bent steel and floors illuminated by undulating pools of iridescent liquids in vinyl pouches.

Probably born on December 30, 1932 (the exact year of her birth is disputed), in Brooklyn, New York, Lila Pell knew that she was going to be an artist, "even when I was in kindergarten." Energetic, red-headed, tall, strong-willed Lila was encouraged to dabble with different art forms, from painting fake wood to working with gilt, by her immigrant grandfather, who had been a court painter in St. Petersburg, Russia. Lila's father died when she was three and a half, and when her widowed mother and her grandfather could not make ends meet, Lila and her two siblings were placed in an orphanage. However, four years later, the family was reunited in Brooklyn. Lila attended Washington Irving, an all-girls high school known for its excellent arts programs; after school she worked for a commercial artist doing drawings and layout design.

In 1948 Pell's application was accepted by Cooper Union School of Art in New York City, where she took night courses so she could work during the day. After six months, her talent was so apparent that she won scholarships enabling her to attend the renowned art school full time. She graduated with a degree in painting and went on to study at the Art Students League, and later with influential abstract painter and teacher Hans Hofmann, at his school in Provincetown, Massachusetts.

At age 19, Pell married Philip Katzen, whom she described as a "very helpful, interested, and stimulating person who encouraged me at all times." Even after the couple had two children, said Katzen, her work was "the focal point of the entire household." The Katzens moved to Baltimore, Maryland, although they maintained a residence in New York City so that the Lila would not, as she put it, "die of aesthetic starvation." While in Baltimore, she befriended Morris Louis, who like her was one of the first expressionistic artists to drip and pour paint. She was also influenced by the gestural canvases of Jackson Pollock. Yet, noted Leslie Ahlander in *Arts Magazine,* "Katzen still retained linear elements and the clean form that have continued to distinguish her work." She rejected the prevalent minimalist style in favor of more rhythmic, continuous lines.

In 1955 Katzen had her first solo show of paintings, mostly canvases with stained surfaces, at the Baltimore Museum of Art. In her quest for a medium that would allow her more freedom—and encouraged by sculptor George Segal, who in 1960 told her she "wanted to be three-dimensional"—Katzen turned to sculpture. She worked with an array of materials including acrylic sheets and Cor-Ten steel. She was fascinated by the effects of fluorescent paint on sheets of plastic that were lit from below, and she discovered that by using black light, the white clothes worn by viewers would appear to glow and thereby include the spectator in the work itself. "Black light will not flood but will hover close to the housing which contains it," she observed.

Katzen received a grant from the Architectural League of New York in 1967. A year later the league exhibited *Light Floors,* a critically successful sculptural installation covering three rooms, with illuminated, multicolored plastic floors. According to Cindy Nemser in *Art Talk,* museum-goers who experienced *Light Floors* felt "enveloped in a beautifully transparent chrysalis of light." A risk taker who nonetheless shunned trendiness, in the late 1960s Katzen stood in the forefront of art. Nemser

described her as "a creator of contained forms at the height of abstract expressionism with its emphasis on the explosive brushstroke, an explorer of shallow space when spatial depth was all the vogue. It was only in the late sixties that the art world and Katzen actually reached an area of mutual understanding."

In 1968 Katzen had a solo exhibition at the Smithsonian Institution in Washington, D.C., and the next year she participated in a group show—one of more than 35 at which her works appeared—at the Museum of Contemporary Crafts in New York City. She went on to create a lunar-inspired work entitled *Universe as Environment* (1969) at New York University's student center; the 65-foot octagonal *Liquid Tunnel* (1970) at the Smithsonian Institution; large-scale commissioned sculptures at Fordham University's campus and Lincoln Center (both in New York); and *Antecedent,* a rolled steel installation placed in front of the new East Wing of the National Gallery of Art in Washington, D.C.

By 1970 Katzen had turned to manipulating steel and welding the forms into large, abstract geometric pieces. Some of these were shown in *Liquid and Solid,* a solo exhibition at the Max Hutchinson Gallery in New York that featured the combined solidity of metal and the liquidity of plastic. She also built sited outdoor sculptures such as *X Notion Like an H* (1978), which was made from rolled, weathered steel and stands at the DeCordova Museum and Sculpture Park in Lincoln, Massachusetts. Katzen had steel-fabricating equipment in her studio in the Soho area of New York City (she commuted from Baltimore), but she relied on industrial rolling mills for her major pieces. Her works were financed through public commissions, grants, and private donations. In 1980 Katzen explained why she chose to create huge, abstract, welded steel works: "My sculpture comes into being with the use of steel and various metals. I want to be able to suspend steel, an intractable material, to swing it into the air, to make it dance." The stainless steel loops of *Oracle* (1974) were literally used for swinging by children who considered the sculpture a jungle gym. "There is a tremendous need for sculpture to be opened to people," Katzen said in an interview in *Art Talk.* "It should enliven and enrich."

Katzen had about 70 one-person shows between 1954 and 1992, in venues ranging from the Alex Rosenberg Gallery in New York City to the Rose Art Museum at Brandeis University in Waltham, Massachusetts. In 1988 she was the American representative at the World Expo in Brisbane, Australia. For many years she taught mixed media (two- and three-dimensional forms) at the Maryland College Institute of Art in Baltimore. As a painter and a sculptor, Katzen concentrated on flowing forms in space, always focusing on the relationship of art to human environments. She wanted, she wrote in an artist's statement, to "use oppositions to create a magical experience . . . a fusion of different textures, materials and conceptions in a scale informed by historical dreams and musing."

Lila Katzen's works can be found in a number of permanent collections, including those of the Baltimore Museum of Art, the Wadsworth Athenaeum in Hartford, Connecticut, and the National Gallery of Art in Washington, D.C. Katzen died on September 20, 1998, at age 66, of liver cancer. She once described her two children as her "source of invention and creativity," adding that her works were like her children. "They are my links to the past. They are what I am."

Further Reading

Ahlander, Leslie Judd. "Lila Katzen: Free Flowing Sculpture." *Arts Magazine* 55:7 (July 1981): 158–159.

Chairmonte, Paula. *Women Artists in the United States,* 679. Boston, Mass.: G.K. Hall, 1990.

Munro, Eleanor. *Originals: American Women Artists.* New York: Simon and Schuster, 1979.

Nemser, Cindy. *Art Talk: Conversations with 15 Women Artists.* New York: HarperCollins, 1995.

Stevens, Elisabeth. "Lila Katzen." *Arts Magazine* 52:10 (June 1978): 23.

— C. K.

KENT, CORITA (Frances Kent, Sister Corita)
(1918–1986)   *Printmaker, Graphic Artist*

A nun who became popular in the 1960s for her vividly rendered silk-screen posters featuring verbal messages, Corita Kent was also a peace activist during the Vietnam War era. Accused of being a "guerilla with a paint brush," she saw herself as relating to "gentle people who are afraid of art." According to the *New York Times,* Sister Corita recognized "the eternal in the ordinary and celebrated it with bursts of brilliant colors and bold abstract shapes."

A native of Fort Dodge, Iowa, Frances Kent (known as Sister Corita or Corita) was born on November 20, 1918, into a large working-class family. She grew up in Los Angeles, California, where she was educated in schools run by the Sisters of the Immaculate Heart Order, a liberal Catholic community of teaching nuns. The sisters encouraged her to pursue art, and she enrolled in drawing and still life classes at Otis Art Institute in Los Angeles. At the age of 18 she entered the convent, graduating from Immaculate Heart College with a bachelor of arts degree in 1941.

Sister Corita taught art to Native Americans at an elementary school in British Columbia, Canada. After five years, she returned to Los Angeles and joined the faculty at Immaculate Heart College. She also studied art history and earned a master's degree in 1951 at the University of Southern California. Around that same time, she found an old screen lying around the university's art department and was shown how to clean and use it by the wife of a Mexican silk-screening muralist. Sister Corita's early serigraphs, such as *The Lord Is with Me* and *As a Cedar of Lebanon,* were semiabstract with figurative religious subjects. *Christ Calming the Storm* (1956) featured a 126-word message scripted in contemporary liturgical Roman letters. During the mid-1950s, she also designed book and record jackets for major American corporations, using representational figures such as doves or sometimes veering off into more

Sister Corita signing her colorful lithographs
at her home in Boston
(AP/Wide World Photos)

abstract patterns as a background for words. "I started early putting words into my prints," Sister Corita said during a 1967 interview, "and the words just got bigger and bigger."

In the early 1960s, she began making posters that were brighter and more colorful, with lively and original designs that had stronger social and religious messages. She silk-screened quotes from a variety of sources, including St. Bernard, Albert Schweitzer, the Beatles, and Ugo Betti. A common theme running through her work was "peace and love." At the 1964–65 World's Fair, Sister Corita created a 50-foot mural entitled *Beatitude Wall* for the Vatican Pavilion. A year later she designed an exhibit for the lobby of IBM headquarters in New York City. She believed that there was nothing wrong with being a commercial artist or working for the mass media and using its vernacular. However, "on closer inspection," pointed out Doug

Harvey in the *L.A. Weekly,* "many of the large blocks of Day-Glo colors are filled with scrawled quotations reflecting on such weighty issues as death, identity and social responsibility."

In 1967 the Morris Gallery in New York hosted a major exhibition of 100 of Sister Corita's serigraphs. By then she was actively supporting the anti–Vietnam War peace movement. "I'm not brave enough not to pay my income tax and risk going to jail," she said. "But I can say rather freely what I want to say in my art." Sister Corita filled her serigraphs with graffiti-like inspirational homilies such as "Handle with Care" and "No Man is a Watermelon." She was influenced by a friend, artist Ben Shahn, who used words in his paintings to make social and political statements. Shahn called Corita a "joyous revolutionary."

A longtime teacher at Immaculate Heart College in Los Angeles, she often produced her silkscreen prints while on vacation or at night after she had finished correcting papers. Finding inspiration from various sources ranging from movies to music, she encouraged her students to find beauty in contemporary "cityscapes." Commenting on her students, she said: "[They] are the greatest thing I've done." For Sister Corita, who is considered one of the most popular American graphic artists of the 1960s and 1970s, art and teaching brought together the religious and secular components of her life. She told a reporter for *Newsweek:* "I get a huge response from people of different religions, and from people of no religion."

After 32 years in the order of the Sisters of the Immaculate Heart of Mary, with visitors flocking in droves to see her, Corita became exhausted and overwhelmed by her celebrity. She resigned from the order and moved to Boston in 1968, where she continued her work as a graphic artist. Chris Braithwaite, an art critic for *Newsweek,* described Corita's "buoyant" serigraphs as "bits of newspaper prints, a grocery list, a philosopher's maxim, or an ad for United Air Lines . . . flitting gaily across abstract patches of orange, red, and yellow like charged-up billboards." He went on to categorize her work as "miniature Gospel billboards ablaze with bright Dayglo colors in which punchy quotes from Beckett, Camus, Macaulay, the Scriptures and fragments of Madison Avenue ad slogans gracefully collide with bouncy abstract designs."

In 1980 the DeCordova Museum in Lincoln, Massachusetts, held a major 30-year retrospective of Sister Corita's prints. Distinguished art institutions, including Boston's Museum of Fine Arts, the Victoria and Albert Museum in London, the Metropolitan Museum of Art in New York, and the Art Institute of Chicago, include her prints in their permanent collections. Sister Corita died of cancer at her home in Boston on September 18, 1986, at age 67. A petite, blue-eyed devout Catholic, she was often described as a "dynamic, extraordinary" woman who lived life fully. The distinguished theologian Harvey Cox wrote that Sister Corita, having produced more than 700 brilliantly colored, widely distributed silk-screen, pop art prints based on advertising design and progressive politics, had stood for a "festive involvement with the world."

Further Reading

Braithwaite, Chris. "The Painterly Nun," *Newsweek,* December 4, 1967, 88–89.

Fiske, Edward B. "Sister Corita," *New York Times,* November 8, 1968, 35.

Harvey, Doug. "Nunconformist: Sister Corita Kent's Pop Subversions," *L.A. Weekly,* February 18–24, 2000.

Kent, Corita. *Sister Corita.* Color print and poster reproductions, with essays by Corita Kent, Harvey Cox, and Samuel A. Einstein. Philadelphia: Pilgrim Press, 1968.

— C. K.

KEYSER, LOUISA (Dabuda, Dat So La Lee)
(ca. 1850–1925)   *Basketmaker*

Widely considered the greatest American Indian basketmaker, Louisa Keyser was born in about 1850 in a Washoe Indian village near the town of Sheridan, Nevada. As a child, she was known by the name Dabuda. By the mid-19th century, the Washoe had lost much of their traditional territory, so most tribe members had to take low-paying menial jobs to survive. By 1871, Dabuda was working as a laundress and cook for white families in California and Nevada. She married a Washoe man named Assu and had two children, but all three soon died. In 1888, she took a second husband, Charley Keyser, a part-Washoe craftsman. After their marriage, she adopted the name Louisa Keyser.

Like most Washoe women, Keyser had learned the basic techniques of basketmaking as a child. Knowing that white tourists were interested in buying Indian craftwork, she showed samples of her basketry to Abe Cohn, the owner of The Emporium, a large clothing shop in Carson City, Nevada. His wife Amy recognized Keyser's superior craftsmanship and urged her husband to sell her work in his store. Soon, Keyser was working full time for the Cohns. In exchange for her baskets, they paid for her food and medical care and eventually built a small house for the Keysers next to their own.

Keyser's arrangement with the Cohns gave her an advantage over other Washoe basketmakers who produced baskets for sale. In order to make a living, they had to sacrifice quality for quantity, since few tourists could distinguish a well-crafted Indian basket from a poorly made one. Keyser, on the other hand, was encouraged by the Cohns to do her best possible work, no matter how long it took. At the Cohns' store, Keyser also had the opportunity to study the basketry of other Indian artisans whose work they sold. She was particularly influenced by the baskets of the Pomo Indians of California. Their ornate, decorative works moved Keyser to see that baskets could be more than utilitarian objects.

With secure patronage, Keyser had the freedom to experiment with new shapes and designs. She made several traditional Washoe basket types, but her favorite style, the *degikup,* was of her own invention. Her *degikups* were small, spherical baskets made from cream-colored willow twigs, blackened fern roots, and red birch bark. Most of Keyser's baskets were decorated with geometric red-and-black shapes, appearing in even intervals over the vessel's light tan surface. The work was difficult and painstaking. Keyser often spent months on a single basket. Late in career, her large, intricate *degikups* took as long as a year to complete.

Washoe Indian basket maker Louisa Keyser displays
her wares, circa 1910.
(Nevada Historical Society)

Keyser soon became well known among Indian art collectors and enthusiasts, both because of her superior artistry and the Cohns' aggressive efforts to promote her work. The Cohns distributed photographs of Keyser surrounded by her baskets and circulated stories about the artist and her people hatched from Amy Cohn's imagination. The Cohns claimed the Washoes considered Keyser a princess and said the designs on her baskets were symbols with secret religious meanings. The Cohns rechristened Keyser "Dat So La Lee," an unflattering Washoe nickname that meant "big hips." To further market her work, the Cohns had Keyser weave her baskets outside their store in the summer, allowing to tourists to stop and gawk.

Adding to this humiliation, Abe Cohn publicly often suggested that Keyser was childish, vain, and dim-witted, accommodating then-common stereotypes of both women and Indians.

Nonetheless, the Cohns always treated Keyser's work with respect. Recognizing that many of her baskets were masterpieces, they asked for prices comparable to those charged for works of fine art. As a result, some of her baskets sold for phenomenal sums even during her lifetime. In 1930, five years after her death, one basket was purchased for $10,000. Recently, her best works have garnered prices of about $250,000. Neither Keyser nor her heirs ever received any of this money, since her arrangement with the Cohns made them the sole beneficiaries of the sale of her work. However, their encouragement and promotion of Keyser were instrumental in building the reputation she holds today as perhaps the most famous basket weaver in the world.

Further Reading

Cohodas, Marvin. "Dat So La Lee's Basketry Designs." *American Indian Art* 1 (autumn 1976): 22–31.
———. "Washoe Innovators and Their Patrons." In *The Arts of the Native North American Indian,* edited by Edwin L. Wade, 203–220. New York: Hudson Hills Press, 1986.
Hirschfelder, Arlene. "Dat So La Lee: Washo Basket Maker." In *Artists and Craftspeople,* 1–8. New York: Facts On File, 1994.
Wilkins Sally. "Dat-So-La-Lee," University of Nevada, Reno. Available online. URL: http://www.unr.edu/wrc/nwhp/biograph/datsola.htm. Updated on January 30, 2001.
— L. S.

KLUMPKE, ANNA ELIZABETH
(1856–1942) *Painter*

Best known for her portraits and genre paintings, Anna Klumpke was the first woman to win the prestigious Pennsylvania Academy of Fine Arts Temple Gold Medal. A resident of France for more than 40 years, she also was the protégée, companion, and biographer of French artist Rosa Bonheur, who is considered one of the outstanding female painters of the 19th century.

Anna Elizabeth Klumpke was born in San Francisco, California, on October 26, 1856, the eldest of seven children of strong-willed parents. John Gerald Klumpke made his way to California from Germany after the discovery of gold, intending to seek his fortune while providing shoes and boots (he was a cobbler by profession) to California gold miners. Dorothea Toll Klumpke, also of German descent, set out in her mid-teens on an extremely difficult journey, alone and mostly by sea, from the East Coast to California—a trip whose midpoint was a trek across the Isthmus of Panama by mule—to visit her sister. All of the Klumpke daughters seem to have inherited a measure of their parents' pioneering spirit, along with considerable other talents. Anna became a noted painter, while her four sisters achieved success as a neurologist, astronomer, violinist/composer, and pianist.

Two events had a major impact on Anna's youth. First, a fall from a chair at the age of two seriously injured her knee, leaving her unable to walk unassisted. A trip to Europe with her mother and three sisters at the age of nine for an almost two-year-long treatment by European orthopedic specialists did not help, although Anna eventually was able to discard her crutches and braces and walk with only the aid of a cane. (Not until their return from Europe did Anna and her younger sisters begin learning English in school, and German remained their primary language until they were adults.) Second, in April 1872, when Anna was 15, her parents divorced. When Dorothea Klumpke left her husband, who was by then a real estate tycoon, she took her children to Germany where, she believed, the education was superior to what was available in America. Recognizing her daughters' talents and their need for self-sufficiency, several years later she moved her family to Paris because of the educational and career opportunities available there for women. Anna herself made this point in a letter to her father in 1881 asking for financial help; despite not having heard from

his children or ex-wife in almost a decade, Gerald Klumpke acceded to his eldest daughter's request.

Klumpke began her formal art training in 1880 in Paris at the Académie Julian, one of the few art schools offering professional art training to women, where she studied with Tony Robert-Fleury and Jules LeFebvre. She made copies of the old masters at the Louvre and won the grand prize for outstanding student of the year at the academy. By 1882 she was exhibiting her work at the prestigious Paris Salon, and in 1885 she won an honorable mention at the salon for a portrait of her sister Augusta. She earned her most important award in 1889 when she won the coveted Pennsylvania Academy of Fine Arts Temple Gold Medal for her genre painting *In the Wash House* (1888), which depicts the camaraderie of a group of French women washing clothes in a communal laundry. That year Klumpke also fulfilled a childhood dream when she met Rosa Bonheur at her home. Bonheur, known for her paintings of animals, had long been her role model.

Klumpke returned to the United States, where she set up a studio in Boston and painted for the next nine years. In 1898 she returned to France to paint her best-known and most critically acclaimed portrait, *Rosa Bonheur* (1898), which she donated to New York's Metropolitan Museum of Art in 1922 to commemorate the 100th anniversary of Bonheur's birth. At Bonheur's request, Klumpke lived with the elderly French artist during the last year of her life and inherited Bonheur's studio-estate in Fontainebleau at her death. As the sole legatee, Klumpke lived there for the next 30 years and published a biography of Bonheur in 1908. She returned to San Francisco in 1934 and published her own autobiography, *Memoirs of an Artist,* in 1940.

Klumpke was honored several times during her lifetime, including being named a chevalier of France's Legion of Honor in 1924 and an officer in 1936. (The Klumpke sisters collectively received five medals from the Legion of Honor: Anna and her neurologist sister, Augusta, each won two, while Dorothea, the astronomer, received one.) Klumpke's paintings are in the permanent collections of New York's Metropolitan Museum of Art, the National Portrait Gallery of the Smithsonian Institution in Washington, D.C., the Pennsylvania Academy of Fine Arts, and other distinguished collections.

Anna Klumpke died in San Francisco, California, in 1942. In 1945 her ashes were buried in Paris alongside the remains of her venerated friend, Rosa Bonheur.

Further Reading

"Anna Elizabeth Klumpke (1856–1942)," Comenos Fine Arts. Available online. URL: http://www.comenos/finearts.com/available/american/Klumpke_bio.htm. Downloaded on July 26, 2001.

Dwyer, Britta C. *Anna Klumpke: A Turn-of-the-Century Painter and Her World.* Boston: Northeastern University Press, 1999.

Fink, Lois Marie. *American Art at the Nineteenth-Century Paris Salons.* Washington, D.C.: Smithsonian Institution Press, and New York: Cambridge University Press, 1990.

Klumpke, Anna Elizabeth. *Memoirs of an Artist,* edited by Lillian Whiting. Boston: Wright and Potter Printing, 1940.

Tufts, Eleanor. *American Women Artists, 1830–1930.* Washington, D.C.: National Museum of Women in the Arts, 1987.

— L. S.

KRASNER, LEE (Lenore Krasner)
(1908–1984)   *Painter, Collagist, Graphic Artist*

A first-generation New York school artist who helped found abstract expressionism, Lee Krasner was a "fabulous draftsman who had an incredible color sense," according to art critic and historian Barbara Rose. Although much of her 50-year career was eclipsed by that of her famous husband, abstract painter Jackson Pollock, since the 1970s Krasner has been recognized as a highly accomplished, versatile, and masterful artist.

Lenore Krasner (known as Lee) was born on October 27, 1908, in Brooklyn, New York, nine months after her family moved from a rural village in Odessa, Russia. She and her five siblings grew up speaking Yiddish, English, and Russian in an impoverished household headed by her Orthodox Jewish parents, who ran a small grocery store. By the time she was 13, Lee was earning her own money. "Everyone had to work," she said in *Originals: American Women Artists.* She also recalled that although she majored in art at Manhattan's Washington Irving High School, her teacher told her that she passed not because she deserved it, but because she had done so well in her other subjects.

Krasner was admitted to the Women's Art School of Cooper Union in 1926; she was considered a "difficult" (independent-minded) student. She took drawing courses at New York's avant-grade Art Students League before graduating in 1929 from Cooper Union and then attended the more mainstream National Academy of Design (1929–32). Again her instructors were disapproving of her work, this time criticizing *Self-Portrait* (1930) because they felt she had painted herself looking too defiant and masculine. Around that same time, Krasner became enamored of paintings by Picasso (with their emphasis on line) and Matisse (with their emphasis on color). "I flipped my lid," was her reaction to seeing their works for the first time in New York's Museum of Modern Art. Although she was at that time a realist, Krasner felt a strong affinity with European modernists. A writer in the *New York Times* pointed out that Krasner's work, while clearly in keeping with the "gestural decisiveness of other abstract expressionists," also had an "inwardness and feelings for color that are close to European artists like Matisse and Bonnard."

In order to paint and also earn a high school teaching degree, Krasner supported herself by waitressing in a café in Greenwich Village, a bohemian neighborhood of Manhattan, where she met and sparred with avant-grade artists, critics, and left-wing intellectuals. A friend, the playwright Edward Albee, once said that Krasner's abrasive personality gave "comfort and ammunition to those who were unwilling to grant her artistic due." Like many of her contemporaries in the

1930s, Krasner worked on the Works Progress Administration's Federal Art Project. Mostly she assisted muralists with their with massive social realist projects. "The whole experience," she explained in *Originals,* "introduced me to scale."

In 1937 Krasner began studying with the German expressionist Hans Hofmann. She was profoundly influenced by his cubist approach to art and started painting "flattened," close-up compositions composed of abstract shapes. Hofmann, meaning to praise Krasner, told her that one of her paintings was "so good you would not know it had been done by a woman." A more forthright compliment came from Dutch abstract painter Piet Mondrian; upon seeing Krasner's paintings at an exhibition sponsored by the American Abstract Artists, he told her: "You have a strong inner rhythm and must never lose it."

There were very few notable American women artists in the male-dominated art world of the 1940s and even fewer who dared to give up representational art for abstract art. In 1941, Krasner was invited to participate in a selective exhibit of modern American and French paintings at New York's McMillan Gallery. Another artist in the show was Jackson Pollock, whose arresting paintings drew Krasner's attention—as did the artist himself. The couple were married on October 25, 1945. A month later they moved from Greenwich Village to a dilapidated farmhouse in The Springs, a community populated by fledgling artists and writers located near East Hampton, Long Island. "Our studios were always separate," recalled Krasner. "We entered by invitation only." They had very little income, except for $150 a month from art patron Peggy Guggenheim. Pollock's work received more critical attention than Krasner's, in part because she spent so much time promoting her husband's work. Pollock would become one of America's premier abstract painters, extolled for his landmark "drop" paintings and archetypal imagery. From him, Krasner learned to treat the canvas as a "thing in itself." However, the artists were very different in their approach to painting. As Cindy Nemser observed in *Art Talk,* while

Lee Krasner was one of the founders of American abstract expressionism.
(Courtesy © Ann Chwatsky)

interviewing Krasner: "Your [Krasner] heavy crusty surfaces are much denser than his thinner, looser applications and your field never thins out at the edges as his does."

In order to express herself more freely, Krasner turned from cubism to what she called her "Little Image" period (1946–49). She produced a series of small, thickly painted canvases packed with abstract calligraphic images. Krasner used a tiny can so that she could move the paint. Her first solo exhibition, featuring the Little Image paintings, was held in New York City in 1951 at Betty Parsons Gallery. But after Pollock left the gallery that same year, Krasner was asked to leave as well.

Insulted and shocked, Krasner recalled that it took her almost a year to recover and begin working again. Two years later she created a series of collages by ripping and cutting sections of some of the paintings that had been on display at the Parsons Gallery and gluing the fragments of canvas together with pieces of her drawings. *Bald Eagle* (1955) is an example of the bold collage paintings, whose subjects were often abstract plant and animal forms.

Krasner and Pollock shared a passionate but tempestuous marriage, in large part because of Pollock's temper, infidelity, and alcoholism. He died, drunk and with a girlfriend, in an automobile accident in 1956, while Krasner was traveling in France. She explained that as artists they had respected and encouraged each other and shared "experience on the same level." After her husband's death, Krasner executed some of her most memorable paintings, such as *The Seasons* (1957), which *New York Times* art critic Michael Kimmelman described as "ripe . . . in terms of maturity and sheer emotion, the emotion mixing elements of violence with sex." Nonetheless, Krasner was considered important mostly because she was Pollock's widow and "keeper" of his legacy. She fought off bouts of depression and eventually produced larger, more colorful works with swirling colors and lush anthropomorphic imagery. In 1958 many of her later paintings were shown at a solo exhibition at the Martha Jackson Gallery in New York. One critic called them "masses burgeoning with growth, within the canvas."

Krasner had a major retrospective at the Whitechapel Gallery in London in 1965 that helped introduce her to an appreciative European audience. In 1968, at a one person show at New York's Marlborough Gallery, it was apparent to critics and viewers, in paintings such as *Combat* and *Courtship,* that her depression had lifted. In 1969, after a decade of painting huge canvases, she turned to small works on paper, including a series of gouaches harking back to her earlier works about nature. Finally, in the 1970s, in part because of the women's movement and in part because

expressionism was back in fashion, critics began to recognize Krasner's artistry and the importance of, as a critic wrote, her "provocatively unquiet paintings in the midst of minimalist quietude." An activist throughout her life, in 1972 Krasner protested against the Museum of Modern Art's apparent reluctance to show works by American women artists. Barbara Rose, who interviewed Krasner for an article in *Vogue* in 1972, described Krasner as a "visionary and a revolutionary personality," who "kept pace with developments in contemporary art, but did it her way."

In 1973 the Whitney Museum of American Art accorded Krasner a major retrospective. Other major honors and accolades followed, as did retrospectives and worldwide solo shows. Belatedly recognized, she was no longer merely "Pollock's wife." Lee Krasner died on June 19, 1984, in New York City, where she had kept an apartment/studio in addition to her home in East Hampton, Long Island. The *New York Times* obituary affirmed Krasner's "mastery of line and color" and her ability to create paintings that were both "elegiac and fierce." In January 2001, Krasner's first full-scale traveling retrospective—including paintings, collages, and drawings from major collections such as New York's Metropolitan Museum of Art and the Philadelphia Museum of Art—completed a national tour. In the *New York Times,* critic Michael Kimmelman wrote that "while Pollock's work influenced Krasner's, she influenced his," and that "Krasner's best paintings are as beautiful as any abstract paintings America has produced."

Further Reading

Baigell, Matthew. "Birth, 1956," Reynolda House, Museum of American Art. Available online. URL: http://www.reynoldahouse.org/birth.htm. Posted in 1998.

Kimmelman, Michael. "A Tough Abstractionist on Her Own Merits," *New York Times,* September 10, 2000, AR91.

Munro, Eleanor. *Originals: American Women Artists.* New York: Da Capo Press, 2000.

Nemser, Cindy. *Art Talk: Conversation with 15 Women Artists.* New York: HarperCollins, 1999.

Rose, Barbara. *Lee Krasner: A Retrospective.* New York: The Museum of Modern Art, 1983.

Tucker, Marcia. *Lee Krasner: Large Paintings.* New York: Whitney Museum of American Art, 1974.

— C. K.

KRUGER, BARBARA
(1945–   )   *Photomontagist, Graphic Artist, Painter*

An internationally recognized conceptual artist, Barbara Kruger is known for evocative montages that combine photography with language. Her overtly political works often feature photographs and phrases or slogans intended to lambast male-dominated economic power and the intrusive influence of the media in American society.

Barbara Kruger was born on January 16, 1945, in Newark, New Jersey, where she was raised in a working-class neighborhood. She enrolled at Syracuse University but after a year transferred to Parsons School of Design in New York City, where she became a pupil of documentary photographer DIANE ARBUS. She also studied with Marvin Israel, a graphic designer and art director of *Harper's Bazaar* magazine. He encouraged her to put together a professional portfolio and was the first person, Kruger later recalled, "who ever told me that I was special and that I could do *anything.*" By 22, she had been appointed chief designer of *Mademoiselle* magazine and for 11 years held various senior positions in art departments at women's fashion magazines owned by Condé Nast in New York City.

Kruger's background as a commercial graphic artist affected her later work as a conceptual artist and social critic. In her photomontages she examines and confronts the world of advertising and mass media, as well as stereotypes and clichés. In the early 1970s Kruger worked on large abstract paintings and soft sculptures in the form of woven and sewn fiber wall hangings; she described the latter as "very decorative, very gorgeous, very sexualized." Her assemblages on canvas often incorporated found materials that were "feminine"

in nature, such as patches of quilted fabric and feathers. In 1973 several of her fiber hangings were included in the highly competitive Biennial exhibition at the Whitney Museum of American Art in New York. (Her work was also represented in Whitney Museum Biennials in 1983 and 1987).

In 1974, Kruger held her first solo exhibition at the Artists Space in New York City. That same year she was named film critic for *Artforum* magazine. Throughout her multifaceted career, Kruger has continued to write art, film, and television criticism, to curate shows, and to publish poetry and participate in poetry readings. In 1976 she left New York City for California, where she taught at the University of California, Berkeley, among other institutions, and was a visiting artist at the California Institute of the Arts.

Around that same time, she stopped painting and sculpting. Assisted by a Creative Artists Public Service grant from the New York State Council on the Arts (1976), Kruger turned to her trademark enamel red-framed, black-and-white photomontages in which she incorporated pithy verbal messages in bold typeface with preexisting photographs. She enlarged and then cropped or cut the photos and superimposed messages on them that usually had to do with sexism or the controlling effects of mass media, such as "I shop therefore I am." For Kruger, content seems to be as important as form, and she has described herself as a "reporter." In working with, "pictures and words," Kruger's goal, as she stated in *ARTnews* (1987), is to "ruin certain representations and welcome the female spectator into the audience of men." Sometimes covering an entire gallery and accompanied by a sound track, her installations are, according to art critic Kate Linker, "assertive, aggressive, and argumentative."

In the Hospital series (1977), Kruger used photographs taken in New York hospitals and combined them with disturbing messages from patients, such as "Go away/Not that." By 1981 she was producing her best-known mixed-media photomontages, including *Untitled (You Invest in the Divinity of the Masterpiece)* (1982), which is owned by the Museum

125

Barbara Kruger's multifaceted work is meant
to be provocative.
(Portrait by Timothy Greenfield-Sanders)

of Modern Art in New York. "The images are usually fragmented in some way, and texts look like self-adhesive labels that were hastily applied," writes Nancy Heller in *Women Artists: Illustrated History.*

Kruger has held several solo exhibitions in venues ranging from New York City and Los Angeles to London, England, and Wellington, New Zealand. In 1982 she earned a National Endowment for the Arts grant and, three years later, a fellowship from the New York Foundation on the Arts. By the 1990s Kruger was working with color photographs, silk-screen prints, photo-lithography, and ribbed plastic screens whose

images change when the viewer shifts position. Kruger has worked on projects and installations with other artists, including JENNY HOLZER, and has designed magazine covers for periodicals such as *Newsweek* and *Esquire.* Her cover for *Ms.* magazine featured the words "Women+Rage=Power." Kruger's sometimes polemical images have also appeared on popular posters, T-shirts, electronic signboards, and billboards.

While some critics are impressed by Barbara Kruger and her "explosive spectacular theater of dissent," as one reviewer described her work, others think little of her "installations-cum-harangue." In 1994 Peter Schjeldahl of the *Village Voice* reluctantly admitted that Kruger was a "consequential graphic inventor" and "an artist of tremendous achievement and really vast influence." As for what Kruger thinks her installations mean, she says it depends on the viewer. "The construction of meaning shifts. And it shifts according to each spectator."

Further Reading

"Artist: Barbara Kruger," The World's Women On-Line!. Available online. URL: http://wwol.inre.asu.edu/kruger.html. Downloaded on June 7, 2001.

"Barbara Kruger," Whitney Museum of American Art. Available online. URL: http://www.tfaei.com/aa/1aa/1aabb7/htm. Updated on August 7, 2000.

Goldstein, Ann. *Barbara Kruger.* Cambridge, Mass.: MIT Press and The Museum of Contemporary Art, Los Angeles, 2000.

Kruger, Barbara. *We Won't Play Nature to Your Culture.* Exhibition Catalog. London, England: Institute of Contemporary Arts, 1983.

Kruger, Barbara, ed. *TV Guides: A Collection of Thoughts about Television.* New York: Kuklapolitan Press, 1987.

Linker, Kate, and Barbara Kruger. *Love for Sale: The Words and Pictures of Barbara Kruger.* New York: Harry N. Abrams, 1990.

Siegel, Jeanne. "Barbara Kruger: Pictures and Words." *Arts Magazine* 51:10 (summer 1987): 17–21.

— C. K.

LANGE, DOROTHEA NUTZHORN
(1895–1965)   *Photographer*

One of the most prominent founders of American documentary photography, Dorothea Lange is renowned for her simple, direct, powerful images of poor, ordinary people. Her insightful photographs, which could be subtly subversive in nature, helped the humanitarian causes she fervently believed in, such as affordable housing for uprooted migrant farmers in the 1930s. Lange portrayed her down-and-out subjects as innately strong, proud, and indefatigable.

Born in Hoboken, New Jersey, on May 26, 1895, to a family of second-generation German immigrants, Dorothea Nutzhorn Lange did not have an easy childhood. After her father deserted the family when Dorothea was 12, she was raised by her mother, a librarian and amateur singer. She took and retained her mother's family name of Lange and never spoke about the father who had abandoned her. Also traumatic was Dorothea's bout with polio when she was seven; it left her with a permanent limp in one leg. She ignored taunts by classmates but became acutely aware of the silent suffering of others; that sensitivity would be reflected later in her compassionate documentary portraits. "The secret places of the heart are the real mainsprings of one's action," Lange once stated.

Soon after graduating from high school in New York City in 1913, Lange realized she wanted to become a photographer. However, at her mother's insistence she attended the New York Training School for Teachers from 1914 to 1917. While there, she apprenticed to portrait photographers and roamed around New York City, captivated by the people she observed. She also enrolled in a photography course at New York's Columbia University taught by the pictorialist Clarence H. White.

Lange left New York City in 1918 to travel with a friend around the world. But when her funds were stolen in San Francisco, California, she decided to settle there. She took a job as a photofinisher at a dry goods store, and a year later, with the financial backing of a friend, she set up a commercial portrait studio. Soon she was earning a good living by taking pictures of the city's social and cultural elite. Her studio became a mecca for San Francisco's bohemian artists, including the landscape painter Maynard Dixon, whom she married in 1920. The couple had two sons, in 1925 and 1928. But Lange, who was petite and shy yet willful and ambitious, felt burdened by the responsibilities of

Documentary photographer Dorothea Lange chronicled
the lives of migrant workers.
(Library of Congress)

motherhood and sent her children to boarding school when they were young; she desperately wanted to work without interruptions. "As a mother, her work came first," noted Linda Morris in *Dorothea Lange: A Visual Life.* "The choice caused her considerable pain."

After more than a decade of working in her comfortable studio as a portraitist, in the 1930s Lange needed something more. "The discrepancy between what I was working on in the printing frames and what was going on in the street was more than I could assimilate," she explained. She and Dixon traveled to the Southwest, where Lange recorded the troubled lives of Native Americans. Once she returned home, she focused on the homeless, hungry, dazed-looking men and women wandering the streets of San Francisco. *White Angel Breadline* (1933), in which a crowd of demoralized unemployed men wait in line for food handouts, is one of her most affecting images from that period. Lange saw in her Great Depression subjects what she called "courage, real courage."

In 1934 Lange held her first solo show of documentary photographs at the studio of avant-grade photographer Willard Van Dyke in Oakland, California. Also in 1934, Lange met economist and social activist Paul Schuster Taylor, and they began working together for the California Rural Rehabilitation Administration, an emergency agency. A year later Lange and Taylor divorced their respective spouses and married each other. Taylor showed his new wife how to take field notes and use them as annotated titles to enhance her prints. From 1935 to 1939, Lange worked for the Farm Security Administration, which had enlisted other accomplished photographers such as Walker Evans and Ben Shahn. Lange began her landmark work of documenting migratory farm laborers in California as they escaped the dust bowl and headed west in search of work. She lived with some of them, would ask their permission to talk with and take pictures of them, and allowed their children to handle her cameras; gradually she won their trust. Lange primarily used a Rolleiflex camera held at her waist and at an angle that "looked up" at her subjects. According to Diana Emery Hulick in *North American Women Artists of the 20th Century*, "detail is subordinated to large effects in Lange's work, and all the people she photographed—most of whom were poor, jobless, or dispossessed—are treated with dignity."

One of Lange's most celebrated and widely reproduced prints, *Migrant Mother, Nipomo, California* (1936), is of a pea-picker's wife struggling to make ends meet during the depression. Nothing interested Lange more than the human face. "I saw and approached the hungry and desperate mother, as if drawn by a magnet," recalled Lange in 1960. "She told me she had sold the tires from her car to buy food. There she sat in that lean-to tent with her children huddled around her, and seemed to know that my pictures might help her, and so she helped me." Lange's classic portrait, made with a simple Graflex camera and selected as one of the 50 best photographs of the century, hangs in the Library of Congress in Washington, D.C.

From 1935 to 1939, Taylor and Lange traveled to most regions of the United States. In 1939, she collaborated with Taylor on a publication entitled *An American Exodus: A Record of Human Erosion.* The critically acclaimed book exposed the shameful conditions faced by poor rural Americans and helped demonstrate the need for federal public housing. In 1941 Lange became the first woman to receive a Guggenheim Fellowship in photography. She was supposed to take pictures of American utopian communities but once World War II broke out, she decided instead to work for the Office of War Information, recording the evacuation and forced resettlement to detention camps of West Coast Japanese Americans. It became obvious that Lange opposed the policy of internment, and some of her photographs were censored by the government. "The neutrality of the lens," wrote an art critic, "allows Lange to clearly show contempt for placing children in internment camps as enemies of the American people. It is this jarring juxtaposition of human values that makes Lange's photographs at once riveting, chilling—and heartbreaking."

Lange's empathy for her subjects—whether wartime shipyard workers or wealthy San Franciscans—without a trace of sentimentality, is one of her greatest virtues as an artist. "See straight and true and fast," she recommended to aspiring young photographers, and she followed her own credo.

In 1945, while covering a United Nations conference in San Francisco, Lange collapsed. Due to a variety of persistent illnesses, she stopped accepting photography assignments until 1951 and then focused more on familial subjects, especially her grandchildren. But she continued to travel and produce photographic essays, including one on Mormon communities in Utah (1954) and another on rural life in Ireland (1955), for *Life* magazine. She also accompanied Taylor on his trips to East Asia, the Middle East, and South America, but she is best remembered for her evocative earlier work, the photos taken during the Great Depression. "Her subjects stand as pioneers and adventurers, often worn down but certainly not worn out," wrote Melissa A. McEuen in *Seeing America: Women Photographers Between the Wars.*

Dorothea Lange, one of the most important documentary photographers of the 20th century, died on October 11, 1965, in Marin County, north of San Francisco. A year later she became the first female artist accorded a retrospective show at New York City's Museum of Modern Art, an exhibition that she helped prepare before her death. Lange also completed a final collection of photographs, *Dorothea Lange Looks at the American Country Woman,* which was published posthumously in 1966. In 1972, the Whitney Museum of American Art in New York exhibited her photographs in a show about the Japanese-American internment during World War II. An art critic for the *New York Times* described those prints as "documents of such a high order that they convey the feelings of the victims as well as the facts of the crime." Thousands of Lange's photographs are housed in collections at the Library of Congress, the National Archives, and the Oakland Museum of California. Robert J. Doherty, in *Contemporary Photographers,* wrote that Lange's "strong sense of justice . . . sparked a silent fury that came to light in the strong emotion of her photographs. With a camera in her hand, she became a giant."

Further Reading

Davis, Keith F. *The Photographs of Dorothea Lange.* New York: Harry N. Abrams, 1996.

Lange, Dorothea, with Paul Schuster Taylor. *An American Exodus: A Record of Human Erosion.* New Haven, Conn.: Yale University Press, 1969.

Meltzer, Milton. *Dorothea Lange: A Photographer's Life.* New York: Farrar, Straus and Giroux, 1978.

Morris, Linda. "A Woman of Our Generation." In *Dorothea Lange: A Visual Life,* edited by Elizabeth Partridge, 14–33. Washington, D.C.: Smithsonian Institution Press, 1994.

Oakland Museum of California. "Dorothea Lange," Oakland Museum of California Art Collections. Available

online. URL: http://www.museumca.org/global/art/collections-dorothea_lange.html. Posted in 1999.

— C. K.

LEIBOVITZ, ANNIE (Anna-Lou Leibovitz)
(1949–)   *Photographer*

Often called icons of popular culture, the celebrity photographs of Annie Leibovitz have made the photographer herself a celebrity. Born Anna-Lou Leibovitz on October 2, 1949, she was one of six children of an air force colonel and a former modern dancer. As military family, the Leibovitzes moved several times a year. Leibovitz later likened looking through her camera's viewfinder to seeing the world through a car window, as she did during her family's frequent moves.

In 1967 Leibovitz began studying painting at the San Francisco Art Institute with the intention of becoming an art teacher. While there, she took a night school course in photography. Discovering her medium, she spent all her free time in the darkroom. She later explained her instant attraction to photography: "To see something that afternoon and have it materialize before your eyes that same day. There was a real immediacy to it."

Leibovitz quickly amassed a portfolio of photographs taken in San Francisco and on a kibbutz in Israel. At the suggestion of a friend, she took her photographs to the offices of *Rolling Stone,* a three-year-old magazine focusing on rock music. *Rolling Stone* publisher Jann Wenner was impressed with the work. He bought one photograph of poet Allen Ginsberg at a peace rally for $25 and put Leibovitz on a retainer of $47 a week. Leibovitz's early photographs for the magazine were primarily candid black-and-white shots of rock celebrities. Her skill at capturing the personalities of her subjects helped define the look and style of *Rolling Stone,* which became the leading chronicler of American youth culture. In 1973 Leibovitz, then 23, was named the magazine's chief photographer.

Her reputation was boosted in 1975 when the Rolling Stones hired her to document their world tour. After spending months with them, Leibovitz wanted to show that touring was "not glamorous. . . . It was a very hard life." She shot not only the band members, but also the audience, creating a picture of celebrity culture from both the performer's and the spectator's points of view. As the intimacy of her photographs of the Rolling Stones suggest, Leibovitz slipped from being merely an observer to a participant in the raucous touring life. She later admitted it took her five years to "get off the tour" as she battled a cocaine addiction that began on the assignment.

After the tour, Leibovitz returned to *Rolling Stone,* which began printing photographs in color in 1974. As Leibovitz taught herself to work in color, she also changed her methods of dealing with subjects. She found that one of her great skills as a portrait photographer was putting people at ease. Growing more comfortable with the idea of staging shots, she convinced celebrities to strike peculiar, sometimes ridiculous poses, that often commented on their public image in a fresh and witty way. Among her notable photographs of the era were portraits of Bette Midler, nude and covered with rose petals; Bruce Springsteen, with the American flag as a backdrop; and John Belushi and Dan Ackroyd as the Blues Brothers, with their faces painted blue.

Her most famous photograph for *Rolling Stone* was one of many she took of former Beatle John Lennon. Snapped two hours before his murder on December 8, 1980, the photograph showed Lennon in the nude, curled like a fetus and clutching the body of his wife Yoko Ono, who was fully clothed. According to Leibovitz, Lennon was enthusiastic about the pose, claiming, "This is our relationship." The photograph appeared on the cover of the *Rolling Stone* issue that reported his death. Aside from the magazine's logo, no other text appeared on the cover, a testament to the power of Leibovitz's image to tell the story to Lennon's grieving fans.

Feeling pigeonholed as a rock-and-roll photographer, Leibovitz left *Rolling Stone* and joined the staff of *Vanity Fair* in 1983. She explained that

Popular, versatile photographer Annie Leibovitz takes pictures of celebrities.
(AP/Wide World Photos)

Rolling Stone "never did want to grow old gracefully. *Vanity Fair* is showing me how to enjoy yourself in the older years and live well." Although Leibovitz continued to photograph celebrities, *Vanity Fair* allowed her broaden her subject matter beyond rock stars and actors; she made portraits of writers, poets, politicians, media moguls, and dancers. They often appeared in portfolios that allowed her to explore a particular group of people, such as one depicting the principal players in the Watergate scandal.

Leibovitz's most notorious image appeared on a 1992 *Vanity Fair* cover. The portrait showed actor Demi Moore, nine months pregnant, in the nude. Banned from newsstands across the country, the cover made national news, sparking debates about American views of pregnancy and female sexuality.

Beginning in 1986, Leibovitz also began producing images for advertisements for companies such as Honda, the Gap, and American Express. Her American Express campaign featured a diverse array of public figures—from novelist Elmore Leonard to record producer Quincy Jones to opera star Luciano Pavarotti—and won Leibovitz a Clio Award, the advertising industry's highest honor. Although advertising work gave her a bigger budget, allowing her to spend more time getting to know her subjects, she later dismissed the campaign's photography as "too slick."

In 1991, the first 20 years of Leibovitz's career were honored with a major exhibition at the National Portrait Gallery. Featuring nearly 200 photographs, the show traveled throughout the United States and to England and Japan. A book based on the show, *Photographs: Annie Leibovitz, 1970–1990* (1991), was also highly successful.

During the 1990s, Leibovitz began to seek out new subject matter. She documented the wars in Sarajevo and Rwanda and became the official photographer of the U.S. Olympic teams for the 1996 Summer Olympics, held in Atlanta, Georgia. Her Olympic photographs were shown at the city's Centennial Olympic Park and collected into the book *Olympic Portraits* (1996).

At the suggestion of a friend, writer Susan Sontag, Leibovitz took on a book project in the late 1990s depicting American women from all walks of life. For three years, she traveled throughout the country, photographing teachers, soldiers, astronauts, athletes, artists, and executives. Although most of her subjects were noncelebrities, she also made portraits of some of the most powerful and influential American women at the end of the 20th century, including Hillary Rodham Clinton, Gloria Steinem, Toni Morrison, and Ruth Bader Ginsburg. The resulting book, *Women* (1999), became the focus of another well-received traveling exhibition. Leibovitz told the *New York Times* that she was initially "intimidated by the subject because it felt so big," but ultimately took on the project because "as I'm older . . . I want to use my talent in some way that feels gratifying."

Further Reading

Annie Leibovitz: Celebrity Photographer. Home Vision Arts, (VHS), 1993.

Leibovitz, Annie. *Olympic Portraits.* Boston: Little, Brown and Company, 1996.

———. *Photographs: Annie Leibovitz, 1970–1990.* New York: HarperCollins, 1991.

———. *Women.* New York: Random House, 1999.

— L. S.

LEVITT, HELEN
(1918–) *Photographer, Filmmaker*

Best known for her photographs of New York City street life, Helen Levitt was born in Brooklyn on August 31, 1918. An enthusiastic reader and moviegoer, she tried to satisfy her creative bent through music, drawing, and dance, but she gave up these pursuits when she was disappointed in the results. After dropping out of high school, she took a job with a family friend who worked as a commercial photographer. As she learned basic camera and darkroom techniques, she realized she had found her art form.

Originally, Levitt aspired to become a portrait photographer, but exposure to museum and gallery exhibitions moved her toward art photography. She was particularly struck by the work of French photographer Henri Cartier-Bresson, whom she befriended in the early 1930s. In his photographs, she saw how the camera could record the poetry of everyday life. Levitt also learned from Cartier-Bresson that even though a photographic image captured a moment in time, it could still be as thoughtfully composed as a painting.

In 1936 Levitt bought a secondhand Leica—a small, light camera she could easily carry without attracting attention. Interested in capturing street life on film, she gravitated to ethnic and working-class neighborhoods where people spent much of the day outdoors. Unlike many photographers of the 1930s, she had little interest in documenting the effects of poverty. Levitt rejected the role of the sociologist, instead aspiring as an artist to create lyrical and intimate images that captured her subjects' internal lives.

To discourage people from playing to the camera, Levitt often used a right angle lens, allowing her to stand a quarter turn away from whatever she was photographing. Most of her photographs, therefore, were taken without the knowledge of the subjects. Because of their lack of self-consciousness, Levitt's favorite subjects were children. She preferred shooting them while they were engaged in imaginative play, creating temporary internal worlds far away from their physical surroundings.

Through a friend, photographer Walker Evans, Levitt met journalist and film critic James Agee. In 1941, she joined him and his wife on a trip to Mexico—a rare vacation that gave her a chance to photograph a location other than her native New York. In 1946 Agee also wrote the introductory essay to a book of her photographs, *A Way of Seeing,* which was published in 1965.

In 1943 Helen Levitt had her first show at New York's Museum of Modern Art (MOMA). For most of the 1940s, however, she abandoned still photography as she began experimenting with film. She had several jobs as a film editor, including one in which she worked with Spanish filmmaker Luis Buñuel on documentaries sponsored by MOMA. Beginning in 1945, she started producing her own films in collaboration with Agee and her friend Janice Loeb. Conceived as the cinematic equivalent of Levitt's still photography, *In the Street* showed images of children playing and fighting to a muscial score. With Loeb and Sidney Meyer, Levitt made a second documentary, *The Quiet One,* about the rehabilitation of a young African-American delinquent.

Winning a Guggenheim grant, Levitt returned to still photography in 1959. She began working in color, while exploring the same subjects of her earlier work. Most of her early experiments were lost when her apartment was burglarized in 1966. Levitt, however, continued to work in color through the 1970s, although she returned to black-and-white occasionally in the following decade.

In 1991 the San Francisco Museum of Modern Art organized a retrospective of Levitt's work, which toured throughout the United States for the next two years. The retrospective helped restore her stature in the history of American photography, in part by challenging the criticism most often leveled by contemporary critics—that her work is mired in sentimentality and nostalgia. A closer examination of her work, however, has convinced many critics of the richness of her vision. As David Levi Strauss wrote in *Artforum* in 1997, "At

first glance, [Helen Levitt's photographs] appear to be as stylistically innocent and guileless as their often young subjects. It is only after prolonged and repeated viewing that these images begin to reveal their complexity and depth."

Further Reading

The Encyclopedia of Photography. "Helen Levitt," Web galleries.com. Available online. URL: http://www.masters-of-photography.com/L/levitt/levitt_articles1.html. Downloaded on July 26, 2001.

Levitt, Helen. *A Way of Seeing,* 3rd edition. Durham, N.C.: Duke University Press, 1989.

Phillips, Sandra S., and Maria Morris Hambourg. *Helen Levitt.* San Francisco: San Francisco Museum of Modern Art, 1991.

— L. S.

LEWIS, EDMONIA (Mary Edmonia Lewis)
(ca. 1845–ca. 1909)   *Sculptor*

Edmonia Lewis overcame three enormous obstacles—being female, African American, and American Indian—to become one of 19th-century America's most successful sculptors. Few firm details are known about her early life. She was probably born Mary Edmonia Lewis in 1843 or 1845 either in Ohio or New York State. Her father was an African American, possibly from Haiti, who worked as a gentleman's servant. Her mother was most likely part African American and part Ojibwa Indian.

As a child, Lewis was orphaned. By her somewhat romanticized account, she spent several years living among the Ojibwa, who called her by an Indian name, Wildfire. Her stepbrother, a successful gold miner, paid for her education, first at a preparatory school in upstate New York, then at Oberlin College in Ohio. When Lewis was admitted in 1859, Oberlin was one of the only colleges in the United States that enrolled women and blacks. While at Oberlin, Lewis began studying drawing and painting. Her first known work was *The Muse Uranus* (1862), a sketch of a Roman sculpture probably based on an engraving.

During her third year in college, Lewis became the focus of a bizarre incident. Two white women with whom she shared a house accused her of poisoning them. Although the citizens of Oberlin considered themselves progressive in racial issues, a mob severely beat Lewis before she could be arraigned. Represented in court by African-American lawyer John Mercer Langston, Lewis was released after the charges against her were dismissed for insufficient evidence. Although legally vindicated, Lewis still was held in suspicion by her classmates. After she was accused of stealing art supplies in February 1863, Oberlin refused to allow her to continue her studies.

Without a diploma, Lewis moved to Boston later that year. Now entertaining the idea of becoming a sculptor, she arrived at the studio of artist Edward Brackett with a letter of introduction from abolitionist William Lloyd Garrison, whom Lewis had met at Oberlin. Brackett took on Lewis as a student. His lessons consisted largely of giving her a fragment of a sculpture and asking her to copy it in clay. This instruction was the only formal art training Lewis ever received.

Lewis quickly established herself as a popular sculptor of medallions and busts, most depicting well-known abolitionists. These subjects appealed to her wealthy, liberal patrons, who included Garrison and social reformer Lydia Maria Child. Having these prominent people as her champions helped Lewis establish her own studio, but she bristled at their efforts to use her in their promotion of civil rights. In 1863 Lewis publicly asked that her work be praised on its merits, not because "I am a colored girl." She also resisted her partrons' often condescending attitude toward her art. Child, for instance, discouraged her from working on a bust of Robert Gould Shaw, a Boston blue blood who commanded African-American troops in the Civil War. Lewis ignored Child's suggestion that the project was beyond her talents. The bust proved to be Lewis's greatest early success. It was so popular that she sold about 100 plaster copies, earning enough to found a tour of Europe.

In the winter of 1865, Lewis arrived in Rome, where she decided to establish a new studio. To Lewis, Rome was attractive for several reasons. She wanted to work in marble, and the city offered a plentiful supply of the material and many skilled craftspeople to help artists carve it. The museums of Rome also gave Lewis many examples of classical sculpture to emulate. At the time, neoclassicism, characterized by a borrowing of classical forms and themes, was the leading style in sculpture.

Perhaps most important to Lewis, Rome offered her some relief from the prejudices she experienced in the United States because of her race and gender. In the city, she also found camaraderie among other expatriate female sculptors, including HARRIET HOSMER, EMMA STEBBINS, and Margaret Foley. Novelist Henry James once wrote of this circle of friends as "that strange sisterhood of American 'lady sculptors.'" Of Lewis, he rather patronizingly added, "one of the sisterhood . . . was a negress, whose colour, picturesquely contrasting with that of her plastic material, was the pleading agent of her fame."

In fact, the novelty of an African-American female sculptor did bring Lewis many of her patrons. Lewis herself was also a memorable figure. A small woman, she often wore mannish clothing and a large crimson cap. Her studio became a favorite stop for Americans on a grand tour of Europe. Many of her visitors described Lewis as a charming host.

To keep her studio solvent, Lewis had to concentrate on producing works that her customers most wanted. She received many commissions for busts of literary and historical figures, such as Henry Wadsworth Longfellow and Abraham Lincoln. Also popular were small figurines of cupids. Lewis, however, aspired to create large sculptures with several figures—a bold ambition for someone with as little training as she had had.

Her first large work in Italy was *The Freed Woman and Her Child* (1866), which depcited an African-American slave in chains with her child clinging to her waist as they learned that they had been freed. She dealt with a similar subject in *Forever Free* (1869), the title of which was taken from the Emancipation Proclamation. She returned to the theme of the suffering of African Americans figuratively in *Hagar* (1875). Based on a biblical story, the work portrayed the Egyptian servant of Sarah, after she had been cast out of her master's home. Since her audience associated Egypt with black Africa, the piece was interpreted as an affecting commentary on the position of African-American women in white society.

Lewis also favored Indians as subject matter. Among her best-known works were *The Wooing of Hiawatha* (1866) and *The Marriage of Hiawatha* (1867), both based on Longfellow's poem *The Song of Hiawatha*. Unlike most artists of her day, Lewis resisted depicting Indians as bloodthirsty killers. She did, however, rely on another stereotype—that of the noble savage—in her depiction of Indian groups.

Lewis's most famous work was *The Death of Cleopatra* (1876). The sculpture became a cause célèbre at the Philadelphia Centennial Exposition. It was displayed with 500 other sculptures, but one journalist noted that it "excites more admiration and gathers larger crowds around it than any other work." Lewis showed the Egyptian queen just at the moment of death from poison. As in many of her works, the drama of the scene revealed an emotionalism uncommon in neoclassicism. This tension between its content and style accounted for much of the excitement the work generated. Seemingly unsure about how to respond to the piece, artist William J. Clark Jr. wrote in 1878 that "the effects of the death are represented with such skill as to be absolutely repellent and it is a question whether a statue of the ghastly characteristics of this one does not overstep the bounds of legitimate art."

With the publicity surrounding *Cleopatra*, Lewis received many commissions in the late 1870s. In the next decade, however, neoclassicism fell out of favor, and Lewis's career floundered. She received her last major commission from a Baltimore church, for which she created *Adoration of the Magi* (1883). Almost nothing is known about the artist's final years. In February 1909 a magazine article mentioned that she was still living in Rome. The date and place of her death, however, remain a mystery.

Lewis was largely forgotten until the 1970s, when a renewed interest in African-American artists once again brought her work to light. Today, she stands out as an artist of tremendous tenacity, who through sheer will carved out a successful career against extraordinary odds.

Further Reading

Hartigan, Lynda R. *Sharing Traditions: Five Black Artists in Nineteenth-Century America.* Washington, D.C.: Smithsonian Institution Press, 1985.

May, Stephen. "The Object at Hand," *Smithsonian Magazine.* Available online. URL: http://www. smithsonianmag.si.edu/smithsonian/issues96/sep96/ object_sep96.html. Posted in September 1996.

Richardson, Marilyn. "Edmonia Lewis's *The Death of Cleopatra*: Myth and Identity." *International Review of African American Art* 12 (summer 1995): 36–52.

— L. S.

LIN, MAYA
(1959–) *Architect, Sculptor*

On the basis of a single work—the Vietnam Veterans Memorial—architect and sculptor Maya Lin has been called by *U.S. News and World Report* "possibly the best known living visual artist in America." On October 5, 1959, she was born Maya Ying Lin in Athens, Ohio. Her parents, Chinese immigrants who fled their native country before the Communist revolution of 1949, were professors at Ohio University. Her father also was a ceramist, and her mother, a poet.

According to Lin's 2000 book *Boundaries*, she led "a very insulated and isolated childhood," which included daily visits to her father's art studio. During her youth, she experimented with various art mediums and techniques, including silversmithing and bronze casting. Lin also attributes her Asian-American heritage to helping her mature into an artist. Her background gave her a "feeling of being other that has profoundly shaped my way of looking at the world—as if form a distance—a third-person observer."

Graduating from high school as a covaledictorian, Lin headed to Yale University with the goal of becoming an architect. During her senior year, she took a seminar in funereal architecture, in which, she later recalled, the class studied "how people, through the built form, express their attitudes on death." When a contest for designing a Vietnam War memorial was announced, she and her classmates were given the assignment of creating a design as a seminar project.

Studying existing war memorials, Lin realized that "most carried larger, more general messages about a leader's victory or accomplishments rather than the lives lost." The memorials of World War I impressed her most. She found that, in trying to address the horror of that war, these treated the realities of battle with more honesty. Lin also noted that many World War I memorials listed the names of soldiers who had died, partly because, due to the nature and location of the fighting, many bodies were never recovered. She was particularly inspired by Sir Edwin Lutyens's memorial in Thiepval, France, commemorating the Battle of the Somme, which bore the names of the conflict's 70,000 casualties. The Memorial Rotunda at Yale—on whose walls the names of alumni killed in war were carved—also left an impression on Lin. During her freshman and sophomore years in college, she often saw stonecutters at work, carving out the names of those who had died in the Vietnam War.

Before learning of the government's criteria for the Vietnam memorial, Lin conceptualized her design. She saw two 200-foot walls of polished black granite forming a 130-degree angle, with one arm pointing toward the Lincoln Memorial and one arm pointing toward the Capitol. As the walls approached one another, they sunk 10 feet into the ground. On the walls, the names of the dead and missing were to be carved. Lin envisioned the

names listed by date of death or disappearance, so that the monument as a whole would read "like a epic Greek poem." She considered adding other elements, but ultimately decided that "the names to be on the memorial would become the memorial; there was no need to embellish the design further." When Lin learned of the government's rules for the competition, she found that her design met them to the letter: The memorial had to be apolitical, had to list the names of the war's 58,000 casualities, and had to take its site between the Lincoln Memorial and Capitol into consideration in the design.

Like all 1,420 entries, Lin's was submitted anonymously. It featured atmospheric watercolor drawings and a proposal that described her monument as "a rift in the Earth—a long polished black stone wall, emerging from and receding into the Earth." While still at Yale, the 21-year-old Lin received a call, telling her that the design committee had unanimously chosen her proposal.

As news of the selection was reported, Lin uncomfortably found herself at the center of a controversy. Some veterans' groups interpreted her design as a negative statement on the war, calling it "a black gash of shame and sorrow." With the history of ill-treatment of Vietnam vets, they saw Lin's design as an affront and demanded a more conventional memorial that would celebrate their heroics in battle. Under pressure, the memorial committee agreed to commission the veterans' choice as well—a more traditional bronze sculpture by Frederick Hart—which would stand 120 feet away from Lin's wall.

In 1981, Lin graduated cum laude from Yale. The next year, her memorial was dedicated. During the ceremony, Lin's name was not mentioned, and Hart's sculpture appeared on the program's cover. The retiring Lin was upset by the resulting controversy. Later, she blamed herself in part for the hysteria surrounding her design's selection. Lin wrote, "It was extremely naive of me to think that I could produce a neutral statement," considering the nation's divided feelings about the war.

Despite the controversy surrounding her memorial, the public responded to it almost immediately. It quickly became a destination for friends and relatives of felled Vietnam veterans, who left flowers and other memorials below the names of loved ones. The emotional outpourings the memorial inspired made it the most famous public sculpture in the United States.

After briefly attending Harvard University, Lin returned to Yale in the fall of 1983, receiving a master's degree in architecture in 1985. The next year, her alma mater granted her an honorary doctorate of fine arts. Since 1987, Lin has worked from her own studio in New York City, where she has concentrated on designing architectural structures and sculpture. Initially, she feared that the Vietnam Veterans Memorial might mark the peak of her career. "I was afraid of becoming a one-hit wonder," she later wrote. "It took me at least 10 years to see that I was more than that."

Lin's next major commission came in 1988 from the Southern Poverty Law Center in Montgomery, Alabama. She was asked to create a memorial for those who had been killed during the civil rights movement. Lin took as her inspiration the biblical phrase from the Book of Amos that Martin Luther King Jr. quoted in his famous "I Have a Dream" speech: "We will not be satisfied until justice rolls down like waters and righteousness like a mighty stream." In the finished monument, Lin had the passage and the names of 40 men, women, and children carved into a black marble slab, over which a thin sheet of water continually flows.

Lin has since made several large public sculptures. At Yale, she created *The Women's Table* in 1993. The granite sculpture lists the number of women who attended during each year of Yale's existence. Since it was an all-male institution until well into the 20th century, a zero follows most of the years listed, driving home how women historically have been excluded from higher education. Lin has expressed her interest in environmental issues through several works, including *TOPO* (1991), a landscape sculpture at

the Charlotte Coliseum in Charlotte, North Carolina, and *Groundswell* (1993), an installation made of 43 tons of recycled glass at the Wexner Center in Columbus, Ohio. In 1993, the Wexner Center held the first one-woman show of Lin's smaller sculptures, which she creates from beeswax, lead, steel, and broken glass.

Lin has also designed houses, most notably the Norton House (1996–98) in New York City, whose shape draws on the principles of origami. The Weber House (1992–94) in Williamstown, Massachusetts, as well displays her affinity for Japanese design. Several of Lin's houses feature movable panels for walls so that occupants came rearrange the interior space to meet their needs.

Although Lin has largely shied away from the limelight since her early fame, she agreed to be filmed for *Maya Lin: A Strong Clear Vision* (1995), an Academy Award–winning documentary. In 2000, she also published *Boundaries,* a book featuring illustrations of her work with commentary on her creative process. The same year, Lin announced that she was working on her final memorial, *Extinction,* which she says will be "about the waves of extinctions taking place across the earth." The piece will feature six structures at different locations throughout the world and a coordinating website. On the impetus behind the work, Lin has explained, "Memorials are not just about the past. If you can make people aware of the extent of extinction, you can also make them aware of what they can do."

Further Reading

Fleming, Jeff, editor. *Maya Lin: Topologies.* Winston-Salem, N.C.: Southeastern Center for Contemporary Art, 1998.

Lin, Maya. *Boundaries.* New York: Simon and Schuster, 2000.

Maya Lin: A Strong Clear Vision. Sanders & Mock Production, VHS, 1995.

Tilsner, Julie. "Maya Lin, Monumental Artist," Women.com. Available online. URL: http://www.womenswire.com/watch/in.html. Downloaded on July 27, 2001.

— L. S.

LOMAS GARZA, CARMEN
(Carmen Lomaz, Garze)
(1948–) *Painter, Printmaker*

A Chicana artist who chronicles Mexican-American history and culture, Carmen Lomas Garza creates neoprimitive paintings and prints, often based on her childhood memories and experiences in Texas. "She recollects and recasts reminiscences in a visual narrative," wrote Victor Zamudio-Taylor in *Latin American Art in the Twentieth Century.*

Born into a bilingual household in 1948, in Kingsville, Texas, Carmen Lomas Garza credits her parents for encouraging her to become an artist. "They started giving me money to buy my art supplies—sketch books, india ink, pencils. They've been invaluable, my first and best teachers," she said during an interview in *In Her Own Image* (1980). In addition, Carmen's mother freely shared stories, in the oral history tradition, about the family's Mexican and Spanish ancestors. Lomas Garza would use the stories as source material in her drawings and paintings. She also used the fetus, which she had studied in a course on the principles of art and biology, as a symbol of "peace and tranquility" in her prints.

Lomas Garza was determined to become an artist. "Art was my main interest in high school," she recalled. "Everything else was something I just had to do." Subjected to racist taunts ("the gringas made me feel inferior and it all went toward destroying my self-image") and punished by teachers for speaking Spanish in school, she described herself as an "introverted and depressed" adolescent. Learning how to draw and paint, she said, gave her "a reason to go to school."

While pursuing a teaching career, Lomas Garza studied art at Texas Arts and Industry University (Texas A & I) in Kingsville. In 1969, while still a student at the university, she was invited by the first national conference of the Mexican American Organization to put on a show of Chicano art. After graduating in 1972 from Texas A & I with a bachelor's degree, she became more involved in the bur-geoning Chicano movement, with its emphasis on Mexican-American ethnic pride; she joined the Con Safos, a group of Chicano artists in San Antonio.

After dabbling with silk-screening and various other forms of printmaking, Lomas Garza began to publicly show her work. She was assisted financially by fellowships from the National Endowment for the Arts, for which she served as a member of the national task force on Hispanic-American art. Meanwhile, Lomas Garza earned a master's degree in education at the Antioch Graduate School in Austin (1973) and a master's degree in fine arts at San Francisco State University (1980). She also studied in Mexico.

In the 1970s Lomas Garza illustrated two books: *The Gypsy Wagon* (1974) and *Chicano Voices* (1975). According to art writer Kevin Hillstrom, by the mid-1980s she was recognized as one of the Hispanic community's best-known artists. Typical of her work is a painting called *Grandparents Cutting Cacti* (1980), which shows three generations of rural Chicanos performing the seasonal task of harvesting cacti (symbols of both the greatness and adversity of life), just as their ancestors had done before them since pre-Columbian times. In 1987 Lomas Garza's paintings and prints appeared in a group show, *Hispanic Art in the United States,* which was held at the Museum of Fine Arts in Houston. Her first solo exhibition, in 1991 at the Laguna Gloria Art Museum in Austin, Texas, was followed by others throughout the United States, including at the Hirshhorn Museum at the Smithsonian Institution in Washington D.C.

Most of her work reflects her own positive, family-oriented memories of the Texan Hispanic community in which she was raised. She depicts traditional quotidian Chicano life, from healing ceremonies to family celebrations. In that way, Lomas Garza is very different from Chicana muralist JUDITH BACA, who considers art a vehicle for social and political protest, or from more overtly feminist conceptual Chicana artists such as Yolanda Lopez and Celia Alvarez Munoz. Lomas Garza has been both praised and criticized by fellow artists for refusing to politicize her work and for her traditional, naive folk-art style. "Lomas Garza chooses to work with a figuration that creates a rich visual language centered on storytelling," explains Victor Zamudio-Taylor, a professor of Mexican and Chicano Art at the University of Texas.

Carmen Lomas Garza currently lives in San Francisco, California. In 1990 she wrote a bilingual children's book, *Family Pictures/Cuadros de familia*. In 1997 she had a solo exhibition at the Steinbaum-Krauss Gallery in New York City, followed in 1998 by a show of her work at the TAEA Conference Center in Corpus Christi, Texas.

Further Reading

Beardsley, John, and Jane Livingston, editors. *Hispanic Art in the United States: Thirty Contemporary Painters and Sculptors.* Houston, Tex.: The Museum of Fine Arts, Houston, 1986.

"Carmen Lomas Garza," Smithsonian American Art Museum. Available online. URL: http://nmaa-ryder.si.edu/webzine/carmen1.htm. Downloaded on July 27, 2001.

Zamudio-Taylor, Victor. "Chicano Art." In *Latin American Art in the Twentieth Century,* edited by Edward J. Sullivan, 321–333. London, England: Phaidon Press, 1996.

Zuver, Marc, et al. *Ancient Roots, New Visions.* Tucson, Ariz.: Tucson Museum of Art, 1977.

— C. K.

LUNDEBERG, HELEN
(1908–1999) *Painter*

A founder of the New Classicism movement and leading figure in the California art scene, Helen Lundeberg was born in Chicago in 1908. When she was four, her family moved to Pasadena, California. She aspired to be a writer until she began taking art courses at the Stickney Memorial School of Art in 1930. There, she flourished under the instruction of painter Lorser Feitelson, whom she soon married. After she had completed only a year of formal art study, one of her paintings was exhibited at San Diego's Fine Arts Gallery. The next year, Lundeberg's *Landscape with Figure* won an honorable mention at a show at the Los Angeles County Museum.

In 1933, Lundeberg and Feitelson founded New Classicism, also known as post-surrealism. In a manifesto published the following year, Lundeberg wrote, "In New Classicism alone do we find an aesthetic which departs from the principles of the decorative graphic arts to found a unique order, an integrity of subject matter and pictorial structure unprecedented in the history of art." It constituted the first formal American response to the surrealist movement of the European avant-garde. Like the surrealists, Lundeberg and Feitelson were interested in exploring the subconscious mind using dreamlike imagery. They, however, eliminated the more fantastic elements of surrealistic art, concentrating on depicting worlds fully understandable by rational thought.

Lundeberg's best known post-surrealistic work is *Double Portrait of the Artist in Time* (1935), now in the collection of the Smithsonian Institution. The painting shows a girl, based on a photograph of the artist as a child, holding a flower and casting a long shadow of an adult. At the top of the otherwise formless shadow is Lundeberg's head, rendered in color and surrounded by a frame. In this painting within a painting, the artist is shown looking at a flower, closely studying its form.

Between 1933 to 1941, Lundeberg spent much of her time working for the Federal Art Project, a program that was administered by the federal government to aid artists during the Great Depression. Supervising staffs of artists and workers, she helped create several public murals in southern California. The most notable was *The History of Transportation* (1940), a mosaic made from colored cement and marble chips that covered a 240-foot wall erected in Centinela Park in Inglewood, a part of Los Angeles.

In the 1940s, Lundeberg was eager to move away from what she called "the impersonal and public aspects of mural painting." She began working on intimate paintings meant "to embody, and to evoke, states of mind, moods, and emotions." Painted in a muted palette, her meticulously composed still lifes and landscapes created a sense of calm and order. In the 1950s Lundeberg's work was often exhibited with the painters of the Hard Edge school. Including Feitelson, John McLaughlin, Karl Benjamin, and Frederick Hammersley, this group of California artists experimented with flat areas of bright, unmodulated color. Unlike the Hard Edge painters, Lundeberg never completely embraced abstraction. Explaining her resistance to nonobjective art, she once said, "I love, too much, the forms, perspectives, and atmosphere of our natural world."

Lundeberg's career was honored in 1979 with a retrospective at the Los Angeles Municipal Art Gallery. The next year, the San Francisco Museum of Modern Art staged a double retrospective featuring her paintings alongside Feitelson's work. Lundeberg briefly stopped painting following Feitelson's death in 1978, though in the 1980s she produced two major series, Grey Interiors and Wetlands. Her health failing, Lundeberg created her final painting, *Two Mountains,* in 1990. She died nine years later in Los Angeles at the age of 91.

Further Reading

Cutajar, Mario. "Helen Lundeberg," Art Scene: The Guide to Art Galleries and Museums in Southern California. Available online. URL: http://artscenecal.com/ ArticlesFile/Archive/Articles1997/Articles1097/ HLundebergB.html. Posted in October, 1997.

Haithman, Diane. "Helen Lundeberg: Artist, Pioneer of the New Classicism Movement," *Los Angeles Times,* April 21, 1999, 23.

Lorser Feitelson and Helen Lundeberg: A Retrospective Exhibition. San Francisco: San Francisco Museum of Modern Art, 1980.

Lundeberg, Helen. *Helen Lundeberg: Paintings Through Five Decades.* New York: Graham, 1982.

— L. S.

 ## MacIVER, LOREN
(1909–1998) *Painter*

Throughout her long career, Loren MacIver expressed a sense of wonder in the everyday in her dreamlike paintings. The daughter of a physician, she was born in New York City on February 2, 1909. At age 10, she began attending classes at the Art Students League. Her year of instruction there was the only formal art training she ever received.

In 1929, MacIver married poet and critic Floyd Frankenberg, who would later write a series of poems inspired by her work. The couple settled in Greenwich Village, where MacIver lived for most of her life. There, she painted for herself, with no thought of pursuing art as a career. Her husband was responsible for sparking public interest in her work. In 1935 he showed her paintings to Alfred H. Barr, the director of New York's Museum of Modern Art (MOMA). Impressed by MacIver's work, he bought *Shack,* an oil painting of the Cape Cod house where she spent her summers as a girl, for the museum's collection.

Beginning in 1936, MacIver spent three years working for the Federal Art Project, a New Deal program designed to provide income for artists during the Great Depression. Two years later, she had her first solo show at the East River Gallery. In the exhibition catalog, photographer Alfred Stieglitz wrote, "This girl should be given a chance to paint, if anybody should be given a chance to paint." In 1946 her paintings appeared in MOMA's influential group exhibition, *Fourteen Americans,* alongside works of Arshile Gorky, Robert Motherwell, Isamu Noguchi, and IRENE RICE PEREIRA. Seven years later, she and Pereira had simultaneous retrospectives at the Whitney Museum of American Art.

MacIver claimed Swiss painter Paul Klee as one of her early influences. Like Klee, she created dreamy images that, though bordering on abstract, never completely abandoned representation of the observable world. By applying thin layers of glazes, she gave her paintings a luminous quality. Writing in *Art in America* in 1994, critic and artist Robert G. Edelman described her style "as a kind of Magic Impressionism, her dreamlike vision seemingly observed through a veil or mist of diaphanous washes."

Many of MacIver's works of the 1940s and 1950s showed scenes of New York, often depicted from an aerial view. Her favorite subjects however, were familiar objects she found around her. In *Red Votive Lights* (1943), for instance, she created a lyrical image out of rows of lit and unlit votive candles. With their close examination of everyday life, her works have been likened to visual poems. In fact, through her husband, MacIver was friends with many of the most notable poets of her day, including e. e. cummings, Marianne Moore, and Elizabeth Bishop.

Beginning in 1961, MacIver spent extended periods in France, where she absorbed the latest in European art. During several summers spent in Provence, she was inspired by the light of the region. Her travels influenced many of her later works, which display a light and airy quality.

In 1989 MacIver became the first recipient of the Lee Krasner Award from the Pollock-Krasner Foundation. Continuing to paint and exhibit her work well into her 80s, MacIver died in her Greenwich Village home on May 3, 1998. Five years earlier, she had described her aesthetic in her only written statement about her work: "My wish is to make something permanent out of the transitory, by means at once dramatic and colloquial. Certain moments have the gift of revealing the past and foretelling the future. It is these moments that I hope to catch."

Further Reading

Baur, John I. H. *Loren MacIver, I. Rice Pereira.* New York: Macmillan, 1953.

Edelman, Robert G. "MacIver's Luminous Vision." *Art in America* 82 (February 1994): 80+.

The Grove Dictionary of Art. "MacIver, Loren," Grove Art. Available online. URL: http://www.artnet.com/library/05/0528/T052868.asp. Posted in 2001.

Loren MacIver: Five Decades. Newport Beach, Calif.: Newport Harbor Art Museum, 1993.

— L. S.

MARGOULIES, BERTA O'HARE
(1907–1996) *Sculptor*

Best known for her expressive sculptures from the 1930s, Berta Margoulies was born in Lowitz, Poland, on September 7, 1907. As an infant, she moved with her family to Belgium. When the Germans invaded the country in 1914, her father was imprisoned. The rest of the Margoulieses fled first to Holland, then to England.

While in her teens, Margoulies and her three siblings migrated to the United States. Settling in New York, she worked her way through Hunter College, graduating with a degree in anthropology in 1927. Fluent in French, German, and English, Margoulies took a job as a translator for a medical magazine.

For her own amusement, she began taking classes at the Education Alliance. An art class there changed the course of her life. As she later remembered, "There was a classroom with all this clay. . . . [T]he minute I got my hands in the stuff I said, 'Oh, my God! This is it.' I went there every evening." Taking classes at the Art Students League, Margoulies progressed quickly. In 1928 she won a scholarship for a year's study in Paris. Margoulies hoped to study with Emile Antoine Bourdelle, who himself had been a student of French master Auguste Rodin, but Bourdelle died while Margoulies was crossing the Atlantic. She enrolled instead at the Académie Julian and Académie Colarossi and attended an anatomy class at Ecole de Beaux-Arts.

Returning to New York City in the early 1930s, Margoulies opened her own studio. At the time, she had little choice, since established sculptors would rarely take on women as apprentices. Her career, however, benefited greatly from New Deal programs for artists administered by the Works Progress Administration (WPA). According to Margoulies, the WPA "gave women sculptors a chance for the first time to compete on an equal basis with men."

After crafting a head of Andrew Jackson for the WPA, Margoulies won a competition to design a statue of a colonial postman for the central U.S. post office in Washington, D.C. Using her brother as a model for the work, Margoulies researched the colonial period and its clothing to ensure the statue's accuracy. In 1939 Margoulies was given another major commission. For the garden court at the Federal Building at the New York World's Fair, she created *Woman and Deer,* a 14-foot plaster sculpture that earned her an award from the National Academy of Arts and Letters. During this period, Margoulies married writer Eugene O'Hare, with whom she had a son, Michael.

In the 1940s, several of Margoulies's most notable works dealt with the struggles of the working class. In *Mine Disaster* (1942), she created in bronze a moving group portrait of relatives of injured and killed mine workers. Her *Strike* (1948) depicted three laborers of different races, united in their cause. Margoulies's Jewish heritage also provided her with subject matter, although she maintained that works such as *Wailing Wall* and *Promised Land* were "humanistic—certainly not religious."

In many of her later works, such as *Panic* (1961), her figures became more expressive and

less naturalistic. While these works moved toward abstraction, Margoulies did not feel comfortbale with completely nonrepresentational work. As she once noted, she wanted her sculptures to express her "interest in people and the human condition." Largely due to her disinterest in form for form's sake, Margoulies's work was largely ignored during the 1960s and 1970s. Collectors have since rediscovered her work, which is represented in several major museums and often featured in group exhibitions of American sculpture. On May 22, 1996, Margoulies died at her home in San Francisco at the age of 88.

Further Reading

Rubinstein, Charlotte Streifer. *American Women Sculptors: A History of Women Working in Three Dimensions.* Boston: G. K. Hall, 1990.

Watson-Jones, Virginia. *Contemporary American Women Sculptors.* Phoenix, Ariz.: Oryx, 1986.

— L. S.

Notable sculptor Berta O'Hare Margoulies at work in her studio
(Courtesy Michael O'Hare)

MARISOL (Marisol Escobar)
(1930–) *Sculptor, Mixed Media Artist*

Known best for her witty pop art sculptures of the 1960s, Marisol Escobar was born on May 22, 1930, in Paris to wealthy Venezuelan parents. The jet-setting Escobars traveled extensively in Europe, Venezuela, and the United States. In Marisol's early teens, her family finally settled in Los Angeles following her mother's death. Rebelling against the Escobars' lavish lifestyle, Marisol fantasized about becoming a saint. Instead, she decided to pursue a career as a painter.

In 1949, with her father's support, Marisol studied art at the Académie des Beaux Arts in Paris. The next year, she moved to New York City, where she has lived ever since. She furthered her education at the Art Students League and the New School, where she studied with painter Hans Hofmann. Through Hofmann, Marisol was introduced to abstract expressionist painters, such as Jackson Pollock and Franz Kline, at their Greenwich Village hangout, the Cedar Tavern. Beautiful, cultured, and elegant, Marisol also attracted the attentions of painter Willem de Kooning, who became a mentor and strong supporter of her work.

Even more influential was Marisol's friendship with sculptor William King. She and King shared a fascination for American folk art. In New York museums, Marisol also began studying pre-Columbian figures. These objects inspired her to give up painting for sculpture. Her early work featured wooden and terra-cotta figures of people and animals, sometimes enclosed in glass-fronted boxes. Her sculptures were soon included in group shows in Tenth Street galleries, then the leading showcase for avant-garde American art. She had her first one-woman show at the Leo Castelli Gallery in November 1957. By that time, she had stopped using her last name, calling herself simply "Marisol."

The success of the Castelli show panicked Marisol. She took a year off in Rome. On returning to New York, she headed into one of her most productive artistic periods. Abstract expressionism had been replaced by pop art as the cutting-edge art style. Pop artists shunned the art-for-art's-sake solemnity of the abstract expressionists in favor of a figurative style that used elements of popular culture to make ironic statements about American society.

Fitting well into this new art scene, Marisol began creating large-scale figures and figure groupings that made use of a variety of materials including wood, plaster, metal, and fabric. Often, the figures' torsos were formed from a rectangular block of wood, on which Marisol drew or stenciled physical details and clothing. Added to the figures were plaster casts and wigs, hats, and other found objects, which Marisol often discovered in the trash. Marisol soon began incorporating images of herself into many of her works, adding plaster casts of her body parts and photographs of her face to her figures. In *Baby Girl* and *Baby Boy*, for instance, she created seven-foot-high toddlers who carried dolls bearing Marisol's photographed face. One of her best-known works, *The Party,* featured 15 representations of herself socializing with one another.

Many of Marisol's sculptures commented on social and political issues, often through depictions

Marisol peers from behind one of her evocative mixed-media assemblages.
(AP/Wide World Photos)

of public figures. In *LBJ Himself,* she depicted President Johnson holding in his hand three small figures representing his wife and daughters, thus suggesting the domination of men over women. Other figure groups that lampooned famous people included *The Kennedys* and *Royal Family.*

As Marisol's work drew more attention, she found herself becoming a celebrity. A friend of painter and provocateur Andy Warhol, Marisol was featured in several of his films. Her clothes, her look, and her circle were discussed in fashion magazines, including *Vogue, Glamour,* and *Cosmopolitan.* Her naturally quiet demeanor seemed to suggest a sense of mystery that made her a fascinating media subject. Marisol later maintained this image was a means of trivializing her work. In 1975 she called it "a way to wipe me out," adding "[I]n the 60s, the men did not feel threatened by me. They thought I was cute and spooky, but they didn't take my art so seriously."

In the late 1960s, Marisol left New York and spent many years traveling. During her travels, she took up scuba diving, which influenced a new stage in her work. In the 1970s, she began exhibiting meticulously carved and painted sculptures of fish with her own face. The sculptures, which satisfied Marisol's desire to create something "very pure," were not as well received as her earlier work.

Marisol has since returned to large figures, though her later work has become more personal. In the 1980s she began showing portrait sculptures of the artists who have influenced her, among them GEORGIA O'KEEFFE, LOUISE NEVELSON, and Pablo Picasso. She has also created her own interpretation of several works by Leonardo da Vinci. In 1991 the National Portrait Gallery opened a popular exhibit of Marisol's portraits. Sculptures from all periods of her career are now found in museum collections throughout the world.

Further Reading

Berman, Avis. "A Bold and Incisive Way of Portraying Movers and Shakers," *Smithsonian,* February 1984, 54+.

Grove, Nancy. *Magical Mixtures: Marisol Portrait Sculpture.* Washington, D.C.: Smithsonian Institution Press, 1991.

Staudek, Tomas. "Marisol," wwwpopArt. Available online. URL: http://www.fi.Muni.CZ/~toms/PopArt/Biographies/Marisol.html. Downloaded on July 27, 2001.

— L. S.

MARTIN, AGNES
(1912–) *Painter*

Her meticulous compositions created from lines and bands of luminous color have made Agnes Martin one of the most celebrated abstractionists in American art. The daughter of a wheat farmer, she was born in Maklin, Saskatchewan, on March 22, 1912. Her grandparents on both sides were Scottish immigrants who traveled to central Canada in covered wagons.

Following her father's death in 1914, Martin spent two years on the farm of Robert Kinnon, her maternal grandfather. She later cited Kinnon as an important influence on her, explaining, "He didn't talk very much, but without ever speaking to little children they knew he liked them. He gave self confidence without talking." Moving with her mother first to Calgary and later to Vancouver, Martin developed a love of drawing, though her only exposure to fine art came from postcards of art masterpieces she collected.

After high school, Martin left for Bellingham, Washington, where she earned a teacher's certificate at the Western Washington College of Education. Between 1937 and 1941, she taught elementary school, although the lack of available jobs during the Great Depression forced her to move frequently to find work. Hoping that further education would give her greater job security, she enrolled at Teachers College at Columbia University in New York City. She graduated with a master's degree in art education in 1952, but by that time, she had set her sights on a different career. Frequent visits to the city's museums convinced her that she could make a living by making art.

During the late 1940s and early 1950s, Martin divided her time between New York and the Santa Fe area, where she was on the faculty at the University of New Mexico. By 1952, she had settled permanently in Taos, New Mexico. Many of her earliest works were still lifes and landscapes, although in the 1950s she was drawn increasingly to abstraction. At the same time, she became interested in Asian thought, particularly in the writings of Chuang Tzu and Lao Tzu.

By 1957, Martin had abandoned representational art and was producing canvases with biomorphic shapes reminiscent of those found in the work of Joan Miró and Jean Arp. They attracted the attention of Betty Parsons, the art dealer who was then representing Jackson Pollack, Barnett Newman, and other leading abstract expressionists. Parsons was eager to show Martin's work, but only on the condition that she move to New York so that Martin would be available to meet with art buyers. After

Parsons bought enough of her paintings to pay her moving expenses, Martin agreed to relocate.

At the age of 45, Martin moved to Coenties Slip, a street in southern Manhattan along an abandoned 19-century seaport. In addition to cheap loft space, Coenties Slip offered Martin the opportunity to get to know young artists, such as Ellsworth Kelly, Jack Youngerman, Lenore Tawney, and Robert Indiana. Kelly later remembered that "Agnes was always the earth mother, a kind of sage. . . . Sometimes she would correct us because of our follies, like a parent would in a way." In part inspired by the hard edges in Kelly's and Youngerman's art, Martin moved away from biomorphic forms and toward geometric shapes.

Initially, she modeled these shapes after materials she found along the abandoned docks. But in about 1960, Martin's art was reshaped by a vision she had of a grid. She developed a new style, in which she drew light horizontal and vertical lines in a gridlike pattern that divided the canvas into a series of rectangles. Working with six-foot-square canvases, Martin extended the lines to their edges, creating an all-over, unified image. She saw the "dissonance" between the drawn rectangles and the square canvas as central to the paintings' effect, maintaining that the rectangle "lightens the weight of the square, destroys its power." For Martin, the new style marked the beginning of her career. She destroyed all the paintings in her possession that she had produced during her first 20 years as an artist.

After 1966, when her work appeared in the *Systemic Painting* exhibit at the Guggenheim Museum, Martin was labeled a minimalist. Minimalism was a movement toward reducing art to its essential elements. Although superficially her paintings resembled those of the minimalists, the purpose of Martin's art was distinctly different. The minimalists disavowed not only the representation of objects in the physical world but also maintained that their work had no metaphorical meaning. As Martin once explained, "The Minimalists were nonobjective. They just recorded beauty, I guess, without the emotions—or at least without personal emotions. My work is a little more emotional than that."

Her move toward the use of geometric shapes served her goal to depict that seen by what she called "the inner eye." Rather than purely formal experiments, her paintings were intended "to make us aware of the perfection of the mind." Her confidence in the transcendent qualities of art linked her philosophically to the abstract expressionists. Their spirit of rebellion and flamboyant public images, however, distinguished them from the more retiring Martin, who strove to make art that was "egoless" and "humble."

Just as she was beginning to receive critical recognition, Martin announced her retirement and left New York. As she once explained, "I came to a place of recognition of confusion that had to be solved. I had to have time and nobody's going to give you time where I was. So I had to leave." In a white pickup truck, she traveled alone through Canada and the American West for a year and half. She then returned to New Mexico, settling on a remote mesa where she built a home and studio from logs and adobe. After a five-year hiatus, Martin began to paint again in the early 1970s. In the work she has produced since, Martin replaced penciled lines with bands of lightly tinted color. Most were produced in series, each exploring variations on a particular compositional format and scheme of colors.

Since the 1970s, Martin's paintings have been hailed by critics. They have often been described in religious terms. Hilton Kramer of the *New York Times,* for instance, maintained in 1976 that "her art has the quality of a religious utterance, almost a form of prayer." Highlighting her paintings' meditative quality, Mark Stevens of *The New Republic* wrote in 1987, "The carefully crafted emptiness invites the mind to fill slowly with its own thoughts, and, perhaps, to glow along with the painting." Martin's reputation was solidified by a major exhibition at the Whitney Museum of American Art in 1992. Two years later, she donated seven canvases to the Harwood Museum in Taos. They are permanently displayed in an octagonal room that has been compared to the famous Rothko Chapel in Houston, Texas.

Now living in a retirement community in Santa Fe, Martin continues to paint three hours a day,

Portrait of Agnes Martin, New Mexico, 1992
(Photograph courtesy Charles R. Rushton
and Pace Wildenstein Gallery)

producing about a dozen canvases a year. Though among the most acclaimed living artists in the United States, she generally eschews awards and honors, maintaining that an unworldly inspiration is responsible for her work. Asked how she began a painting, Martin once explained, "I say to my mind, 'What am I going to paint next?' Then I wait for the inspiration. . . . You have to clear out your mind, to have a quiet and empty mind."

Further Reading

Agnes Martin. New York: Pace Wildenstein, 2000.

Brandauer, Aline Chipman. *Agnes Martin: Works on Paper.* Santa Fe: Museum of New Mexico, 1998.

Cotter, Holland. "Profiles: Agnes Martin. (Abstract Painter)," Art Journal. Available online. URL: http://www.findarticles.com/M0425/3_57/53286459/p1/article.jhtml. Posted in fall 1998.

Haskell, Barbara. *Agnes Martin.* New York: Whitney Museum of American Art, 1992.

— L. S.

MARTINEZ, MARIA (Maria Montoya)
(ca. 1887–1980)   *Potter*

Even during her lifetime, Maria Martinez was recognized as one of the greatest ceramists in the world. In the late 1880s, she was born Maria Montoya at San Ildefonso Pueblo in what is now north-central New Mexico. When she was about seven, she was taught to make pottery by her aunt, Tia Nicolasa. Maria also attended day school at San

Prizewinning potter Maria Martinez with her
husband Julian, circa 1940
(AP/Wide World Photos)

Ildefonso and spent two years at St. Catherine's Indian School in Santa Fe.

In 1904, Maria Montoya married Julian Martinez. The couple honeymooned at the St. Louis World's Fair, where they performed as part of a troupe of Pueblo dancers. Maria also demonstrated pottery making at the fair. Settling in San Ildefonso, the Martinezes eventually had four sons.

A farmer, Julian supplemented the family income by working for archaeologist Edgar Lee Hewitt of the University of New Mexico. Hewitt supervised the excavation of Frijoles Canyon—the site of a village of the Anasazi, the ancient ancestors of the Pueblo. Hewitt hired Julian and several other locals to help him with the dig, while Maria was employed as a cook for the laborers.

Learning of Maria Martinez's skill as a potter, Hewitt encouraged her to replicate Anasazi pots based on the shards his crew excavated. The shards were thinner and more polished than contemporary Pueblo pottery. Through trial and error, Martinez discovered that by adding very fine sand to her clay, she could reproduce the earlier pottery styles. Following Pueblo custom, she gave her pottery to Julian

to paint with designs found on the shards. Hewitt bought their pots and urged her to make more.

The Martinezes continued their study of Anasazi pottery at the Museum of New Mexico, where Julian took a job as a janitor. They were particularly fascinated by shards with a black surface and discovered that they could create the same effect in the firing process. Pueblo pottery was fired in an open flame. The Martinezes found that adding dung to the flame produced a smoke cloud that darkened a pot's surface. Through further experimentation, they learned that by painting a design with slip—clay mixed with water—before using their new firing method, they could create a shiny black design on a matte black background. This black-on-black style became the Martinezes' trademark.

With Hewitt's help, the Martinezes began selling their pottery to tourists. Their black-on-black pieces were particularly popular with art collectors. By the early 1920s, the Martinezes' work was found in many private and public collections. In addition to sharing her substantial income with needy friends and neighbors, Maria Martinez was generous with her knowledge of pottery making. At San Ildefonso and at the Indian school in Santa Fe, Martinez taught other Pueblo potters the techniques she and her husband had developed.

After Julian's death in 1943, Maria's work was painted by Santana Martinez, the wife of her son Adam. In 1956 she began a new collaboration with her son Tony, also known as Popovi Da. Well-regarded by art collectors and experts, Popovi Da's painting revived many of the red-and-black designs used by Anasazi potters.

By the 1950s Maria Martinez's work was internationally known. She was given several honorary doctorates and visited the White House four times. In 1954 she was awarded the Palmes Académiques by the French government for her contributions to the world of art. By the time of her death on June 10, 1980, Maria Martinez had become the most famous Indian artist in history and had helped to make the sale of Indian art a substantial industry. Because of her willingness to teach others her techniques, today dozens of distinguished San Ildefonso Pueblo potters—including her grandson Tony Da and great-granddaughter Barbara Gonzales—work in the Martinez tradition.

Further Reading

"Maria Martinez and San Ildefonso Pottery," J. Mark Sublette, Medicine Man Gallery, Inc. Available online. URL: http://www.Mariapottery.com/bio/frame.html. Downloaded on July 27, 2001.

Morse, Juddi. *Tending the Fire: The Story of Maria Martinez.* Flagstaff, Ariz.: Rising Moon, 1997.

Peterson, Susan. *The Living Tradition of Maria Martinez.* New York: Kodansha International, 1989.

Spivey, Richard L. *Maria.* 1979. Revised and Expanded. Flagstaff, AZ: Northland, 1989.

— L. S.

MASON, ALICE TRUMBULL
(1904–1971)   *Painter, Printmaker*

One of the earliest champions of abstractionism in American art, Alice Trumbull Mason was born into a wealthy and prominent family in Litchfield, Connecticut, in 1904. On her father's side, she was related to John Trumbull, the great history painter of the Revolutionary War era. During her youth, she frequently traveled to Europe with her family. In the 1920s, she spent several years in Florence and Rome, where she received her first formal art training at the British Academy.

By 1927, Alice Trumbull had settled in New York City. She took classes at the National Academy and the Grand Central Art Galleries, where she was taught by painter Arshile Gorky. He introduced Trumbull to European modernists, including the cubists and Wassily Kandinsky, thus sparking an interest in nonrepresentational experimentation. She later wrote that her total commitment to abstraction came in 1929, while she was traveling in Greece: "[A]fter happily painting these realistic things, I said to myself, 'What do I really know?' I knew the shape of my canvas and the use of my colors and I was completely joyful not to be governed by representing things anymore."

In 1928 Trumbull married sea captain Warwood Mason, with whom she had two children.

While her children were young, she had trouble finding time to paint and turned instead to writing poetry and experimental prose for self-expression. By the mid-1930s, however, Alice Trumbull Mason had emerged as one of the leading abstractionists in New York. At the time, abstract art was virtually ignored by critics, galleries, and museums. To gain more attention for their work, Mason and 38 other artists formed American Abstract Artists. Throughout her life, Mason was active in the organization and served as its president in 1951–52.

Through her association with American Abstract Artists, Mason secured her first one-woman show in 1942 at the Museum of Living Art at New York University. Her work of the 1930s and 1940s consisted largely of formal experiments using biomorphic shapes reminiscent of those of Kandinsky and Joan Miró. During the mid-1940s, she became fascinated by the work of Dutch painter Piet Mondrian. Under its influence, Mason increasingly worked with geometric forms in a style she called "architectural abstraction." Although her basic forms rarely changed, she used a varied and vivid palette. Mason created her own paints, grinding pigments herself and mixing them with oil.

In 1944 Mason began studying etching with Stanley Hayter at the New York printmaking studio Atelier 17. By 1949, she had an etching press in her studio. Mason later experimented with other methods of printmaking, including making woodcuts and using stencils.

Whether creating paintings or prints, Mason worked very methodically. She made extensive preparatory sketches and developed theories about the interaction of colors and forms. She often worked through an idea in a series of works. One of her print series, for instance, included *Interference of Closed Forms, Labyrinth of Closed Forms,* and *Orientation of Closed Forms.* As the titles indicate, she enjoyed repeatedly reworking an image, each time slightly shifting its emphasis.

In Mason's later years, she became more reclusive, especially after the death of her son in 1958.

(Her surviving child is the artist Emily Mason Kahn.) Her works moved toward greater simplicity, employing fewer shapes and more muted colors. Mason's last work, *Urban White,* was painted in 1969. She died in 1971 in New York City. Two years later, the Whitney Museum of American Art exhibited a small retrospective of her work. Since then, her paintings have often appeared in major exhibitions, securing her place in the early history of nonrepresentational art.

Further Reading

Alice Trumbull Mason: Etchings and Woodcuts. New York: Taplinger, 1985.

Bailey, Brooke. *The Remarkable Lives of 100 Women Artists.* Holbrook, Mass: Bob Adams, 1994.

Brown, Marilyn. *Alice Trumbull Mason, Emily Mason: Two Generations of Abstract Painting.* New York: Eaton House, 1982.

Mecklenburg, Virginia M. "Alice Trumbull Mason," National Museum of American Art and Smithsonian Institution Press. Available online. URL: http://nmaa-ryder.si.edu/collections/exhibits/abstraction/Mason.html. Downloaded on July 27, 2001.

— L. S.

MENDIETA, ANA
(1948–1985)   *Body Artist, Earth Artist, Sculptor, Performance Artist*

Using avant-garde art forms pioneered in the 1970s, Ana Mendieta created passionate art that explored her identity as a woman and as a Cuban American. Born on November 8, 1948, she grew up in an affluent family in Havana, Cuba. To protect their children from the violence of the Castro regime, her parents sent 12-year-old Ana and her sister Raquel to live in the United States through the Catholic-sponsored relocation program Operation Pedro Pan. Mendieta spent the rest of her youth in a series of orphanages and foster homes, separated from her family and her homeland.

In 1969 Mendieta graduated with a bachelor's degree from the University of Iowa. She continued on at the university and received a master's of fine arts (MFA) degree in painting three years later.

During her studies, however, Mendieta had grown disillusioned with her work. As she wrote, "My paintings were not real enough for what I wanted the images to convey, and by real I mean I wanted my images to have power, to be magic." Her quest led her to the university's recently established Multimedia and Video Art program. Studying there for a second MFA, she was exposed to the various forms of experimental art—including earth art, body art, and performance art—in which she would work for most of her career.

Mendieta was also strongly influenced by the women's movement of the 1970s. One of her first performance pieces was a feminist response to the rape and murder of a fellow student. Mendieta invited friends to her apartment, where they found her smeared with blood, half nude, and tied to a table as she reenacted the victim's ordeal.

Other performances challenged social assumptions about gender. In "Facial Hair Transplants" (1972), a male student shaved his facial hair, which Mendieta then affixed to her own face. During "Glass on Body Imprints" (1972), she shoved parts of her body flat against a pane of glass as a commentary on expectations about women's physical appearance.

Although continuing to use her body in her art, Mendieta shifted toward creating outdoor artwork with her Silueta series (1973–77). The series was inspired by her research into pre-Columbian cultures and her frequent visits to Mexico during this period. In each work, Mendieta made an outline of her five-foot-tall frame using natural materials, such as stones, flowers, and earth, and allowed the elements to destroy the silhouette. In one Silueta piece, she dug an outline of herself on a beach, poured red paint onto it, and let the tide carry it away. Over four years, Mendieta made 200 Siluetas in Mexico and Iowa, which she documented in more than 80 short films and slides.

Mendieta claimed that the relation between her body and the earth in her art was a response to her removal from Cuba as an adolescent. She explained, "I am overwhelmed by the feeling of having been cast from the womb. My art is the way I re-establish the bonds that united me to the universe." The frequent use of blood in her art was also a reference to her fascination with the Santería religion developed by black Cubans, which involves animal sacrifice. Her sister once recalled that she and Ana as children were fascinated with the stories of Santería legends and rituals told to them by their nannies.

In 1978 Mendieta moved to New York City, where she quickly became involved in the experimental art scene. She joined the AIR Gallery, a cooperative gallery that showed the work of feminist artists. There, in 1979, she had her first solo exhibition, which featured photographic documentation of the Silueta series. The following year, Mendieta helped organize a group show at the AIR Gallery titled, *Dialectics of Isolation: An Exhibition of Third World Women Artists in the United States.*

Mendieta returned to Cuba for the first time in 1979. On a subsequent visit, she created her Rupestrian sculpture series. Supported by the Cuban Ministry of Culture, the series included images that resembled fertility symbols carved on the rocks and caves of Jaruco Park, outside Havana. Photographs of the carvings were shown at the AIR Gallery and the Hartford Art School.

By 1982, Mendieta began experimenting with more traditional forms of art. Using bark paper and dry leaves, she created a series of drawings featuring abstracted female figures. While in Rome on a fellowship in 1983, she made her first freestanding sculptures from tree trunks. Mendieta seemed interested in continuing in this direction. In a 1985 proposal for a commission from the Otis Art Institute of Los Angeles, she planned to create an outdoor installation in MacArthur Park composed of seven tree trunks marked with carved and burned images.

In January 1985, Mendieta married minimalist sculptor Carl Andre. During a violent argument on his birthday on September 8, Mendieta fell through the window of their 34th-floor New York apartment and was killed. Andre was tried for second-degree murder, but he was acquitted in 1988. The year after her death, the University of Iowa's School of Art created the Ana Mendieta Memorial Scholarship in her honor.

Further Reading

Blocker, Jane. *Where Is Ana Mendieta?: Identity, Performativity, and Exile.* Durham, N.C.: Duke University Press, 1999.

Clearwater, Bonnie, editor. *Ana Mendieta: A Book of Works.* Miami Beach, Fla.: Grassfield Press, 1993.

Nederend, Gabriëlle. "Ana Mendieta," Galerie Akinci. Available online. URL: http://www.akinci.nl/Ana_Mendieta/Mendieta.htm. Posted in 1999.

Mendieta, Ana. *Ana Mendieta: A Retrospective.* New York: New Museum of Contemporary Art, 1987.

— L. S.

MISS, MARY
(1944–) *Sculptor*

One of the United States's leading environmental sculptors, Mary Miss was born in New York in 1944. Her father was an officer in the military, so the family moved frequently. Miss spent most of her youth at army posts in the western United States, and the landscape of the West would later play a crucial role in her development as an artist.

Miss graduated from the University of California, Santa Barbara, in 1966 and the Rinehart School of Sculpture at the Maryland Art Institute in 1968. Even while a student, Miss began experimenting with materials, including wood and wire mesh, as she tried to create her own sculptural vocabulary. She initially made large sculptural works in her New York City studio, but increasingly she began designing sculptures for large outdoor spaces. At the time, other sculptors, most notably Robert Smithson, were exploring large-scale environmental art, but Miss had difficulty relating to their work. "They were using the landscape as a large canvas, making their mark on it," as she later explained. Her experiences living in the West had taught her the "futility of attempting to do this in the vast landscapes found, for example, in Canada or Colorado."

Miss instead wanted to create art on a more human scale that would allow viewers to see the landscape surrounding the piece in a new way. One of her early works, installed on Ward's Island in New York's East River, made use of lengths of white rope attached to stakes set up along the shore. From a distance it was invisible, but, according to Miss, "you discovered it as you walked around the edge of the island—an accumulated experience." Like many of Miss's works, the piece guided viewers from place to place, thus creating an experience that involved the viewers' perception of both space and time.

In her first outdoor sculptures, Miss frequently used fencelike structures. She said they were inspired by the large stretches of western land that were empty except for "a beautiful ribbon of fence which never dominate[d] the landscape," but appeared instead as "just a subtle structure marching off into the distance." In 1973 Miss employed fence imagery in creating a site sculpture on a landfill in southern Manhattan. She erected five wooden sections 50 feet apart along the river's shore. Each was cut with an eyehole, providing five different views of the surroundings.

One of Miss's most ambitious early works was *Perimeters/Pavilions/Decoys* (1978), a temporary sculpture that covered acres on the grounds of the Nassau County Museum of Fine Arts in Roslyn, New York. The work included a wooden tower, a sunken pit, and underground rooms, with each element producing a distinct spatial experience. Other notable pieces from this period included *Veiled Landscapes* (1980), which invited the viewer to look at particular vistas through wire screens, and *Field Rotation* (1981), which featured wooden posts that, through an optical isolation, appeared to spin around a central pit.

In 1988 Miss was given her most important commission. Working with architect Stanton Eckstut and landscape architect Susan Child, she designed *South Cove,* a large site sculpture at Battery Park City, an exclusive waterfront development in Manhattan. The piece includes a public walkway that curves over the river. Miss later explained, "I tried to imagine the experience of coming from the density of lower Manhattan and walking over the water on the curving pier. . . . Once you're at the point where the land, the water

and the structure come together, you've reached the heart of the place. The culminating circle is defined on one side by the built and on the other by the organic."

Among Miss's more recent works is *Greenwood Pond, Double Site* (1996), an installation at the Des Moines Art Center. The piece offers a variety of vantage points from its bridges, walkways, seating areas, and observation tower. Miss has also worked with New York's Metropolitan Transportation Authority on the renovation of the Union Square subway station. At 115 locations in the station, she placed architectural elements from the original building in frames of red stainless steel, thus relating the new construction to the original building.

Further Reading

The Grove Dictionary of Art. "Miss, Mary," Grove Art. Available online. URL: http://www.artnet.com/library/05/0586/T058636.asp. Posted in 2001.

Miss, Mary. *Mary Miss: Projects 1966–1987.* London: Architectural Association, 1987.

———. *Mary Miss: Photos/Drawings.* Reading, Pa.: Freedman Gallery, 1991.

Onorato, Ronald J. "Illusive Spaces: The Art of Mary Miss." *Artforum* 17 (December 1978): 28–33.

— L. S.

MITCHELL, JOAN
(1926–1992) *Painter*

One of the few female abstract expressionists, Joan Mitchell was born into a wealthy family in Chicago on February 21, 1926. Her father, a physician and amateur painter, introduced her to fine art through visits to the Art Institute of Chicago. She began painting as a child and soon decided she wanted to become an artist.

After two years at Smith College, Mitchell enrolled at the Art Institute and graduated with a bachelor of fine arts degree in 1947. She spent the following year in New York City, where she studied with Hans Hofmann. While in New York, Mitchell was first introduced to the work of Jackson Pollock and Arshile Gorky, leaders in the abstract expressionist school. The abstract expressionists were experimenting with a unique American form of abstraction that emphasized brush stroke and texture and embraced spontaneity in the painting process.

On a year-long fellowship, Mitchell made her first trip to Paris in 1948. While she was there, her work became progressively more abstract. After returning to New York, she married her childhood friend Barney Rosset, the founder of Grove Press. She also began a close association with the abstract expressionists. She was particularly influenced by the slashing brush strokes and bold colors of Willem de Kooning and Franz Kline. Mitchell embraced the aggressive and competitive personal style of the abstract expressionists as well, often joining her fellow artists for drinking sessions at Greenwich Village's Cedar Tavern.

Two years after receiving her master's degree in fine arts from New York University in 1950, Mitchell had her first one-woman show. An *Artnews* (later *ARTnews*) review called it "a savage debut" and described her paintings as "heroic-sized cataclysms of aggressive color-lines." The same year, Mitchell divorced Rosset. She had a brief second marriage to financial analyst Alan Greenspan, the future chairman of the Federal Reserve Board.

Feeling that the celebrity-driven New York art world was stifling her creativity, Mitchell returned to France. There, in 1955, she met Canadian painter Jean-Paul Riopelle, who remained her companion for 12 years. By 1959, Mitchell had settled permanently in the countryside north of Paris.

Working in relative isolation, Mitchell emerged in the 1960s as a powerful colorist. Most of her paintings were inspired by nature. Rather than a literal representation of an outdoor setting, Mitchell's work, in her own words, was "about a feeling that comes to me from the outside, from landscape." While still working in the abstract expressionist style, she developed a highly organized working method. Rejecting the spontaneity that characterized the approach of artists such as Pollock, Mitchell painted slowly and deliberately, often working from preliminary drawings. As Mitchell once said, "I want to know what my brush is doing."

In the United States of the 1960s, where painting was moving toward pop art and minimalism, Mitchell's work was largely ignored. Still, Mitchell remained a force in French art and was frequently visited by young artists at her estate in Vétheuil. Often personally abrasive, Mitchell was alternately supportive and dismissive of the work of her friends and visitors. One friend, anticipating her withering criticism, once wrote on the back of an announcement she sent to Mitchell of an upcoming show, "Don't tell me. I know."

Some critics have noted that Mitchell's home overlooked the same countryside Claude Monet painted during the 1870s. Mitchell, however, bristled at the suggestion that her work was derivative of Monet, though she clearly shared with the French impressionists a fascination with the light and terrain of northern France. Her kinship with the impressionists made her unusual among American modernists, most of whom in the 1960s were more interested in rejecting rather in embracing the masters of the past.

By the 1970s, the American art world had renewed its interest in Mitchell. In 1974 she had a museum show at the Whitney Museum of American Art in New York. Her reputation was solidified in 1988 with a career retrospective at Cornell University. Many critics maintained that her work during the 1980s was among her best, despite her increasingly poor health. After years of relative obscurity, Mitchell was recognized as a major American artist at the time of her death on October 30, 1992.

Further Reading

Bernstock, Judith E. *Joan Mitchell.* New York: Hudson Hills Press, 1988.

"Joan Mitchell," Geocities. Available online. URL: http://www.geocities.com/Athens/oracle/1318/Joan_Mitchell.html. Downloaded on July 27, 2001.

Kertess, Klaus. *Joan Mitchell.* New York: Harry N. Abrams, 1997.

— L. S.

MORGAN, JULIA
(1872–1957)   *Architect*

Arguably America's greatest woman architect, Julia Morgan is best remembered for her design of William Randolph Hearst's mansion, San Simeon. On January 26, 1872, Morgan was born into a wealthy family in San Francisco. Her mother pushed Julia and her younger sister Emma to excel academically. Though physically small and sickly, Julia showed an early interest in athletics and feats of daring.

Morgan was introduced to architecture by Pierre LeBrun, her mother's cousin and a prominent New York architect known for his design of the Metropolitan Life Insurance Tower. She decided to study at the University of California at Berkeley, which at the time had no architecture school. Morgan instead earned her degree in civil engineering, becoming the first woman to do so at Berkeley.

By graduation, Morgan had a thorough grounding in building construction, but little training in design. She turned for help to her drawing professor, Bernard Maybeck, who taught informal architecture classes from his home. For two years, she worked as a draftsperson for Maybeck, who encouraged her to continue her study of architecture at his alma mater, the Ecole des Beaux-Arts in Paris. She left for Europe in 1896 and devoted the next two years to seeking admission to the rigorous school. Once admitted, Morgan was harassed by male students and professors, but she excelled nevertheless, winning several coveted prizes for her student work. In 1902 she was awarded her degree, becoming the architecture school's first female graduate.

Returning to the San Francisco Bay area, Morgan was hired by the firm of John Galen Howard, which was then helping to redesign the Berkeley campus. Much of the work was financed by Phoebe Apperson Hearst, whose husband had made a fortune in mining. Hearst was impressed by Morgan and possibly encouraged her to create her own firm in 1904. Among Morgan's early

commissions were the reconstruction of the Fairmont Hotel, which had been leveled in the 1906 San Francisco earthquake. During the project, she spoke with a reporter, who assumed she was the hotel's interior decorator because of her gender. It was the last interview Morgan ever gave.

The Fairmont made Morgan's reputation. Her firm was soon in demand, particularly for housing designs. Working on both cottages and mansions, Morgan became known for her comfortable, practical interiors and simple, well-proportioned exteriors. Instead of developing a signature style, she adapted her work to suit her clients' needs and tastes. Morgan, however, was instrumental in pioneering a distinctive northern California style that featured the use of exposed wood inside and out and attempted to integrate buildings into their natural surroundings.

In addition to private houses, Morgan designed numerous public buildings, including St. John's Presbyterian Church in San Francisco and the library and bell tower at Mills College in Oakland. She also worked for many nonprofit women's organizations, most notably the Young Women's Christian Association (YWCA). In 1913 she designed the organization's Asilomar Conference Center near Monterey. Now the site of a state park, the structure created a warm atmosphere through the use of exposed redwood and local stone. Morgan also designed YMCA residence halls throughout the United States.

In 1919 Phoebe Apperson Hearst died, leaving her fortune to her son, William Randolph Hearst. The same year, he commissioned Morgan to build several bungalows on a family ranch along the Pacific coast, midway between San Francisco and Los Angeles. The project quickly became more ambitious. For the next two decades, both Morgan and Hearst became consumed with constructing what became known as San Simeon. With a castle of 127 rooms, several guest mansions, multiple pools and courtyards, and a zoo, it would eventually be the most elaborate personal residence in the United States.

In many ways, Morgan and Hearst seemed an unlikely team. Morgan was as shy as Hearst was flamboyant. Hearst's capriciousness also proved a formidable challenge. From day to day, he would change his mind about what he wanted. It was Morgan's responsibility to persuade the crew of as many as 90 construction workers and craftspeople to cater to her client's whims.

From a design standpoint, the project was equally daunting. Hearst wanted San Simeon to showcase thousands of art objects he purchased in Europe. Morgan had to meld together many different architecture styles to accommodate his massive and highly eclectic collection.

During the more than 20 years Morgan worked on Hearst's estate, she spent nearly every weekend at San Simeon. She continued to take on many other commissions, aided by a large staff. At her firm's height, she employed 16 architects. Morgan enjoyed nurturing young talent and supported the careers of many female architects and draftspeople, often funding their education with her profits.

During the war years, Morgan's work on San Simeon slowed down as Hearst struggled with financial setbacks. She had little trouble finding other work, however. In addition to being known for keeping costs down, Morgan was experienced in working with concrete, a desirable skill when other building materials were scarce due to wartime restrictions.

Morgan retired in 1946 and spent several years touring Europe, Mexico, and South America. She closed her office in 1951, after designing more than 700 buildings. Six years later, Morgan died of a stroke in her hometown on February 2, 1957. Though now honored as an important pioneer in American architecture, during her lifetime she shied away from publicity and acclaim, preferring instead for people to know her by her work. As she once explained, "My buildings speak for me."

Further Reading

Boutelle, Sara Holmes. *Julia Morgan, Architect.* New York: Abbeville Press, 1988.

"Julia Morgan Biography," Special Collections Department, Robert E. Kennedy Library, California Polytechnic State University. Available online. URL: http://www.lib. calpoly.edu/spec_Coll/Morgam/bio/bio.html. Posted in 1996.

Kastner, Victoria. *Hearst Castle: Biography of a Country House.* New York: Harry N. Abrams, 2000.

— L. S.

MOSES, GRANDMA (Anna Mary Robertson Moses)
(1860–1961) *Painter*

Rising to international fame in the 1940s, Grandma Moses became the best-known folk artist in American art. Her landscapes, peopled by tiny figures, offered a view of rural life still popularly celebrated for representing uniquely American virtues and values. Moses was born Anna Mary Robertson on September 7, 1860, on a flax farm in Washington County, New York. One of 10 children, she received little schooling and no formal education in art. However, her father, himself an amateur painter, nurtured her artistic inclinations by giving her sheets of paper on which she drew pictures with berry and grape juice. In her 1952 autobiography, Moses recalled that her mother was less encouraging: "[She] was more practical, thought that I could spend my time other ways."

At age 12, Anna went to work on a neighbor's farm. There, she met farmhand Thomas Moses, whom she married in 1887. The couple settled on a farm in Staunton, Virginia, and had 10 children, only five of whom survived infancy. In addition to Anna Moses's work as a farmwife, she used her savings to buy a cow so she could start a butter-making business. She later explained, "[I] always wanted to be independent. I couldn't bear the thought of sitting down and Thomas handing out the money."

In 1905 the Moses family returned to New York State, moving to a farm in the village of Eagle Bridge near Anna's childhood home. After Thomas's death in 1927, Anna continued to run the farm with the help of several of her grandchildren. In her seventies, she began to retire from farm work, instead filling her days by making embroidered pictures from scraps of yarn. When her arthritis made it too difficult to handle a needle at age 78, Moses took up painting at the suggestion of her sister.

Moses made her first work using leftover house paint and canvas cloth from the cover of a threshing machine. She soon bought by mail order a box of artist's paints and brushes and began painting on masonite, which she cut to fit old frames she collected. Initially, Moses copied postcard illustrations and Currier and Ives prints. Using her bedroom as her studio, she gradually moved toward painting landscapes based on her memories of the Virginia and New York countryside. Moses painted first the sky, then the ground, and finally small, highly detailed figures engaged in the everyday activities of rural families, such as apple-picking, sleighing, tapping maple trees, and catching wild turkeys. Moses's art depicted a seemingly timeless world that changed only with the seasons. Her palette defined the season depicted, with her winter scenes dominated by white; spring scenes, by light green; summer scenes, by dark green; and autumn scenes, by brown.

As she began painting, Moses gave away many of her works, although she exhibited several at local fairs. With characteristic wryness, she remembered how at one fair she showed a few paintings alongside examples of her canning: "I won a prize for my fruit and jam, but no pictures."

In 1938 Moses displayed four of her paintings in the window of a nearby drugstore, which as a sideline sold local women's handiwork. There, they were spotted by Louis Caldor, a New York City engineer and art collector who was vacationing upstate with his family. Caldor bought the lot and, on a visit to Moses the next day, purchased about a dozen more. He promised Moses that he would promote her work to New York galleries.

For the next year, Caldor showed Moses's work to his friends in the art world, but no one showed much interest. Finally, he convinced Sidney Janis of the Museum of Modern Art to feature three of her paintings in its *Contemporary Unknown Painters* exhibition in October 1939. The show, assembled in the museum's Members' Room, was not open to the public, so it received scant attention. But the exhibition was just a small part of the growing interest in American folk art. At the time, modern American art was often dismissed as an inferior imitation of the work of European modernists. In search of a unique identity for American art, some in the avant-grade began looking for a new idiom in the homespun work of folk artists.

One such folk art enthusiast was Otto Kallir, a gallery owner who had recently arrived in New York from Vienna. In his early shows, he introduced to the United States the work of the great Austrian modernists Gustav Klimt, Egon Schiele, and Oskar Kokoschka. With his interest in folk and primitive art, Kallir agreed to stage Moses's first one-woman show at his Galérie St. Étienne. Opening in October 1940, the exhibition of 35 paintings, titled *What a Farm Wife Painted*, was well attended but received little press. A short, unsigned article on the show that appeared in the *New York Herald Tribune*, however, referred to the artist as "Grandma Moses," a quaint nickname that helped pave the way for her future popularity.

Executives at Gimbels department store, however, were impressed enough to re-create the exhibit as part of their Thanksgiving promotion. The event brought Moses's art to a larger audience and started her career as a celebrity. Touting her in advertisements as "the biggest artistic rave since Currier and Ives," Gimbels invited Moses to attend the exhibition's opening. On her first trip to New York City in more than 20 years, she charmed the press by telling the crowd about her canning techniques, avoiding the subject of her painting altogether. One resulting headline—"Grandma Moses Just Paints and Makes No Fuss About It"—communicated the humility that helped shape Moses's legened.

The publicity brought Moses a wave of commissions, which she called "those dreadful orders." Resentful of intrusions into privacy, she wrote Caldor in 1942, "I have too much of it. . . . Every day or so there is a call for paintings, for an exhibit or to buy." She was equally annoyed by the press and generally refused to grant interviews. In another letter, Moses complained of her folksy image, citing that a neighbor had asked her sons "if it was so that I could not read or write, being a primitive."

Grandma Moses was a world famous, self-taught folk artist.
(AP/Wide World Photos)

Moses also initially resisted the conventions of art sales and promotion. While Caldor acted as her agent, working primarily with Kallir's gallery, Moses continued to sell her paintings directly to the public, often for $50 or less apiece. As her reputation grew, she became appalled at the high prices Kallir charged for her work. She once wrote Caldor, telling him to stop Kallir from "ask[ing] such extortion prices for some of those shopworn paintings. He must come down on his prices or not sell." Still, Moses always viewed her painting as a business, maintaining that if her work stopped selling, she could always raise chickens or take in boarders to bring in extra income.

In 1944 Kallir began taking a traveling exhibition of Moses's work to museums and art associations throughout the country. Over the next 15 years, her work appeared in hundreds of shows in the United States and 15 in Europe. Even more instrumental in popularizing her work, Kallir signed a deal with the Brundage greeting card company, licensing several of Moses's works for a line of Christmas cards. After a tremendous initial response, Hallmark took over the license the next year and eventually sold more than 35 million cards featuring color reproductions of Moses's works. Through Grandma Moses Properties, a company established by Kallir, her paintings were also reproduced on drapery fabrics, on plates, and in framed prints.

By the end of the 1940s, Grandma Moses had become a national phenomenon. Her birthday was annually noted in the press, and she was regularly the subject of media attention during the Thanksgiving and Christmas season. With her fame, Moses became more comfortable with the press. She appeared occasionally on radio and television, most notably in a special color edition of Edward R. Murrow's talk show, *See it Now,* in 1955. The public responded well to her down-to-earth witticisms, which echoed one of the most appealing aspects of her work. For many, her paintings seemed to represent a quiet world of the past, preserved and protected from the anxieties of modern postwar America.

Her popularity also rested on the story of how she came to painting late in life, which was told repeatedly in press accounts. Her example was held up as proof of the appealing notion that one was never too old to take on something new. Largely because of Moses, mid-20th century America saw a vogue for amateur painting.

High art circles were less enthusiastic about Moses and her work. Her rise to fame coincided with the development of abstract expressionism, the first major art movement initiated in the United States. To critics, Moses's representational paintings were discounted as the antithesis of new American abstract art. Her very popularity was often cited as evidence that she was not an important artist. On the other hand, many who were disturbed by abstractionism held Moses up as paragon because the accessibility of her work.

A media star for nearly 20 years, in September 1960 Moses saw her 100th birthday celebrated with a cover story in *Life* magazine. She continued to paint until she fell ill the following April. On December 13, 1961, Moses died in a nursing home in Hoosick, New York. Her paintings now hang in major museums throughout the world, but her work is even better known through the reproductions that are still hung in homes throughout the country. Perhaps more than the work of any other artist, Moses's vision penetrated the national consciousness, providing images that continue to influence how the world defines what it means to be American.

Further Reading

"Anna Mary Robertson: Grandma Moses and Her Place in History," World Wide Arts Resources Corp. Available online. URL: http://www.absolutearts.com/artnews/2001/03/16/28245.html. Downloaded on July 27, 2001.

Kallir, Jane. *Grandma Moses in the 21st Century.* Alexandria, Va.: Art Services International, 2001.

———. *Grandma Moses: The Artist Behind the Myth.* New York: Clarkson N. Potter, 1982.

Kallir, Otto. *Grandma Moses.* New York: Harry N. Abrams, 1973.

Kallir, Otto, editor. *Grandma Moses: My Life's History.* New York: Harper, 1952.

— L. S.

MURRAY, ELIZABETH
(1940–)   *Painter*

In 1997 *Art in America* magazine described Elizabeth Murray's witty paintings as "Walt Disney meets Edvard Munch and Salvador Dali, but without the esprit, angst or enigma." Born in Chicago in 1940, Murray graduated from the city's Art Institute in 1962. Two years later, she earned a master's of fine arts degree from Mills College in Oakland, California.

During the 1960s, Murray's primary influences were the works of painters Jasper Johns and Robert Rauschenberg. In her early paintings, she built up the canvas surface with thick paint, often attaching objects, such as stuffed fabric and parts of furniture, to her work. Several paintings included images of Dick Tracy and Little Orphan Annie, a reference to her fascination with cartoons and animated figures. Displaying her interest in narrative, Murray also crafted "books" with painted and embroidered pages and gave friends a newspaper, called *The Monthly,* with stories she had written and illustrated. Murray destroyed much of her early work, which art critic Roberta Smith once described as "conventional, unoriginal, and frequently close to awful."

In the fall of 1967, Murray moved to New York City. There she had two daughters, Daisy and Sophie, with her husband, performance artist and poet Bob Holman. Although Murray was exhilarated by living in the center of the American art world, she was disturbed by her introduction to minimalism. Then the pervasive school among the avant-garde, minimalism embraced abstraction using only the most basic forms and a limited palette—a style at odds with Murray's pop art–influenced assemblages. Murray spent her first years in New York trying to reconcile the new art with her own. As she later remembered, "The mood was that painting was out, that hip people, people who were avant, weren't involved with painting."

Murray reached a turning point in 1971, when her friend, artist Jennifer Barnett, responded to her recent work by saying, "You can do better than this." Murray gave up working in three dimensions, replaced her acrylics with oils, and moved toward more pure abstraction. In 1972 one of Murray's new pieces, *Dakota Red,* was shown in the Whitney Biennial, marking her first major exposure.

Through the late 1970s, Murray continued to embrace abstraction. She later said that during this period, "I felt that the work was really about clearing the decks. . . . I began to work with the shapes and focusing on the paint and thinking in very simple terms about what a painting could be." Slowly, she began working on larger canvases, sometimes cutting them in irregular shapes, and started using bolder color.

By the end of decade, almost unconsciously, Murray also began moving back toward representation. As she once explained, "[T]he shapes started to show me that they became real things." In works such as *Brush's Shadow* (1981) and

Painters' Progress (1981), brushes and her own hands could be seen in the shapes on the canvas. In others such as *Yikes* and *Just in Time,* she began to explore what would become her favorite motif—the coffee cup.

Throughout the 1980s and 1990s, Murray concentrated on depictions of household objects that seemed energetic and alive, with parts twisting and turning in unexpected and impossible ways. *Stirring Still* (1997), for example, shows two undulating coffee cups with intertwined handles, while *Moonbeam* (1995–96) depicts a bed with its twining legs looping into U shapes on top of the blankets. The edges of many of her later works also appear to have a mind of their own. With as many as 20 oddly shaped canvases pieced together, Murray's paintings jut out in all directions heightening the manic sensation they provoke in the viewer. While humorous and whimsical, her work also communicates a sense of chaos, which Murray has likened to the moment of panic she feels when working on a painting just before all its elements come together.

In 1988 Murray had her first major solo show at the Whitney Museum of American Art in New York. She has since emerged as a leading American painter, particularly renowned for her ability to meld abstraction and representation. Her paintings are at once exercises in form and depictions of objects that stir the emotions.

Further Reading

Doktorczyk-Donohue, Marlena. "Elizabeth Murray," *Art Scene: The Guide to Art Galleries and Museums in Southern California.* Available online. URL: http://artscenecal.com/Articlesfile/Archive/Articles 1997/Article0297/EMurray.html. Posted in February 1997.

Elizabeth Murray: Recent Paintings, February 12–March 13, 1999. New York: Pace Wildenstein, 1999.

Elizabeth Murray: Recent Paintings, May 1–June 20, 1997. New York: Pace Wildenstein, 1997.

Graze, Sue, and Kathy Halbreich. *Elizabeth Murray: Paintings and Drawings.* New York: Harry N. Abrams, 1987.

— L. S.

NAMPEYO

(ca. 1860–1942)   *Potter*

The work of Nampeyo helped convince non-Indian collectors that American Indian pottery could be considered as art. Nampeyo was born in about 1860 in the Hopi village of Hano in present-day Arizona. Few details are known about Nampeyo's youth, though she likely learned to make pottery from her grandmother. Pottery making traditionally was a highly respected skill among the Hopi. But when Nampeyo was a young woman, it was becoming a lost art. Able to acquire metal pots and china bowls from non-Indian traders, few women bothered to make even the most utilitarian pottery, much less the intricately painted vessels crafted by their ancestors.

In the late 1870s, Nampeyo married a man named Kwivioya, but they never lived together. In 1881 she wed her second husband, Lesou. The couple had at least five children before his death in 1932. Some scholars have speculated that Lesou guided Nampeyo's career as a potter. While the extent of his involvement is not clear, he certainly took an interest in her work.

In 1891 Lesou was one of about 15 men hired by archaeologist Jesse Walter Fewkes to help him excavate the ruins of the old village of Sityatki. The men found many shards and some whole pots that were made hundreds of years before. Lesou brought some of these artifacts home. Their beautiful painted designs inspired Nampeyo to visit the excavation site and sketch the patterns of the unearthed pots.

Most likely, Nampeyo was familiar with Sityatki designs from pot shards she had found herself years earlier. But with the new discoveries, she began studying the ancient pottery decorations and creating her versions of the designs. She also adapted some of the shapes of the Sityatki artifacts in her own work. Her favorite shape became a wide, squat water jar, which she decorated in a thick band along its shoulder placed between two black horizontal stripes.

Nampeyo had little trouble finding buyers for her art. Traders usually gave her about two to five dollars for large pots, which they could easily resell for a high profit. Her superior artistry was so obvious that even tourists unfamiliar with Indian art were eager to purchase her pieces. Fewkes even feared that she had so captured the spirit of Sityatki works that "unscrupulous traders" were driving up prices by telling their customers that Nampeyo's pots were prehistoric artifacts.

One of the earliest admirers of Nampeyo's art was Walter Hough of the Smithsonian Institution.

Acclaimed potter Nampeyo in the Pueblo village
of Hano in 1875
(Courtesy Museum of New Mexico, Neg. No. 49806)

Visiting Fewkes's dig site in 1896, he met Nampeyo and bought several pots for the collection of the U.S. National Museum. In an article in *American Anthropologist* magazine, Hough wrote that Nampeyo's pottery had "attained the quality of form, surface, fire change, and decoration of the ancient ware which give it artistic standing."

In 1898 and 1910, Nampeyo and Lesou were invited to demonstrate pottery making at the Chicago Coliseum. Nampeyo also gave demonstrations at the Fred Harvey Company's luxury hotel at the Grand Canyon. The company's promotional materials touted Nampeyo as a star attraction, making her face and name familiar to non-Indians throughout much of the United States. In Hano, her success inspired others to imitate her work. Many women in Hano, including Nampeyo's four daughters, Annie, Cecelia, Fannie, and Nellie, began making and selling pots in the

Sityatki style. Though Nampeyo had gone blind by the 1920s, she continued to work with the help of her family. Relying on her sense of touch, she molded clay in the shapes she desired, then handed her work to Lesou and her daughters for painting.

In 1942 Nampeyo died in her home in Hano. During her 70-year career, she played a crucial role in popularizing Indian pottery and establishing it as an important art form. Her work also helped create a market for Hopi art, inspiring nearly 75 members of her family to make pottery their vocation.

Further Reading

Ashton, Robert, Jr. "Nampeyo and Lesou." *American Indian Art* 1 (summer 1976): 24–33.

Hirschfelder, Arlene. "Nampeyo: Hopi Potter." In *Artists and Craftspeople,* 9–15. New York: Facts On File, 1994.

McCoy, Ronald. "Nampeyo: Giving the Indian Artist a Name." In *Indian Lives: Essays on Nineteenth- and Twentieth-Century Native American Leaders,* edited by L. G. Moses and Raymond Wilson, 43–57. Albuquerque: University of New Mexico Press, 1985.

"Nampeyo Hopi Master Potter," Canyon Country Originals: Art of the Southwest. Available online. URL: http://www.canyonart.com/Nampeyo.htm. Posted in 1998.

— L. S.

NEEL, ALICE
(1900–1984)   *Painter*

"I have felt that people's images reflect the era in a way that nothing else could," Alice Neel once said to explain her devotion to portraiture. During her 60-year career, her incisive portraits—with subjects ranging from her family to famous artists to society's outcasts—created a panorama of American urban life in the mid-20th century.

Alice Hartley Neel was born in Merion Square, Pennsylvania, on January 28, 1900. The daughter of a railroad clerk, she enrolled in the Pennsylvania School of Design for Women (now Moore College of Art) in 1921. She chose a women's art school to avoid the distracting influence of men so that she could better concentrate on her art.

After her graduation in 1925, Neel married fellow artist Carlos Enriquez. The couple moved to his native Cuba, where their bohemian lifestyle was challenged by his conservative, upper-class parents. Neel's early watercolors, such as the tension-filled *The Family* (1927), reflect her growing difficulty reconciling her art career with a conventional family life.

In 1927 Neel and Enriquez moved to New York City, where they settled in Greenwich Village. Their relationship soon began to unravel, however, when their infant daughter, Santillana, died of diphtheria. Neel recorded the child's death in her paintings *Futility of Effort* (1930) and *After the Death of a Child* (1928), which juxtaposes a haunting image of a grieving mother with children at play.

Neel gave birth to a second daughter, Isabella (nicknamed Isabetta) in 1928, but within two years Enriquez had given up on their marriage. He left Neel and returned to Havana with Isabella, where she was raised by his family. Neel saw her daughter only two more times. During one of these visits, she painted *Isabetta* (1934), which depicted the then seven-year-old Isabella in the nude staring defiantly at the viewer.

With her marriage over and her career stalled, Neel suffered a mental breakdown. After two suicide attempts, she spent a year recuperating in hospitals and sanitariums. In the fall of 1932, she was well enough to return to New York, where she lived with her lover Kenneth Doolittle. She recorded their life together in a series of intimate watercolors. Most, however, were destroyed when, in a fit of jealousy, Doolittle burned nearly 300 of her watercolors and drawings as well as some 50 oil paintings. The event was later fictionalized in the crime thriller *The Big Clock* (1946), written by Neel's friend Kenneth Fearing.

Beginning in 1933, Neel made a modest income working for the Federal Art Project of the Works Progress Administration (WPA). Most notable were *Investigation of Poverty at the Russell Sage Foundation* (1935) and *Nazis Murder Jews* (1936). Less controversial were her New York City landscapes, such as *Ninth Avenue El* (1935). Most of these works are now lost, because the federal government later sold WPA canvases as scrap at four cents a pound.

In the 1930s, Neel turned increasingly to portraiture. She primarily painted friends, family, and acquaintances who struck her as interesting, creating a visual diary of the people in her life. Her most notorious early portrait was *Joe Gould* (1933), which portrayed a Harvard-educated street person well known to Greenwich Village bohemians. In her daring painting, Neel depicted Gould not only in the nude but also with three sets of genitalia.

Perhaps Neel's greatest work of this period was *T. B. Harlem* (1940). The portrait depicted a young Puerto Rican victim of tuberculosis in his hospital bed after having his lung removed. Characteristic of many Neel portraits, the painting showed its subject at a moment of vulnerability, yet it communicated a respect for the person's dignity and individuality. The image also revealed Neel's interest in depicting experiences of the poor rarely seen in fine art.

Her commitment to the subject only grew after she moved to Spanish Harlem, a neighborhood in upper Manhattan, in 1938 with her lover José Santiago. She and Santiago had a son, Richard, the following year. In 1941 Neel gave birth to a second son, Hartley, by photographer Sam Brody, with whom she lived on and off for two decades.

In 1943 Neel lost her financial support from the WPA. Raising two small children as a single mother, she had to rely on public assistance and the help of friends to get by. Although she occasionally exhibited her work in group shows, the exposure led to few sales. Her style, reminiscent of the German expressionists of the early 20th century, also discouraged commissions. Her somber portraits of the 1940s and 1950s depicted their subjects with such a ruthless honesty that she usually had to talk people into sitting for her. Her most frequent subjects were her friends and neighbors, though two of her most powerful portraits of this period depicted her parents. *Dead Father* (1946) showed the body of her father in his coffin, while *Last Sickness* (1953) depicted her mother's fearful face as she was dying from cancer.

Alice Neel, a highly regarded expressionist portraitist, poses with portraits she did of her two sons.
(AP/Wide World Photos)

Neel's productivity declined in the late 1950s as she experienced several changes in her personal life. During this time, her sons left home, and she broke off her relationship with Sam Brody for good. After two years of therapy, she emerged from this difficult period no longer content to work in obscurity. In 1960 she asked poet Frank O'Hara, then a curator at the Museum of Modern Art, to sit for her. The O'Hara portrait later appeared in *Artnews* (now *ARTnews*), which ran a glowing appreciation of Neel's work in 1962. In addition to praising her paintings, it hailed her as a risk taker for painting "portraits as works of art during a time when this genre is widely suspected for not being art at all." Indeed, in the previous decades, abstraction had so dominated the American art world that figurative work, such as Neel's, had been virtually ignored by art critics.

Just as a renewed interest in representational art was developing, Neel made changes in her subject matter and style that helped bring her work into the mainstream. Increasingly, she painted art-world notables, including artists Robert Smithson and Andy Warhol, curator Henry Geldzahler, and art historians Linda Nochlin and Meyer Schapiro. Although there was an obvious element of self-promotion in inviting these figures to sit for her, Neel hardly flattered her famous subjects. Generally less gloomy than her earlier works, these later portraits were still unrelenting in their depiction of scars and imperfections as a means of communicating the sitters' inner lives. Usually painted on large canvas, most of these works show the subjects' full body, with the figures' postures or even individual body parts, particularly hands, as expressive of their state of mind as their facial features.

In the 1970s, the women's movement also inspired more interest in Neel and her work. Much of this attention focused on new portraits featuring mothers and their children. Although mother-and-child portraits had long been a favorite subject for female artists, Neel's works were notable for their lack of sentimentality and suggestion of the psychological complexity of the mother-child relationship. Neel was also praised for her nudes of pregnant women, a subject then rarely explored in fine art. Particularly of note was her 1978 portrait *Margaret Evans Pregnant,* in which the sitter's wide eyes convey both the joys and anxieties of pregnancy.

An even more daring nude was Neel's 1980 self-portrait—the only one she painted. *Self-Portrait* shows Neel at 80 and unflinchingly depicts the effects of age on her body. Fittingly, she holds a paintbrush and a rag, the tools of her trade. Her face is turned to the viewer, with one eyebrow raised, suggesting an unspoken challenge.

Neel continued to paint until her death on October 13, 1984. By this time, she had finally earned the recognition that had escaped her in her youth. Her reputation, however, rested largely on her late works, particularly those of her famous sitters. Since her death, studies of her early work have helped solidify Neel's place as one of the most important portrait painters of the 20th century.

Further Reading

Alice Neel: The Woman and Her Work. Athens: Georgia Museum of Art, 1975.

"Artist Profile Alice Neel," National Museum of Women in the Arts. Available online. URL: http://www.nmwa. org/Legacy/bios/bneel.htm. Downloaded on July 27, 2001.

Hills, Patricia. *Alice Neel.* New York: Harry N. Abrams, 1983.

Temkin, Ann, editor. *Alice Neel.* New York: Harry N. Abrams, 2000.

—L. S.

NEVELSON, LOUISE (Louise Berliawsky)
(1900–1988) *Sculptor*

Credited by John Russell of the *New York Times* with bringing "mystery back into sculpture," Louise Nevelson emerged during her lifetime as one of the most influential American sculptors of the 20th century. She was born Louise Berliawsky on September 12, 1900, near Kiev, Russia. At four, she moved with her mother to Rockland, Maine, where her father had already established a successful contracting business. Even as a young child, she gathered wood scraps from her father's lumberyard and crafted them into crude sculptures. Encouraged by her doting parents, Louise had great ambitions for herself and dreamed of becoming a famous actress or artist.

Eager to leave Rockland, at 20 she married Charles Nevelson, a wealthy older man, with whom she later had a son, Myron. Soon after their wedding, the Nevelsons moved to New York City, where Louise refused to settle into the role of a society wife. Finding marriage and motherhood confining, she spent much of the 1920s taking classes in painting, music, acting, dance, and voice. By 1928, she enrolled full time at the Art Students League. There, she heard of painter Hans Hofmann's classes in modern art and became determined to travel to Munich, where he was then teaching. In 1931 she left her husband, put her son in her parents' care, and headed to Europe. After studying with Hofmann, she traveled to Paris, where she was introduced to the works of Picasso and the African art displayed at the Musée de l'Homme.

After returning to New York, Nevelson briefly worked as an assistant to Mexican muralist Diego Rivera. In her own art, she moved away from painting and toward sculpture, which she studied under Chaim Gross. Working in wood, terra-cotta, plaster, and stone, Nevelson drew inspiration for her early work from various sources, including cubism, African sculpture, and pre-Columbian art.

In the late 1930s, Nevelson was hired as an art teacher by the Works Progress Administration. When she lost her job, she scrambled to make a living, relying heavily on help from her parents. Determined to improve her finances, Nevelson sought out Karl Nierendorf of the Nierendorf Gallery and insisted he show her work. Nierendorf became, in Nevelson's words, her "spiritual godfather." They developed a seven-year business and romantic relationship, during which he provided her with the financial and emotional support she needed.

Between 1941 and 1946, Nevelson had five one-woman shows at the Nierendorf Gallery, but few of her pieces were sold. Her most innovative work during this period was shown at the Norlyst Gallery in a 1943 exhibition titled *The Circus: The Clown Is the Center of His World.* The exhibition showed Nevelson's new fascination with using found objects—from bed knobs to whiskey glasses—in her sculpture. It also marked her first effort to design the exhibition space to create a near-theatrical experience. The show featured abstracted circus figures and animals made of wood, with circus posters on the wall and sand and marbles on the floor. To Nevelson's disappointment, none of the pieces in the show were purchased. She disassembled the exhibit and destroyed it, along with many other sculptures and paintings, for lack of storage space.

In the late 1940s, Nevelson became depressed following the deaths of her father and Nierendorf. She struggled with her art as well, until she had a creative breakthrough during a trip to Central America. In the ruins of Maya architecture, Nevelson found "a world of geometry and magic" that provided her with new inspiration. As she later explained, "The Yucatan was a world of forms that at once I felt was mine."

Returning to New York, Nevelson settled into a Manhattan townhouse on Thirteenth Street that her family purchased for her. The house became a gathering place for artists. Nevelson often hosted meetings of the Sculptors' Guild and the Federation of Modern Painters and Sculptors. During this period, Nevelson became determined to use her contacts to draw attention to her art. As she

Louise Nevelson with one of her works at the World Trade Center in New York, 1978
(AP/Wide World Photos)

later explained, she decided to "flood the market with my work until they know I'm here."

Her efforts attracted the attention of Colette Roberts, director of the Grand Central Moderns Gallery. The gallery staged a series of exhibitions—including *Ancient Games, Ancient Places* (1955), *The Royal Voyage* (1956), and *The Forest* (1957)—to showcase her latest works. But it was not until her 1958 show, *Moon Garden + One,* that Nevelson received the recognition she craved. The exhibition featured constructions made from wooden boxes stacked to form walls and columns. Inside the boxes were collections of wooden objects, many crafted from pieces of furniture and architectural ornaments. The boxes and their contents were painted black, both to unify the sculptures' compositions and to make it difficult to identify the found objects used. The exhibit space was bathed in a blue light, lending the sculptural installation an air of mystery. The light also intensified the shadows cast by the sculptures' various elements. Nevelson considered these shadows as integral to the work as the wooden forms themselves.

Moon Garden + One established Nevelson's reputation as an important sculptor. Of the works in the exhibition, *New York Times* art critic Hilton Kramer wrote, "[They are] utterly shocking in the way they violate our received ideas on the limits of sculpture." In some respects, Nevelson's work was considered the three-dimensional equivalent of the painting of the abstract expressionists, who were then dominating the New York art world. Similar to the abstract expressionists' penchant for compositions that filled their large canvases, Nevelson designed sculptures that covered the whole of her exhibition space. She also shared their interest in incorporating improvisation into their work. Nevelson assembled her works without models or preliminary drawings, instead allowing inspiration and chance to guide their creation.

Nevelson's newfound fame was fanned by her flamboyant personality. With a flair for the theatrical, she carried herself like royalty and adopted an eccentric style of dress. Her odd combinations of clothing often included kimonos, work shirts, and Mexican skirts, which she wore with heavy jewelry of her own design.

In 1962 Nevelson was one of four artists selected to represent the United States at the Venice Biennale. Although still sometimes working with black paint, by this time she was creating works in white and gold as well. In the early 1960s, she also began experimenting with new materials, such as Plexigas, Formica, aluminium, and Lucite. Perhaps in response to the rise of minimalism, the edges of her sculptures became cleaner and sharper during this period.

Nevelson was honored with a major retrospective at the Whitney Museum of American Art in 1967. Two years later, she produced her first large outdoor steel sculpture, *Atmosphere and Environment X,* on commission from Princeton University. Many more commissions followed, making Nevelson one of the most sought-after creators of public art in the United States. Among her most notable works of this period were her gleaming white *Chapel of the Good Shepherd* (1977), designed for New York's St. Peter's Lutheran Church, and her series of seven black sculptures erected on Maiden Lane in lower Manhattan in 1979. The site has since been renamed the Louise Nevelson Plaza.

Hailed as one of America's greatest sculptors, Louise Nevelson died in New York City on April 17, 1988. Although she cultivated celebrity, her passion for her work sprang from her own personal need to create. "It is not really for an audience," she once explained, "it is really for my visual eye. It is a feast for myself."

Further Reading

Barret, David. "Louise Nevelson," Sheldon Memorial Art Gallery and Sculpture Garden. Available online. URL: http://sheldon.unl.edu/HTML/ARTIST/Nevelson_L/SSll.html. Updated on January 5, 2001.

Lipman, Jean. *Nevelson's World.* New York: Hudson Hills Press, 1983.

Lisle, Laurie. *Louise Nevelson: A Passionate Life.* New York: Summit Books, 1990.

Nevelson, Louise. *Dawns + Dusks: Taped Conversations with Diana MacKown.* New York: Scribner, 1976.

Wilson, Laurie. *Louise Nevelson: Iconography and Sources.* New York: Garland, 1981.

— L. S.

NORMAN, DOROTHY
(1905–1997)   *Photographer*

Owing in part to her long relationship with Alfred Stieglitz, photographer Dorothy Norman was an influential force in the New York art world of the 1930s and 1940s. She was born Dorothy Stecker on March 28, 1905, into a wealthy Philadelphia family. She attended Smith College and the University of Pennsylvania before marrying Edward A. Norman, the son of the founder of Sears, Roebuck & Company, in 1925. The couple had two children before they divorced in 1951.

Soon after their wedding, the Normans moved to New York City. Dorothy resisted settling into the life of a socialite, an existence that she described as full of "bridge and mah-jongg and petty gossip." Instead, she became devoted to several social causes that were considered radical at the time. Norman conducted research for the American Civil Liberties Union and was an early supporter of the Planned Parenthood Federation.

In New York, Norman also developed a passion for modern art. In 1927 she wandered into the Intimate Gallery, which was operated by famed photographer Alfred Stieglitz. Stieglitz considered the gallery a "laboratory center," where artists and photographers could meet and exchange ideas. Norman became a frequent visitor, coming to the gallery, as she later recounted, "to listen to Stieglitz, read about him, watch him function, look at his photographs, talk with him, and begin to fathom that he represents an approach to life I have been seeking in the world around me but had not found." Although 40 years her senior and married to painter GEORGIA O'KEFFE, Stieglitz soon became Norman's lover and mentor.

Beginning in 1931, Stieglitz made a series of portraits of Norman, with their small size echoing the intimacy of their relationship. He also gave her a camera and, though he generally refused to teach, he began to instruct her in photography. Stieglitz made elaborate notes on the back of her photographs, offering gentle criticism and enthusiastic praise. His notes often included "ILY" for "I love you" or "IBO" for "I bow out," which he reserved for images he deemed so perfect that he had nothing to say about them.

Beautifully lit and composed, many of Norman's photographs showed the New York cityscape and the architecture of Cape Cod, where her family spent its summers. Norman also made photographic portraits, including many of Stieglitz. The famous artists and writers who frequented Stieglitz's gallery were also favorite subjects. Among those she photographed were writers Lewis Mumford and Theodore Dreiser and composer John Cage.

In 1932 Norman was instrumental in establishing Stieglitz's new gallery, An American Place. In addition to raising funds for its operation from family and friends, she oversaw the gallery's daily operations for nearly 15 years. Norman's work made her an intimate of Stieglitz's circle of friends, which included painters John Marin, Marsden Hartley, and Charles Demuth. At An American Place, she also became acquainted with writers William Carlos Williams, Sherwood Anderson, Hart Crane, and e.e. cummings.

With her strong connections in New York's artistic and literary avant-garde, in 1938 Norman founded *Twice a Year: A Semi-Annual Journal for Literature, the Arts and Civil Liberties.* Initially financed by a $10,000 wedding gift, the journal reflected her faith in the ability of the arts and artists to improve society. One issue summed up her beliefs with the statement, "art without action in its image is as valueless as mere action that is performed without mirroring the feeling embodied in art." Published for 10 years, *Twice a Year* featured works by writers Albert Camus, Jean-Paul Sartre, Bertolt Brecht, Thomas Mann, and Federico García Lorca. During the 1940s, Norman also wrote "A World to Live In," a column in the *New York Post,* for seven years.

In 1946 Norman's longtime association with Stieglitz ended with his sudden death. Determined to preserve his legacy, she assembled *America and Alfred Stieglitz,* a collection of essays about the photographer's place in American culture. During Stieglitz's lifetime, Norman also recorded many of their conversations about art and life. These recordings formed the basis of her book *Alfred Stieglitz: An American Seer* (1973), the first full-length biography of the photographer.

After Stieglitz's death, Norman closed An American Place, leaving her with more time for her work on social and political causes. She became particularly committed to the Indian independence movement. In 1949 she met Jawaharlal Nehru on one of his first visits to New York. Norman became one of Nehru's staunchest supporters in the United States and edited two volumes of his speeches and writings. She also developed a friendship with Nehru's daughter Indira Gandhi, which she documented in the book *Indira Gandhi: Letters to an American Friend* (1985).

By the late 1950s, Norman had largely given up photography due to her failing eyesight. In 1963 she gave the Philadelphia Museum of Art her extensive collection of photographs, helping to establish the museum's Alfred Stieglitz Center. Her own works were shown in a retrospective at the International Center of Photography in New York City in 1993. Having distinguished herself as an artist, a journalist, an author, and a social reformer, Dorothy Norman died at her home in East Hampton, Long Island, on April 12, 1997.

Further Reading

Barth, Miles, editor. *Intimate Visions: The Photographs of Dorothy Norman.* San Francisco: Chronicle Books, 1993.

Norman, Dorothy. *Alfred Stieglitz: An American Seer.* Reprint. New York: Aperture, 1990.

———. *Beyond a Portrait: Photographs.* N.Y.: Aperture, 1984.

———. *Encounters: A Memoir.* San Diego: Harcourt Brace Jovanovich, 1987.

— L. S.

 ## O'KEEFFE, GEORGIA
(1887–1986)   *Painter*

Public response to both her bold paintings and her extraordinary life have made Georgia O'Keeffe an American icon. She was born Georgia Totto O'Keeffe on November 15, 1887, on a Wisconsin dairy farm near the town of Sun Prairie. Her mother arranged for her and her six siblings to receive art lessons in their home. By age 12, Georgia had announced her intention of becoming an artist.

After her family moved to Williamsburg, Virginia, O'Keeffe continued her art studies at a girls' boarding school. She then attended the Art Institute of Chicago (1905–06) and the Art Students League (1907–08) in New York City. While at the league, she first visited photographer Alfred Stieglitz's gallery at 291 Fifth Avenue, a meeting place for American and European avant-garde artists and writers. It was there she was first introduced to the works of European modernists, including Henri Matisse, Paul Cézanne, and Pablo Picasso.

Her formal art studies, however, were less inspiring. Frustrated with her training in the realist tradition, O'Keeffe gave up painting and took a job as a commercial artist in Chicago. She soon returned to Virginia, where her interest in art was rekindled at a University of Virginia summer school class taught in 1912 by Alon Bement of Teachers College. He adopted the teaching methods of his colleague Arthur Wesley Dow, who encouraged students to create their own forms rather than merely copying the works of old masters. O'Keeffe was inspired by Dow's contention that the goal of art was to express the artist's emotions and ideas. She left the class with a renewed commitment to pursuing a career in fine art.

While spending summers as Bement's assistant, O'Keeffe found work as the "supervisor of drawing and penmanship" in the Amarillo, Texas, school system. The job gave her her first experience with the western landscape. She wrote of her excitement over her new surroundings, "It was loud and raw under the stars in that wide empty country."

In 1915 O'Keeffe took another teaching post at Columbia College in South Carolina. That winter, she made a series of abstract charcoal drawings based on natural forms. She sent several to her friend Anita Pollitzer, who showed them to Alfred Stieglitz. He called them "the purest, finest, sincerest things that have entered 291 in a long while" and in 1916 exhibited 10 of them without O'Keeffe's permission. While visiting New York,

O'Keeffe confronted Stieglitz, insisting that he take down her work, but he persuaded her to let him continue the exhibition.

O'Keeffe left to teach at the West Texas State Normal College, in Canyon, Texas, where she kept up a correspondence with Stieglitz. He convinced her to return to New York in June 1918. A month later, he left his wife of 25 years and moved in with O'Keeffe. They were married in 1924.

O'Keeffe at once became part of Stieglitz's circle of intimates, which included painters John Marin, Arthur Dove, and Marsden Hartley. Stieglitz displayed her work alongside theirs at the 291 gallery and gave O'Keeffe her first one-woman show in 1923. She was already known in art circles through a series of photographic portraits of her, many in the nude, that Stieglitz had exhibited at a retrospective at the Anderson Galleries in 1921. With Stieglitz's heavy promotion of the artist and her art, O'Keeffe was well established by the late 1920s. Her work was showed at the Brooklyn Museum in 1927 and the Museum of Modern Art in 1929.

During this period, many of O'Keeffe's paintings depicted flowers, leaves, rocks, and other natural objects. Although representational, the forms were so simplified that the images approached abstraction. Influenced by photographic techniques, O'Keeffe showed the object in extreme close-up on large canvases, lending her work a certain monumentality. The exaggeration of the objects' sizes also gave the paintings an emotional intensity that characterized O'Keeffe's best works throughout her career. In cityscapes such as *New York with Moon* (1926), O'Keeffe also explored the New York skyline, emphasizing its geometric shapes and the flow of light around city structures.

In the early 1920s, O'Keeffe and Stieglitz spent summers with his family on Lake George in upstate New York. Needing time away from the Stieglitz clan, O'Keeffe soon began spending weeks alone along the Maine coast. During a month-long period in 1926, she produced a series of paintings of clamshells, using a much more muted palette than her flower images and reflecting the increasing chilliness of her marriage. In 1928, Stieglitz began an affair with journalist and photographer DOROTHY NORMAN. In the same year, a commission for O'Keeffe to paint a mural at Radio City Music Hall fell through. O'Keeffe's personal and professional problems led to her hospitalization for depression.

As O'Keeffe recovered, she experienced a renewed enthusiasm for her work. She wrote Stieglitz, "I am not sick anymore. Everything in me begins to move." She drew new inspiration from the landscape of New Mexico, where she spent her summers, beginning in 1929. Living at Ghost Ranch, she painted the bright sky and multicolored sandstone around her in rich color and near-abstract compositions. Animal skulls and bones found in the desert also became a favorite subject.

O'Keeffe had her first retrospective at the Art Institute of Chicago in 1943. Three years later, she had a one-artist exhibition at New York's Museum of Modern Art, the first at that institution to show the work of a woman. Also in 1946, Stieglitz died at 82. O'Keeffe spent three years in New York settling his estate, then moved permanently to New Mexico. She bought an adobe house in the village of Abiquiu, which she transformed into an artist's studio. During the 1950s, the shape of the door of her Abiquiu house inspired a series of paintings. Notable among her late works was her *Sky Above the Clouds* series of the mid-1960s. Inspired by the view from an airplane, the works depicted rows of fluffy clouds floating in calm, blue sky.

The myth that grew around O'Keeffe claimed that she lived as a virtual recluse in her last years, although in truth she had frequent visitors at Abiquiu—some welcome, others not. As Letitia Frank, the granddaughter of O'Keeffe's friend Mabel Dodge Luhan, once explained, "She had many friends, and visitors from all over. But being a friend of Georgia, you had to accept her privacy. One violated it at their peril. She did not suffer fools."

In 1973 one uninvited visitor, a 27-year-old potter named Juan Hamilton, developed a strong friendship with O'Keeffe. Living with her first as her assistant and later as her caretaker, Hamilton was her companion for the next 13 years. By this

One of America's major painters, Georgia O'Keeffe died at 98 in 1986.
(AP/Wide World Photos)

time, O'Keeffe's eyesight began to fail, making painting increasingly difficult. With Hamilton's encouragement, O'Keeffe experimented with working in clay. He also helped her finish her 1976 autobiography, *Georgia O'Keeffe*.

On March 6, 1986, O'Keeffe died in Santa Fe at the age of 98. In accordance with her wishes, her ashes were scattered on the landscape surrounding Ghost Ranch. In a codicil to her will signed two years earlier, O'Keeffe gave Hamilton the majority of her $76 million estate—one of the largest ever left by an American artist. Her niece and nephew contested the will, and in a settlement Hamilton's share of the inheritance was drastically reduced. The bulk of the estate was subsequently used to create the nonprofit Georgia O'Keeffe Foundation. In July 1997 the Georgia O'Keeffe Museum was opened in Santa Fe.

By the time of her death, Georgia O'Keeffe had long been a legend. Since the 1920s, her paintings have been celebrated for their formal innovations and dramatic power. But much of her notoriety arose from her biography, particularly her stormy relationship with Stieglitz and her later years in isolation from public view. Celebrated as a feminist role model for decades, O'Keeffe has become as famous for her independent spirit as for her artistic vision.

Further Reading

"About Georgia O'Keeffe, Biography," Georgia O'Keeffe Museum. Available online. URL: http://www. OkeeffeMuseum.org/background/index.html. Downloaded on August 1, 2001.

Lisle, Laurie. *Portrait of an Artist: A Biography of Georgia O'Keeffe*. Albuquerque: University of New Mexico Press, 1986.

Merrill, Christopher, and Ellen Bradbury, editors. *From the Faraway Nearby: Georgia O'Keeffe as Icon*. Reading, Mass.: Addison-Wesley, 1992.

O'Keeffe, Georgia. *Georgia O'Keeffe*. New York: Viking, 1976.

Robinson, Roxana. *Georgia O'Keeffe: A Life*. New York: Harper and Row, 1989.

— L. S.

P

PALMER, FANNY (Frances Flora Bond)
(1812–1876)   *Printmaker*

One of the leading lithographers of her day, Fanny Palmer was born Frances Flora Bond in Leicester, England, on June 26, 1812. In the early 1830s, she married Edmund Seymour Palmer, with whom she had two children, Flora and Edmund. Initially, the family lived well on Fanny's substantial inheritance, but they fell into financial difficulties in the 1840s. With Fanny's brother and sister, the Palmers moved to New York City in 1844 to seek their fortunes.

As children, Fanny and her siblings had been well schooled in art. All three tried to use their artistic talents to make a living, but Fanny had the greatest success. With her husband, she established a lithography business, F. & S. Palmer. Her early work included landscapes and flower prints, often based on original paintings by other artists. Although her business failed in 1851, she gained a reputation as one of New York's finest lithographers.

With two prints of Manhattan made in 1849, Palmer began working as a staff artist at the lithography firm N. Currier. She was soon producing lithographs from her own drawings. In 1852 she created a series of bird-hunting scenes depicting her husband and his friends. But her specialty quickly became atmospheric landscapes. Particularly successful were her series American Farm Scenes (1853) and American Country Life (1855). Although Palmer never traveled outside New York, she created images of areas from New England to California, often relying on photographs for reference.

In the late 1850s, Palmer became less prolific, possibly because she was distracted by family troubles. In 1859 her husband died after falling down a flight of stairs, leaving her as the sole provider for her family. Soon afterward, Palmer entered her most productive period. Between 1860 and 1868, she made more than 100 lithographs on a wide variety of subjects. Palmer moved toward more dramatic scenes in prints such as *American Express Train* (1864) and *A Midnight Race on the Mississippi* (1860). She also illustrated literary works, most notably in a series of lithographs based on poems by Henry Wadsworth Longfellow. Her best late works, however, had an epic scope. Particularly effective were her images of the westward migration, including *The Rocky Mountains, Emigrants Crossing the Plains* (1866) and *Across the Continent, Westward the Course of Empire Takes Its Way* (1868).

Palmer was renowned in her day for her panoramic scenes. She was less skilled at drawing human figures, however. After 1857, when James M. Ives joined N. Currier as a partner, many of the figures in her works were drawn by Ives. The incompatibility of Palmer's and Ives's styles, unfortunately, lessened the appeal of some of her later work. Nevertheless, during the 20 years she worked for N. Currier and Currier and Ives, she produced about 200 prints, many of which counted among the firm's most popular. Long after she left Currier and Ives in 1868, her images appeared on calendars, cards, and advertisements.

Little is known about Palmer's final years. She lived with her sister Maria, a music teacher, in her Brookyn home, where Palmer may have given private art lessons. On August 20, 1876, Fanny Palmer died of tuberculosis at the age of 64.

Further Reading

Ayers, William, editor. *Picturing History: American Painting, 1770–1930.* New York: Rizzoli, 1993.

Cowdery, Mary Bartlett. "Fanny Palmer, An American Lithographer." In *Prints: Thirteen Illustrated Essays on the Art of the Print,* edited by Carl Zigrosser, 217–234. New York: Holt, Rinehart and Winston, 1962.

DeWan, George. "The Picture of a Workhorse, Long Island: Our Past." Available online. URL: http://www.lihistory.com/histpast/past1006.htm. Downloaded on August 1, 2001.

Peters, Harry Twyford. *Currier & Ives: Printmakers to the American People.* Garden City, N.Y: Doubleday, 1942.

— L. S.

PEALE, SARAH MIRIAM
(1800–1885) *Painter*

Portrait painter Sarah Miriam Peale was the first American woman to have a professional career in the visual arts. Born on May 19, 1800, she was the youngest of the six children of James Peale and Mary Claypoole. James was the brother of famed painter and scientist Charles Willson Peale, who encouraged James to become a professional artist. In addition to adding backgrounds to many of Charles's works, James Peale emerged as a noted painter of miniatures and still lifes.

Sarah's art training started early. She began painting as a child and probably added details, such as lace and flowers, to her father's works. In aspiring to paint, Sarah followed in the footsteps of two of her older sisters, Anna and Margaretta. Anna established herself as a miniaturist, while Margaretta specialized in still lifes. Sarah instead chose to concentrate on a genre rarely explored by female artists—portraiture. In 1818 she produced her first large-scale canvas painting, a self-portrait depicting herself as an attractive, confident 18 year-old. The same year, Sarah Peale began showing portraits at the annual Pennsylvania Academy of the Arts exhibition. She and Anna were elected into the academy in 1824—the first women to be so honored.

As Peale carved out her career, she received needed support from her uncle Charles, who praised her "great talents." On several occasions, he invited her to social events in Washington, D.C., where she could meet potential patrons. Peale also found work by sharing commissions with her sister Anna. Peale would paint a full-size portrait of their patron, while Anna would make a miniature copy of the work. The arrangement was particularly helpful because the sisters could travel together to meet with patrons; at the time, it would have been considered highly inappropriate for a woman to travel alone.

Peale was aggressive in seeking out commissions. In 1825 she learned that the Marquis de Lafayette, the famous Revolutionary War hero, was planning a visit to Washington. Peale wrote Lafayette, asking for the chance to paint him. He sat for the young artist four times. The resulting portrait, however, is now lost.

The same year, Peale left Philadelphia for Baltimore, where her cousin, painter Rembrandt Peale, had a studio. Peale soon established herself as one of the city's leading portraitists. She was certainly its most prolific. Over the next decade, she painted more than 100 of Baltimore's most prominent citizens and visiting dignitaries. In the early 1840s, Peale also made frequent trips to Washington, where she painted many politicians, soldiers, and diplomats. Among her subjects were Senators Thomas Hart Benton, Henry A. Wise, and Daniel Webster.

In Peale's portraits, her subjects appear respectable, yet warm and down-to-earth. Her precise draftsmanship reveals the influence of her father and uncle, although her works also demonstrated her own interest in decorative detail, colorful patterns, and rich textures. Particularly in her portraits of women, Peale enhanced her paintings with landscapes in the background or detailed still lifes in the foreground.

In 1846 Peale exhibited four of her portraits at the Missouri Bank in St. Louis. A local journalist wrote that "her portraits have indeed a living expression about them, only attainable by the highest order of artistical skill." Equally impressed, several leading St. Louis families encouraged Peale to relocate to their city. The next year, Peale made the move to St. Louis, then still a fairly unsophisticated western frontier town. Although her reasons for the move are uncertain, possibly she wanted more independence from her famous family.

Peale quickly became St. Louis's most sought-after portraitist. Over the next 30 years, she painted many individual and family portraits. By 1860, she also began painting still lifes in oil and in watercolor. Like those produced by her father, her early still lifes were highly formal compositions that depicted fruits and flowers with extreme precision. Later in life, she experimented with a looser brush stroke and more naturalistic style, often depicting objects in the open air. Peale's still lifes won prizes at many St. Louis agricultural fairs, where they were seen by thousands.

In 1878 Peale returned to Philadelphia, where she spent her final years sharing a house with her sister Anna. She continued to paint until her death on February 4, 1885, at the age of 84. Unique among women of her day, Sarah Peale succeeded in supporting herself through her art for more than 60 years.

Further Reading

Hunter, Wilbur H., and John Mahey. *Miss Sarah Miriam Peale, 1800–1885: Portraits and Still Life.* Baltimore: Peale Museum, 1967.
Miller, Lillian B., editor. *The Peale Family: Creation of a Legacy, 1770–1870.* New York: Abbeville Press, 1996.

"Sarah Miriam Peale," Brigham Yang University Museum of Art. Available online. URL: http://www.byu.edu/Moa/exhibits/current%20Exhibits/150years/840033100.html. Downloaded on August 1, 2001.

— L. S.

PEÑA, TONITA (Maria Antonia Peña, Quah Ah)
(1893–1949) *Painter*

Tonita Peña was the first American Indian woman to establish herself as a painter. She was born Maria Antonia Peña on May 10, 1893, at San Ildefonso Pueblo in present-day New Mexico. At four, she was given the Indian name Quah Ah, meaning "little bead" or "pink shell."

After her mother died of influenza in 1905, Tonita was sent to live with her maternal aunt, Martina Montoya, at Cochiti Pueblo. From Montoya, she learned the Cochiti techniques for making pottery. Montoya was considered one of the Pueblo's greatest potters. As a teenager, Peña was trained in a new art form at St. Catherine's Indian School in Santa Fe. Using watercolors, Peña painted Pueblo pottery designs and scenes of Pueblo life on paper.

At 15, Peña married Juan Rosario Chavez, the first of her three husbands. Arranged by her aging aunt and uncle, the union produced two children, Richard and Helia, before Juan died in 1912. The next year, Peña married Felipe Herrera. He was killed in a mining accident in 1919, two months after Peña gave birth to Hilario J. Herrera. (Hilario grew up to become the acclaimed painter Joe H. Herrera.) Peña had five more children by her third husband, Epitacio Arquero, a Cochiti farmer who became a leader in tribal politics in the 1940s and 1950s.

During her marriages to Herrera and Arquero, Peña returned to painting. She was offered encouragement by Edgar Lee Hewitt. A professor of archaeology at the University of New Mexico, Hewitt supervised the excavation of the ancient Indian site of Frijoles Canyon. He was fascinated by the drawings made by some of his Pueblo laborers, in which they copied the designs on the pottery shards they found. Hewitt gave the men watercolors and asked them also to try painting pictures of Pueblo ceremonies and daily life. When he learned of Peña's interest in painting, he also paid her to produce watercolors for him.

Hewitt was instrumental in the development of a school of Pueblo watercolorists, who were among the first Indians to paint on paper and canvas. Known as the San Ildefonso Group, this group included Peña, her cousin Romando Vigil, Fred Kabotie, and Awa Tsireh. Most of their works are similar in both style and subject matter, featuring highly detailed, linear Pueblo figures, usually dressed in ritual garb and set against a stark white background. Peña, the only woman in the San Ildefonso Group, focused on depicting female figures. In addition to their artistic value, her works have provided anthropologists and historians with visual documentation of the everyday activities of women in traditional Pueblo society.

In the 1920s, Peña sold her paintings to the tourists in the city square of Santa Fe. Her works and those of the other artists of the San Ildefonso Group were soon in demand. As her reputation grew, her paintings were displayed in galleries, where they were marketed to collectors and museums. By the early 1930s, Peña had received a commission by the federal government to help paint a series of murals for the Santa Fe Indian School. The school also hired Peña to instruct its students in molding and painting pottery.

Peña's success often brought her into conflict with her own people. Although she reared eight children and had a long, happy marriage to Epitacio Arquero, some Pueblo condemned Peña for working outside the home. Their resentment was possibly fueled by the high prices she received from her work. Others disapproved of her depicting Pueblo ceremonies in paintings intended for a non-Indian audience, although at the time white tourists routinely attended religious rites when visiting Pueblo reservations.

Peña died on May 1, 1949, having paved the way for many Native American painters, both male and female. One artist she inspired was PABLITA VELARDE, who respected Peña for being a "good wife

Native American painter Tonita Peña, circa 1935
(Photo by T. Harmon Parkhurst, Courtesy Museum of New Mexico, Neg. No. 46988)

like a good woman" but also admired the "little bit of rebellion" in her. As Velarde once explained, "She always wanted to show the men that not only a man can paint a good picture, and she did it."

Further Reading

Gray, Samuel L. *Tonita Peña: Quah Ah*. Albuquerque, N.M.: Avanyu Publishing, 1990.

Jantzer-White, Marilee. "Tonita Peña (Quah Ah), Pueblo Painter: Asserting Identity through Continuity and Change." *The American Indian Quarterly* 18 (summer 1994): 24–30.

"Pena, Tonita Vigil (Quah Ah)," AskART. Available online. URL: http://www.askart.com/biography.asp. Posted in 2000.

— L. S.

PEPPER, BEVERLY
(1924–   ) *Sculptor*

A pioneer in environmental sculpture, Beverly Pepper was born Beverly Stoll in Brooklyn, New York, on December 20, 1924. At 16, she enrolled at Brooklyn's Pratt Institute, where she studied photography, advertising design, and industrial design. After graduating, she worked as an art director at an advertising agency, while studying drawing at the Art Students League and art theory at Brooklyn College.

Dissatisfied with her job, Beverly Stoll headed in 1949 to Paris, where she studied painting with French artists André Lhote and Fernand Léger. While visiting Rome, she met journalist Bill Pepper, whom she married several months later. The couple had two children, John and Jorie, the latter of whom would grow up to become the poet Jorie Graham.

In 1952 the Peppers moved to Italy. Exposure to Rome's ancient ruins and Renaissance and Baroque monuments had a great influence on Beverly Pepper's aesthetic. Even more important were her travels in Japan and Cambodia in 1960. Seeing the Khmer temple at Angkor Wat in the Cambodian jungle became a turning point in her career. The structure, particularly its integration into its environment, sparked a new desire to work in three dimensions. As Pepper later said, "I walked into Angkor Wat a painter and I left a sculptor."

Returning to Rome, Pepper found that several trees in a grove near her villa had been cut down. Untrained in sculpture, she made her first works by carving the trunks with saws and electric drills. Soon she was incorporating bronze and steel elements into her large wooden pieces. In 1962 she was invited to exhibit new works at the *Sculpture in the City* show at the piazza of Spoleto. Among the other 10 artists in the exhibition were American sculptors Alexander Calder and David Smith. Teaching herself welding techniques, Pepper produced five large steel pieces, marking her first foray into public sculpture.

Through her friendship with Smith, Pepper secured her first major commission in 1962. For the exterior of the Marine Midland Bank in Manhattan,

Beverly Pepper, who lives in Italy and New York, erects large abstract sculptures.
(Courtesy Beverly Pepper)

she created an 18-foot sculpture from stainless steel. The work was one of the first abstract outdoor sculptures displayed in the United States.

Throughout the 1960s, Pepper continued to work in stainless steel. In works such as *Excathedra* (1968) and *Zig Zag* (1967), she created geometric forms that were polished to create mirrorlike surfaces. The metal reflected the sculpture's surroundings, giving the illusion that its environment was part of the sculpture itself. Pepper once said of her reflective sculpture that "from whatever angle you view it, the voids seem filled and the solids seem empty."

By the 1970s, Pepper began experimenting with horizontally oriented works that were even more closely integrated into the landscape. In *Dallas Land Canal and Hillside* (1971–75), she dug a 300-foot trench with wedge-shaped sides of steel. Her other environmental sculptures included *Amphisculpture* (1974–75) in Bedminister, New Jersey, and *Thel* (1977) at Dartmouth College in Hanover, New Hampshire. Of these works, critic Barbara Rose wrote, "Her outdoor environmental projects are not an assault on nature but a collaboration with the landscape."

In 1980 Pepper returned to vertical forms with *Todi Columns*, four sculptures ranging in height from 28 to 36 feet. She has also explored wedge shapes in a series of monumental works, which she refers to as "urban altars." Eighteen feet high and weighing more than 4,000 pounds, *Cleopatra's Wedge,* erected at Battery Park in Manhattan in 1993, is among Pepper's best-known later works. Pepper's career has been chronicled in several major retrospectives in the United States and Italy, including *Beverly Pepper: Sculpture in Place,* which toured the United States in 1986.

Further Reading

Krauss, Rosalind E. *Beverly Pepper: Sculpture in Place.* New York: Abbeville Press, 1986.

Rose, Barbara. *Beverly Pepper: Three Site-Specific Sculptures.* Washington, D.C.: Spacemaker Press, 1998.

— L. S.

PEREIRA, IRENE RICE (I. Rice Pereira)
(1907–1971) *Painter*

Through her experiments in abstraction, painter Irene Rice Pereira attempted both to create a visual equivalent of modern science and to find her own sense of meaning in the universe. Born in Chelsea, Massachusetts, on August 5, 1907, she was encouraged in the arts by her mother, Hilda, herself an amateur artist. In Irene's teenage years, the Rices moved to Brooklyn, New York. Soon after, Irene's father died, leaving her the sole breadwinner for her family. Rice worked as a stenographer and studied fashion and literature at night.

Determined to become an artist, she began taking night classes at the Art Students League in 1927. There she studied European modernism with Jan Matulka and Richard Lahey and met sculptor David Smith, a fellow student who remained a friend throughout her life. Rice married commercial artist Humberto Pereira in 1929, but they soon separated.

In 1931 Irene Rice Pereira took a year-long trip to Europe and North Africa. She studied at the Académie Moderne in Paris, but her travels through the Sahara had a far greater impact on her art. The harsh sunlight and vast expanses of desert inspired an interest in light and space that proved a driving force throughout her career as a painter.

Returning to New York, Pereira began painting anchors, boats, and marine gear. These evolved in semiabstract works, such as *Man and Machine* (1936), that combined machine forms with human shapes. Pereira's early paintings appeared in solo shows at New York's Contemporary Arts Gallery in 1933, 1934, and 1935.

In 1935 Pereira helped found the New York Laboratory School of Design, established under the auspices of the Federal Art Project. Modeled after the German design school known as the Bauhaus, the Design Laboratory sought to apply fine arts training to industrial design. Students were encouraged to experiment with a wide variety of materials and to study an array of subjects—including psychology, chemistry, and physics—in addition to the conventional art school curriculum.

While teaching at the Design Laboratory, Pereira moved toward pure abstraction in her own work. She developed a vocabulary of geometric shapes, primarily rectangles, that appeared suspended in space. Pereira explained that through a "geometric system of aesthetics" she sought "to find plastic equivalents for the revolutionary discoveries in mathematics, physics, biochemistry and radioactivity." But she also ascribed a mystical quality to the forms she chose. In an unpublished autobiography, Pereira wrote, "Why . . . I have used geometric symbols I cannot answer. They make themselves from an inner rhythm. I never plan a picture: I am simply the medium for communication."

In her mature paintings, Pereira became increasingly preoccupied with light. Working from her belief that "the light source belongs in the depth of the picture," she experimented with unusual materials, such as gold leaf and radium paint, and scraped forms made with oil paint to manipulate their degree of luminosity. In 1939 she also began painting on glass. Initially, her glass paintings were composed of one painted glass sheet placed against a painted background. But in later works, such as *Transversion* (1949) and *Shooting Stars* (1952), Pereira joined several layers of glass to create a complex play of shadows and light. She often used pebbled and corrugated glass to make reflections that changed when viewed at various angles. In her work with glass and other unfamiliar materials, such as plastic and metal, she was aided by her second husband, George Wellington Brown, who was an engineer. They were married from 1942 to 1950.

By the late 1940s, Pereira was regarded as one of New York's leading modernists. Her work was included in the Museum of Modern Art's pivotal 1946 exhibition, *Fourteen Artists,* which also featured paintings by Robert Motherwell, Arshile Gorky, and LOREN MACIVER. In 1953 Pereira and MacIver became the first women to receive retrospectives at the Whitney Museum of American Art in New York.

Despite her renown, Pereira found herself out of favor in art circles of the 1950s as abstract expressionism became the prevailing nonrepresentational style. Increasingly, she felt more comfortable among writers than artists. Among her friends were Irish poet George Rainey, whom she married in 1950. They divorced nine years later.

Pereira also turned to poetry and essays to articulate her philosophy of art. Drawn from her study of science, alchemy, and occult, her writings did not achieve much influence, perhaps due to their denseness. Her books included *Light and the New Reality* (1951), *The Transformation of Nothing and the Paradox of Space* (1952), and *The Lapis* (1957). Pereira continued to paint and write until she died in Marbella, Spain, on January 11, 1971. Largely forgotten at her death, Pereira's work has since been rediscovered, as has her significance in the history of American modernism.

Further Reading

Baur, John I. H. *Loren MacIver, I. Rice Pereira.* New York: Whitney Museum of American Art, 1953.

Bearor, Karen A. *Irene Rice Pereira: Her Paintings and Philosophy.* Austin: University of Texas Press, 1993.

I. Rice Pereira. New York: Andrew Crispo Gallery, 1976.

Mecklenburg, Virginia M. "Irene Rice Pereira," National Museum of American Art and Smithsonian Institution Press. Available online. URL: http://nmaa-ryder.si.edu/ collections.exhibits/abstraction/pereira.html. Downloaded on August 1, 2001.

— L. S.

PERRY, LILLA CABOT
(1848–1933)   *Painter*

As a portraitist and landscape painter, Lilla Cabot Perry helped introduce impressionism to the United States. Born Lilla Cabot on January 13, 1848, she was the oldest of eight children in a distinguished Boston family. Such luminaries as Ralph Waldo Emerson, Louisa May Alcott, and James Russell Lowell were friends of the Cabots.

Lilla was a devoted student, especially proficient in the arts. In 1874 she married Thomas Sargeant Perry, the grandnephew of Commodore Matthew C. Perry and a professor of literature at Harvard University. The couple had three daughters—Margaret, Edith, and Alice. While raising their family, the Perrys relied heavily on an inheritance Lilla received after her father's death.

At the age of 30, Perry produced her first painting, an intimate study of her daughter Margaret. She began formal art study six years later, inviting critiques of her work from noted portrait painter Alfred Quentin Collins. Her favorite subject was her own children, whom she often posed with a book or musical instrument.

In 1887 the Perrys moved to Paris, then the center of the international art world. Perry took instruction in several well-regarded academies and frequented museums to study the old masters with art critic Bernard Berenson, a friend of her husband's. She submitted two paintings—one of her husband and one her daughter Edith—to the Salon de la Société des Artistes Français in 1889. Both were accepted, marking the beginning of Perry's professional career.

In the same year, Perry attended an exhibition of the works of Claude Monet at the Galérie Georges Petit—an event that would have a profound effect on her own art. Perry was particularly taken with Monet's approach to landscape. His loose brush strokes and concentration on depicting light marked him as a member of the avant-garde school of French impressionism.

The Perrys were so impressed by Monet's work that they spent the next summer in Giverny, the

French village where Monet lived. It was the first of nine summers they would enjoy in the village over the next 20 years. Though Giverny attracted a small colony of American painters, including Theodore Robinson and John Breck, Lilla Perry forged the closest relationship with Monet. Inspired by her friendship with the master, she began painting her own landscapes. While she used an impressionist brush stroke and soft palette, Perry's early landscapes still reflected the influence of her traditional French academy training.

Returning to Boston in 1891, Perry began promoting the work of Monet. She exhibited his works in her home and delivered a lecture about his technique to the Boston Art Students' Association in 1894. The conservative art circles in her hometown, however, were leery of Monet's innovations. They had far more enthusiasm for Perry's work, particularly her portraits. When in 1897 Perry had her first solo show at the St. Botolph Club, a critic for the *Boston Evening Transcript* wrote, "Mrs. Perry is one of the most genuine, nononsense, natural painters that we known of. . . . Such work must be taken seriously." Seven of Perry's paintings also caused a sensation at the 1893 World's Columbian Exposition in Chicago.

In 1897 Thomas Perry accepted a position as a English professor at the Keiogijiku University in Tokyo. Lilla Perry welcomed the opportunity to study Japanese prints and paintings, which already had had an impact on impressionist compositions. While in Tokyo, Perry became acquainted with Okakura Kakuzo, the cofounder of the Imperial Art School. Kakuzo organized an exhibition of Perry's work in Tokyo in October 1898. During her two years in Japan, Perry also found a new subject—Fujiyama, or Mount Fuji. She later exhibited 35 views of the mountain and painted many more.

The Perrys divided the next decade between Boston and Paris. As Lilla's inheritance dwindled, the family increasingly relied on the sale of her work as its primary source of income. Perry often found the pressure to complete more and more commissions exhausting. She once recalled having

to paint "thirteen portraits in thirteen weeks, four sitters a day at two hours each." Perry was also frustrated that, after settling in Boston permanently in 1908, she had to devote herself primarily to portraiture, since her landscapes were considered too experimental by her conservative patrons. She found a more receptive audience in New York, where she had her first solo exhibition in November 1922. Featuring 42 paintings and including many of her Giverny and Japanese landscapes, the show was called "one of the most interesting exhibitions given by a woman in this city in years" by a reviewer at the *New York Morning Telegraph*.

In her final years, Perry returned to landscape, painting a series of winter scenes at her vacation home in Hancock, New Hampshire. Although she denounced modernists such as Henri Matisse, her late work moved increasingly toward abstraction. Divisions of sky and ground are almost indistinguishable in *Mist on the Mountain* (1931), her last exhibited landscape. Devoted to her art for more than 50 years, Lilla Cabot Perry continued painting daily until her death on February 28, 1933.

Further Reading

"Artist Profile: Lilla Cabot Perry," National Museum of Women in the Arts. Available online. URL: http://www.nmwa.org/legacy/bios/bperry.htm. Downloaded on August 1, 2001.
Lilla Cabot Perry, Days to Remember: An Exhibition of Paintings. Santa Fe, N.M.: Santa Fe East Gallery, 1983.
Martindale, Meredith. *Lilla Cabot Perry: An American Impressionist.* Washington, D.C.: The National Museum of Women in the Arts, 1990.

— L. S.

POWERS, HARRIET
(1837–1911) *Quiltmaker*

The Bible quilts of Harriet Powers are the best surviving examples of the quilting tradition of the 19th-century American South. Powers was born into slavery on October 29, 1837. After the Civil War, she and her husband, Armstead, ran a small farm near Athens, Georgia, and reared three children.

Like many African-American women, Powers added to her family's income by sewing for her African-American and white neighbors.

Aside from tax and census records, the only information about Powers documented in her lifetime comes from Jessie Smith, a noted local artist. Smith saw one of Powers's Bible quilts at a craft exhibit held at a county fair in 1886. Smith was fascinated by the quilt, which featured nine panels. Each was decorated with simple figures and told a biblical story. Beginning with Adam and Eve and ending with the crucifixion, the quilt, taken as a whole, traced the path from the first humans' fall from grace to humankind's redemption through Jesus's death.

Now displayed at the Smithsonian Institution's National Museum of American History, Powers's work was in the tradition of narrative quilts, a craft most often practiced by African-American women. But unlike most narrative quilts, its panels were "read" from left to right, rather than from top to bottom. It was also almost square, instead of being longer than it was wide, as one would expect a bed quilt to be. Its composition and shape suggest that it might have been used as a teaching tool, with its panels acting as mnemonic devices for retellings of Bible stories.

On the quilt, Powers depicted people, animals, and celestial bodies using the technique of appliqué. Each shape was cut from scraps of cloth, hemmed with a sewing machine, and sewn by hand onto the quilt fabric. Some scholars have noted similarities between Powers's appliqués and those created by the male artisans of the Fon people of Dahomey (now Benin) in Africa. It is possible that knowledge of Dahomey appliqué may have been passed along to Powers by other slaves.

Struck by the originality and beauty of Powers's quilt, Jessie Smith tracked down the artist and asked to buy it. Powers initially refused, but in about 1890 she approached Smith with an offer to sell because her family was having severe financial problems. Powers asked for $10, but accepted Smith's counteroffer of five. Smith wrote that Powers was heartbroken to give up her work, but she came to Smith's home "several times to visit the darling offspring of her brain. She was only in measure consoled for its loss when I promised to save her all my [fabric] scraps."

As painful as it was for Powers, selling the quilt ironically helped preserve her work and establish her place in the history of American folk art. Based on conversations with Powers, Smith wrote an 18-page description of her encounters with the artist and explanations of the images on each panel. Smith was also responsible for having Powers's work displayed at the Cotton States Exposition in Atlanta in 1895. The quilt appeared in the Negro Building, an exhibition funded by African-American communities and featuring items made by African-American tradespeople and craftspeople from 11 southern states. There, Powers's work was seen by a group of faculty wives from Atlanta University. They commissioned another Bible quilt from Powers as a gift for Reverend Charles Cuthbert Hall, a member of the university's board of directors and the president of Union Theological Seminary in New York City.

The resulting quilt, today part of the collection of Boston's Museum of Fine Arts, is made up of 15 panels, most of which told Old and New Testament stories. A few, however, recounted events of the recent past that relatives must had told Powers about when she was a child. One panel depicted May 19, 1780—popularly known as the "dark day" because smoke from massive forest fires turned the sky black. Another showed Powers's interpretation of the Leonid meteor storm of November 13, 1833. Both events were widely interpreted at the time as the coming of the apocalypse. Powers's second Bible quilt also depicted popular folk legends, such as one about a hog that ran all the way from Virginia to Georgia.

Little is known about the remainder of Powers's life. Records suggest that she and Armstead separated, and she lived alone until her death in 1911. Her legacy, however, is preserved by her two Bible quilts, which rank as among the greatest treasures of American folk art.

Further Reading

"African-American Story Bible Quilts by Harriet Powers," *Women's Early Art*. Available online. URL: http://womensearlyart.net/powers/#Illustration. Downloaded on August 1, 2001.

Fry, Gladys-Marie. *Stitched from the Soul: Slave Quilts from the Ante-Bellum South*. New York: Dutton, 1990.

Perry, Regenia A. *Harriet Powers' Bible Quilts*. New York: Rizzoli, 1994.

— L. S.

PROPHET, ELIZABETH
(Nancy Elizabeth Prophet)
(1890–1960)   *Sculptor*

Plagued by poverty and self-doubt, Elizabeth Prophet created sculptures that acted as physical manifestations of her emotional turmoil. Born Nancy Elizabeth Prophet on March 19, 1890, in Warwick, Rhode Island, she was the daughter of an African-American father and a Narragansett-Pequot Indian mother. Throughout her life, Prophet was ambivalent about her ancestry, at times embracing her ethnic heritage, at others denying it.

Working as a housekeeper to pay her tuition, in 1918 Prophet graduated from the Rhode Island School of Design in Providence with a degree in painting and drawing. For four years, she tried to make a living as a portraitist but found little success. Frustrated with the course of her career, she moved to Paris in 1922. Prophet left behind her husband, Francis Ford, whom she had married while still a student.

In Paris, Prophet turned to sculpture. She took classes with the well-known sculptor Victor Segoffin at the Ecole des Beaux-Arts and produced her first two busts in 1923. One was exhibited at the Salon d'Automne the following year.

Despite this early success, Prophet was overwhelmed by poverty. She made some money by selling batiks, but she was often hungry. With little to eat but the vegetables she grew in a small garden, she was hospitalized for malnutrition. Looking back on this period, she later wrote in her journal, "It was then interesting to feel how I felt each day, my mind was very clear, I could think with a great ease, though my belt was always dropping around my feet."

Prophet also suffered from frequent bouts of melancholy. She was often intensely disappointed in her work. In 1926 she smashed to bits her first full-size work, *Volonté,* when it did not live up to her expectations. The same year, she moved to a tiny studio in Montparnasse and began work on *Poverty,* an androgynous figure with a snake circled around its legs. Other sculptures she completed during this period included *Discontent, Bitter Laughter,* and *Silence.* Prophet wrote in her journal that her works communicated "an experience, something I have lived—or its result." Prophet worked in a variety of mediums, including marble, wood, granite, terra-cotta, and bronze. In attempting to convey a universal emotional state, her style had similarities to that of French sculptor Auguste Rodin and his student Emile Antoine Bourdelle.

Prophet exhibited works in the Salon d'Automne in 1925, 1926, and 1927, yet her art earned her little income. To feed herself and pay her rent, she had to rely on friends such as sculptor Mabel Gardner and painter Henry Ossawa Tanner to help her obtain grants. Another of her influential friends was African-American intellectual W. E. B. DuBois, with whom she kept up a lively correspondence. In October 1929, Prophet returned to the United States to promote her work with DuBois's help. She was welcomed into elite social circles and was able to show her work in several galleries and salons. Prophet sold *Discontent* to two wealthy patrons, who then donated the work to her alma mater.

Prophet succeeded in making new contacts, but the trip yielded her only $500 in sales. Missing her life in France, she wrote author Countee Cullen, the son-in-law of DuBois, in January 1930: "What is dear Paris doing these days? I long to be there in the solitude of my own studio, I do not like being famous, Cullen." By the end of the year, Prophet returned to Paris, where she briefly enjoyed the patronage of French writer Edouard Champion.

Prophet exhibited three works in the Société des Artistes Français in 1931 and 1932. On a visit to the United States in 1932, she also saw five of her sculptures featured in the Art Association of Newport's annual exhibition. *Discontent* won the exhibition's grand prize, while *Congolais*—a wooden head depicting a Masai warrior—was purchased by the Whitney Museum of American Art in New York City.

The following year, Prophet was back in Paris, starving and more than 10,000 francs in debt. DuBois and Atlanta University president John Hope came to her rescue by arranging for her to take a teaching post at Spelman College in Atlanta, Georgia. Arriving at Spelman in 1934, Prophet initially embraced the campus community and the craft of teaching. She exhibited her work at important shows at the Whitney and the Philadelphia Museum of Art, but she soon grew frustrated as her job took time away from her art. During her 10 years at Spelman, Prophet became increasingly isolated and eccentric. Wearing a black cape, she spoke in barely audible whispers and often carried a live chicken around campus.

In 1944 Prophet left Atlanta to live with friends in Providence. The next year, her work was shown at the Providence Public Library. It was the last known exhibit of Prophet's sculpture. She spent the final years of her life working odd jobs. On December 18, 1960, she died of a heart attack while working as a housekeeper. Her employer collected funds for her burial expenses.

Prophet made fewer than 40 sculptures in her lifetime. About 10 are now found in public and private collections. The others are known only through the black-and-white photographs Prophet took to document her work.

Further Reading

Davis, Karen A. "Sculptor Went Overseas to Gain Recognition Here," Providence Journal Company. Available online. URL: http://www.projo.com/special/history/prophet.htm. Posted in 1997.

Kirschenbaum, Blossom S. "Nancy Elizabeth Prophet, Sculptor." *SAGE* 4 (spring 1987): 45–52.

Leininger, Theresa. "Elizabeth Prophet." In *Notable Black American Women,* edited by Jessie Carney Smith, 215–217. Detroit: Gale Research, 1992.

— L. S.

R

◈ **REAM, VINNIE** (Vinnie Ream Hoxie)
(1847–1914)   *Sculptor*

At age 18, Vinnie Ream was chosen to create a marble sculpture of Abraham Lincoln, making her the first female artist awarded a major commission from the U.S. government. Ream was born on November 20, 1847, in a log cabin in Madison, Wisconsin. She grew up in remote settlements in Missouri, Iowa, and Kansas, where her father, a surveyor, plied his trade. Ream briefly attended Christian College in Columbia, Missouri, where she displayed a flair for music.

With the outbreak of the Civil War, the Reams moved to Washington, D.C. By lying about her age, Vinnie secured a clerkship at the dead letter office of the U.S. Postal Service when she was 14. Soon she became reacquainted with Missouri congressman James S. Rollins, whom she had first met in college. Through Rollins, Ream was introduced to Clark Mills, the most famous sculptor in the capital. She later wrote that "as soon as I saw the sculptor handle the clay, I felt at once that I, too, could model." During her first visit to Mills's studio, she grabbed a ball of clay and modeled it into a medallion featuring the head of an Indian chief. Mills was impressed enough to take her on as a part-time student.

At the studio, Ream met many of the most prominent men in Washington. Slight and pretty, with voluminous brown curls framing her face, she was able to convince several of them to sit for her. Among her subjects were Congressman Thaddeus Stevens, Senator James Nesmith, journalist Horace Greeley, and Lieutenant Colonel George Armstrong Custer.

One sitter who eluded Ream, however, was President Abraham Lincoln. Several of her important friends pressed the president to sit for her. But in the end, according to Ream, it was she who persuaded him. Ream maintained that she caught Lincoln's attention while in the crowd that gathered daily as he walked from his living quarters to his office. Touched that she was trying to support herself with her art, Lincoln agreed to sit for her for a half an hour a day over the next five months.

After Lincoln's assassination, Congress authorized $10,000 for a memorial sculpture for the Capitol Building. With her bust of Lincoln completed, Ream set about winning the prestigious and lucrative commission. She arranged for her busts and medallions to be displayed in Washington jewelry stores and began to assemble an impressive collection of letters of recommendation from her powerful admirers. She also wrote Mary Todd

Lincoln, hoping to win her support. Lincoln's widow, however, refused in a curt reply. She said she had never heard her husband speak of Ream, so she doubted Ream's claim that he had ever sat for her. Mary Todd Lincoln's letter has led some scholars to conclude that Ream's stories of her personal contact with the president were fabricated. Her mentor Clark Mills had created a life mask of Lincoln several months before his death; therefore, it is possible that Ream based her bust on this mask rather than on sittings with her subject.

Normally, a congressional committee commissioned sculpture by asking for models from competing artists, which were then judged by a group of impartial experts. The House and Senate then voted on who should get the commission, largely based on the group's recommendations. For the Lincoln commission, however, Ream's friend Congressman Thaddeus Stevens tried to circumvent the procedure. As the congressional session of 1866 was drawing to an end, Stevens introduced a resolution that would give the commission to Ream without an evaluation of the works of the other competitors, who included Mills and noted female sculptor HARRIET HOSMER. Ream had armed Stevens with a written endorsement that she was an "accomplished young lady [of] rare genius in the beautiful art of sculpture." It was signed by 30 senators, 111 representatives, and President Andrew Johnson.

Immediately passed by the House, Stevens's resolution was met with passionate opposition in the Senate. Leading the fight against awarding Ream the commission was Senator Charles Sumner of Massachusetts. He expressed doubt that such an inexperienced artist would be able to make a work worthy of the Capitol, if she could complete the sculpture at all. One of Ream's supporters, James W. Nesmith, countered that her very lack of experience was what made her the ideal choice. Unlike a well-trained sculptor, she would come to the project fresh, without the preconceptions of the classical tradition, allowing her to produce an exact likeness of her subject. Calling Ream "this young scion of the West, from the same land from which

Lincoln came," Nesmith also argued that she could best capture Lincoln because they were from similar backgrounds. On July 28, 1866, Stevens and Nesmith convinced a firm majority of senators to give Ream the commission.

The story was reported in newspapers throughout the country, making Ream an instant celebrity. Western papers were almost unanimous in their praise of Ream. Several eastern journalists, however, echoed Sumner's concern about Ream's inexperience and youth. A number implied that she had used her feminine wiles to win the commission. Journalist Jane Gray Swisshelm, who had favored Hosmer's design, described Ream as "a young girl of about twenty who has been studying art for a few months, never made a statue, has some plaster busts on exhibition, including her own minus clothing to the waist, has a pretty face, [and] . . . sees members at their lodgings."

Ream set up a studio in the Capitol, which became a popular tourist attraction. Among her many visitors were General Ulysses S. Grant, painter George Caleb Bingham, and photographer Mathew Brady. For two years, she crafted her work first in clay, then in plaster.

Once her plaster model was approved, she headed to Europe to watch as Italian artisans carved it into marble. She traveled to London, Munich, Berlin, and Florence, and she briefly studied with sculptor Léon J.F. Bonnat in Paris. Ream established a studio in Rome, which was frequented by famous friends, such as Franz Liszt and Dante Gabriel Rossetti. One of her European admirers, the Danish literary critic Georg Brandes, wrote that "she had a mind of many colours. And there was the very devil of a rush and Forward! March! about her, *always in a hurry.*"

On January 25, 1871, Ream's sculpture of Lincoln was unveiled in a ceremony in the Capitol Rotunda. Most of the hundreds present were Ream's supporters, who applauded loudly at their first glimpse of her work. While acknowledging that he knew nothing about art, Wisconsin senator Matthew H. Carpenter praised it, saying "it is

Abraham Lincoln all over." Another friend of Ream's declared that the sculpture represented a new American aesthetic, developed by artists who were "very like nature herself" and who "speak and act as they feel." Eastern critics, however, were soon criticizing the work in the press. They called Ream's Lincoln "lifeless and soulless" and "a gaunt, shameful spectacle" and derided Ream herself as a "fraud" and "humbug." Hiram Powers, a leading sculptor of the day, condemned Ream as "a female lobby member, who has no more talent for art than the carver of weeping willows on tombstones."

Despite the scathing criticism, Ream hoped that the Lincoln sculpture would lead to more commissions. None came her way, however, perhaps because of the controversy she had provoked. Also, her greatest champions were westerners, who were generally not inclined to build and pay for grand sculpted memorials.

Vinnie Ream executed a marble statue of President Abraham Lincoln.
(Library of Congress)

The sole breadwinner for her family, Ream was finally heartened with announcement of an open competition for a memorial sculpture of Civil War hero David A. Farragut. As she began work on her model, she wrote his widow, Virginia, who became one of her most enthusiastic supporters. Virginia Farragut gave Ream a list of her friends, whom Ream also wrote seeking endorsements.

In the 1870s, she found another important correspondent in General William Tecumseh Sherman. Clearly smitten with the young artist, he used his influence to lobby for Ream's entry into the competition. He also walked her down the aisle at her wedding to Richard Leveridge Hoxie, a lieutenant in the Army Corps of Engineers, in 1878. Five years later, she gave birth to a son, Richard Ream Hoxie.

In February 1874, Congress turned the matter of resolving the Farragut commission to Secretary of the Navy George Robeson. Ream appealed to congressmen she knew to place the final decision in the hands of a committee of three, consisting of Robeson, Sherman, and Virginia Farragut. Not surprisingly, Sherman and Farragut voted for Ream's design, winning her the $20,000 commission.

By the spring of 1878, Ream had created a 10-foot plaster model. The sculpture was then cast in bronze at the Washington Navy Yard. The metal used for the project came from melting down the propeller of Farragut's ship, *The Hartford.* In April 1881, the work was unveiled in Washington's Farragut Square before a crowd of 4,000, including President James A. Garfield.

After fulfilling the Farragut commission, Ream retired at the insistence of her husband. Although they summered in Iowa City, her husband's hometown, they spent much of the year at their home on Farragut Square. There Ream continued to entertain her many friends, presiding over one of the liveliest salons in Washington, D.C.

Ream returned to her profession in 1906 when the state of Iowa asked her to make a statue of former governor Samuel Kirkland for the Capitol's Statuary Hall. Six years later, Oklahoma commissioned from her a sculpture of Sequoyah, creator of the Cherokee syllabary, also for Statuary Hall. She finished a model before dying of a chronic kidney ailment on November 20, 1914. The Sequoyah sculpture was cast in bronze by her friend George Zolnay. Her husband also asked Zolnay to sculpt a bas-relief on her gravesite memorial in Arlington National Cemetery. The carving depicts Ream as the beautiful young woman she was when she rose first to fame.

Further Reading

Jacob, Kathryn Allamong. "Vinnie Ream." *Smithsonian,* July 2000, 104–115.

Prioli, Carmine A. "'Wonder Girl from the West': Vinnie Ream and the Congressional Statue of Abraham Lincoln." *Journal of American Culture* 10 (winter 1989): 58–67.

Sherwood, Glenn V. *A Labor of Love: The Life and Art of Vinnie Ream.* Hygiene, Colo.: SunShine Press, 1997.

"Vinnie Ream Hoxie," Tarzanna Graphics. Available online. URL: http://www.awomanaweek.com/ream.html. Downloaded on August 2, 2001.

— L. S.

RINGGOLD, FAITH (Faith Willie Jones)
(1930–) *Quiltmaker, Illustrator, Painter, Sculptor, Performance Artist*

Using various styles and mediums, Faith Ringgold has devoted her art to exploring the experiences of contemporary African-American women. She was born Faith Willie Jones on October 8, 1930, in New York City. After her parents separated when she was a toddler, her mother, Willi Posey, became a successful dressmaker and fashion designer. Living in the affluent Sugar Hill neighborhood, Faith and her mother frequently attended museum shows, films, and jazz clubs.

Intent on a career in the arts, Faith Jones enrolled in City College in 1948. Two years later, she married Earl Warren, her high school sweetheart, but they soon separated after Faith discovered his drug problem. Their marriage was annulled in 1956. In January 1952, she gave birth to their child Michele; she had a second daughter, Barbara, in December of that year.

Faith Jones earned a bachelor's degree in 1955 and a master's degree in 1959. While working as an art teacher in the New York public schools, she married Burdete Ringgold in 1962. She also began painting scenes of African-American life, taking on issues associated with the fight for civil rights. These early works were often angry political statements. *Flag for the Moon: Die Nigger* (1969), for instance, spoke out against the vast sums the government was spending on the space program while African-American families lived in poverty.

Influenced by the women's movement of the 1970s, Ringgold began experimenting with materials traditionally used by craftswomen. From fabric and thread, she first made needlepoint sculptures in the style of African masks. For several of these masks, her mother sewed costumes to create full-length figures of African-American heroes, such as Martin Luther King Jr. and Adam Clayton Powell. Ringgold also made doll-sized representations of the people she knew from her neighborhood.

In 1980 Ringgold began making art by quilting, a skill she had learned as a child from her grandmother. Her first quilt, *Echoes of Harlem* (1980), featured faces of her Harlem neighbors with a frame-like border sewn by her mother. In later works, Ringgold added paint and text to create her well-received story quilts. Her *Slave Rape Story* told of a young girl on a southern plantation, while *Flag Story Quilt* offered a story of a wounded Vietnam veteran. Ringgold called her story quilts feminist art because they "came out of being a woman, and the use of craft."

In the 1980s, Ringgold also explored performance art. One of her performance pieces was called "Change: Faith Ringgold's Over 100 Lbs. Weight Loss Performance Story Quilt." During the performance, she wore a quilted jacket while talking about her substantial weight loss. In the end, she shed the jacket, as a symbol of how her artistic successes had given her the confidence to lose her excess weight.

Ringgold's art reached a mass audience with the publication of *Tar Beach* (1991). Based on one of her story quilts, this children's book told of an eight-year-old girl who dreams of flying as a way of escaping the bitter realities of poverty. *Tar Beach* was named a Caldecott Honor Book. Ringgold has since written and illustrated many other books for children, including *Aunt Harriet's Underground Railroad in the Sky* (1992), *Dinner at Aunt Connie's House* (1993), and *If a Bus Could Talk: The Story of Rosa Parks* (1999). In 1995, her autobiography *We Flew over the Bridge* was published.

Among Ringgold's recent works are her French Collection series of quilt paintings. The quilts explore in text and image the fictional experiences of Ringgold's character Willia Marie Simone, an African-American artist who studies art in Paris in the 1920s. Taken as a whole, the quilts reevaluate the history of art from the perspective of a black woman. Through the series, Ringgold maintains, "I'm rewriting history," adding that "the life of African American women artists has been so bleak that if I dealt with it factually, it would be too depressing."

Further Reading

Authors Online Library. "About Faith Ringgold," Scholastic. Available online. URL: http://teacher.scholastic.com/authorsandbooks/authors/ringgold/bio.htm. Downloaded on August 2, 2001.

Cameron, Dan, et al. *Dancing at the Louvre: Faith Ringgold's French Collection and Other Story Quilts.* Berkeley: University of California Press, 1998.

Farrington, Lisa E. *Art on Fire: The Politics of Race and Sex in the Paintings of Faith Ringgold.* New York: Millennium Fine Arts, 1999.

Ringgold, Faith. *Tar Beach.* New York: Crown Publishers, 1991.

———. *We Flew over the Bridge: The Memoirs of Faith Ringgold.* Boston: Little, Brown and Company, 1995.

— L. S.

ROTHENBERG, SUSAN
(1945–   )   *Painter*

Susan Rothenberg is best known for her paintings featuring horse imagery, which helped mark the return of representational painting in the 1970s. Born on January 20, 1945, in Buffalo, New York,

she studied painting and sculpture at Cornell University, graduating with a degree in fine arts in 1966. In Washington, D.C., she continued her art education at the George Washington University and the Corcoran Museum School.

Rothenberg moved to New York in 1969, but she found the art scene there hostile to painting. Performance and installation art were instead the preferred forms of progressive artists. Rothenberg participated in these experimental art forms first as an assistant to installation artist NANCY GRAVES, then as a member of the performance group led by Joan Jonas. In 1971 Rothenberg married George Trakas and gave birth to their daughter, Maggie, the following year.

Painter and printmaker Susan Rothenberg is renowned for her depiction of horses.
(Courtesy © Ann Chwatsky)

Beginning in 1973, Rothenberg began making large paintings featuring faint outlines of horse figures. Most were monochromatic, painted in a cool blue, gray, black, or white that added to their otherworldly quality. Her departure from abstraction drew an enthusiastic response from critics, who often compared her powerful images to ancient cave paintings. In 1979 *Artforum* critic Peter Schjeldahl praised her exhibition at the Williard Gallery, calling it "an emotionally clenched, even grueling show, fantastically well painted."

Rothenberg's professional success coincided with the failure of her marriage. Divorced from Trakas in 1979, she began painting violent images incorporating human body parts. One showed a head vomiting, while another depicted several fingers being thrust into the eyes of a face. Rothenberg later explained, "Many of those are divorce images. . . . My energies [were] being blocked and the flow [was] being screwed up." During this period, Rothenberg also struggled to overcome an addiction to alcohol.

In the 1980s, Rothenberg began depicting full human figures using a looser, more feathery brush stroke. Among other new images she employed were bones, the Buddha, and bike riders. She also incorporated in several pieces a small figure of Danish painter Piet Mondrian, whose abstract works of the early 20th century combined horizontal and vertical blocks of color in highly ordered compositions. Rothenberg explained that her representation of Mondrian symbolized her "desire to build a painting correctly."

By the end of the decade, Rothenberg was romantically involved with sculptor Bruce Nauman. They married in 1989, and Rothenberg came to live in Nauman's home in New Mexico. In this new setting, Rothenberg's palette shifted toward reds and yellows, inspired by the southwestern landscape. She also returned to horse imagery, also adding figures of dogs, rabbits, goats, and other animals found on her ranch. Personal experiences and anxieties became the subject of several important works of the 1990s. *Accident* (1991–92) recalled her terror of seeing Nauman thrown from a horse, while *Impending Doom* (1996–97) referred to a near-fatal bee sting she suffered.

With these recent works, Rothenberg has continued to earn critical accolades. Regarded as a "painter's painter" because of her technical proficiency, she is also hailed for her committment to using paint on canvas to create art that speaks to a postmodern audience. As Mark Stevens wrote in *The New Republic* in 1993, "She has attracted attention not only because she has made some good pictures, but because she seems to be struggling to maintain the world of painting."

Further Reading

Brutvan, Cheryl. *Susan Rothenberg: Paintings from the Nineties*. New York: Rizzoli, 1999.

Rothenberg, Susan. *Susan Rothenberg: Paintings and Drawings*. New York: Rizzoli, 1992.

Simon, Joan. *Susan Rothenberg*. New York: Harry N. Abrams, 1991.

— L. S.

S

SAAR, BETYE (Betye Brown)
(1926–) *Mixed Media Artist, Sculptor*

Through her assemblages and installations, Betye Saar has explored her personal history and challenged society's stereotypes of African-American women. She was born Betye Brown in Pasadena, California, on July 30, 1926. Her mother believed Betye had special powers, which possibly contributed to her lifelong fascination with mysticism and the occult. Another early influence was the Watts Towers, monumental works of folk art created by Italian immigrant Simon Rodia in her grandmother's Los Angeles neighborhood. Constructed from a steel frame covered with pieces of broken tile, glass, and other castoff objects, the towers showed Betye how found materials could be used to create a work of art.

In 1949, she graduated from the University of California at Los Angeles with a degree in graphic design. Two years later, she married Richard W. Saar, with whom she had three daughters—Lezley, Alison, and Tracye—before their divorce in 1968. While raising her children, Betye Saar attended Long Beach State University, hoping to become an art teacher. Her printmaking instructor, however, helped changed her mind. He encouraged her to think of herself as an artist, inspiring her to pursue a career in the fine arts.

Initially, Saar was a printmaker, but by the end of the 1960s, she began placing her prints in boxes, juxtaposing them with other objects. As a child, she had enjoyed collecting objects that appealed to her and arranging them in a frame. Saar found further inspiration in the similarly styled work of artist Joseph Cornell, whose shadow boxes were shown in an exhibition at the Pasadena Art Museum in 1966. His work helped her see assemblage as an art form.

Many of Saar's early boxed works dealt with the occult and featured images from tarot cards and the zodiac. In pieces such as *Nine Mojo Secrets* (1971), she started incorporating elements from African art. Saar also used her box sculptures to recount her family history. In *Record: For Hattie* (1975), she paid tribute to her recently deceased great aunt in an assemblage that included her relative's jewelry and cosmetics, a baby photograph, and pressed flowers.

Saar's most influential work of the 1970s, however, dealt with derogatory representations of African Americans in popular culture. Following the assassination of civil rights leader Martin Luther King Jr. in 1968, Saar used images of Black

Sambo, Uncle Remus, and other stereotyped figures to protest racism. Her seminal piece was *The Liberation of Aunt Jemima* (1972), which depicted a smiling "mammy" doll holding a broom in one hand and a gun in the other. With pride, Saar said, "I turned Aunt Jemima into a warrior." Presenting African-American stereotypes in a new context, Saar sought to reclaim the images as symbols of empowerment. Her works from this period were shown in a solo exhibit at the Whitney Museum of American Art in New York in 1975.

Saar's first assemblages were intended to be hung on the wall like a canvas. By the mid-1970s, however, she was gravitating toward freestanding sculptural works. She began creating what she called "altars," such as *Spirit Catcher* (1976–77), from objects she found at flea markets and yard sales. Rather than having a preconceived notion about what materials to use, she was guided by intuition to items she felt contained a certain power that would embue her altars with a mystical quality.

Over time, Saar began creating installations by incorporating the space surrounding her sculptures into the work. Her installations were in part a reaction to the pressure to sell her art in the marketplace. As Saar once explained, "Installation art . . . frees you from that kind of pressure—it's art that's not for sale. You still reach audiences with your work, but the critics have less influence over its value." One example of Saar's installations is *Mojotech,* which she created for the List Visual Arts Center at the Massachusetts Institute of Technology in 1987. Its eight panels integrated radio parts and circuit boards with organic materials, such as leather, fur, and wool.

In the late 1980s and 1990s, Saar received many commissions for installations in public spaces. In many of these works, she invited the people who used the space to participate in creating her art. In *On Our Way* (1987) for the Martin Luther King Metrorail Station in Miami, she organized a party during which she asked commuters to hold a pose so she could trace their shadows. The finished piece featured their silhouettes re-created in enamel-painted steel.

Mixed-media artist Betye Saar was given a solo show at New York's Whitney Museum in 1975.
(Portrait by Timothy Greenfield-Sanders)

Saar's art inspired her daughters to follow in her footsteps. Tracye has worked as her assistant, Lezley is a painter, and Alison is a sculptor. At the Wight Art Gallery in Los Angeles, Betye and Alison Saar had a two-artist exhibition in 1990, in which they collaborated on the installation *House of Gris Gris.*

In 1997 Saar threw herself in the center of a controversy when she launched a letter-writing campaign criticizing the work of the 28-year-old African-American artist Kara Walker. Widely hailed by critics, Walker's art depicts images of sex and sadism on Southern plantations, created using the 19th-century art form of cut-paper silhouettes. Saar maintained that Walker's work "makes white people feel relief. They don't have to feel guilty about slavery because here's an African-American woman mocking it." Saar's actions led to a two-day conference at Harvard University in the spring of 1998, at which leading artists and critics debated the ethical use of stereotypical images of African Americans in art.

Saar herself reexamined her earlier use of such images in a 1999 exhibition titled *Workers + Warriors: The Return of Aunt Jemima.* It featured 30 assemblages, in which old washboards were decorated with illustrations and collectibles of mammy figures from the 1940s and 1950s. Less politically aggressive than her famous *Liberation of Aunt Jemima,* the works emphasized the day-to-day work performed by Saar's ancestors. Incorporating printed text from the works of Langston Hughes and Henry Dumas, Saar's new Aunt Jemimas also featured her own aphorisms, including appropriately the statement, "Extreme measures call for extreme heroines."

Further Reading

Betye Saar: Workers + Warriors: The Return of Aunt Jemima. New York: Michael Rosenfeld Gallery, 1998.

Clothier, Peter. *Betye Saar.* Los Angeles: Museum of Contemporary Art, 1984.

Shepherd, Elizabeth, editor. *Secrets, Dialogues, Revelations: The Art of Betye and Alison Saar.* Los Angeles: Wight Art Gallery, 1990.

Sherman, Ann Elliot. "Soaring Saar," Metro Publishing and Virtual Valley, Inc. Available online. URL: http://www.metroactive.com/papers/metro/02.08.96/saar-9606.html. Posted on Februray 8, 1996.

— L. S.

SAGE, KAY
(1898–1963)   *Painter*

A surrealistic painter known for her precise architectural forms, Kay Sage was born into a wealthy family in Albany, New York, on June 25, 1898. She spent much of her youth traveling through Europe, where she became fluent in Italian and French. During World War II, Sage returned to the United States, where she briefly attended the Corcoran Art School in Washington, D.C. However, she rarely attended class, preferring to carve out her artistic vision without the interference of instructors.

In 1918 Sage traveled to Italy, where she rented a dilapidated villa in Rome and began to focus on her painting. Although she studied at several academies, she found more encouragement in the circle of artist Onorato Carlandi. In the company of her artist friends, she later recalled, "I simply drew and painted until I really knew how to draw and paint." Sage remembered this period as the happiest of her life.

In 1925 Sage married Ranieri di San Faustino, an Italian prince. During their marriage, she painted little. In 1935, the year after her divorce, Sage returned to her art and soon displayed recent landscapes and portraits in her first one-woman show. While in Italy, she also wrote and illustrated a children's book, *Piove in Giardino,* under the name K. di San Faustino.

Selling jewelry to earn her keep, Sage moved to Paris in 1937. One of her paintings in a group exhibition attracted the attention of André Breton, a leader in the surrealistic movement. The surrealists used fantastic imagery and peculiar juxtapositions to explore the unconscious. After meeting Breton, Sage became one of the few woman associated with the style.

With the outbreak of World War II, Sage moved to New York, where she used her resources to help bring several of her friends from Paris to the United States. Among them was the painter Yves Tanguy, whom she married in 1940. They bought a large country house in Woodbury, Connecticut, which they decorated with their collection of paintings by such modernists as Giorgio de Chirico, Max Ernst, Joan Miró, and René Magritte. They converted the estate's barn into two separate studios, where they worked in isolation. Although they had one joint show in 1954, Sage generally played down Tanguy's influence on her for fear that her work would be judged as derivative of his.

Sage's first 15 years in Connecticut were her most productive. Reminiscent of de Chirico's work, her mature style featured architectural structures resembling scaffolding in barren settings, all bathed in eerie light that lent the objects a mysterious quality. The disturbing effect of works such as

Small Portrait (1950)—a self-portrait in which one of her architectural forms takes the place of her head—contrasted with the smooth surfaces produced by Sage's almost invisible brush stroke.

In 1955 Tanguy died suddenly—a blow from which Sage never completely recovered. She also struggled to continue painting as her eyesight began to fail. Overwhelmed by despair, Sage attempted suicide in 1959. Her friend and art dealer, Catherine Viviano, tried to reinterest Sage in her work by organizing a retrospective of her paintings. For a time, Sage experimented with new forms, particularly collage and creating sculptures from found materials, such as doorknobs and tinfoil. She also turned to writing, publishing a book of poems titled *Mordicus* (1962). Despite her efforts to renew her will to live, Sage committed suicide by shooting herself in the heart on January 8, 1963. Her works were bequeathed to several friends who distributed them to museums around the world. She also willed her personal art collection and a large monetary donation to the Museum of Modern Art in New York.

Further Reading

Chadwick, Whitney. *Women Artists and the Surrealist Movement.* Boston: Little, Brown and Company, 1985.

Sage, Kay. *Kay Sage, 1898–1963.* Rochester, N.Y.: Great Lakes Press, 1977.

"Sage, Kay (Katherine Lynn Tanquy)," AskART. Available online. URL: http://www.askart.com/Biography.asp. Posted in 2000.

Suter, Judith D. *A House of Her Own: Kay Sage, Solitary Surrealist.* Lincoln: University of Nebraska Press, 1997.

— L. S.

 SAVAGE, AUGUSTA
(Augusta Christine Fells)
(1892–1962) *Sculptor*

Through teaching and example, sculptor Augusta Savage helped open doors for African-American artists. The daughter of a minister, she was born Augusta Christine Fells in Green Cove Springs, Florida, in 1892. As a child, she took to molding ducks and other animals from the area's rich red clay. Convinced she was making graven images, her father beat her when he discovered her early attempts at sculpture. She later remembered that he "almost whipped all the art out of me."

At 15, Fells married John T. Moore, with whom she had a daughter, Irene. Soon after Moore's death, she married James T. Savage, whom she divorced in the early 1920s. Once they separated, she went to live with her parents, who had moved to West Palm Beach.

While attending high school there, Augusta Savage so impressed the principal with her sculpture that he hired her to teach a clay modeling class. Her dollar-a-day job sparked her lifelong passion for teaching. With an eye toward becoming an art instructor, she briefly attended State Normal and Industrial School in Tallahassee, but she soon dropped out to devote herself to her sculpture.

Savage had her first professional success while running a booth at the Palm Beach County Fair. Although fair officials were initially hesitant to let an African-American woman sell her wares, her small sculptures of farm animals were extremely popular. She earned $175 and a $25 prize for the most original exhibit. At the fair, she also met official George Graham Currie, who commissioned a bust from her. Currie suggested she pursue her career in New York City and gave her a letter of introduction to sculptor Solon Borglum.

With less than five dollars in her pocket, Savage arrived at Borglum's studio in 1921. Borglum told her that she could not afford classes from him, suggesting instead that she apply to Cooper Union, a New York City school that charged no tuition. A letter from Borglum and a bust Augusta made of an African-American minister convinced the Cooper Union to admit her. While there, she studied sculpture with George T. Brewster. Her talents were so appreciated that when she had trouble paying her living expenses, Cooper Union's advisory council voted to give her enough money that she could complete her education.

During her years as a student, Savage schooled herself in art history at the 135th Street branch of the New York Public Library. A librarian there arranged for the library to commission her to create a bust of writer W. E. B. DuBois. Savage was also asked to sculpt a bust of black nationalist leader Marcus Garvey. Through Garvey, she met Robert L. Poston, a lawyer whom she married in 1923. Poston died four months later while traveling home from a trip to Africa.

In 1923 Savage was thrust into the national news after applying to—and being rejected by—a summer art school at Fontainebleau that was funded by the French government. She was devastated when she was rejected, particularly because many of the students admitted were far less qualified. Savage elicited the help of Alfred W. Martin, a prominent New Yorker who headed the city's Ethical Culture Society. Martin got the Fontainebleau admissions committee to admit that it had turned down Savage because it feared that, as an African American, her presence would make other students from the South uncomfortable.

The story of Savage's rejection was published in New York newspapers, receiving front-page coverage for months. The exposure of such blatant racism in the art world was condemned by noted intellectuals, including anthropologist Franz Boas. Savage herself added to the fray in a letter to the *New York World,* printed on May 20, 1923. Stating that her troubles were shared by all African-American artists, she wrote that "we do want—and we have a right to seek—the chance to prove that we are men and women with powers and possibilities similar to those of other men and women." Although many luminaries came out in support of Savage, the controversy also helped brand her as a troublemaker, giving galleries and museums an excuse to ignore her work.

Appalled by Savage's treatment by the Fontainebleau school, one member of its admission committee, National Sculpture Society president Hermon MacNeil, offered to help her. He accepted her as a student, and soon her work was being exhibited by the Harmon Foundation, an organization established to recognize the achievements of African Americans. Despite the exposure,

Savage made little money from her art. To support her aged parents and other family members, she had to take away valuable time from her art to earn money as a laundress. In 1926 DuBois helped secure Savage a scholarship to study in Rome, but she had to give up the award when she failed to raise enough money to pay her travel expenses.

Savage's sculpture *Gamin* (1929) soon provided her with a second chance to visit Europe. Inspired by her nephew Ellis Ford, the portrait bust is a sensitive study of an African-American boy that suggests both a youthful vitality and a hard-won sense of dignity. On the basis of this well-received work, Savage was awarded a Julius Rosenwald Fellowship for two years of foreign study. She also received substantial financial help from the African-American community, where many still felt bitter about the Fontainebleu scandal. When news of the fellowship spread, black women's groups sent her contributions, while other supporters held parties to raise money for her trip.

In 1929 Savage arrived in Paris, where she studied at Académie de la Grande Chaumière. A Carnegie Foundation grant also allowed her to tour Belgium and Germany before returning to New York in 1931. She resumed her career with commissions to sculpt several famous African Americans, including writer James Weldon Johnson and entertainer Ted Upshure. The Upshure bust won her election to the National Association of Women Painters and Sculptors, the first African American so honored. Soon, however, commissions dried up as the Great Depression worsened. To make ends meet, Savage opened the Savage Studio of Arts and Crafts, where she taught art classes from her apartment. Savage's home also became a center for African-American intellectuals to meet and exchange ideas. Among Savage's frequent guests were DuBois, writer Claude McKay, and painter Romare Bearden.

Savage also devoted her energies to challenging the Fedral Art Project (FAP), a Works Projects Administration program designed to provide income for artists. She held that the FAP virtually ignored African-American artists, and she demanded that images from black history be included in the public murals it funded. Her past experience with the media helped Savage wage an effective campaign to reform the FAP. In 1937 she was named director of the government-funded Harlem Community Art Center, which became the largest art center in the United States. Under her watch, the center offered art classes to more than 1,500 Harlem residents, including artists Jacob Lawrence and Gwendolyn Knight. Alternately offering enthusiastic support and withering criticism, Savage was an inspiring teacher and influential force in promoting young African-American artists. During this period, Savage also served as the president of the Harlem Artists Guild and organized the Vanguard Club, which allowed Harlem artists to meet and discuss their work.

Savage's work on behalf of other artists left her frustrated with her own career. She had little time to sculpt, and the works she did complete rarely sold. Savage wanted to create multifigured, monumental works, but the Great Depression made it impossible to find patrons willing to fund the ambitious sculptures she envisioned.

Just as she had given up her dream, Savage won her most prestigious commission in 1939. The committee organizing the New York World's Fair asked, her to make a sculpture to celebrate "the American Negro's contribution to music, especially to song." Inspired by Rosamond and James Weldon Johnson's song "Lift Every Voice and Sing," she created a 16-foot sculpture depicting a harp, with a choir of boys and girls as its strings. Placed at the entrance to the *American Art Today* exhibit, the plaster sculpture was enormously popular. Many fair visitors purchased miniatures and postcards depicting the piece. The sculpture itself, however, was destroyed when Savage could not raise the money to have it cast in bronze.

Forced out of her art center job because of budget cuts, Savage established the Salon of Contemporary Negro Art in Harlem, the first gallery of African-American art in the United States. Although 500 people attended its opening, Savage discovered that few local residents had the money to buy art, and few white art buyers were willing to travel to Harlem. The gallery closed within months.

Still hoping to capitalize on the publicity surrounding her success at the World's Fair, Savage organized a nine-city tour of her work. It opened in Chicago in 1940, but failed to generate many sales. Savage had to abandon not only the exhibition but also many of her works, because she could not afford to ship them back to New York.

Savage's frustration with the art world only grew in the early 1940s. By 1945, she felt so defeated that she retired to a farm in Saugerties, New York. Although she taught some children's art lessons, she all but gave up sculpting. In her final years, she came to live with her daughter in New York City, where she died on March 27, 1962. Few of her works have survived. A number of those lost were probably destroyed by her own hand.

Savage's disappointment with her career once led her to write, "I have created nothing really beautiful, really lasting." Despite her harsh self-assessment, she did recognize her enormous contribution to the promotion of African-American art and artists. "If I can inspire one of these youngsters to develop the talent I know they possess," Savage wrote, "then my monument will be in their work."

Further Reading

Bearden, Romare, and Harry Henderson. *A History of African-American Artists from 1792 to the Present.* New York: Pantheon Books, 1993.

Perry, Regenia. *Free within Ourselves: African-American Artists in the Collection of the National Museum of American Art.* Washington, D.C.: National Museum of American Art, 1992.

"Savage, Augusta Christine." AskART. Available online. URL: http://askart.com/Biography.asp. Posted in 2000.

— L. S.

SCHAPIRO, MIRIAM

(1923–) *Collagist, Mixed Media Artist, Painter, Sculptor*

One of the leading artists of the feminist art movement of the 1970s, Miriam Schapiro was born in

Toronto, Ontario, on November 15, 1923, but she spent much of her youth in New York City. Her father, Theodore, was an industrial designer who first introduced her to the world of art. In addition to giving her weekly drawing assignments, he instilled in her what Schapiro later called "a sensible attitude about humanism." She added, "My feminism grew out of that humanism, a belief that men were in as much trouble as women were when it came to being victimized."

After two years at New York City's Hunter College, Schapiro enrolled at the Iowa State University. She received a bachelor's degree in graphics in 1945, a master's in printmaking in 1946, and a master of fine arts degree in 1949. While at Iowa, Schapiro married fellow student Paul Brach, with whom she had a son, Peter.

In 1951 Schapiro moved to New York City, where she was influenced by abstract expressionism, an abstract American art style characterized by an attention to surface qualities, such as brush stroke and texture. As a member of the second generation of abstract expressionists, she saw her work featured in the Museum of Modern Art's *New Talent Exhibition* in 1957 and in the Whitney Museum of American Art's biennial exhibition in 1959. In the 1960s, however, she moved toward a more minimalist style. By the middle of the decade, she had produced her Shrine series, a collection of works featuring framed compartments stacked on top of one another. After her family's move to California in 1967, she also began experimenting with using computers to design her work, becoming one of first artists to employ this new technology.

Schapiro began feeling frustrated in her career and personal life in the late 1960s. She soon found relief in the growing feminist movement. As she once explained, "The reason I was drawn to feminism was the sense of community. I had never had that kind of support before. Feminism allowed me to be myself as an individual and an artist." With artist JUDY CHICAGO, she founded the Feminist Art Program at the California Institute of Arts in 1971. The next year, the program rented an aban-

doned mansion in Hollywood. Schapiro, Chicago, and their students renovated the house and created in the rooms art environments that expressed their experiences and fantasies about being female. The project, known as *Womanhouse,* drew national press attention and became a center for feminist groups in Los Angeles.

During this period, Schapiro largely put her own art aside to devote herself to teaching. When she returned to painting in 1972, she began working in a completely new style. Combining paint and craft materials, such as fabric and lace, she created mixed media works that she called "femmages"—a conflation of "female" and "collage." By using craft materials associated with female artisans, she challenged art traditions that favored men's creations over women's. She explained that "our culture insists that ornamentation and decoration are innately female. But unfortunately, it then follows that what is female is considered inferior." Schapiro further worked to blur the distinction between high and low art by helping to found the Pattern and Decoration Movement in 1974. This alliance of artists sought to raise the status of decoration in contemporary art.

Returning to New York in 1975, Schapiro began using in much of her work fans, hearts, and kimonos—all objects and shapes associated with women. She also toured extensively, lecturing on feminist art. Her efforts to increase the visibility and promote the validity of the work of female artists earned her the nickname "Miriam Appleseed."

In 1987 Schapiro began exploring the medium of sculpture with *Anna and David,* a monumental work in aluminum that depicts two dancers and which stands outside an office building in Roslyn, Virginia. She also used dancers as a motif in *Rondo,* an accordion-style book published in 1989. More recently, Schapiro has paid homage to great female artists of the past—among them MARY CASSATT, Frida Kahlo, and Sonia Delaunay—in several series of works on paper and canvas. These series she refers to as "collaborations," as she incorporates paintings by these artists into her own.

Further Reading

Gouma-Peterson, Thalia. *Miriam Schapiro: Shaping the Fragments of Art and Life.* New York: Harry N. Abrams, 1999.

"Miriam Schapiro: A Retrospective of Paintings 1954–1997." Traditional Fine Art Online, Inc. Available online. URL: http://www.tfaoi.com/aa/iaa/iaaioz.htm. Downloaded on August 2, 2001.

Schapiro, Miriam. *Rondo: An Artist Book.* San Francisco: Bedford Arts, 1989.

———. *Miriam Schapiro, Works on Paper: A Thirty Year Retrospective.* Tucson, Ariz.: Tucson Museum of Art, 1999.

— L. S.

SHERMAN, CINDY
(1954–) *Photographer, Filmmaker*

Hailed for her explorations of how American society views women, photographer Cindy Sherman has become one of the most widely exhibited artists of her generation. She was born Cynthia Morris Sherman on January 19, 1954, in Glen Ridge, New Jersey, and raised in the suburbs of Long Island, New York. As a child, she loved to play "dress up," a game that would inform much of her later work.

In 1972 she enrolled at the State University of New York at Buffalo as an art education major. She developed an interest in painting, generally working in photorealism—a style characterized by meticulous attention to realistic detail. Sherman had less success with photography: She failed an introductory course in the subject because she was unable to master the technical aspects of printing.

Through her boyfriend, painter Robert Longo, Sherman was introduced to conceptual and performance art, which freed her notion of what art could be. She returned to her childhood fascination with dressing up and began spending hours to completely alter her appearance as a performance piece. Longo suggested she use photographs to record her transformations. Soon photography had became her art form of choice. As she later explained, "I started to question why I should

paint; it just seemed not to make sense. Using a camera, I don't have to spend so much time, hours and hours, copying something that I could take a picture of. I can put the time into the concepts." While still a student, Sherman made her first series of photographic works, *Cutouts* (1975), which were created from photographs of herself that she cut out and placed on panels.

In 1977 Sherman graduated, won a small grant from the National Endowment for the Arts, and moved to New York. There she began work on a new series of small black-and-white prints, again featuring herself as the model. Each mimicked a film still from a B-movie of the 1950s or 1960s, with Sherman dressed as a stock female type— from a librarian to a runaway to a seductress. The images did not suggest a set narrative; instead, each invited viewers to make their own story about Sherman's character.

Over three years, Sherman created 69 images known as Untitled Film Stills. Now considered a seminal work in contemporary art, the entire series was exhibited at the Hirshhorn Museum in Washington, D.C., in 1980. The series struck an immediate chord with viewers of Sherman's generation, particularly women, who like Sherman had spent their childhoods looking to mass-media images for clues about their role in society. To many viewers, the photographs seemed both to parody the film stills they pretended to be and to comment on modern women's often painful search for identity.

The series was an enormous critical and popular success. Sherman, though, felt uncomfortable with the attention she received, particularly because it far outshone that paid to her artist friends. She once said, "I felt guilty about being singled out. It seemed just too fast to deal with." With her new prominence, Sherman was hired to photograph several fashion layouts, which she used to skewer the ideals of beauty promoted by conventional magazine spreads. Many of these photographs pictured Sherman wearing haute couture while also sporting fake scars and prosthetic attachments.

For *Vanity Fair,* Sherman created several photographs, in which she used fake noses, horns, and makeup to transform herself into creatures inspired by fairy tales. Though the magazine declined to print them, the assignment lead to Sherman's Fairy Tales series. These often disturbing images emphasized the violence, horror, and sexuality that serve as subtext for many traditional children's stories.

Equally daring was Sherman's next series, History Portraits (1988–90). Drawing from works by famous painters such as Raphael, Michelangelo Merisi da Caravaggio, and Jean-Auguste-Dominique Ingres, Sherman made herself up to resemble the subjects of classic portraits. Adding incongruent elements, such as large fake breasts, the photographs commented on the history of art, particularly on the idealized vision of women found in many works of the old masters.

Sherman continued to receive critical acclaim, much to her discomfort. Explaining her move to darker subject matter, she said, "I started feeling uncomfortable about being successful. I wanted to make something that would be difficult for some collector to hang over his couch." She met her goal with a variety of works that featured such repellent objects as garbage, rotting food, and vomit in vivid colors. She was even accused of creating pornography in her surreal photographs of body parts, prosthetic devices, sexual toys, and children's dolls. By presenting these grotesque images in visually rich photographs, Sherman challenged the viewers to reexamine their ideas of what is beautiful. "I think there's more to beauty than what we traditionally think of as beautiful," she once told an interviewer, adding, "Things that are not considered to be pleasant to look at or think about can be just as interesting. I think the things I made are beautiful in their own way. It's just a different sensibility."

Despite the extremity of her new vision, Sherman remained a critical darling. In 1995 she was awarded a "genius grant" from the MacArthur Foundation. In the same year, the Museum of Modern Art bought the entire Untitled Film Stills series for $1 million. Although the sum would not be considered extravagant for a painting, it was notably high for a photographic work, especially one created by a female artist. The purchase ensured that all the photographs of the series would remain together in a public collection.

Sherman made a foray into film in 1997 as the director of *Office Killer*. The low-budget horror movie/art film failed to find an audience. More successful was a series of new works Sherman began exhibiting in 2000. Again turning the camera on herself, she created portraits of imagined characters—all aging starlets, bit players, and other disappointed hopefuls on the margins of the glitz and glamour of the film industry. Depicting their subjects in sloppy wigs, ill-fitting clothes, and too much makeup, the images were celebrated for their humorous, yet melancholy portrayal of vulnerable women facing the failure of their Hollywood dreams.

Further Reading

Helfand, Glen. "Cindy Sherman From Dream Girl to Nightmare Alley." Salon. Available online. URL: http:www.salon.com/Media/1997/12/08Media.html. Posted December 8, 1997.

Schjeldahl, Peter. *Cindy Sherman*. New York: Pantheon, 1984.

Smith, Elizabeth, et al. *Cindy Sherman: A Retrospective*. New York: Thames & Hudson, 1997.

— L. S.

SHORE, HENRIETTA
(1880–1963) *Painter*

Though largely forgotten today, Henrietta Shore was considered by many of her contemporaries to be one of the 20th century's most important artists. The youngest of seven children in a middle-class family, Shore was born in 1880 in Toronto, Ontario. As a young woman, she moved to New York and studied with painters William Merritt Chase and Robert Henri. She also attended the Art Students League, where GEORGIA O'KEEFFE was among her fellow students. Early in Shore's career, critics often likened her work to O'Keeffe's, with O'Keeffe usually suffering in the comparison.

On a tour of Europe, Shore briefly studied at London's Heatherly Art School. When she returned to the United States, she joined her brother in Los Angeles in 1913. During her seven years in the city, she won several prestigious awards and founded the Los Angeles Society of Modern Artists. In 1920 she returned to New York for several years, further establishing herself as a rising star in the American art scene.

Back in California, Shore was introduced to photographer Edward Weston on February 14, 1927. At the time, Shore was the far-better-known artist. In his journal, Weston wrote of a friend taking him to Shore's studio, where he saw her work for the first time. "[T]he response was immediate," he recorded, "[T]hose deeply felt, finely executed paintings moved me at once. . . . That work held the amazement of discovery, had all the force released by an artist who in a period of transition reaches toward new horizons." Working on small canvases, Shore painted rigorously simplified natural forms, such as flowers and shells, often cropping them so that they filled the picture plane. She built up color slowly, in layers of glaze that made the objects seem illuminated from within. Although Shore's work represented forms found in nature, her style invested in them a sense of mystery that made them seem almost unreal. Inspired by Shore's paintings, Weston began photographing shells in a manner that echoed their style. These works helped make him one of the most heralded photographers in the history of American art.

For many years, Shore and Weston maintained a close friendship. They frequently exchanged letters and exhibited together. In 1930 Shore moved to Carmel, California, probably because Weston had made the town his home. Weston's journal entries, however, show that Shore frequently tried his patience, especially when she relentlessly criticized his womanizing. Nevertheless, Weston contributed a glowing tribute to Shore in a monograph of her work published in 1933. Printed in a limited edition of 250 copies, it was the only book about Shore published in her lifetime.

As Weston's reputation grew, Shore's began to fade. Increasingly, her work was shown only by the Carmel Art Association, which she founded in 1934. Unable to sell her work during the Great Depression, she began teaching art classes. Her financial difficulties were briefly relieved in the late 1930s, when she was hired by the federal government's Treasury Relief Art Project. Under its auspices, she created murals for post offices in Santa Cruz and Monterey.

There are no known paintings produced by Shore after 1939. Her life after this date is equally obscure. She lived in poverty in Carmel, supported by funds from her nephews and from the sale of photographs Weston had given her. In the late 1950s, she was committed to an asylum in San Jose, where she died in 1963. The Monterey Peninsula Museum of Art staged a Shore retrospective in 1986. It was the first time her paintings had been shown publicly for more than 30 years. Since the exhibit, interest in Shore's work has been slowly but steadily growing.

Weston once called Shore "an artist of destiny . . . lost in Carmel," implying her physical isolation from American art centers was to blame for her lack of acclaim. Undoubtedly equally important, however, was Shore's complete disinterest in marketing her work and her open contempt for art critics. (Her contemporary O'Keeffe, in contrast, benefited from her relationship to her husband, Alfred Stieglitz, a famous photographer who eagerly took over the task of promoting her painting.) Writing in 1939, artist Jean Charlot, a friend of Shore's, gave his own succinct assessment of her lack of popular and commercial success: "That more than many she has worked, loved, and suffered, that she buttresses each stroke with the full impact of brain and heart, does not weigh in the balance against the fact that she is a woman, that she paints flowers, and that her technique is crystal clean."

Further Reading

Aiken, Roger. "Henrietta Shore and Edward Weston." *American Art* 6:1 (winter 1992): 43–61.

Armitage, Merle. *Henrietta Shore.* New York: E. Wehye, 1933.

"Shore, Henrietta." AskART. Available online. URL: http://askart.com/Biography.asp. Posted in 2000.

— L. S.

SIMPSON, LORNA
(1960–   )   *Photographer, Filmmaker*

Juxtaposing photographs and text, Lorna Simpson's art forces the viewer to confront issues of race and gender. She was born on August 14, 1960, in Brooklyn, New York. After graduating from New York's High School of Art and Design, she earned a bachelor's degree from the School of Visual Arts (SVA). However, an internship at the Studio Museum of Harlem, where she met many working African-American artists, had a far greater influence on her work than her formal art training.

At SVA, Simpson abandoned painting for documentary photography. But while studying for a master's degree at the University of California, San Diego, she grew disillusioned with this medium as well. Simpson was frustrated that in traditional photography the viewer came to the work with preconceived assumptions about "how one should read the work and the photographer's intentions." To challenge her audience to see photographic images in a new way, she began creating series of large-scale photographs, which she placed alongside panels featuring fragments of text. Her first major work in this style, *Gestures/Reenactments* (1985), included six 4 × 5–foot panels showing portions of the body of an African-American man dressed in white. The accompanying text suggested several everyday incidents, including a job search and an argument between a man and a woman. Simpson explained that "this work strives to remind the viewer of the cultural and societal interpretations of gesture, their importance and range."

In most of her work from the late 1980s, Simpson explored the stereotypes assigned to African-American women and their degraded position in American society, often using photographs of model Alva Rogers with her face obscured. Among the most famous of these works was *Easy for Who to Say* (1989). It featured five photographs of a woman's head. On each the face was covered by a white oval marked with one of the five vowels. Underneath the disturbing images were panels with the words "Amnesia," "Error," "Indifference," "Omission," and "Uncivil."

Simpson's work caused an immediate sensation in the New York art world. In 1989 she had a successful exhibition at the Josh Baer Gallery. The next year, she became the first African-American woman to represent the United States at the prestigious Venice Biennale and to have a solo exhibition in the Museum of Modern Art's Profiles series.

In the early 1990s, Simpson began using hair as a motif in her art. For instance, in *Flipside* (1991), she juxtaposed two photographs—one of the back of her model's head, one of an African mask—with the words, "the neighbors were suspicious of her hairstyle," as a commentary on the societal importance placed on black women's hair. Simpson eliminated the figure altogether in her monumental *Wigs* (1994), an installation measuring 6 × 13 feet and featuring images of 21 wigs made for African Americans.

More recently, Simpson has moved into filmmaking. While an artist-in-residence at the Wexner Center for the Arts in Columbus, Ohio, she made her first work incorporating film, *Interior/Exterior, Full/Empty* (1994). The work included six black-and-white films, showing men and women in interior spaces, projected onto two walls. On a third wall, a seventh film showed a series of couples talking with one another, though their speech was inaudible. The films seemed to suggest that the characters' stories were somehow interrelated, but exactly how was left to the viewer's interpretation. Among her other films are *Recollection* (1998), in which a character tries to reconstruct the past through fragmented memories, and *Call Waiting* (1997), in which Simpson explores the nature of interpersonal communication through a series of interrupted telephone calls. Enjoying the collaborative process in filmmaking, Simpson has explained that she is particularly drawn to working with actors: "I find actors to be fascinating in the way that they can jump from one character into another and come up with something completely different than they did five minutes ago. To play with that skill is quite interesting."

Further Reading

Sadowski, Paul. "Lorna Simpson and Carrie Mae Weems," *Photography and the Critical Imagination.* Available online. URL: http://www.comwood.org/afroam21.htm. Downloaded on August 2, 2001.

Willis, Deborah. *Lorna Simpson.* San Francisco: The Friends of Photography, 1992.

Wright, Beryl J. *Lorna Simpson: For the Sake of the Viewer.* New York: Universe, 1992.

— L. S.

SMITH, JAUNE QUICK-TO-SEE
(1940–)   *Painter, Mixed Media Artist*

Among the most successful contemporary Native American painters, Jaune Smith was born on January 15, 1940, on the Flathead Indian Reservation in southwestern Montana. She is of mixed Indian and French ancestry—the latter of which is reflected in her first name, the French word for "yellow." Her grandmother gave her the middle name Quick-to-See as a tribute to her powers of observation.

As a child, Jaune traveled throughout the West with her father, who made his living as a horse trader. He was also an amateur artist, particularly skilled in sketching animals. With his encouragement, she grew determined to become an artist. After graduating from high school, Smith worked her way through a two-year associate program at Olympia Junior College in Washington State. She wanted to pursue a bachelor's degree in art, but lacked the necessary funds. During the next 18 years, she raised a family of three children while working and taking classes. Finally, in 1976, she was awarded a degree in art education from Framingham State College in Massachusetts. Four years later, she received a master's degree in fine art from the University of New Mexico.

In the 1970s and 1980s, Smith looked to the rock paintings, cave paintings, and petroglyphs of ancient Indian peoples for inspiration. Many of her paintings were landscapes that featured abstract forms representing humans, horses, and tipis, painted in muted earth tones. According to Smith, the warm grays and deep browns in these works were drawn from memories of the smoky air and leather tools and equipment in her father's bunkhouse.

As Smith explained in a 1995 interview, by the late 1980s she "began to throw caution to the winds and experiment with more materials and mixed media. I also began to see that what I had to say was equally as important as the painting surface. Perhaps more so." Smith's paintings also took on politically charged subject matter, especially environmental issues. Her painting *Rain* (1990), for instance, incorporated several stainless-steel spoons, with the bowls pointed down, which were meant to represent acid rain. She made the work after visiting the Mohawk Akwesasne Reservation in New York State, where acid rain has nearly destroyed the area's forests.

Another recurring theme in Smith's work was the injustices Indian peoples have suffered, particularly in regard to the theft of their land. In the mixed-media work *Trade* (1992), she hung tourist trinkets—such as a plastic tomahawk and a Cleveland Indians sports cap—above a canoe as a commentary on the "trades" in treaty negotiations, in which the U.S. government took Indian land in exchange for cheap trade goods. In response to celebrations of the 500-year anniversary of Christopher Columbus's arrival in North America, Smith made *Paper Dolls for a Post-Columbian World with Ensembles Contributed by the U.S. Government* (1992). The work depicted paper dolls called Ken and Barbie Plenty Horse. The dolls' clothing included a housekeeper's uniform, a comment on the menial work poor Indians perform for whites at low wages, and a "smallpox suit," a reference to smallpox-infested blankets given to Indians by government officials. Smith's sardonic humor was also evident in *The Red Mean: Self-Portrait* (1993), in which Smith reworked Leonardo da Vinci's sketch of the ideal man, putting her image in his place and encasing herself in a medicine wheel, an ancient Indian religious structure.

When she is not in her studio in Corrales, New Mexico, Smith travels frequently, teaching classes and delivering lectures. She has also established two artists' cooperatives and organized many exhibits to help young Indians sell their artwork. Her most successful exhibit was *Women of Sweetgrass, Cedar and Sage* (1985), which featured the work of 30 female Indian artists ranging in age from their 20s to their 70s.

Further Reading

Abbott, Lawrence, editor. *I Stand in the Center of the Good: Interviews with Contemporary North American Artists.* Lincoln: University of Nebraska Press, 1994.

"Artist Profile Jaune Quick-To-See Smith," National Museum of Women in the Arts. Available online. URL: http://www.nmwa.org/legacy/bios/bigSmith.htm. Downloaded on August 2, 2001.

Hammond, Harmony, and Jaune Quick-to-See Smith. *Women of Sweetgrass, Cedar and Sage.* New York: Gallery of the American Indian Community House, 1985.

Hirschfelder, Arlene. "Jaune Quick-to-See Smith: Salish/Shoshone/Cree Painter." In *Artists and Craftspeople*, 109–116. New York: Facts On File, 1994.

— L. S.

SMITH, JESSIE WILLCOX
(1863–1935)   *Illustrator, Painter*

Jessie Willcox Smith's portraits of children made her one of the most successful illustrators of her day. The youngest of four children, she was born in Philadelphia on September 8, 1863. As a teenager, she moved to Cincinnati, Ohio, to attend high school with her cousins. Although her family was financially comfortable, they could not afford to support her after graduation. Smith decided on a career as a kindergarten teacher, but unable to control unruly children, she determined that she was an "utter failure" at her chosen profession.

By chance, Smith took her first art class at age 17. A friend of hers was asked to give drawing lessons to a young male teacher. Attending the classes as her friend's chaperone, Smith tried drawing for the first time in her life. Her first sketch, which depicted a desk lamp, was impressive enough to convince her that she had discov-

ered a hidden and potentially lucrative talent. She later wrote that "that lamp was the turning point in my life."

Smith gave up teaching and enrolled at the School of Design for Women in Philadelphia in 1884. She initially tried sculpting, but quickly gravitated to painting. Unsatisfied with the instruction she was receiving, Smith convinced her family to send her to the more progressive Pennsylvania Academy of Fine Arts, where she briefly studied with painter Thomas Eakins.

Smith finished her studies in 1888, the same year her first illustration was published in *St. Nicholas,* a magazine for children. For the next five years, she worked mostly as an illustrator for magazine advertisements. In 1894 Smith returned to school, attending a class taught by the famous illustrator Howard Pyle at the Drexel Institute of Arts and Sciences. She emerged as one of Pyle's most promising students. With Pyle's help, she secured a commission to produce illustrations for two books for boys about American Indians. When the publisher asked her to illustrate a third Indian book, Smith hesitated, saying that she would prefer an assignment that allowed to her depict children. She was then commissioned to illustrate an edition of Louisa May Alcott's *Little Women,* a project much more to her liking. During her lifetime, Smith illustrated nearly 40 books, including children's classics such as Robert Louis Stevenson's *A Child's Garden of Verses,* Charles Kingsley's *Water Babies,* and Johanna Spyri's *Heidi.*

In 1900 Smith and her Drexel classmates Violet Oakley and Elizabeth Shippen Green moved into the Red Rose Inn, an estate in Villanova, Pennsylvania. They were joined by their friend Henrietta Cozens, who kept house. Pyle nicknamed the four women "the Red Rose Girls." The women called themselves the Cogs family, taking their name from the first letters of their surnames. In an era when female artists were often torn between their work and their obligations to their families, the living arrangement was extremely congenial to furthering the housemates' artistic careers. Although the friends vowed to live together forever, the household broke up in 1911 with Green's decision to marry.

In addition to her work on books, Smith was a prolific magazine illustrator. She was in so much demand for high-paying magazine commissions that her friends called her "the Mint." Smith worked for many leading magazines, including *Ladies' Home Journal, Collier's, Scribner's,* and *Harper's.* Her best-known work, however, was produced for *Good Housekeeping,* which hired her as its cover artist in 1917. Announcing the appointment, the magazine declared that Smith's art represented "the highest ideals of the American home, the home with that certain sweet wholesomeness that one associates with a sunny living room—and children." Working for *Good Housekeeping* until 1933, Smith produced more than 200 covers for the magazine, which paid her as much as $1,800 for each. Most of the covers showed children at play or interacting with their mothers. Though somewhat sentimental by today's standards, the images so well capture the personality and innocence of their young subjects that Smith's work still remains popular.

Late in her career, Smith began accepting commissions to paint the children of wealthy Philadelphia families. However, she found working with young sitters difficult, so few of these portraits rank among her best work. Smith continued to paint until 1933, when her ill health and failing eyesight left her unable to work. She died at her home on May 3, 1935, at the age of 71.

Further Reading

Carter, Alice A. *The Red Rose Girls: An Uncommon Story of Art and Love.* New York: Harry N. Abrams, 2000.
"Jessie Willcox Smith (1863–1935)," Women Children's Book Illustrators. Available online. URL: http://homepage.feqnetworks.net/tortakales/Illustrators/Smith.html. Updated on September 4, 2000.
Mitchell, Gene. *The Subject Was Children: The Art of Jessie Willcox Smith.* New York: Dutton, 1979.
Nudelman, Edward D. *Jessie Willcox Smith: American Illustrator.* Gretna, La.: Pelican, 1990.

— L. S.

SMITH, KIKI
(1954–) *Mixed Media Artist, Sculptor*

Kiki Smith's explorations of the human body, its beauty, and its fragility have made her one of the most critically acclaimed young American artists. She was born on January 18, 1954, in Nuremberg, Germany, but her family soon moved to South Orange, New Jersey. There she grew up in a large Victorian house, the family home of her father, minimalist sculptor Tony Smith. As a girl, she was fascinated by old objects she found in the attic, which she once referred to as "the dead things in the dead parts of the house."

Initially, Smith had little interest in being an artist, in part because she did not want to compete with her famous father. She attended Hartford Art School, but lost interest in her studies after about a year. In 1972 she moved to New York City, where she worked as a cook and an electrician's assistant. By the late 1970s, Smith had joined Collaborative Projects, an artists' collective that displayed some of her early drawings in its 1980 show.

The death of her father in 1980 helped unleash Smith's creativity. She began working seriously on her art, much of which focused on bodily deterioration. Her *Hand in Jar* (1983), for instance, featured a latex hand covered with algae floating in a mason jar, an object that suggested the decay of flesh as well as the beginning of new life. Smith has explained that she "chose the body as a subject, not consciously, but because it is the one form that we all share; it's something that everybody has their own authentic experience with."

To gain a knowledge of human anatomy, Smith studied to be an emergency medical technician in 1985. Her research inspired a series of works depicting internal organs, such as *Second Choice* (1987), a large bowl filled with a ceramic lung, liver, and heart. Many of her works of this period depicted the reproductive system, including an installation that featured 200 giant sperm, handcrafted in lead crystal.

Although Smith did not identify herself as a feminist artist, she had an interest in using imper-

Kiki Smith is a controversial figurative artist who investigates the anatomy of the human body.
(Portrait by Timothy Greenfield-Sanders)

manent craft materials associated with women artisans in her work. In a 1990 installation, for instance, she strung white paper cutouts of male figures from the ceiling of a room with red paper covering its walls. The piece was a commentary on AIDS, which killed her sister in 1988. Smith also experimented with printmaking, using lithography to create a series of self-portraits in her work *Banshee Pearls* (1991).

By 1990, Smith's work was regularly exhibited at the Fawbush Gallery and had been shown at the Museum of Modern Art in New York and the Dallas Museum of Art. Just as she had received widespread critical attention, she took her work in a new direction as she began to work in the more traditional form of full-size sculpture. Many of her first sculptures were created from beeswax, including a male and a female nude, whose reddened

skin implied physical and psychic pain. Most of her works, however, concentrated on the female body, emphasizing its day-to-day functions. In *Pee Body* (1992), she showed a female figure squatting over yellow glass beads, suggestive of urine.

To counter the depiction of women purely as victims in much contemporary art, Smith in 1993 showed a series of sculptures of female deities from various cultures. The exhibition included a nude Virgin Mary in bronze, with her skin stripped back to show her muscles and tendons. A Catholic, Smith has identified her religion as a central inspiration for her work. As she has explained, "One of the things about Catholicism is, it's a religion that's about . . . taking emotional and spiritual ideas and making them physical."

Again changing the focus of her work, Smith exhibited a series of lithographs based on doily patterns at the Pace Wildenstein Gallery in 1994. Her recent installations have also explored her interest in animals and human interactions with them. In *Jersey Crows* (1994), she used bronze sculptures to represent crows killed by pesticide, while an installation in her *Of Her Nature* show (1999) included a full-size figure of a girl transforming into a wolf.

Further Reading

"Kiki Smith: Works on Paper, Multiples and Editioned Prints," Greg Kucera Gallery Home. Available online. URL: http//www.gregkucera.com/smith.htm Downloaded on August 2, 2001.

Lahs-Gonzales, Olivia. *My Nature: Works with Paper by Kiki Smith*. St. Louis, Mo.: St. Louis Art Museum, 1999.

Posner, Helaine. *Kiki Smith*. Boston: Bulfinch, 1998.

— L. S.

SPENCER, LILLY MARTIN
(Angélique Marie Martin)
(1822–1902) *Painter*

Famed for her genre paintings, Lilly Martin Spencer was born Angélique Marie Martin in Essex, England, on November 26, 1822. Her French-born parents were passionate supporters of liberal social causes, especially temperance and women's suffrage.

In 1830 her family moved to the United States, where her father, a French teacher, hoped to establish an academy. After a brief stay in New York City, the Martins moved to a farm in Marietta, Ohio.

Angélique, nicknamed Lilly, was schooled at home with her three siblings. Her parents encouraged her artistic tendencies, allowing her to paint the walls of their house with full-sized portraits of family members going about their daily activities. By age 18, Lilly had finished more than 50 oil paintings. Local artists arranged her first exhibition in a church in 1841. Most of the paintings shown were portraits and domestic scenes, subjects that would dominate her later art.

The exhibition attracted a patron, who offered to send Martin to New York to study. She instead moved to Cincinnati, then an art center for the western United States. Martin took lessons from John Insco Williams, one of the city's leading portraitists. She married businessman Benjamin Rush Spencer in 1844, but true to the liberal ideals imbued in her by her parents, she chose to continue her career. Even more remarkable for the time, her husband took charge of their household, while she worked as the family's sole breadwinner. Financially supporting their family was soon a daunting task. Lilly Martin Spencer gave birth to as many as 13 children, although only seven survived to adulthood.

In the late 1840s, Spencer's work was displayed in several New York shows. Eager to advance her career and improve her earnings, she moved her family to New York in 1848. Spencer found competing with the city's many well-trained artists intimidating. She took night classes at the National Academy of Design to improve her draftsmanship, continually a sore point with critics of her work. Spencer painted scenes of Shakespeare's works and did some commercial illustration for periodicals, such as *Godey's Lady's Book*. Increasingly, though, she concentrated on domestic subjects, showing everyday family life, often with a touch of humor.

By the 1850s, Spencer's works were frequently reproduced as lithographs. Although overly sentimental to modern tastes, her images such as *Domestic Happiness* (ca. 1849), *Peeling Onions* (ca. 1852), and *The Gossips* (1857) were extremely popular with the American middle class of her time. More than 1 million of her prints were sold and hung in American homes. Spencer, however, was paid only for the original work. Despite her success, she was constantly scrambling to earn enough to feed her family. To save money, the Spencers moved in 1859 to a house in Newark, New Jersey, after she arranged to execute several portraits in lieu of rent.

During the Civil War era, Spencer's paintings became darker and more serious. For example, *The War Spirit at Home—Celebrating the Victory at Vicksburg* (1866) showed children at play while their concerned mother read news from the battlefield. Spencer also experimented with grand allegorical paintings, possibly in imitation of French works then in vogue. She established a studio in New York to create *Truth Unveiling Falsehood* (1869), which in her lifetime was hailed as her masterpiece. The finished work was exhibited at the Women's Pavilion at the Philadelphia Centennial in 1876 and received enthusiastic reviews in newspapers throughout the nation.

Despite this triumph, Spencer's popularity soon declined. In her later years, however, she adopted a looser style in her portraits, which are now considered among her strongest works. In 1900 Spencer returned to New York City, where, though in her late seventies, she continued to seek commissions to make ends meet. On May 22, 1902, she died at her easel. Though earning a living through her art was an unending struggle, Lilly Martin Spencer even in her day was hailed a pioneer, blazing a trail for many female American artists to come.

Further Reading

Blake Benton Fine Art. "Spencer, Lilly Martin." AskART. Available online. URL: http://askart.com/Biography.asp. Posted in 2000.

Bolton-Smith, Robin, and Truettner, William H. *Lilly Martin Spencer, 1822–1902: The Joys of Sentiment.* Washington, D.C.: Smithsonian Institution Press, 1973.

Lubin, David. *Picturing a Nation.* New Haven, Conn.: Yale University Press, 1994.

— L. S.

STEBBINS, EMMA
(1815–1882) *Sculptor, Painter*

Best known as the sculptor of *Angel of the Waters* in New York's Central Park, Emma Stebbins was born in New York City on September 1, 1815. The daughter of a bank president, she enjoyed a privileged upbringing, during which she dabbled in music, literature, and art. Among her eight siblings was Henry George Stebbins, who became a congressman and the president of the New York Stock Exchange.

In New York society, Stebbins established herself as a talented amateur artist by painting portraits of friends. Her work attracted the attention of Henry Inman, a successful portraitist, who instructed her in oil painting in his studio. In addition to portraits in oil, watercolor, and crayon, Stebbins's early work included illustrations for a manuscript of poetry, "A Book of Prayer." In 1843 Stebbins was elected to the National Academy of Design. She exhibited several paintings, including *A Portrait of a Lady* (1845), at the Pennsylvania Academy of Fine Arts in the late 1840s.

With the support of her brother Henry, Stebbins moved to Rome in 1857. At the age 42, she embarked on a new career as a sculptor. She received encouragement from the English sculptor John Gibson, who suggested she study with Benjamin Paul Akers. Stebbins developed a close friendship with Akers and HARRIET GOODHUE HOSMER, another expatriate American sculptor.

During her first winter in Rome, Stebbins also met Charlotte Cushman, one of the most famous actresses of her day. Cushman's home was a popular meeting place for wealthy Americans living in Italy. As ambitious and strong-willed as Stebbins, Cushman was immediately drawn to the sculptor and became a great champion of her art. Stebbins and her new friend became lifelong companions.

Stebbins's first sculpture, which depicted the biblical hero Joseph as a boy, was exhibited at the Dublin International Exhibition in 1865. Her early commissions included a sculpture of Cushman, which was donated to the Handel and Haydn Society of Boston. She also produced figures of a miner and a sailor, meant to represent industry and commerce. These sculptures, commissioned by Pennsylvania mine owner Richard Heckscher, were among the first allegorical figures in modern dress designed by an American sculptor.

Cushman helped secure Stebbins an important commission for a bronze statue of educator Horace Mann by courting his wife with free theater tickets. Showing Mann wearing a Roman cloak over contemporary clothes, the work was installed in front of the State House in Boston in 1865. Stebbins also probably profited from her brother Henry's position on the Central Park Commission. Possibly because of his support, she was commissioned to design the sculpture for the park's Bethesda Fountain, which was unveiled in May 1873 to great critical acclaim. The work drew on the biblical story of an angel who gave the waters of the Bethesda Pool the power to heal. At the sculpture's base were four ornamental cherubs that represented health, temperance, purity, and peace.

In the early 1870s, Stebbins and Cushman returned to the United States, spending most of the year at Cushman's mansion in Newport, Rhode Island. After Cushman's death in 1876, Stebbins compiled a biography of the celebrated actress titled *Charlotte Cushman: Her Letters and Memories of Her Life* (1878). Six years later, Stebbins died on October 24,1882, in New York City at the age of 73.

Further Reading

Gerdts, William H. "Stebbins, Emma." In *Notable American Women: 1607–1950*, edited by Edward T. James, 354–355. Cambridge, Mass.: Belknap Press, 1971.
Rubinstein, Charlotte Streifer. *American Women Sculptors: A History of Women Working in Three Dimensions.* Boston: G. K. Hall, 1990.

— L. S.

STEPHENS, ALICE BARBER
(1858–1932) *Illustrator*

In her day Alice Barber Stephens was dubbed "the dean of female illustrators." She was born Alice

Barber on July 1, 1858, near Salem, New Jersey. Her earliest memories were of making pencil drawings of the Barber family farm. When Alice was in grade school, the Barbers moved to Philadelphia, where she had her first opportunity for formal art training. Her parents arranged for her to take classes at the School of Design for Women. By age 15, Alice Barber was earning her own keep with her skill at wood engraving. Her early works included a series of portraits of prominent women reproduced in the magazine *Women's World.*

In 1876 Barber became one of the first women admitted to the prestigious Pennsylvania Academy of Fine Arts. There she was taught by painter Thomas Eakins, who supervised her translation of several of his works into engravings. At school, Barber joined a group of female students in petitioning for more life drawing classes. When *Scribner's Monthly* wrote an article on the school, she was commissioned to create an illustration titled "Women's Life Class," which was accompanied by her first published credit.

Financial need forced Barber to leave the academy in 1880 and become a full-time engraver. For several years, she worked exclusively for the *Harper's* magazines, with most of her work appearing in *Harper's Young People.* Her heavy work load took a toll on her health. Near physical collapse, Barber traveled to Europe in 1886 to recover. She toured Italy, Holland, England, and France. In Paris, she studied at the Académie Julian and displayed several works in the Salon of 1887.

Returning to Philadelphia, Barber resumed her career, while painting in oil on her own time. In 1890 her painting *Portrait of a Boy* won the Mary Smith Prize when exhibited at the academy. The same year, she married painter Charles Hallowell Stephens, whom she had met when they were both students. Their son, Daniel Owen, grew up to become a noted artist of astronomical bodies.

The 1890s saw Alice Barber Stephens at the peak of her career. Frustrated with engraving, she had moved into illustration, working in oils, charcoal, and watercolors. During this period, Stephens was in steady demand by magazine publishers. She worked for periodicals such as *Century, Cosmopolitan,* and *Frank Leslie's Illustrated Weekly,* before becoming a regular illustrator for *Ladies' Home Journal.* In 1897 she created for this magazine perhaps her most popular works—the American Women series. The six illustrations included conventional images of women reading the Bible and entertaining, as well as several images showing the so-called New Woman, who was then beginning to explore life outside the home. One illustration, titled *Women in Business,* showcased a female clerk assisting a shopper at Philadelphia's Wanamaker department store. In glowing press accounts, Stephens herself was lauded as a New Woman for continuing to work after marriage. One reporter for the *Philadelphia Press Fiction Magazine* wrote, "In Alice Barber Stephens there is a confluence of two of the most noble strains in humanity—the mother and the artist. . . . Together they have given her love, happiness, and work that is a joy and a compensation for leisure and ease."

In addition to her magazine work, Stephens was well regarded as a book illustrator. Her illustrations adorned works by George Eliot, Louisa May Alcott, Bret Harte, and Henry Wadsworth Longfellow. Among Stephens's best illustration work were paintings for a special edition of Nathaniel Hawthorne's *The Marble Faun.* They were exhibited at the Exposition Universelle in Paris, where they won a bronze medal.

Prominent in Philadelphia art circles, Stephens founded two art organizations in 1897. With Emily Sartain, she established the Plastic Club, which brought together professional female artists for lectures and exhibitions. She also established the Fellowship of the Pennsylvania Academy to promote and support her alma mater. It was the first such organization in the United States open to both women and men.

Again working herself to the point of exhaustion, Stephens traveled to Europe in 1901. Returning 15 months later, her family settled in Rose Valley, Pennsylvania, where they remodeled a barn into a house and artist's studio. Although her illustration style went out of fashion in the early 20th century, she continued to work until 1926. Three years later, the Plastic Club staged a retrospective of her work. Stephens died following a stroke at her home on July 13, 1932.

Further Reading

Brown, Ann Barton. *Alice Barber Stephens: A Pioneer Woman Illustrator.* Chadds Ford, Pa.: Brandywine River Museum, 1984.

Gilchrist, Agnes Addison. "Stephens, Alic Barber." In *Notable American Women: 1607–1950,* edited by Edward T. James, 359–360. Cambridge, Mass.: Belknap Press, 1971.

Kitch, Carolyn. "The American Women Series: Gender and Class in The Ladies' Home Journal, 1897." *Journalism and Mass Communication Quarterly* 75:2 (summer 1998): 243–262.

"Stephens, Alice Barber," AskART. Available online. URL: http://askart.com/Biography.asp. Posted in 2000.

— L. S.

STETTHEIMER, FLORINE
(1871–1944)   *Painter*

In her complex, decorative paintings, Florine Stettheimer playfully satirized the world of wealthy New Yorkers in the 1920s and 1930s. Born on August 19, 1871, in Rochester, New York, she was the fourth of five children born to a successful businessman. After her father abandoned the family, Florine spent her youth traveling through Europe with her mother and her sisters, Carrie and Ettie. In the early 1890s, they briefly returned to New York, where Florine studied painting at the Art Students League. By 1895 they were back in Europe. They traveled abroad almost constantly for the next 19 years.

Stettheimer's early work was conventional and undistinguished. She began to find her artistic voice only after seeing Vaslav Nijinsky dance with the Ballet Russes in Paris in 1912. Nijinsky inspired her to create her own ballet, which she titled *Orphée des Quat'z Arts.* The ballet was never produced, but Stettheimer did craft a series of small models, showing her designs for the costumes in taffeta, beads, and tinfoil. These models were her first step toward developing the elegant, etheral figures that peopled her mature paintings.

With the outbreak of World War I, the Stettheimers settled permanently in New York City. At their townhouse, they established a popular salon frequented by such luminaries as artists Marcel Duchamp, GEORGIA O' KEEFFE, and Gaston Lachaise, and writers H. L. Mencken and Sherwood Anderson. A frequent visitor in the 1920s, critic Paul Rosenfeld, wrote, "The celebrities in the world of art and literature . . . felt themselves entirely at home in their company. Art was an indispensable component of the modern, open intellectual life of the place."

In 1916 Stettheimer's friend Maria Sterner offered to organize a one woman show of her paintings at the Knoedler Gallery. Stettheimer enthusiastically designed the gallery space herself, draping the walls with white muslin. To her disappointment, the show received bad reviews, and none of her works sold. After the fiasco, Stettheimer never had another solo show. She would only allow her paintings to be shown in group exhibitions or at parties she held to unveil her latest works to sympathetic friends.

With no interest in displaying her art to a wider audience, Stettheimer felt free to develop her own idiosyncratic style. After 1917, her paintings generally showed the leisure class at play, enjoying boating parties, picnics, and shopping expeditions. Scattered over the canvas, her figures were small and slender, often painted in unnaturally bright pinks, yellow, and blues. In such works as *La Fête à Duchamp* (1917), which depicted a birthday party for her friend Duchamp, Stettheimer showed the same figure at different moments, suggesting a narrative spread over time in a single image. In the 1920s, she also painted numerous portraits that, through details offering clues to the subject's personality and past, attempted to serve as visual biographies.

In 1934 Stettheimer had her greatest public success as the set and costume designer of *Four Saints in Three Acts,* an experimental opera with music by Virgil Thomson and a libretto by Gertrude Stein. Stettheimer's designs, which featured unusual materials such as cellophane, feathers, lace, and tinsel, were universally praised in the work's otherwise mixed reviews. Considered a pivotal event in the history of American modernism, the opera's premiere marked the first time a noted artist in the United States had channeled her talents into the theater design.

Energized by the success of *Four Saints,* Stettheimer began work on her Cathedral series of paintings. The first three explored New York's entertainment, social, and financial worlds by depicting Broadway, Fifth Avenue, and Wall Street. Her final work, *Cathedrals of Art,* was a satiric tribute to the luminaries of the art world, which included a portrait of the artist, smiling and dressed in a white flapper dress. The canvas was unfinished when Stettheimer died of cancer on May 11, 1944. Although she had asked that her paintings be destroyed after her death, her sister Ettie instead donated them to museums across the country. In 1946 Duchamp organized a retrospective of Stettheimer's paintings, the first exhibition of her work in 30 years.

Stettheimer and her art soon fell into obscurity. Although little known to the public and seldom exhibited, her work, nonetheless continued to attract a small legion of devotees. Later artists, including Andy Warhol, Jasper Johns, and KIKI SMITH, were vocal admirers of Stettheimer. Her work has reached a large audience only since 1995, when a retrospective at the Whitney Museum of American Art and a biography by Barbara J. Bloemink introduced Stettheimer to a new generation.

Further Reading

Bloemink, Barbara J. *The Life and Art of Florine Stettheimer.* New Haven: Yale University Press, 1995.

Nares, Mario, "Florine Stettheimer Manhattan Fantastica," The New Criterion Online. Available online. URL: http://www.newcriterion.com/archive/14/sept95/neves.htm. Downloaded on August 2, 2001.

Sussman, Elizabeth. *Florine Stettheimer: Manhattan Fantastica.* New York: Whitney Museum of American Art, 1995.

— L. S.

STEVENS, MAY
(1924–)   *Painter*

Throughout her long career, May Stevens has remained committed to the power of art to enact social change. Born in Boston on June 9, 1924, she was raised in a working-class family in Quincy, Massachusetts. After attending the Massachusetts College of Art, she moved to New York in 1947. While taking classes at the Art Students League, she met and married painter Rudolf Baranik in 1948. The couple had one son, photographer Steven Baranik.

Soon after their wedding, Stevens and Baranik moved to Paris, where Stevens had her first solo show. They returned to the United States in 1951, eventually settling in New York City. Beginning in 1961, Stevens taught at the School of Visual Arts for 35 years.

The first works to earn Stevens critical attention were those of her Big Daddy series (1967–76). Made during the Vietnam War, these paintings expressed her opposition to the war and to militarism, while also commenting on her authoritarian father, whom she considered a racist. This combination of the political and personal became a familiar feature in her art. Stevens's work was also distinguished by its rejection of minimalist, abstract, and conceptual art, which then dominated the New York art scene. She instead remained wedded to art that was figurative and narrative in order to directly address the social and political issues that engaged her.

By the mid-1970s, Stevens was chanelling her energies into the cause of feminism. With MIRIAM SCHAPIRO, Joan Snyder, and Lucy Lippard, she helped found a feminist collective that published the magazine *Heresies.* She also began work on her best-known series, Ordinary/Extraordinary. Including paintings, collages, and an artist's book, the series juxtaposed images of the two women Stevens considered her mothers: Her "intellectual mother" was Rosa Luxemburg, a Polish-German revolutionary who was assassinated in Berlin in 1919. Her biological mother was Alice Stevens, whom the artist has described as a "housewife, mother, washer and ironer, inmate of hospitals and nursing homes." The grouping of these two figures suggests the range of female experience—from Luxemburg's determination to change the world to Alice Stevens's depressed withdrawal from it. The artist, however, was careful to lend dignity to both women. Explaining her goal in creating Ordinary/Extraordinary, Stevens said, "I want Rosa and her work to be remembered. But I also want Alice to be remembered, to validate the lives of women like her, women who are discounted when they are old and heavy and no longer glamorous or charming." Among the most moving images of the series are *Go Gentle* (1983), which shows Alice as a child, a young woman, and an elderly invalid, and *Forming the Fifth International* (1985), in which the Alice and Rosa figures seem engaged in an imaginary conversation with one another.

In the 1990s, Stevens began the "Women, Words and Water" series, which also addressed the place of women in American society. The paintings depict small female figures in rowboats, sailing on an ocean formed from barely legible words, painted in gold ink, from the works of Virginia Woolf, Julia Kristeva, and others. Four of these works and 10 from the Ordinary/Extraordinary series were displayed in *May Stevens: Images of Women Near and Far,* an 1999 exhibition at the Boston Museum of Fine Arts.

Further Reading

Shapiro, Barbara Stern. "May Stevens: Images of Women Near and Far," Museum of Fine Arts. Available online. URL: http://www.mfa.org/exhibitions/Stevens.html. Posted in 2000.

May Stevens: Ordinary/Extraordinary, A Summation, 1977–1984. Boston: Boston University Art Gallery, 1984.

Stevens, May. *May Stevens: Images of Women Near and Far, 1983–1997.* New York: Mary Ryan Gallery, 1999.

———. *Rosa, Alice: Ordinary Extraordinary May Stevens.* New York: Universe Books, 1998.

— L. S.

T

TAFOYA, MARGARET
(Maria Margarita Tafoya)
(1904–2001) *Potter*

A master of the Pueblo pottery making tradition, Margaret Tafoya was born Maria Margarita Tafoya on August 13, 1904. Raised in Santa Clara Pueblo in northeastern New Mexico, she was the daughter of Sara Fina Gutierrez Tafoya, herself one of the best Pueblo potters of her day. As a child, Margaret accompanied her parents on clay-gathering expeditions, during which she often grabbed a ball of clay and molded it into animal shapes. She learned the art of making pottery by watching her maternal aunts and by direct instruction from her mother. A strict perfectionist, Sara Fina frequently recruited Margaret to work her own pottery, telling the girl how to knead clay and polish shaped pots and where to gather fuel needed for the firing process.

Margaret Tafoya briefly attended high school at the Santa Fe Indian School, but dropped out to help her family during the 1918 flu pandemic. For several years, she worked as a cook and a waitress before marrying Alcario Tafoya in 1924. The couple had 10 children and adopted three more. Despite her ample responsibilities at home, Tafoya continued to make pottery, which she traded for children's clothing and other necessities. The Tafoyas also regularly loaded her works into a horse-drawn wagon and headed to Taos and Santa Fe, where they sold the pots to tourists and traders. Tafoya frequently showed her work at nearby Indian art fairs, such as the Santa Fe Indian Market and the Inter-Tribal Ceremonial in Gallup. In addition to giving her a chance to market her work, attending these fairs allowed her to study the works of potters from other pueblos.

During the 1930s and 1940s, Tafoya experimented with new decorations and forms. She explored polychrome painting and even dabbled in adapting forms from Greek and Roman pottery. In her later works, however, she generally returned to more traditional forms. Most were elegant, simple pieces in red or black, well-polished to create an extremely shiny surface.

Beginning in the 1960s, Tafoya started receiving recognition as an artist, particularly for her large black jars. Measuring as high as three feet, these vessels took months to mold and polish. They also required an enormous amount of technical skill, particularly to keep them from breaking while being fired.

In 1978 and 1979, Tafoya won the Best in Show award at the Santa Fe Indian Fair. The Wheelwright

Museum of the American Indian presented the first major exhibition of her work in 1983. Among the many awards she received for her work was the New Mexico Governor's Award in 1985. The previous year, she was named folk artist of the year by the National Endowment for the Arts.

Despite these accolades, Tafoya was extremely modest about her achievements, as befitted a traditional Pueblo woman. However, she was far from shy about sharing with her family her knowledge of pottery making. Before her death on February 25, 2001, she helped instruct nearly 75 of her relatives in her traditional techniques. Her teaching helped preserve the old ways of making pottery. She insisted that her protégés make the clay, rather than using a commercial product, and that they mold their work by hand without the aid of a potter's wheel or molds.

Tafoya could be a harsh critic, demanding in others the perfection she expected from herself. Her granddaughter, the renowned potter Nancy Youngblood, once explained that Tafoya "didn't mince any words. She would say, 'I don't think you polished this as well as you could have.' At first it hurt, but later I appreciated it." But Youngblood also noted that, beyond technical excellence, Tafoya also stressed the spiritual side of her art. Youngblood recalled Tafoya telling her, "You have to have a good heart when you sit down to make this pottery. . . . You have to live a good life, because the clay knows."

Further Reading

Blair, Mary Ellen, and Laurence R. Blair. *Margaret Tafoya: A Tewa Potter's Heritage and Legacy.* West Chester, Pa.: Schiffer, 1986.

Dillingham, Rick. *Fourteen Families in Pueblo Pottery.* Albuquerque: University of New Mexico Press, 1994.

Martin, Douglas. "Pueblo Potter Margaret Tafoya Dies," Houston Chronicle. Available online. URL: http://www.chron.com/CS/CDA/printstory.hts/death/art/840843. Downloaded on August 2, 2001.

Morgan, Brandt, and Susan Roller Whittington. "A Good Heart, A Good Life: The Legacy of Santa Clara Pueblo Potter Margaret Tafoya." *Indian Artist* (spring 1997): 42–46.

— L. S.

TANNING, DOROTHEA
(1910–) *Painter, Sculptor*

A leading painter in the surrealist movement, Dorothea Tanning was born on August 25, 1910, in Galesburg, Illinois. The small town—which Tanning once described as "where nothing happens but the wallpaper"—did little to excite Tanning's rich imagination. She retreated into the world of books and art, painting and drawing constantly. By age seven, she was declaring her intention to become an artist.

After two years at Knox College, Tanning briefly attended the Art Institute of Chicago. She found formal training stifling, however, and decided that she could learn more by studing works at art museums on her own. With $12 in her pocket, she moved to New York in 1935. Painting at night, she supported herself with odd jobs, including working as an extra at the Metropolitan Opera and writing vignettes for *Ladies' Home Journal.*

In 1936 Tanning saw *Fantastic Art, Dada, Surrealism,* an exhibition at the Museum of Modern Art. She was immediately drawn to the surealists' exploration of the unconscious and use of dreamlike imagery. Hoping to join the circle of European surrealists, Tanning traveled to Paris in 1939, carrying letters of introduction to such artists as Max Ernst and Yves Tanguy. Unfortunately for Tanning, the artists she wanted most to meet had fled France at the onset of World War II. Disappointed, she left Paris and lived briefly in Stockholm with relatives before returning to New York.

Back home, Tanning found work in the advertising office of a department store. Her boss showed her paintings to gallery owner Julien Levy, who began showing her work in 1941. At about this time, Tanning became acquainted with many of the European surrealists, including Tanguy, KAY SAGE, and André Breton, who congregated in New York during the war years. Tanning became closest to Max Ernst. He met her in 1943 when he came to pick up a painting for his wife, gallery owner Peggy Guggenheim, who was putting together a show

211

titled *31 Women.* Tanning and Ernst became fast friends, often playing chess at Guggenheim's gallery. As Guggenheim remembered, "Soon they were more than friendly and I realized that I should only have had thirty women in the show." Following Ernst and Guggenheim's divorce, Tanning married Ernst in 1946 in a double ceremony with artist Man Ray and Juliet Browner. After the war, Tanning and Ernst moved to Sedona, Arizona, where several other of the surrealists had gathered.

By the early 1940s, Tanning had fully adopted the surrealist aesthetic, although her gender placed her at the margins of the movement. She once wrote that she "noticed with a certain consternation that the place of women among the surrealists was no different from that which they occupied among the population in general, the bourgeoisie included." Many of her meticulously painted surrealist works, such as *Children's Games* (1942) and *Eine Kleine Nachtmusik* (1946), depicted young women or girls in erotically charged settings that suggested sexual menace. Other paintings, such as *Maternity* (1946), included strange-looking Pekingese dogs, one of Tanning's favorite motifs. Her most famous work from this period was *Birthday* (1942). Painted when she was 32, *Birthday* includes a self-portrait, showing Tanning staring at the viewer, dressed in an exotic costume, with both her breasts and her feet bare. Behind her are a series of doorways, and a strange and sinister winged creature crouches in the foreground.

In 1952 Tanning and Ernst moved to France, where they lived for nearly 20 years. In the 1950s and 1960s, she began to paint in a new style, using softer colors and a looser brush stroke. Amorphous forms in these semiabstract works suggested human figures that seemed to meld into one another and move in and out of focus. Tanning also designed set for ballets and theater productions in New York, London, and Paris.

While listening to the work of electronic composer Karlheinz Stockhausen in 1969, Tanning had a vision that shifted her work in still another direction. She imagined soft sculpted forms made of cloth and felt. As she recalled, "I saw them so clearly, living materials becoming living sculptures, their lifespan something like ours." Tanning worked in cloth sculpture throughout the early 1970s. In 1974 she created *Hôtel du Pavot,* an installation in which her sculptures appeared to grow out of the walls, the floors, and pieces of furniture.

Tanning returned to New York after Ernst's death in 1976. She continued to paint until the mid-1990s, when a stroke left her bedridden. In June 1997, she emerged from bed, eager to work again. As Tanning explained, "I had a vision of a mauve flower. I said, 'I'll do that on one of those canvases.' Then more and more crept into my mind and wanted to be painted. I could hardly finish one before I'd start the next one." By April 1998, she had completed 12 large canvases, each depicting abstracted flowers in modulated greens, blues, and purples. The paintings were displayed at the Boston University Art Gallery in 1999 alongside 12 poems, each inspired by one of Tanning's works. Many of the poets who contributed pieces were friends of Tanning's and included W.S. Merwin, Adrienne Rich, and John Ashbery. The paintings and poems were collected in the book *Another Language of Flowers* (1999).

Further Reading

Dorothea Tanning. New York: George Braziller, 1995.

Tanning, Dorothea. *Another Language of Flowers.* New York: George Braziller, 1999.

———. *Between Lives: An Artist and Her World.* New York: W. W. Norton, 2001.

"Dorothea Tanning," Masterworks Fine Art. Available online. URL: http://www.masterworksfineart.com/inventory/tanning.htm. Posted in 2001.

— L. S.

TAWNEY, LENORE
(Leonora Agnes Gallagher)
(1907–) *Textile Artist, Collagist*

Beginning in the 1950s, Lenore Tawney's experimental textiles helped elevate weaving to a respected fine art form. Born Leonora Agnes Gallagher on May 10, 1907, she was raised in

Lorain, Ohio, where she attended parochial schools. At age 20, she moved to Chicago. Working as a proofreader, she attended art classes at night at the city's art institute. In the early 1940s, she married George Tawney, a psychologist. The marriage ended less than two years later, when George died after a sudden illness.

Grief-stricken, Lenore Tawney moved to Urbana, where she began studying art at the University of Illinois. After several years, she returned to Chicago and enrolled at the Chicago Institute of Design. From 1946 to 1948, she studied drawing, sculpture, watercolor, and weaving. Taken under the wing of sculpture instructor Alexander Archipenko, Tawney began working in his studio in Woodstock, New York. Her early sculptures were abstract figures made from clay. Finding the studio atmosphere too tense, Tawney headed home to Chicago. She abandoned sculpture and bought a secondhand loom. Her experimentation with weaving was interrupted by a two-year trip to Paris, during which time she also traveled extensively through Europe and North Africa.

Returning to the United States, Tawney committed herself to weaving after studying for six weeks with Martta Taipale at the Penland School of Crafts in North Carolina. She later recalled that "Martta [was] a warm and wonderful person and an inspiring teacher. She said, 'Color is like music,' and I could see color soaring like Gothic arches in the sky." By 1955 Tawney was developing her own unique weaving techniques. She often began a piece with a black-and-white sketch, then spontaneously translated it into color while working on the loom. Tawney also created compositions that juxtaposed tightly woven areas with open patches that revealed the warp (the vertical threads strung on the loom). Hung away from the wall, the open compositions allowed for a play of light and shadow not possible in traditional opaque weavings.

In 1957 Tawney received her first major commission from the Marshall Field department store. Developing a system she would use in future commissions, she refused to make preparatory sketches, but gave the company the opportunity to reject the finished work. For the Marshall Field commission, Tawney ended up creating two weavings—one that satisfied what she thought the company wanted and one that pleased herself. Marshall Field purchased both pieces.

The same year, Tawney moved to New York. In her journal, she wrote, "I left Chicago to seek a barer life, closer to reality, without all the *things* that clutter and fill our lives." She settled in the Coenties Slip section of lower Manhattan, then a popular area for avant-garde artists. Tawney soon established a studio in a sailmaker's loft. The high ceilings allowed her make tapestries on a monumental scale. For example, her *Nativity in Nature* (1959), commissioned by the Interchurch Center, measured 10 by 12 feet.

In the early 1960s, Tawney began to simplify her work, using primarily undyed and black fibers. She also invented a reed that allowed her to change the shape of the weaving as she worked and began incorporating dowels into pieces to make them more three-dimensional. For these more sculptural works, she coined the term *woven forms. Woven Forms* became the title of an influential exhibit at the Museum of Contemporary Crafts (now the American Craft Museum) in 1961. The first major show of nontraditional weaving in the United States, the exhibition featured 22 pieces by Tawney and established her as the leading innovator in American textiles.

Tawney started experimenting with new forms in mid-1965. She began making small assemblages by placing feathers, eggs, pebbles, bird skeletons, and pages of rare books in boxlike enclosures. She also created collages, often sending them to friends as postcards. Later collages were made from Japanese paper inscribed with small, unreadable writing from Zen and Siddha Yoga texts.

In 1977 Tawney received a commission for a public work for the lobby of the federal building in Santa Rosa, California. Abandoning her loom, she constructed the piece, titled *Cloud Series IV* (1978), from a blue-painted canvas, on which she strung more than 2,500 linen threads in a grid pattern. Though controversial, the work led to more commissions for works in the series in the 1980s. Now in her 90s, Tawney continues to be prolific. Among her most recent works are the small, sculptural works of her Shrine series. These pieces feature webs of threads holding small natural objects, such as shells, bones, and twigs, enclosed in Plexiglas boxes. Displaying Tawney's ability to create a sense of mystery from the simplest of forms, these works were described in 1996 in *Art in America* as "cat's cradles elevated to the level of the awesome."

Further Reading

Lenore Tawney: Celebrating Five Decades of Work. Wilton, Conn.: Browngrotta Arts, 2000.

"Lenore Tawney," The School of the Art Institute of Chicago. Available online. URL: http://www.artic.edu/saic/alumni/news/spotlight/archives/tawney.html. Downloaded on August 2, 2001.

Mangan, Kathleen Nugent, editor. *Lenore Tawney: A Retrospective.* New York: Rizzoli, 1990.

— L. S.

TEICHERT, MINERVA
(Minerva Bernetta Kohlhepp)
(1888–1976) *Painter*

Mormon artist Minerva Teichert used her art to celebrate her faith and the courage of female pioneers. She was born Minerva Bernetta Kohlhepp on August 28, 1888, in North Ogden, Utah. Her mother was the daughter of a bodyguard for Mormon leader Brigham Young. Her father was a convert to Mormonism, whose wealthy family disowned him because of his religious beliefs.

The second of 10 children, Minerva grew up on a ranch in Idaho. Because her father suffered from tuberculosis, earning the family's keep fell largely to her mother, who sold handmade lace, fruits, and vegatables to make ends meet. Her example inspired in Minerva a respect for strong rural women. Her mother's gift of a set of watercolors when she was four also incited her passion for art.

After finishing high school, Minerva Kohlhepp worked as a teacher, and she handpainted china and pillows for sale. Although she gave most of her income to her family, she was able to save enough to attend the Art Institute of Chicago, where she studied academic painting with John Vanderpoel. She was also influenced by lecturer Edwin Blashfield, an advocate of public murals.

Kohlhepp continued her education on scholarship at the Art Students League in New York City in 1915. To earn a living, she took any job she could, from sketching cadavers for medical schools to working as a trick rider in a Wild West show. While at the league, Kohlhepp developed a friendship with instructor and painter Robert Henri, who nicknamed her "Miss Idaho." In her memoirs, she remembered Henri asking, "Has anyone ever told your great Mormon story?" to which she replied, "Not to suit me." She claimed the exchange persuaded her to return to the West and paint the history and religious stories of the Mormon people.

Settling on a ranch in Cokeville, Wyoming, Kohlhepp married Herman Teichert, a cowboy, with whom she had five children. While cooking for the ranch hands and raising her family, Minerva Teichert wrote *Drowned Memories,* a book of short stories, and *A Romance of Fort Hall,* a novel. Every night after her children were asleep, she painted in a makeshift studio in her living room. On her obsession to paint daily, she once said, "I must paint. It's a disease." In addition to canvases, she painted almost any available surface, from discarded doors to paper bags to the margins of books.

Many of her paintings, such as *Madonna at Dawn* and *Handcart Pioneers,* depicted early western settlers. Unlike most artists of the region, she emphasized the role of female pioneers, depicting them as hardy and capable. Teichert's most famous works, however, were her interpretations of Scripture and scenes from the Book of Mormon. Of her passion for these subjects, Teichert wrote, "[T]he story of the building of a mountain empire and the struggles of my people drive me on and unless I can paint a little each day on the great pageant of the West I think the day is lost. It seems like a call to me that I sin if I while my time away and do not answer."

Continuing to paint until her death in 1976, Teichert created more than 500 works. Honored as one of the greatest Mormon artists, her paintings often appear in church publications. Forty paintings of her Book of Mormon series are now in the collection of Brigham Young University.

Further Reading

"Art of the West, Biographical Information," State Wide Art Partnership. Available online. URL: http://www.shs.nebo.edu/Museum/swap/awteichert.html. Updated on March 8, 2001.

Cannon, Elaine, and Shirley A. Teichert. *Minerva!: The Story of an Artist with a Mission*. Salt Lake City, Utah: Bookcraft, 1997.

Welch, John W., and Doris R. Dant. *The Book of Mormon Paintings of Minerva Teichert*. Salt Lake City, Utah: Bookcraft, 1997.

— L. S.

THOMAS, ALMA W.
(Alma Woodsey Thomas)
(1891–1978)   *Painter*

In 1972, while in her eighties, painter Alma W. Thomas became the first African-American woman to have a solo exhibition at the Whitney Museum of American Art in New York. The eldest of four daughters, Thomas was born into a prosperous family in Columbus, Georgia, on September 22, 1891. Disturbed by race riots in Atlanta, the Thomases moved to Washington, D.C., in 1907. Thomas would live in the house they purchased there for much of the rest of her life.

In high school, Thomas excelled in math and science and considered studying to become an architect. An art class, however, changed her mind. She later recalled that "when I entered the art room, it was like entering heaven." At the time, however, it was unimaginable to Thomas that an African-American woman could have a career as a fine artist. She opted instead to become a teacher, earning her certificate at the Miner Teachers Normal School in 1913.

After several years of teaching, Thomas enrolled at Howard University with the intention of studying costume design. Immediately recognizing her talent, Thomas's professor and mentor James

Herring convinced her to enter the fine arts program he had recently created. In 1924 Thomas became the program's first graduate and one of the first African-American women to earn a degree in fine arts.

The next year, Thomas began teaching at the Shaw Junior High School in Washington, D.C., where she would work for the next 35 years. In the late 1920s and early 1930s, she spent her summers in New York City studying at Columbia University's Teachers College. She was awarded her master's degree in art education in 1934. While in New York, Thomas frequented the city's museums and galleries, becoming well-versed in the work of both the old masters and the avant-garde.

As vice president of the Barnett-Aden Gallery, Thomas also became a central figure of art circles in Washington, D.C. Beginning in 1943, the gallery was the first in the Washington area to exhibit modern American art. It also broke a color barrier by showing the work of both black and white artists.

Thomas returned to school in 1950, enrolling in night classes in painting and art history at American University. Under the instruction of Joe Summerford and Robert Gates, she moved from painting representational still lifes toward works of pure abstraction. With artists such as Kenneth Noland and Morris Louis, she became associated with the Washington Color Field painters, an abstract school that emphasized pure areas of color, often formed from thinned paint poured on a large unprimed canvas. Her art, however, shared little more with the group than a preference for vibrant color.

Following her retirement from teaching in the 1960s, Thomas began devoting herself full time to her art. By 1964, she "decided to try to paint something different from anything I'd ever done. Different from anything I'd ever seen." Her new style featured small rectangular shapes of color arranged to create mosaic-like patterns. Although abstract, her paintings were directly inspired by objects in nature, as their titles, such as *Iris, Tulips, Jonquils and Crocuses* (1969), implied. Among her best-received works were her Earth Paintings series, which referred to the flower beds outside her kitchen window. Also notable was the series called

215

Space Paintings, which Thomas explained was inspired by the "heavens and stars and my idea of what it is like to be an astronaut, exploring space."

In addition to her historic Whitney show, Thomas was the focus of an even larger exhibition at the Corcoran Gallery in 1972. As part of the exhibition festivities, September 9 was declared "Alma Thomas Day" in Washington, D.C.

Despite ill health, Thomas continued to paint into the mid-1970s. During a heart operation, she died in February 25, 1978, at age 86. Thomas left behind a distinguished legacy as an art educator and painter of colorful forms expressing the joyousness with which she approached both life and art. As she once said, "I never bothered painting the ugly things in life. . . . I wanted something beautiful that you could sit down and look at."

Further Reading

"Artist Profile Alma Thomas," The National Museum of Women in the Arts. Available online. URL: http://www.nmwa.org/legacy/bios/bthomas.htm. Downloaded on August 2, 2001.

Foresta, Merry A. *A Life in Art: Alma Thomas, 1891–1978.* Washington, D.C.: Smithsonian Institution Press, 1981.

Perry, Regenia. *Free within Ourselves: African-American Artists in the Collection of the National Museum of American Art.* Washington, D.C.: National Museum of American Art, 1992.

Thomas, Alma. *Alma W. Thomas: A Retrospective of the Paintings.* Rohnert Park, Calif.: Pomegrante, 1998.

— L. S.

TREIMAN, JOYCE (Joyce Wahl)
(1922–1991)   *Painter*

With her constant experimentation with new styles and subject matter, California painter Joyce Treiman was dubbed by *Los Angeles Times* art critic William Wilson "a painter's painter and artist's artist." She was born Joyce Wahl on May 29, 1922, in Evanston, Illinois. At eight, she began drawing, immediately displaying a prodigy's skill. She later remembered that as soon as she picked up a pencil,

"[I] knew then that what I really wanted was to make art. There was never any doubt although doubts happened along the way."

Throughout her teens, Wahl took classes at the Art Institute of Chicago, where she first learned about art history by wandering though the institution's collections. After spending two years at Stephens College in Columbia, Missouri, Wahl enrolled at the Iowa State University, then one of the few American universities that offered a bachelor's of fine arts degree. There, she was taught by painter Philip Guston, whose style would influence her art for the next decade. Under his instruction, she began to paint for the first time. She once explained, "I could draw as easily as I could breathe. Painting I had to learn."

Wahl graduated in 1943 and briefly worked as a commercial artist in Chicago. In 1945 she married businessman Kenneth Treiman. Six years later, they had a son, Donald.

Awarded a grant from the Louis Comfort Tiffany Foundation in 1947, Joyce Treiman had the financial stability to devote all her time to her art. Her early works included paintings of skid row residents and interpretations of mythic figures such as Prometheus and Icarus. In the early 1950s, Treiman was excited by abstract expressionism, which had become the prevalent style of the American avant-garde. Although in response to that style her work moved toward abstraction, her nonobjective works usually featured humanlike forms.

In 1960 Treiman and her family moved to Los Angeles. Initially, she found the new setting disorienting. Treiman wrote,"I think it took a while for it to sink in artistically—in terms of the light and color—so different from the inward-looking and soul searching of the Middle West." In California, Treiman returned to figurative art. Initially, figures in paintings such as *Dream Sequence* (1962) emerged from a dreamlike atmosphere. Her paintings soon became more focused on the figures themselves. In works such *The Secret* (1965–66) and *The Birthday Party* (1966), she created groupings of ghoulish figures that seemed to capture a moment just before some unspecified disaster.

During several trips to Europe in the late 1960s, Treiman studied the works of the old masters, cementing her commitment to the figurative tradition. She embraced the painterly quality of the works of Diego de Velázquez, Francisco de Goya, and most of all Rembrandt van Rijn, whose melding of formal expertise with an emotional understanding of humanity particularly inspired her.

Her research resulted in a series of group portraits in the late 1960s. Though handling paint like the old masters she admired, Treiman delved into contemporary subject matter, especially feelings of alienation in modern life. *Anomie* (1969–70), for example, depicts eight exotically dressed men and women, including a self-portrait. Most of the figures are staring at the viewer, but they seem wholly unconnected to one another, creating a sense of anxiety and tension.

Treiman's tone and palette became lighter in the 1970s. Early in the decade, she painted herself and friends in fanciful settings, often depicting them as cowboys on horseback. Later, she created a series of tributes to famous artists of the past. Using bright colors and looser brush strokes, she painted fantasy meetings between herself and the artists she admired, including John Singer Sargent, Thomas Eakins, and Pierre Bonnard. Picturing herself alongside modern masters, she flaunted her confidence in her talents and her willingness to challenge the male authority in the art world.

In 1983 Treiman's work became far darker than ever before. That year, she created several paintings dealing with death, including *Thanatopsis* and *The Parting,* which are now considered among her best. She also made a series based on the labors of Hercules. On this subject, she wrote, "Those stories had it all: death-defying challenges, the refusal to accept defeat even against impossible odds. . . . And what wonderful subjects for all-out, give-'em-hell paintings."

At the end of this landmark year, Treiman was diagnosed with lung cancer. After surgery and chemotherapy, she returned to painting in 1984, with a looser style and a more exuberant use of color. Many of her last works explored the theme of departure. In *Me and Big Ship,* she depicted herself before a cruise ship, while in *Sailing Away* (1985), the ship has disappeared, heading off for its destination. In her later years, her interest in abstraction was renewed as she showed a new preference toward flat forms and warmer colors. With her art again moving in a new direction, Treiman died suddenly of a heart attack on June 2, 1991.

Further Reading

Duncan, Michael. *Joyce Treiman.* New York: Hudson Hills Press, 1997.

Folkart, Burt A. "Joyce Treiman: Eclectic Painter," *Los Angeles Times,* June 4, 1991, 26.

"Painting Is a Lonely Arena: Joyce Treiman and the Old Masters," Traditional Fine Art Online, Inc. Available online. URL: http://www.tfaoi.com/newsm1/n1m440.htm. Downloaded on August 2, 2001.

— L. S.

U

ULMANN, DORIS
(1884–1934)   *Photographer*

Through her sensitive photographic portraits, Doris Ulmann documented the lives of people in the rural Southeast during the early 20th century. On May 29, 1884, she was born into a wealthy family in New York City. In her youth, she had several operations for stomach ailments, which nevertheless continued to plague her throughout her life.

Beginning in 1900, Ulmann attended New York's Ethical Culture School, intending to become a teacher. As part of the Ethical Culture movement, the school emphasized the equality of people from all backgrounds, a philosophy displayed in her later work. Ulmann also attended Columbia University, where she studied psychology and law. During this time, she probably took up photography as a hobby.

Ulmann's formal training in photography began at Columbia's Teachers College, where she took a course from Clarence H. White. She continued her instruction from White at an independent school he subsequently established. While studying with White, she met and married Charles Jaeger, an orthopedic surgeon who shared her pas-

sion for photography. Ulmann and Jaeger became involved with White's organization Pictorial Photographs of America and often had photographs they had taken published in its annual journal, *Pictorial Photography in America.*

Setting up a darkroom in her Park Avenue apartment, Ulmann concentrated on landscapes and portraits, photographing many noted artists, writers, and musicians. She also produced figure studies of laborers, dockworkers, and tradespeople she encountered in New York City. In 1925 she went to Virginia, New York, and Pennsylvania, to photograph the Shaker and Mennonite communities—the first of many trips she took to document rural American cultures.

The same year, Ulmann divorced Jaeger and met John Jacob Niles, who would become her companion for the rest of her life. An entertainer and folklorist 10 years her junior, Niles was probably Ulmann's lover by the time she hired him as her assistant in 1927. From 1928 to 1934, the couple made annual expeditions to the Appalachian Mountains, where Ulmann photographed poor workers and farmers while Niles collected their traditional ballads. Originally from Kentucky, Niles most likely made the first contact with Ulmann's subjects, putting them at ease before they were asked to pose for her camera. Her images of them, shot in soft focus, were warm and respectful, emphasizing their inherent dignity above the difficult circumstances of their lives. Unlike the works of later photographers such as Walker Evans and DOROTHEA LANGE, Ulmann's photographs of the poor were less of a call for action than an attempt to document their traditional way of life.

Beginning in 1929, Ulmann collaborated with her close friend Julia Peterkin, a Pulitzer Prize–winning novelist. With Peterkin providing the text, Ulmann produced a book of photographs called *Roll, Jordan, Roll* (1933), depicting African-American cultures in the South, particularly lifeways of the Gullah people of South Carolina. Ulmann was also asked to contribute illustrations to *Handicrafts of the Southern Highlands* (1937). Written by Allen H. Eaton, the book was sponsored by the Russell Sage Foundation, an organization founded to further social work in the United States.

During Ulmann's lifetime, her work also appeared in many magazines and exhibitions, including the *International Photography* show held by the Harvard Society for Contemporary Art in 1930. In 1934 the Library of Congress acquired and exhibited 40 of her works, prompting First Lady Eleanor Roosevelt to invite Ulmann to dinner at the White House. In frail health throughout her life, she died on August 28 of that year at the age of 50.

Further Reading

"Doris Ulmann," Getty Explore Art. Available online. URL: http://www.getty.edu/art/collections/bio/a1603-1.html. Downloaded on August 2, 2001.

Featherstone, David. *Doris Ulmann: American Portraits.* Albuquerque: University of New Mexico Press, 1985.

Jacobs, Philip Walker. *The Life and Photography of Doris Ulmann.* Lexington: University Press of Kentucky, 2001.

Ulmann, Doris. *Doris Ulmann: Photographs from the J. Paul Getty Museum.* Malibu, Calif.: J. Paul Getty Museum, 1996.

— L. S.

V

VELARDE, PABLITA
(Tse Tsan, "Golden Dawn")
(1918–) *Painter*

Painter Pablita Velarde has earned an international reputation for her beautiul images of traditional Pueblo society. She was born on September 19, 1918, in Santa Clara Pueblo in northeastern New Mexico and given the name Tse Tsan (Golden Dawn). As a young child, she suffered an infection that left her blind. Treated with traditional medicines, she regained her sight two years later. The experience made her want to memorize every visual detail of her world. As she later recalled, "I wanted to see everything."

At six, Tse Tsan was sent to St. Catherine's, an Indian boarding school in Santa Fe. Christened "Pablita" by her teachers, she learned English and academic subjects. After some years, she left St. Catherine's to start the eighth grade at the Santa Fe Indian School. There a new teacher, Dorothy Dunn, had established the Studio, a center for art training for Native Americans. Dunn taught her students to use charcoal and paint to create pictures on paper and canvas. In her determination to instruct Indians in nontraditional art forms, Dunn was inspired by the San Ildefonso Group, a group of Pueblo artists, including TONITA PEÑA, who had begun painting scenes of Indian life with watercolors in the 1910s. Like the San Ildefonso artists, Dunn's students were encouraged to use their art to record the traditional customs of their people. They were told not to draw from life but instead to tap their childhood memories for subject matter. Since by the 1930s the Pueblo had been affected by many non-Indian influences, Dunn was convinced that these memories would provide a more "authentic" vision of Indian ways.

Also in imitation of the San Ildefonso Group, Dunn instructed her students to paint flat, unshaded figures against a stark background. The figures themselves, however, were very detailed, with their clothing, hair, and other features meticulously rendered. Velarde took to this style immediately. Because of her keen attention to her surroundings, she was able to remember and represent everyday scenes from her youth with extreme accuracy.

Displayed in a student show at the Museum of New Mexico, several of Velarde's works caught the attention of Santa Fe artist Olive Rush. She invited Velarde and two other students to help her paint a series of murals on the theme "A Century of Progress" for the 1933 Chicago World's Fair. The next year, Rush asked Velarde to assist her on murals commissioned by the Works Progress Administration (WPA), a federal government program that hired artists to create public artwork during the Great Depression.

In 1936 Velarde graduated from the Santa Fe Indian School, becoming the first person in her family to earn a high school diploma. She returned to Santa Clara, where she taught at an Indian day school. There Rush asked her to contribute one mural to a series to be exhibited outside of the Maisel Trading Post in Albuquerque, New Mexico. The mural depicted a row of Pueblo women in richly patterned calico dresses, standing behind a display of traditional pottery.

In 1938 Velarde was hired by the National Park Service to paint a series of murals at the Bandelier National Monument Museum. The series took nearly two years to complete and depicted traditional Pueblo activities, which Velarde researched extensively through historical research and interviews with Santa Clara elders. The scenes portrayed Pueblo ceremonies and rituals; craft activities such as basketmaking and beadwork; and daily work such as house building, farming, and gathering wild plants. Because of their detail, these paintings are today valued not only as art but also as rare visual documents of Pueblo life.

Laid off by the National Park Service as World War II loomed, Velarde moved to Albuquerque, where she worked as a telephone operator. There she met Herbert Hardin, a white man whom she married in 1942. The couple had two children, Helen Hardin and Herbert Hardin II. After the war, Velarde was rehired by the National Park Service. She also started exhibiting her work in local shows and competitions. In 1948 Velarde won her first major prize, in a competition sponsored by the Philbrook Art Center in Tulsa, Oklahoma. Many more honors followed, and she quickly became a favorite of Indian art collectors who had embraced "Traditional Indian Painting," the name given to the style shared by the Santa Fe Studio artists and the San Ildefonso watercolorists.

Velarde's new celebrity caused tensions in her marriage. After she and Herbert Hardin divorced in

Pablita Velarde, circa 1955, next to one of her striking paintings
(Courtesy Museum of New Mexico, Neg. No. 174192)

1959, Velarde returned to Santa Clara, where she renewed her relationship with her father. On visits, she often asked him to share old Pueblo stories, which she then wrote down and translated into English. The project inspired her to create a new series of paintings to illustrate the ancient stories. One of these works, *Old Father, the Story Teller,* became her most famous painting. It depicted her father telling a group of children the story of how the Pueblo people were created and how all creatures came to earth from a lower world. In 1960 the stories Velarde transcribed were combined with her illustrations and collected in a book titled after this painting.

For her contributions to Native American art, Velarde has received many honors. They include the 1954 Palmes Académiques from the French government, the 1977 New Mexico Governor's Award, and the 1990 award from the Women's Caucus of Art. Her career also blazed a trail for other Indian artists, including her daughter Helen, who emerged as one of the next generation's finest Native American painters.

Further Reading

Gridley, Marion E. "Pablita Velarde, Artist of the Pueblo." In *American Indian Women,* 94–104. New York: Hawthorn Books, 1974.

Hirschfelder, Arlene. "Pablita Velarde: Santa Clara Potter." In *Artists and Craftspeople,* 53–60. New York: Facts On File, 1994.

Nelson, Mary Carroll. "Pablita Velarde." *American Indian Art* 3 (1978): 50–57, 90.

Velarde, Pablita. *Old Father, the Storyteller.* Santa Fe: Clear Light Publishers, 1989.

"Velarde, Pablita (Tse Tsan)," AskART. Available online. URL: http://askart.com/Biography.asp. Posted in 2000.

— L. S.

VON WIEGAND, CHARMION
(ca. 1896–1983) *Collagist, Painter*

Through the medium of collage, Charmion Von Wiegand explored her fascination with Eastern mysticism. The daughter of foreign correspondent Karl Von Wiegand, she was born in about 1896 in Chicago, but she grew up in San Francisco. Visits to the city's Chinatown excited her interest in both Chinese culture and in the uses of color. As she once recalled, "I always liked color. I got it early from the Chinese in the streets . . . [with their] dragons and firecrackers." Her father's belief in Theosophy, a sect that incorporated elements of Buddhism, was also an early influence.

After living with her father in Berlin for three years, Charmion Von Wiegand traveled to New York City to attend Barnard College and Columbia University, where she studied journalism and art history. Bowing to her mother's ambitions for her, she married an affluent man and had a brief career as a society wife. Bored with this life, she underwent psychoanalysis. She discovered her passion when her analyst asked her what she wanted to do most. Without hesitation, she answered that she wanted to paint. By 1926, she was divorced

and again living in New York, working as a journalist by day while painting at night. Three years later, she went to Moscow, where she worked as a correspondent for the Hearst Press until 1932.

Returning to the United States, Von Wiegand married journalist and novelist Joseph Freeman. She began writing articles on art exhibitions for *The New Masses,* a magazine that her husband founded, and editing *Art Front,* a publication of the Artists' Union. Her work brought her into contact with the avant-garde, particularly with leading abstractionists such as Joseph Stella and Max Weber. Von Wiegand's growing interest in abstraction coincided with her increasing disappointment with her own paintings, which at the time were mostly landscapes.

In the spring of 1941, Von Wiegand began work on an article about European artists who had recently come to the United States to escape the devastation of World War II. While researching the piece, she interviewed Dutch painter Piet Mondrian. Intrigued by the spiritual aspects of his work, Von Wiegand became a close friend of Mondrian and helped him translate and edit his writings for publication in the United States. For the *Journal of Aesthetics and Art Criticism,* she also wrote the first American article about his work. On Mondrian's recommendation, Von Wiegand joined the American Abstract Artists in 1941. She served as its president from 1950 to 1953.

During the late 1940s, Von Wiegand began experimenting with abstraction in her work. The process moved her away from painting and toward collage. Her early works combined paper and cloth with found objects. *Transfer to Cathay* (1948), for instance, incorporated pieces of a bus ticket, a menu, and a matchbox. She also often added Chinese characters, either from printed text or by painting them directly on the work. Like the work of Mondrian, Von Wiegand's collages were largely composed of rectangles, but generally her compositions were less rigid and her color choices more varied.

By the late 1950s, her study of Eastern thought and religion increasingly informed her work. In *Gouache #88: Southern Sanctuary* (1958), the combination of rectangles she created was inspired by the ground plan of a Tibetan temple. Many later works, including *Kundalini Lotus* (1968–69), drew on mandalas, geometric designs symbolizing the universe that are often used in meditation. Several years before feminist artists began depicting female dieties, Von Wiegand was creating images that evoked goddesses in such works as *Invocation of the Winter Goddess* (1969).

Well into her 70s, Von Wiegand continued to write and lecture about religion and art. She died in her mid-80s in New York City on June 9, 1983.

Further Reading

Bailey, Brooke. *The Remarkable Lives of 100 Women Artists.* Holbrook, Mass.: Bob Adams, 1994.

Larsen, Susan C. "Charmion Von Wiegand: Walking on a Road with Milestones." *Arts* 60:3 (November 1985): 29–31.

Mecklenburg, Virginia M. "Charmion Von Wiegand," National Museum of American Art and Smithsonian Institution Press. Available online. URL: http://nmaa-ryder.si.edu/collections/exhibits/abstraction/vonWiegand.htm. Downloaded on August 2, 2001.

Rubinstein, Charlotte Streiffer. *American Women Artists: From Early Indian Times to the Present.* New York: Avon Books, 1982.

Three American Purists: Mason, Miles, Von Wiegand. Springfield, Mass.: Museum of Fine Arts, 1975.

— L. S.

VONNOH, BESSIE POTTER
(Bessie Onahotema Potter)
(1872–1955) *Sculptor*

Bessie Potter Vonnoh is best remembered for sensitive sculptures of women and children. She was born Bessie Onahotema Potter on August 17, 1872, in St. Louis, Missouri. After her father died in a railroad accident, her family moved to Chicago. While still a toddler, Bessie contracted a mysterious ailment that left her an invalid, confined in plaster casts and wheelchairs for 10 years. The illness stunted Bessie's height at four feet, eight inches and possibly left her infertile.

Returning to school, Bessie Potter discovered a passion for modeling clay. She later recalled that in art class "the touch of the clay and joy of creating gave me a sense of deep contentment." At 14, she began studying sculpture at the Art Institute of Chicago, financing her schooling by working as an assistant to modeling instructor Lorado Taft, who would remain a friend and mentor throughout her life. Potter was one of several female students, nicknamed the "White Rabbits," who assisted Taft in making a sculpture for the World's Columbian Exposition in 1893. Potter was also awarded an $800 commission to make her own eight-foot work, *Art,* for the Illinois State Building. Also at the fair, she saw the small works of Russian sculptor Paul Troubetskoy, which inspired her to experiment with making intimate sculptures about one foot in height.

After five years at the Art Institute, Potter established her own studio. Her customers were largely wealthy women, who hired her to make small plaster portraits of them and their children. These small works reflected Potter's belief that simple figures in contemporary dress could render "as perfect a likeness and as much beauty" as monumental sculpture. She once wrote of her work in portrait sculpture, "What I wanted was to look for beauty in the every-day world, to catch the joy and swing of modern American life."

Selling her works at $25 apiece, Potter saved enough to fund a trip to Paris, where she met the French master Auguste Rodin. Returning to Chicago, she continued to produce portrait sculpture, while also making small-sized uncommissioned works. Her sculpture *The Young Mother* (1896), depicting a woman rocking her baby to sleep, created a modern scene that also expressed the universal theme of parents' love for their children. Cast in bronze in multiple editions, the work helped solidify Potter's reputation.

In the late 1890s, she won two major commissions, producing a bust of Major General Samuel Wylie Crawford for the Smith Memorial in Philadelphia and a six-foot statue of actress Maude Adams for the Exposition Universelle in Paris.

After completing the Adams sculpture, Potter married her longtime friend and suitor, impressionist painter Robert Vonnoh, in 1899. Throughout their marriage, the Vonnohs often exhibited their work together.

While known for depicting women in modern dress, Bessie Potter Vonnoh began creating a series of works, including *Maidenhood* (1906) and *In Grecian Drapery* (1913), that depicted classically posed female figures dressed in loose tunics. Rather than drawing from Greek sculpture, they were probably inspired by the costumes of modern dancer Isadora Duncan. Vonnoh also started working on large pieces with the garden sculpture *Water Lilies* (1914–20). In 1921 she became the first woman to become a permanent member of the National Academy of Design.

In the 1920s, Vonnoh was awarded two major commissions for outdoor sculptures—the *Bird Fountain* (1924–27) at the Theodore Roosevelt Memorial Bird Sanctuary in Long Island, New York, and the *Frances Hodgson Burnett Memorial Fountain* (1926–37) in New York City's Central Park. Both works depicted children at play. Vonnoh became less productive after the death of her husband in 1933. She remarried in 1948 to physician Edward Keyes, but he died nine months after their wedding. Vonnoh continued to make small works like those that first established her career before suffering a stroke in 1952. She died in New York City on March 8, 1955, at the age of 82.

Further Reading

Aronson, Julie A. "Vonnoh, Bessie Potter." In *American National Biography.* Volume 22. Edited by John Arthur Garraty and Mark C. Carnes, 401–403. New York: Oxford University Press, 1999.

"Bessie Potter Vonnoh," Sheldon Memorial Art Gallery and Sculpture Garden. Available online. URL: http://sheldon.unl.edu/HTML/ARTIST/Vonnoh_B/ss.html. Updated on March 10, 2000.

Rubinstein, Charlotte Streifer. *American Women Sculptors: A History of Women Working in Three Dimensions.* Boston: G. K. Hall, 1990.

— L. S.

W

WARING, LAURA WHEELER
(1887–1948)   *Painter, Illustrator*

Known for her portraits of prominent African Americans, Laura Wheeler Waring was born on May 27, 1887, in Hartford, Connecticut. One of six children, she was reared in a middle-class African-American household. Her father was a minister, and her mother was a schoolteacher.

As a teenager, Waring began working in watercolors, winning several awards for her paintings while she was still in high school. She continued her education at the Pennsylvania Academy of Fine Arts, where she studied with Henry McCarter, William Merritt Chase, and Thomas Anshutz. While there, she began teaching art part time at Cheyney State Teachers' College in Pennsylvania, then the only African-American state college in the North.

In 1914 Waring won the Cresson Travel Scholarship, which allowed her to travel to Europe. Visiting museums throughout the continent, she was exposed for the first time to the works of the old masters. After three months, Waring returned to Cheyney. By the end of the decade, she was also illustrating covers for *The Crisis,* the magazine of the National Association for the Advancement of Colored People (NAACP). In 1920 she began providing illustrations for *The Brownies' Book,* a children's periodical produced by the NAACP to instill racial pride in young African Americans. Waring contributed artwork to each of the magazine's 24 issues.

Waring returned to Europe in 1924. In addition to traveling through Italy and North Africa, she lived briefly in Paris, where she enrolled at the Académie de la Grande Chaumière. Her studies and her exposure to French impressionism led her to work with a looser brush stroke and a brighter, more colorful palette. While in France, Waring became acquainted with several other notable African Americans living abroad, including the sculptors ELIZABETH PROPHET and AUGUSTA SAVAGE, the writers Countee Cullen and Langston Hughes, and the actor Paul Robeson.

Returning to the United States, Waring became a full-time professor at Cheyney in 1926, a post she filled for the next 21 years. The following year, *Anne Washington Derry* (1927)—a portrait of the elderly mother of a friend—won a gold medal at the annual Harmon Foundation Salon. The Harmon Foundation, established to promote African-American achievement in all fields, was then the primary patron of black artists. In addition to the Harmon shows, Waring's portraits, landscapes, and still lifes were featured in exhibits at the Art

Institute of Chicago, the Pennsylvania Academy of Fine Arts, and the Howard University Art Gallery throughout the late 1920s and 1930s.

In 1943 the Harmon Foundation commissioned Waring and Betsy Graves Reyneau, a white artist, to produce portraits of famous African Americans. Among Waring's subjects were the writers W.E.B. DuBois and James Weldon Johnson and singer Marian Anderson. Waring and Reyneau had 23 of their portraits displayed in *Portraits of Outstanding Americans of Negro Origin,* an exhibition that opened at the Smithsonian Institution on May 2, 1944. The Harmon Foundation envisioned the show as a means of combating racial prejudice. In the promotional material, the foundation celebrated the Waring-Reyneau collaboration as "two races and two women banded together to fight social injustice." For the next 10 years, *Portraits* toured 32 cities. Most of the paintings were later given to the National Portrait Gallery, which partially reconstructed the historic show in a 1996 exhibition.

A year after retiring from her teaching post, Laura Wheeler Waring began work on a series of paintings based on African-American spirituals. Following a long illness, she died on February 3, 1948.

Further Reading

Campbell, Susan. "Laura Wheeler Waring," Hartford Courant. Available online. URL: http://court.ctnow.com/projects/bhistory/waring.htm. Posted in 1999.

Johnson-Feelings, Dianne, editor. *The Best of the Brownies' Book.* New York: Oxford University Press, 1996.

Lewis, Samella S. *Art: African American.* New York: Harcourt Brace Jovanovich, 1978.

Reynolds, Gary A., and Beryl J. Wright. *Against the Odds: African-American Artists and the Harmon Foundation.* Newark, N.J.: Newark Museum, 1989.

— L. S.

WAYNE, JUNE (June Claire Klein)
(1918–) *Printmaker, Painter, Textile Artist*

As the founder of the Tamarind Lithography Workshop, June Wayne revived interest in lithography as an American fine art form. Born June Claire Klein in Chicago on March 7, 1918, she was raised by her mother and grandmother, strong women who instilled in her a spirit of independence. A voracious reader, June stopped attending school in her early teens, preferring to spend her days in the library. She dropped out completely at 15, and after briefly working in a factory, decided to become an artist.

Inspired by the benday dots used to print comic books, Klein's first works were drawings made from colored dots. She soon taught herself to paint and at 17 was given her first one-woman show at Chicago's Boulevard Gallery. She also found employment with the Federal Art Project, a Works Progress Administration program designed to provide income for artists. While still in her teens, Klein lobbied in Washington on behalf of the Artists Union to prevent planned layoffs.

In 1939 Klein moved to New York City, where she worked as a costume jewelry designer. Two years later, she married George Wayne, with whom she had one daughter. (She divorced Wayne in 1960 and married her second husband, Arthur Henry Plone, in 1964.)

In the late 1940s, June Wayne moved with her family to Los Angeles. For a time, she worked as an illustrator in the aircraft industry and as a scriptwriter for radio programs. But while studying at Lynton Kisler's graphics studio, Wayne found her true calling. There she was introduced to the art of lithography. As she later remembered, "I took a small [lithography] stone home from his studio and started fooling around. . . . It was like a first shot of heroin. I was hooked right off." With little opportunity for advanced training in lithography in the United States, Wayne headed for Paris in 1957 and began studying with the greatest European masters of printmaking. While in Europe, she created a book of prints illustrating the poems of John Donne.

After returning to the United States, Wayne met with W. McNeil Lowry, an executive of the Ford Foundation. She submitted to the organization a proposal to create a lithography studio in Los Angeles. Wayne later explained that she envisioned it as not "just a training place. It was to be

. . . an attempt to revive a dying art and give it the means to thrive."

With financing in place, Wayne designed a print-making studio on Tamarind Avenue and filled it with used lithography stones and presses. Over the next 10 years, she invited hundreds of artists and printers to the Tamarind Lithography Workshop's intensive two-month program. More than 3,000 print editions were produced at the studio by such artists as LOUISE NEVELSON, Josef Albers, and David Hockney. Many of Tamarind's alumni opened their own print studios, thereby spreading the renaissance of American lithography across the United States. In addition to training artists in print techniques, under Wayne's direction, Tamarind produced important written materials on lithography and set new standards for documenting art prints. Wayne also encouraged the production of limited editions as a means of driving up the price of each print. Stating that "I do not believe in permanent subsidy," she wanted to ensure that the lithographers she trained "could flourish in a free-market society."

In 1970 the Tamarind workshop was renamed the Tamarind Institute and relocated to the University of New Mexico. Assured that the studio would have regular funding, Wayne resigned as Tamarind's director. While helping others experiment with printmaking, she had had no time to create any herself. Since leaving Tamarind, she has devoted herself completely to her own art.

In the 1970s, Wayne ventured into tapestry with a series of works depicting giant waves, reminiscent of those in Japanese prints. During this period, Wayne also created perhaps her most acclaimed lithography—the Dorothy Series (1975–79), a collection of 20 prints that together provide a visual biography of her mother. The prints incorporate family photographs and personal documents to tell how Dorothy Klein emigrated from Russia, survived two bad marriages, and found success and financial freedom as a corset saleswoman. The *L. A. Weekly* called the series "artistic feminism at its toughest, most poignant and most opulent." Although Wayne did not identify herself as a feminist artist during this period, she organized "Joan of Art" seminars to allow

Printmaker June Wayne founded the Tamarind Lithography Workshop.
(AP/Wide World Photos)

female artists to discuss their careers and help them make a living from their work.

More recently, many of Wayne's prints have shown the influence of minimalism, particularly her stark, one-color series from the 1980s, Cognitos and The Djuna Set. Her work also continues to reflect her lifelong fascination with science; the print *Nacelle* (1996), for instance, incorporates a technical drawing of an airplane she made in the 1940s. Wayne's creation of *Knockout* (1996), inspired by a childhood memory of a horse-drawn wagon, was documented in an episode of the Public Broadcasting Service's World of Art series. Although still best-known for her promotion of American printmaking, Wayne's own art received overdue recognition with a major retrospective at the Neuberger Museum of Art in Purchase, New York, in 1997.

Further Reading

"June Wayne, Artist Extraordinaire," Women's International Center. Available online. URL: http://www.wic.org/bio/jwayne.htm. Downloaded on August 2, 2001.
Tamarind: From Los Angeles to Albuquerque. Los Angeles: University of California, 1984.
Wayne, June. *June Wayne: A Retrospective.* Purchase, N.Y.: Neuberger Museum of Art, 1997.

— L. S.

WHEELER, CANDACE
(Candace Thurber)

(1827–1923)   *Textile Artist, Interior Designer*

With her innovative design sense and business acumen, Candace Wheeler helped open the field of interior design to American women. She was born Candace Thurber on a dairy farm in Delhi, New York, on March 24, 1827. Like most young women of the day, she learned home crafts, such as weaving, sewing, and embroidery, from her mother. After attending Delaware Academy, at age 18 she married businessman Thomas M. Wheeler. At homes in Brooklyn and Long Island, she raised four children.

The Wheelers' interest in art led them to attend openings and lectures at the Tenth Street Studio, operated by painter William Merritt Chase, in New York City. They also entertained such artists as Frederic Church and Albert Bierstadt at their country home. With the encouragement of her artist friends, Candace Wheeler briefly studied painting in Dresden, Germany, during one of her family's extended sojourns abroad.

In 1876 Wheeler attended the Philadelphia Centennial Exposition, an event that changed the course of her life. There she saw an exhibit sponsored by the Royal School of Art Needlework, a London institution that helped impoverished gentlewomen make a living by selling handicrafts. Wheeler, then nearly 50 years old, was inspired by the school's goal of giving women a means to support themselves. As she later wrote, "Women of all classes had always been dependent upon the wage-earning capacity of men, and although the strict observance of the custom had become inconvenient and did not fit the times, the sentiment of it remained. But the time was ripe for a change."

With the help of other prominent women in New York society, Wheeler founded the Society of Decorative Art in 1877. Like the Royal School, the society operated a gallery and a shop featuring crafts made by women and offered classes on such subjects as embroidery and china painting. When Wheeler established the Women's Exchange, another organization intended to market female-made goods, her associates at the Society of Decorative Art accused her of disloyalty. Then vice president of the society, Wheeler resigned, which allowed her to enter her own work in the organization's annual competition. In 1879 she won first prize for portière (curtain) design for her textile *Consider the Lillies of the Field*.

The same year, Wheeler was asked by Louis Comfort Tiffany, a leader in the art nouveau movement, to join his new design firm, Associated Artists. Art nouveau works featured sinuous lines that often formed flowing flower and leaf designs. At Associated Artists, Wheeler oversaw all textiles, embroidery, tapestry, and needlework for the interiors the firm designed. Among its commissions were Mark Twain's house in Hartford, Connecticut, and four rooms in the White House. One of Wheeler's greatest triumphs was the stage curtain she created for New York's Madison Square Theater, which depicted a realistic landscape using velvet and silk appliqué. She also ventured into wallpaper design, winning first prize in an international contest staged by Warren, Fuller, and Company. Fourth prize went to her daughter Dora, whom Wheeler saw was given the formal design training she lacked.

In 1883 Associated Artists disbanded, although Wheeler used the name for a new design firm she founded. Assisted by Dora, she assembled a staff of female artisans to create what Wheeler considered distinctly American textiles. She tried to move away from the two-dimensional patterns of English textile design by creating landscapes and scenes with figures, often depicting stories from American literature. Wheeler also sought to elevate textiles to the status afforded other art forms. She once explained that, in her eyes, the textile artist "using a needle expresses . . . [what] the pencil or brush expresses for the painter."

In addition to creating large embroidered tapestries for prominent clients, including the actresses Ellen Terry and Lillie Langtry, Wheeler contracted with several fabric houses to design fabric patterns. Hoping to encourage middle-class families to appreciate fine design, she insisted that her fabrics be available not only in silk, but also in affordable fabrics such as cotton and denim. Her firm soon expanded into wallpaper design, and by 1893, it was taking commissions for entire interiors.

Perhaps the pinnacle of Wheeler's career was her work on the New York State display at the World's Columbian Exposition in Chicago in 1893. She was charged with overseeing the interior decoration of the Women's Building, which included murals by Dora and tapestries produced by Associated Artists. Among them was an enormous tapestry based on Raphael's *The Miraculous Draught of Fishes.*

By the turn of the 20th century, Wheeler turned over to one of her sons the management of Associated Artists, which closed in 1907. She spent much of her final years writing books about the decorative arts and home decoration. In addition, she wrote a children's book, a gardening book, and an autobiography appropriately titled *Yesterdays in a Busy Life* (1918). At age 96, Wheeler died on August 5, 1923, at Dora's New York apartment. Long before, she had achieved her life's mission of translating the "feminine skill in the use of the needle into a means of art-expression and pecuniary profit."

Further Reading

Blanchard, Mary W. "Wheeler, Candace Thurber." In *American National Biography.* Volume 22. Edited by John Arthur Garraty and Mark C. Carnes, 131–133. New York: Oxford University Press, 1999.

Burke, Doreen Bolger, et al. *In Pursuit of Beauty: Americans and the Aesthetic Movement.* New York: Rizzoli, 1986.

The Grove Dictionary of Art. "Wheeler, Candace (Thurber)," Grove Art. Available online. URL: http://www.artnet.com/library/09/0913/T091353.asp. Posted in 2001.

— L. S.

WHITNEY, GERTRUDE
(Gertrude Vanderbilt)
(1875–1943)   *Sculptor*

A sculptor passionately devoted to her work, Gertrude Whitney is best known as one of the greatest patrons of modern American art. Born as Gertrude Vanderbilt on January 9, 1875, in New York City, she was the daughter of Cornelius Vanderbilt II, one of the wealthiest men in the United States. After attending the Brearley School, she made her debut, though even as a child she felt constrained by the manners and mores of high society.

Wary of fortune hunters, Gertrude in 1896 married a neighbor, Harry Payne Whitney, who was also from an extremely privileged background. The couple had three children—Cornelius, Flora, and Barbara. Their marriage, however, quickly faltered, in large part due to Harry's infidelities. By 1900, Gertrude began committing her time to a new interest—the art of sculpture. Her status in society, however, led teachers to assume she was not serious enough to take on as a student. Rejected by Daniel Chester French and Augustus Saint-Gaudens, she finally began studying privately with Hendrik Christian Andersen. In 1903 she enrolled in classes at the Art Students League, where she was instructed by James Earle Fraser. Seven years later, she studied briefly in Paris. During the trip, she had her work critiqued by French sculptor Auguste Rodin, whose expressive sculptures were an important influence on Whitney.

Initially, Whitney exhibited her sculpture under an assumed name, fearing that it would otherwise be dismissed as the work of a dilettante. Only after her Rodinesque *Paganism Immortal* (1907) was given an award by the National Academy of Design in 1910 was she willing to attach her name to her art. She soon became known for her public sculptures. In an open competition, she won a commission for a memorial to the men who gave up their seats on lifeboats to women and children as the Titanic sank. *Titanic Memorial* (1914) in Potomac Park in Washington, D.C., depicts a male figure with his arm spread outward, standing on top of a 30-foot stone base decorated with dolphins. Whitney's monumental bronze sculpture *El Dorado Fountain* (1915) featured 40 writhing figures reminiscent of those in Rodin's *The Gates of Hell.* It was awarded a bronze metal at the Panama-Pacific International Exposition in San Francisco.

With the outbreak of World War I, Whitney headed to Europe, where she founded the American Field Hospital for war victims in Juilly, France. The horror of the war had a resounding impact on her art. She began creating small bronze figures, with such titles as *Gassed* and *Blinded,* inspired by the soldiers she encountered. Made in a much looser, expressionistic style, these works communicated far more emotion than her previous work. One provided the basis for her *Washington Heights War Memorial* (1921), which earned her a medal from the New York Society of Architects in 1922. Two years later, Whitney won a bronze medal from the Paris Salon for *The Scout,* a sculpture of William "Buffalo Bill" Cody commissioned by the state of Wyoming.

Despite her successes, Whitney still felt patronized by high society for her artistic ambitions. In 1919 she told the *New York Times,* "Let a woman who does not have to work for her livelihood take a studio and she is greeted by a chorus of horror-stricken voices, a knowing lift of eyebrows." She found much more acceptance among the artists living in Greenwich Village, where she established a studio in 1907. Sympathetic to their struggles to feed themselves and keep a roof over their heads, she offered financial help to many young artists, sometimes sending money anonymously when she heard one was in need. She also began purchasing the work of modernists that most art buyers then scorned. In 1908 she bought four of the seven paintings sold through *The Eight* exhibit. This important show displayed the works of Robert Henri, John Sloan, Arthur B. Davies, and other painters of the Ashcan school, pioneering American realists who embraced gritty urban subjects. She also contributed one-tenth of the budget for the 1913 Armory Show, which introduced the American public to the innovations of modern European painters, such as Marcel Duchamp and Henri Matisse.

In 1914 Whitney bought the house next door to her studio. There she established the Whitney Studio Club as a meeting place and exhibition space for young artists. She also contributed funds to the Society of Independent Artists, which exhibited art that was considered too avant-garde for traditional galleries and museums. To administer her projects, Whitney hired former secretary Juliana Force.

Through her generous patronage, Whitney amassed a collection of more than 500 works by American painters and sculptors. In 1929 she offered to give them to New York's Metropolitan Museum of Art along with the funds needed to maintain a new wing for their display. The Metropolitan's director refused the gift, writing "We have a basement full of American work. We don't need any more." Outraged, Whitney decided to build a museum of her own to house her collection. In 1931 the Whitney Museum of American Art opened, with Juliana Force as its first director. In keeping with Whitney's wishes, the museum continues to provide a showcase for the work of living American artists and remains an institution receptive to experimental art.

Despite championing the avant-garde, Whitney's own sculpture remained highly traditional, which cost her commissions late in her career. Among her last works were the *Peter Stuyvesant Memorial* (1936–39) for Stuyvesant Square Park in New York City and *To the Morrow (The Spirit of Flight)* for the 1939 World's Fair. Following Whitney's death on April 18, 1942, Force organized a memorial exhibition of her work at the museum that remains Whitney's richest legacy.

Further Reading

Biddle, Flora Miller. *The Whitney Women and the Museum They Made: A Memoir.* New York: Arcade, 1999.

Friedman, B.H. *Gertrude Vanderbilt Whitney: A Biography.* Garden City, N.Y.: Doubleday, 1978.

"Whitney, Gertrude Vanderbilt," AskART. Available online. URL: http://askart.com/Biography.asp. Posted in 2000.

— L. S.

WRIGHT, PATIENCE (Patience Lovell)
(1725–1786) *Sculptor*

With innate talent and a forceful personality, Patience Wright carved out a career as the United

States's first professional sculptor. She was born Patience Lovell in 1725 in Oyster Bay, Long Island (New York), but spent most of her youth in Bordentown, New Jersey. Her father, a prosperous farmer, was a Quaker and freethinker. Opposed to the killing of animals, he insisted his family live as strict vegetarians and wear only wooden shoes. Patience and her nine siblings were also expected to dress completely in white, as an expression of their moral purity. The children rebelled against their colorless upbringing by secretly painting pictures from vegetable dyes and berry juice and crafting "graven images" out of clay and dough.

Eager to escape her father's rules, Patience ran away to Philadelphia in 1745, possibly accompanied by Robert Feke, a cousin who later became a noted portrait painter. Little is known about how she survived in the city. By 1748, however, she was back in Bordertown, where she married Joseph Wright, an older, successful cooper. She bore him four children, but as an early account of her life noted, "she modeled him an hundred [more children] in Clay, but not one to his *Gout* [taste]." Apparently, her husband had little respect for her hobby of molding small figurines.

In 1769 Joseph Wright died, leaving Patience with a family to raise on her own. At the suggestion of her sister Rachel, she decided to sell her sculptures to make a living. Wright's ambition to become a professional sculptor was at the time unique. The only "sculptors" then in the American colonies were stone and wood carvers who created objects such as tombstones, furniture, and figureheads for ships.

Wright began her new career crafting figures in wax because the material was readily available, inexpensive, and did not require any special tools or training to manipulate. She soon moved to New York, where her personal charm helped convince many of the city's luminaries to sit for her. In time, Wright created an entire waxwork exhibit. Unlike most such exhibits in Europe, which depicted historical personages or allegorical figures, Wright's showed living celebrities. To add to their realism, she dressed them in appropriate costumes, adorned them with real hair and glass eyes, and posed them

with props. Wright's exhibit toured Charleston, Philadelphia, and other cities before a fire accidentally set by one of her children destroyed most of her wax sculptures in 1771.

Hoping to revive her career, Wright set off for London. She immediately called on Benjamin Franklin, who was then in the city, armed with a letter of introduction from his sister. After meeting Wright, Franklin wrote back, "I have this day received your kind letter by Mrs. Wright. She has shown me some of her work which appears extraordinary. I shall recommend her among my Friends if she chuses to work here." Establishing a studio near Buckingham Palace, Wright took full advantage of Franklin's offer of help. She regularly entertained dukes, actors, political figures, and other celebrities, who allowed her to add their likenesses to her burgeoning collection of waxworks. Glowing reports of her exhibit appeared in many periodicals, most of which were probably written by Wright herself.

Wright was as much of an attraction as the wax sculptures. According to sitters' accounts, she created her sculpted heads by working with a ball of wax held under her apron, where her body heat made the wax malleable. When the head was almost complete, she pulled it free of her clothing, often surprising her subject with the accuracy of the portrait. She then added the finishing touches. While working, Wright talked constantly, expounding on any issue of the day that interested her. Her uncensored, bawdy monologues impressed her English visitors, many of whom considered her manner as emblematic of the freedoms enjoyed by Americans. One acquaintance wrote that "her strong mind poured forth an uninterrupted torrent of wild thought, and anecdotes and reminiscences of men and events. . . . She would utter language in her incessant volubility, as if unconscious to whom directed, that would put her hearers to the blush." Among Wright's greatest champions were George III and Queen Charlotte, whom she, disregarding all formalities, called "George" and "Charlotte."

Not everyone found Wright's lack of propriety so charming. Abigail Adams, wife of colonial leader John Adams, was so offended by her vulgar language and habit of kissing male acquaintances that she described Wright as "quite the slattern" and "the very queen of the sluts." Yet even Adams conceded that her work was remarkable. Like many visitors to Wright's studios, she mistook a sculpture for a living being: "There was an old clergyman sitting reading a paper in the middle of the room; and though was prepared to see strong representation of real life, I was effectively deceived in this figure for ten minutes."

Despite Wright's friendship with the English king and queen, she was a fervent supporter of the American colonies when they declared their independence in 1776. Although perhaps just a legend, when she learned of the fighting at Lexington and Concord, she supposedly stormed into the royal palace and berated George III for his treatment of the American rebels. Although there is little solid evidence, Wright may also have passed along gossip she heard about English war strategies to members of the Continental Congress. She was said to have given some of this information to the colonies in letters encased in wax sculptures that she sent to her sister Rachel in Philadelphia.

Wright's outspoken support for the American cause began to rankle the English. The last straw, however, was a painting by her son Joseph, which he submitted for display at a 1780 exhibition of the Royal Academy. The work depicted his mother molding a head of Charles I, the British monarch beheaded in 1649 during a political coup. Watching her work were George III and Queen Charlotte, whom Wright was giving a knowing look. Even Wright seemed to understand that the portrait was too much for the monarchy to take. Perhaps fearing for her life, she left England for France for the duration of the war.

Wright hoped to establish a new exhibit in Paris but decided she could not compete with the show created by Philippe Curtius (the uncle of Madame Tussard, who would later operate the world's most famous waxwork exhibit). She was also disap-

pointed in her efforts to depose the English king and queen. Reunited with Benjamin Franklin in Paris, she tried to get his support for her plot to assemble an army to storm England and liberate the English people from their rule. Franklin, though, showed no interest in scheme, which then fell apart.

After the war, Wright returned to England, moving in with her daughter Phoebe and Phoebe's husband, painter John Hoppner. To her dismay, she found her wax sculptures no longer in vogue. With characteristic resilience, she planned a new career. Intending to return to the United States, she wrote George Washington, saying that she wanted to him to sit for her. Washington sent an encouraging reply, in which he said, "I should be proud to see a person so universally celebrated; and on whom Nature has bestowed such rare and uncommon gifts." Possibly hoping to secure commissions for public sculptures of the founding fathers, she then wrote Thomas Jefferson in 1785, using Washington's note as a calling card. Before she could return to the United States to pursue her goal, however, she died after an accidental fall on March 23, 1786.

Only one of Wright's sculptures—a figure of William Pitt at London's Westminster Abbey—survives today. As a result, she is better known for her role as a celebrity than as an artist. Yet, she holds an important place in the history of art, as one of the first successful artists, male or female, born on American soil.

Further Reading

Rubinstein, Charlotte Streifer. *American Women Sculptors: A History of Women Working in Three Dimensions.* Boston: G. K. Hall, 1990.

Sellers, Charles Coleman. *Patience Wright: American Artist and Spy in George III's London.* Middletown, Conn.: Wesleyan University Press, 1976.

"Wright, Patience Lovell," Encyclopedia Britannica, Inc. Available online. URL: http://www.britannica.com/women/articles/Wright_Patience_Lovell.html. Posted in 1999.

— L. S.

Z

ZORACH, MARGUERITE THOMPSON
(1887–1968)   Painter, Textile Artist

Marguerite Thompson Zorach was one of the first American artists to embrace fauvism and other European modernist innovations. She was born Marguerite Thompson in Santa Rosa, California, on September 25, 1887, but her family soon moved to Fresno, which then was still a relatively small pioneer town. The daughter of a lawyer, Thompson graduated from high school in 1906, well trained in painting and drawing and fluent in French and German. Thompson enrolled at Stanford University, but she abandoned her studies when her aunt, Harriet Adelaide Harris, invited Thompson to join her in Paris. En route for Europe, Thompson stopped in Chicago, where she saw her first impressionist works. At the time, impressionism was considered radical art in the United States.

In the fall of 1908, Thompson arrived in Paris. The same day, a friend of her aunt's took her to the Salon d'Automne, which was showing works of Henri Matisse, André Derain, Albert Marquet, and other fauves. The fauves embraced simplified forms and used color for its own sake, rather than only as a means of visually describing objects. Although her aunt insisted she take traditional art lessons at the Ecole de la Grande Chaumière, Thompson was immediately impressed by this avant-garde style, which would influence her art for decades. She was also one of the first Americans exposed to cubism, a style that experimented with perspective and the use of space. At the home of art patrons Leo and Gertrude Stein, friends of her aunt Harriet, she was able to study the cubist works of Pablo Picasso before they appeared in major exhibitions. Another early influence on Thompson was the boldly colored paintings of the Blaue Reiter artists, whose works she saw during a 1910 trip to Germany.

While living in Paris, Thompson studied at the progressive La Palette school. In 1911 she befriended fellow student William Zorach, a Lithuanian-born painter from Cleveland, Ohio. She encouraged Zorach to embrace modernist innovations in his work, telling him that he should "let his colors go wild."

Thompson and her aunt left Paris in 1911 and spent seven months traveling around the world. The next spring, Thompson returned to California, an environment she now found stifling. Her family showed little enthusiasm for her art and hid her paints, as they pressed her to become a proper society lady. She felt some relief in the summer of

1912, when she vacationed with her family in the Sierra Mountains. Painting for the first time since leaving Europe, she created a series of fauve-inspired landscapes, painted in blues and greens and accented in brilliant oranges and yellows. These and some earlier works were shown in Los Angeles and Fresno in her first one-woman shows. Nevertheless, Thompson felt she had to leave her family if she were to grow as an artist. Before heading for New York City, she framed some of her more traditional work as gifts for her parents and took most of her other paintings to the city dump.

Thompson arrived in New York on December 24, 1912. The same day, she married William Zorach. Establishing a joint studio in their apartment, the Zorachs were to have a close personal and professional relationship throughout their marriage.

New York immediately presented new opportunities for Marguerite Zorach. A month after her arrival, one of her works and two of her husband's were selected for the now famous Armory Show of 1913, which introduced the works of Matisse, Picasso, and other European modernists to the United States. Their association with the Armory Show immediately thrust the Zorachs into the center of the American avant-garde. Three years later, they furthered their reputations for showing work in the *Forum Exhibition of Modern American Painters* at the Anderson Galleries, alongside paintings by American artists Thomas Hart Benton, Arthur Dove, Marsden Hartley, and John Marin. The Zorachs also associated with cutting-edge writers and actors while designing scenery for the Provincetown Players during summers spent in Provincetown, Massachusetts.

Although well known in bohemian circles, the Zorachs had little success selling their paintings. Their financial troubles worsened by 1917, when they had two small children, Tessim and Dahlov, to care for. As a young mother, Marguerite struggled to find time for her art. She largely gave up oil painting in favor of creating embroidered versions of her art, which she referred to as tapestries. Her devotion to embroidered works during the 1920s and 1930s cost her respect in the art world, since working with fabrics, with its association with women artisans, was generally denigrated. Ironically, Marguerite's textiles proved far more marketable than paintings by either of the Zorachs. Through sales and commissions of her embroidered works, Marguerite provided much of her family's income during their leanest years.

While vacationing in New Hampshire in the summer of 1917, the Zorachs began experimenting with ceramic sculpture. The form was quickly embraced by William, who by 1922 had given up painting for sculpture. As a sculptor, William's reputation far eclipsed Marguerite's as a painter or textile artist. Although her paintings were regularly exhibited at the Kraushaar Galleries in New York, by her death in 1968 her work was largely forgotten. Two years later, however, several of her paintings from 1911 and 1912 were discovered, renewing interest in her career. She is now known mostly for her early work, particularly for its effective melding of various modernist styles developed in the 20th century's first decades.

Further Reading

Bailey, Brooke. *The Remarkable Lives of 100 Women Artists.* Holbrook, Mass.: Bob Adams, 1994.

Hoffman, Marilyn Friedman. *Marguerite and William Zorach: The Cubist Years, 1915–1918.* Mancester, N.H.: Currier Gallery of Art, 1987.

"Marguerite Zorach," Sheldon Memorial Art Gallery and Sculpture Garden. Available online. URL: http://sheldon.unl.edu/HTML/ARTIST/Zorack_M/AA.html. Updated February 23, 2000.

Zorach, Marguerite. *Marguerite Zorach: The Early Years, 1908–1920.* Washington, D.C.: Smithsonian Institution Press, 1973.

— L. S.

RECOMMENDED SOURCES ON AMERICAN WOMEN IN THE VISUAL ARTS

Books

Agosin, Marjorie, ed. *A Woman's Gaze: Latin American Women Artists.* Fredonia, N.Y.: White Pine Press, 1998.

Antler, Joyce. *The Journey Home: Jewish Women and the American Century.* New York: The Free Press, 1997.

Atkinson, Edwin. *Black Dimensions in American Contemporary Art.* New York: New American Library, 1971.

Bailey, Brooke. *The Remarkable Lives of 100 Women Artists.* Holbrook, Mass.: Bob Adams, 1994.

Bank, Mirra. *Anonymous Was a Woman.* New York: St. Martin's Press, 1979.

Bataille, Gretchen M., ed. *Native American Women: A Biographical Dictionary.* New York: Garland Publishing, 1991.

Beardsley, John, and Jane Livingston, eds. *Hispanic Art in the United States: Thirty Contemporary Painters and Sculptors.* Houston, Tex.: The Museum of Fine Arts, Houston, 1986.

Behr, Shulamith. *Women Expressionists.* New York: Rizzoli, 1988.

Benitez, M. *The Latin American Spirit: Art and the Artists in the United States.* New York: Harry N. Abrams, 1988.

Biller, Geraldine P. *Latin American Women Artists, 1915–1995.* Milwaukee, Wisc.: Milwaukee Art Museum, 1995.

Biren, Joan E. *Seeing Women: One Hundred Years of Women's Photography.* Trumansburg, N.Y.: Crossing Press, 1984.

Broder, Patricia Janis. *Earth Songs, Moon Dreams: Paintings by American Indian Women.* New York: St. Martin's Press, 1999.

Broude, Norma, and Mary D. Garrard, eds. *The Power of Feminist Art: The American Movement of the 1970's, History and Impact.* New York: Harry N. Abrams, 1994.

Callen, Anthea. *Women Artists of the Arts and Crafts Movement.* New York: Pantheon, 1979.

Chadwick, Whitney. *Women, Art, and Society.* New York: Thames and Hudson, 1990.

Chiarmonte, Paula. *Women Artists in the United States: A Selective Bibliography and Resource Guide on the Fine and Decorative Arts, 1750–1986.* Boston: G. K. Hall, 1990.

———. *Women Artists and the Surrealist Movement.* Boston: Little, Brown and Company, 1985.

Chicago, Judy, and Edward Lucie-Smith. *Women and Art: Contested Territory.* New York: Waston-Guptil, 1999.

Clark, Garth. *American Ceramics: 1896 to the Present.* New York: Abbeville Press, 1987.

Cline, Ann. *A Hut of One's Own: Life Outside the Circle of Architecture.* Cambridge, Mass.: M.I.T. Press, 1998.

Cole, Doris. *From Tipi to Skyscraper: A History of Women in Architecture.* New York: George Braziller, 1973.

Collins, Jim, and Glenn B. Opitz, eds. *Women Artists in America: Eighteenth Century to the Present*

(1780–1980). Revised edition. Poughkeepsie, N.Y.: Apollo, 1980.

Cummings, Paul. *Dictionary of Contemporary American Arts.* New York: St. Martin's Press, 1994.

Dewhurst, C. Kurt, Betty MacDowell, and Marsha MacDowell. *Artists in Aprons: Folk Art by American Women.* New York: E. P. Dutton, 1979.

Diamonstein, Barbaralee. *American Architecture Now II.* New York: Rizzoli, 1985.

Driskell, David. *Two Centuries of Black American Art.* New York: Knopf, 1976.

Dunford, Penny. *A Biographical Dictionary of Women Artists in Europe and America Since 1850.* Philadelphia: University of Pennsylvania Press, 1989.

Ebert, John, and Katherine Ebert. *American Folk Painters.* New York: Charles Scribner's Sons, 1978.

Emanuel, Muriel, ed. *Contemporary Architects.* Farmington Hills, Mich.: St. James Press, 1994.

Farris, Phoebe, ed. *Women Artists of Color: A Bio-Critical Sourcebook of 20th Century Artists in America.* Westport, Conn.: Greenwood Press, 1999.

Fowler, Carol. *Contributions of Women in Art.* Minneapolis, Minn.: Dillon Press, 1976.

Frueh, Joanna, Cassandra L. Langer, and Arlene Raven, eds. *New Feminist Criticism: Art, Identity, Action.* New York: IconEditions, 1994.

Garb, Tamar. *Women Impressionists.* New York: Rizzoli, 1986.

———. *Bodies of Modernity: Figure and Flesh in Fin-de-Siècle France.* London: Thames and Hudson, 1998.

Gaze, Delia, ed. *Dictionary of Women Artists.* Chicago, Ill.: Fitzroy Dearborn Publications, 1997.

Gerdts, William H. *Artists of America, 1707–1964.* Newark, N.J.: Newark Museum, 1965.

Gusson, Allan. *A Sense of Place: The Artist and the American Landscape.* New York: The Saturday Review Press, 1971.

Hammond, Harmony. *Lesbian Art in America: A Contemporary History.* New York: Rizzoli, 2000.

Harris, Ann Southerland, and Linda Nochlin. *Women Artists 1550–1950.* New York: Knopf, 1976.

Harrison, Helen A. *Women Artists of the New Deal Era.* Washington, D.C.: The National Museum of Women in the Arts, 1988.

Heard Museum. *Watchful Eyes: Native American Women Artists.* Phoenix, Ariz.: Heard Museum, 1994.

Hedges, Elaine, and Ingrid Wendt, eds. *In Her Own Image: Women Working in the Arts.* Old Westbury, N.Y.: The Feminist Press, 1980.

Heller, Jules, and Nancy G. Heller, eds. *North American Women Artists of the Twentieth Century: A Biographical Dictionary.* New York: Garland, 1995.

Heller, Nancy G. *Women Artists: An Illustrated History.* 3rd edition. New York: Abbeville, 1997.

———. *Women Artists: Works from the National Museum of Women in the Arts.* New York: Rizzoli, 2000.

Hemphill, Herbert W., Jr., and Julia Weissman. *Twentieth-Century American Folk Art and Artists.* New York: E.P. Dutton, 1976.

Henkes, Robert. *American Women Painters of the 1930s and 1940s: The Lives and Work of Ten Artists.* Jefferson, N.C.: McFarland, 1991.

———. *The Art of Black American Women: Works by Twenty-Four Artists of the Twentieth Century.* Jefferson, N.C.: McFarland, 1993.

———. *Latin American Women Artists of the United States.* Jefferson, N.C.: McFarland, 1999.

Hess, Thomas B., and Elizabeth C. Baker, eds. *Art and Sexual Politics.* New York: Collier Books, 1971.

Hillstrom, Laurie C., and Kevin Hillstrom. *Contemporary Women Artists.* Farmington Hills, Mich.: St. James Press, 1999.

Hughes, Robert. *American Visions.* New York: Knopf, 1997.

James, Edward T., ed. *Notable American Women.* Cambridge, Mass.: Belknap Press of Harvard University Press, 1971.

Kovinick, Phil, and Marian Yoshiki-Kovinick. *An Encyclopedia of Women Artists of the American West.* Austin: University of Texas Press, 1998.

La Duke, Betty. *Women Artists: Multi-Cultural Visions.* Trenton, N.J.: Red Sea Press, 1992.

Lipman, Jean, ed. *What Is American in American Art.* New York: McGraw-Hill, 1963.

Lippard, Lucy. *From the Center: Feminist Essays on Women's Art.* New York: Dutton, 1976.

———. *Pop Art.* New York: Praeger, 1966.

Lucie-Smith, Edward. *American Realism.* New York: Harry N. Abrams, 1994.

Marcoci, Roxanna, et al., eds. *New Art.* New York: Harry N. Abrams, 1997.

Marling, Karal Ann. *Seven American Women: The Depression Decade.* Poughkeepsie, N.Y.: Vassar College Art Gallery and A.I.R. Gallery (New York), 1976.

McDarrah, Gloria S., et al., eds. *The Photography Encyclopedia.* New York: Schirmer Books, 1999.

Meyer, Ursula, ed. *Conceptual Art.* New York: Dutton, 1972.

Mitchell, Margaretta. *Recollections: Ten Women of Photography.* New York: Viking Press, 1979.

Moutoussamy-Ashe, Jeanne. *Viewfinders: Black Women Photographers.* New York: Dodd, Mead, 1986.

Munro, Eleanor. *Originals: American Women Artists.* New York: Da Capo Press, 2000.

Munsterberg, Hugo. *A History of Women Artists.* New York: Clarkson N. Potter, 1975.

Nemser, Cindy. *Art Talk: Conversations with 15 Women Artists.* New York: HarperCollins, 1995.

Nochlin, Linda. *Women, Art, and Power, and Other Essays.* New York: Harper and Row, 1989.

Parker, Rozsika. *Old Mistresses: Women, Art, and Ideology.* New York: Pantheon, 1981.

Patton, Sharon F. *African-American Art.* New York: Oxford University Press, 1998.

Peterson, Karen, and J. J. Wilson. *Women Artists: Recognition and Reappraisal from the Early Middle Ages to the 20th Century.* New York: Harper and Row, 1976.

Petteys, Chris. *An International Dictionary of Women Artists Before 1900.* Boston: G.K. Hall, 1985.

Quirarte, Jacinto. *Mexican-American Arts.* Houston: University of Texas Press, 1953.

Remer, Abby. *Pioneering Spirits: The Lives and Times of Remarkable Women Artists in Western History.* Worcester, Mass.: Davis Publications, 1997.

Rennolds, Margaret B., ed. *The National Museum of Women in the Arts.* New York: Harry N. Abrams, 1987.

Robins, Corinne. *The Pluralist Era: American Art, 1968–1981.* New York: Harper and Row, 1984.

Robinson, Hilary, ed. *Visibly Female: Feminism and Art: An Anthology.* New York: Converse, 1988.

Robinson, Jontyle Theresa. *Bearing Witness: Contemporary Works by African American Artists.* New York: Rizzoli, 1996.

Rose, Barbara. *American Painting: The 20th Century.* New York: Skira, 1973.

Rosen, Randy, et al., eds. *Making Their Mark: Women Artists Move into the Mainstream, 1970–1985.* New York: Abbeville Press, 1989.

Rosenbaum, Robert. *On Modern Art.* New York: Harry N. Abrams, 1999.

Rosenblum, Naomi. *A History of Women Photographers.* 2nd edition. New York: Abbeville, 2000.

Rubinstein, Charlotte Streifer. *American Women Artists: From Early Indian Times to the Present.* Boston: G.K. Hall, 1982.

———. *American Women Sculptors: A History of Women Working in Three Dimensions.* Boston: G.K. Hall, 1990.

Sawelson-Gorse, Naomi. *Women in DADA: Essays on Sex, Gender and Identity.* Cambridge, Mass.: MIT Press, 1998.

Sills, Leslie. *Visions: Stories About Women Artists.* Morton Grove, Ill.: Albert Whitman and Company, 1993.

Slater, Elinor, and Robert Slater. *Great Jewish Women.* Middle Village, N.Y.: Jonathan David Publishers, 1994.

Slatkin, Wendy. *Women Artists in History: From Antiquity to the Twentieth Century.* Englewood Cliffs, N.J.: Prentice Hall, 1985.

Sochen, June, ed. *Women's Comic Visions.* Detroit, Mich.: Wayne State University Press, 1991.

Sonneborn, Liz. *A to Z of Native American Women.* New York: Facts On File, 1998.

Sontag, Susan. *On Photography.* New York: Dell, 1977.

Stofflet, Mary. *American Women Artists: The Twentieth Century.* New York: Harper and Row, 1979.

Sullivan, Constance, ed. *Women Photographers.* New York: Harry N. Abrams, 1990.

Sullivan, Edward J., ed. *Latin American Art in the 20th Century.* London: Phaidon Press, 1996.

237

Swenson, Lynn F., and Sally Swenson. *Lives and Work: Talks with Women Artists.* Metcuchen, N.J.: Scanecrow Press, 1981.

Tighe, Mary Ann, and Elizabeth Ewing Lang. *Art America.* New York: McGraw-Hill, 1977.

Torre, Susana, ed. *Women in American Architecture: A Historic and Contemporary Perspective.* New York: Whitney Library of Design, 1977.

Trenton, Patricia, ed. *Independent Spirits: Women Painters of the American West, 1890–1945.* Berkeley: University of California Press, 1995.

Tucker, Anne. *The Woman's Eye.* New York: Knopf, 1973.

Tufts, Eleanor. *American Women Artists, Past and Present: A Selected Bibliographic Guide.* 2 vols. New York: Garland, 1984–89.

———. *American Women Artists, 1830–1930.* Washington, D.C.: The National Museum of Women in the Arts, 1987.

Upton, Dell. *Architecture in the United States.* New York: Oxford University Press, 1998.

Wagner, Anne Middleton. *Three Artists, Three Women: Modernism and the Art of Hesse, Krasner, and O'Keeffe.* Berkeley: University of California Press, 1996.

Watson-Jones, Virginia. *Contemporary American Women Sculptors.* Phoenix, Ariz.: Oryx Press, 1986.

Weatherford, Doris. *American Women's History.* New York: Prentice Hall, 1994.

Wheeler, Kenneth W., and Virginia Lee Lussier, eds. *Women, the Arts, and the 1920s in Paris and New York.* New Brunswick, N.J.: Transaction Books, 1982.

The White Marmorean Flock: Nineteenth Century American Women Neoclassical Sculptors. Poughkeepsie, N.Y.: Vassar College Art Gallery, 1972.

Women of Sweetgrass, Cedar, and Sage. New York: Gallery of the American Indian Community House, 1985.

Periodicals

The Feminist Art Journal
Feminist Art News
Heresies: A Feminist Publication on Art and Politics
Matriart
Women Artists
Women in the Arts

Websites

http://www.artnet.com (Grove Dictionary of Art, 2000)
http://www.askart.com
http://www.distinguishedwomen.com (Encyclopedia Britiannica, 1999)
http://www.masters-of-photography.com
http://www.nmwa.org (National Museum of Women in the Arts)

ENTRIES BY MEDIUM

Architecture

Goody, Joan Edelman
Griffin, Marion Lucy
    Mahony
Lin, Maya
Morgan, Julia

Collage

Fine, Perle
Itami, Michi
Krasner, Lee
Saar, Betye
Schapiro, Miriam
Tawney, Lenore
Von Wiegand, Charmion

Filmmaking

Sherman, Cindy
Simpson, Lorna

Illustration

Aycock, Alice
Bacon, Peggy
Bridges, Fidelia
Brownscombe, Jennie
    Augusta
Dwight, Mabel Jacque
    Williamson
Frank, Mary Lockspeiser

Grossman, Nancy
Hokinson, Helen Elna
Lomas Garza, Carmen
O'Keeffe, Georgia
Ringgold, Faith
Smith, Jessie Willcox
Stephens, Alice Barber
Waring, Laura Wheeler

Interior Design

Wheeler, Candace

Mixed Media

Bartlett, Jennifer Losch
Chase-Riboud, Barbara
Chryssa
Flack, Audrey
Fuller, Sue
Goldin, Nan
Holzer, Jenny
Itami, Michi
Katzen, Lila Pell
Kruger, Barbara
Marisol
Saar, Betye Brown
Schapiro, Miriam
Smith, Jaune Quick-to-See
Smith, Kiki

Painting

Alvarez, Mabel
Baca, Judith Francisca
Bacon, Peggy
Bartlett, Jennifer Losch
Bascom, Ruth Henshaw
    Miles
Beaux, Cecilia
Bishop, Isabel Wolff
Blaine, Nell
Bourgeois, Louise
Bridges, Fidelia
Brooks, Romaine
Brownscombe, Jennie
    Augusta
Cassatt, Mary Stevenson
Chicago, Judy Cohen
Chryssa
Coman, Charlotte Buell
de Kooning, Elaine Marie
    Catherine Fried
Dewing, Maria Oakey
Dreier, Katherine Sophie
Dwight, Mabel Jacque
    Williamson
Eakins, Susan Hannah
    MacDowell
Fine, Perle
Fish, Janet
Flack, Audrey

Frank, Mary Lockspeiser
Frankenthaler, Helen
Freilicher, Jane Niederhoffer
Goodridge, Sarah
Graves, Nancy Stevenson
Greenwood, Marion
Grossman, Nancy
Hall, Anne
Hartigan, Grace
Hesse, Eva
Hunter, Clementine
Itami, Michi
Katzen, Lila Pell
Klumpke, Anna Elizabeth
Krasner, Lee
Kruger, Barbara
Lomas Garza, Carmen
Lundeberg, Helen
MacIver, Loren
Martin, Agnes
Mason, Alice Trumbull
Mitchell, Joan
Moses, Grandma
Murray, Elizabeth
Neel, Alice
O'Keeffe, Georgia
Peale, Sarah Miriam
Peña, Tonita
Pereira, Irene Rice
Perry, Lilla Cabot
Ringgold, Faith
Rothenberg, Susan
Sage, Kay
Schapiro, Miriam
Shore, Henrietta
Smith, Jaune Quick-to-See
Smith, Jessie Willcox
Spencer, Lilly Martin
Stebbins, Emma
Stettheimer, Florine
Stevens, May
Tanning, Dorothea
Teichert, Minerva
Thomas, Alma W.

Treiman, Joyce
Velarde, Pablita
Von Wiegand, Charmion
Waring, Laura Wheeler
Wayne, June
Zorach, Marguerite
  Thompson

Photography

Abbott, Berenice
Arbus, Diane
Bourke-White, Margaret
Cunningham, Imogen
Eakins, Susan Hannah
  MacDowell
Goldin, Nan
Käsebier, Gertrude Stanton
Kruger, Barbara
Lange, Dorothea Nutzhorn
Leibovitz, Annie
Levitt, Helen
Norman, Dorothy
Sherman, Cindy
Simpson, Lorna
Ulmann, Doris

Pottery

Itami, Michi
Martinez, Maria
Nampeyo
Tafoya, Margaret

Printmaking

Albers, Anni
Alvarez, Mabel
Bacon, Peggy
Bartlett, Jennifer Losch
Bourgeois, Louise
Bridges, Fidelia
Brownscombe, Jennie
  Augusta
Cassatt, Mary Stevenson
de Kooning, Elaine Marie
  Catherine Fried

Dwight, Mabel Jacque
  Williamson
Eakins, Susan Hannah
  MacDowell
Fine, Perle
Frankenthaler, Helen
Fuller, Sue
Greenwood, Marion
Itami, Michi
Kent Corita
Kruger, Barbara
Lomas Garza, Carmen
Mason, Alice Trumbull
Palmer, Fanny
Saar, Betye
Spencer, Lilly Martin
Wayne, June

Quilting

Powers, Harriet
Ringgold, Faith

Sculpture

Asawa, Ruth
Aycock, Alice
Bartlett, Jennifer Losch
Bourgeois, Louise
Burke, Selma Hortense
Chase-Riboud, Barbara
Chicago, Judy Cohen
Chryssa
Eberle, Mary Abastenia
  St. Leger
Flack, Audrey
Frank, Mary Lockspeiser
Frankenthaler, Helen
Fuller, Meta Vaux Warrick
Fuller, Sue
Graves, Nancy Stevenson
Grossman, Nancy
Hesse, Eva
Hoffman, Malvina Cornell
Hosmer, Harriet Goodhue

Huntington, Anna Vaughn
   Hyatt
Johnson, Adelaide
Katzen, Lila Pell
Lewis, Edmonia
Lin, Maya
Margoulies, Berta
Marisol
Mendieta, Ana
Miss, Mary
Nevelson, Louise
Pepper, Beverly
Prophet, Elizabeth
Ream, Vinnie
Ringgold, Faith
Saar, Betye

Savage, Augusta
Schapiro, Miriam
Smith, Kiki
Stebbins, Emma
Tanning, Dorothea
Vonnoh, Bessie Potter
Wayne, June
Whitney, Gertrude
Wright, Patience

Textiles and Basket Making

Albers, Anni
Frankenthaler, Helen
Keyser, Louisa
Tawney, Lenore
Wayne, June

Wheeler, Candace
Zorach, Marguerite
   Thompson

Works on Paper

Albers, Anni
Bishop, Isabel Wolff
Blaine, Nell
Bridges, Fidelia
Brooks, Romaine
Frank, Mary Lockspeiser
Hesse, Eva
Grossman, Nancy
Johnston, Henrietta
   Deering
Krasner, Lee

ENTRIES BY ARTISTIC STYLE

Abstract Expressionism

de Kooning, Elaine Marie Catherine Fried
Fine, Perle
Frankenthaler, Helen
Freilicher, Jane Niedeshoffer
Graves, Nancy Stevenson
Hartigan, Grace
Krasner, Lee
Mitchell, Joan

Art Nouveau

Wheeler, Candace

Ashcan School

Eberle, Mary Abastenia St. Leger

Bauhaus/Geometric Art

Albers, Anni
Fuller, Sue
Von Wiegand, Charmion

Body Art

Mendieta, Ana

Earth Art

Mendieta, Ana
Miss, Mary

Fauvism

Zorach, Marguerite Thompson

Feminist Art

Bourgeois, Louise
Chicago, Judy Cohen
Goldin, Nan
Grossman, Nancy
Holzer, Jenny
Johnson, Adelaide
Kruger, Barbara
Mendieta, Ana
Ringgold, Faith
Schapiro, Miriam
Sherman, Cindy
Stevens, May

Folk Art

Bascom, Ruth Henshaw Miles
Hunter, Clementines
Lomas Garza, Carmen

Moses, Grandma
Powers, Harriet

Genre Art

Bishop, Isabel Wolff
Brownscombe, Jennie Augusta
Klumpke, Anna Elizabeth
Spencer, Lilly Martin

Impressionism

Alvarez, Mabel
Cassatt, Mary Stevenson
Fuller, Meta Vaux Warrick
Perry, Lilla Cabot

Installation Art

Aycock, Alice
Bartlett, Jennifer Losch
Chicago, Judy Cohen
Holzer, Jenny
Katzen, Lila Pell
Kruger, Barbara

Miniature Art

Goodridge, Sarah
Hall, Anne

Minimalism

Hesse, Eva
Martin, Agnes
Pepper, Beverly

Neoclassicism

Flack, Audrey
Hosmer, Harriet Goodhue

New Classicism

Lundeberg, Helen

New Image

Rothenberg, Susan

New Realism

Fish, Janet
Flack, Andrey
Neel, Alice

Pattern and Decoration

Albers, Anni
Chicago, Judy Cohen
Frankenthaler, Helen
Keysen, Louise
Schapiro, Miriam
Tawney, Leonore

Photography

Abbott, Berenice
Arbus, Diane

Bourke-White, Margaret
Goldin, Nan
Käsebier, Gertrude Stanton
Lange, Dorothea Nutzhorn
Ulmann, Doris

Photomontage Art

Kruger, Barbara
Itami, Michi

Performance Art

Mendieta, Ana
Ringgold, Faith

Pop Art

Chryssa
Marisol, Escobar

Pre-Raphaelite Art

Bridges, Fidelia

Public Art

Asawa, Ruth
Baca, Judith Francisca
Bartlett, Jennifer Losch
Burke, Selma Hortense
Chase-Riboud, Barbara
Chryssa
Flack, Audrey
Fuller, Meta Vaux Warrick
Greenwood, Marion

Hosmer, Harriet Goodhue
Johnson, Adelaide
Lin, Maya
Miss, Mary
Pepper, Beverly
Shore, Henrietta

Satirical Art

Bacon, Peggy
Dwight, Mabel Jacque
    Williamson
Hokinson, Helen Elna
Marisol

Surrealism
and Postsurrealism

Alvarez, Mabel
Bourgeois, Louise
Lundenberg, Helen
Sage, Kay
Tanning, Dorothea
Vallejo, Linda

Tonalism

Coman, Charlotte Buell

Western American Art

Alvarez, Mabel
Baca, Judith Francisca
O'Keeffe, Georgia
Teichert, Minerva

ENTRIES BY YEAR OF BIRTH

Before 1800

Bascom, Ruth Henshaw
Miles
Goodridge, Sarah
Hall, Anne
Johnston, Henrietta
Deering
Wright, Patience

1800–1809

Peale, Sarah Miriam

1810–1819

Palmer, Fanny
Stebbins, Emma

1820–1829

Spencer, Lilly Martin
Wheeler, Candace

1830–1839

Bridges, Fidelia
Coman, Charlotte Buell
Hosmer, Harriet Goodhue
Powers, Harriet

1840–1849

Cassatt, Mary Stevenson
Dewing, Maria Oakey

Lewis, Edmonia
Perry, Lilla Cabot
Ream, Vinnie

1850–1859

Beaux, Cecilia
Brownscombe, Jennie
Augusta
Eakins, Susan Hannah
Macdowell
Johnson, Adelaide
Käsebier, Gertrude Stanton
Keysen, Louise
Klumpke, Anna Elizabeth
Stephens, Alice Barber

1860–1869

Moses, Grandma
Nampeyo
Smith, Jessie Willcox

1870–1879

Brooks, Romaine
Dreier, Katherine Sophie
Dwight, Mabel Jacque
Williamson
Eberle, Mary Abastenia
St. Leger
Fuller, Meta Vaux Warrick

Griffin, Marion Lucy
Mahony
Huntington, Anna Vaughn
Hyatt
Morgan, Julia
Stettheimer, Florine
Vonnoh, Bessie Potter
Whitney, Gertrude

1880–1889

Cunningham, Imogen
Hoffman, Malvina Cornell
Hunter, Clementine
Martinez, Maria
O'Keeffe, Georgia
Shore, Henrietta
Teichert, Minerva
Ulmann, Doris
Waring, Laura Wheeler
Zorach, Marguerite
Thompson

1890–1899

Abbott, Berenice
Albers, Anni
Alvarez, Mabel
Bacon, Peggy
Hokinson, Helen Elna
Lange, Dorothea Nutzhorn
Peña, Tonita

INDEX

Locators in **boldface** indicate main entries.
Italic locators indicate photographs.